# NEW YORK

The Politics of Urban
Regional Development

**A publication of the Franklin K. Lane Memorial Fund, Institute of Governmental Studies, University of California, Berkeley**

The Franklin K. Lane Memorial Fund takes its name from Franklin Knight Lane (1864–1921), a distinguished Californian who was successively New York correspondent for the San Francisco *Chronicle*, City and County Attorney of San Francisco, member and later chairman of the United States Interstate Commerce Commission, and Secretary of the Interior in the cabinet of President Woodrow Wilson.

The general purposes of the endowment are to promote "better understanding of the nature and working of the American system of democratic government, particularly in its political, economic and social aspects," and the "study and development of the most suitable methods for its improvement in the light of experience."

**Lane Studies in Regional Government:**

*Governing the London Region: Reorganization and Planning in the 1960s*, by Donald L. Foley

*Governing Metropolitan Toronto: A Social and Policy Analysis*, by Albert Rose

*Governing Greater Stockholm: Policy Development and Urban Change in Stockholm*, by Thomas J. Anton

# NEW YORK

## The Politics of Urban Regional Development

Michael N. Danielson and Jameson W. Doig

Published for the Institute of Governmental Studies
and the Institute of International Studies

UNIVERSITY OF CALIFORNIA PRESS
BERKELEY   LOS ANGELES   LONDON

University of California Press
Berkeley and Los Angeles, California

University of California Press, Ltd.
London, England

1  2  3  4  5  6  7  8  9

Library of Congress Cataloging in Publication Data

Danielson, Michael N.
  New York, the politics of urban regional development

  (A Publication of the Franklin K. Lane Memorial
Fund, Institute of Governmental Studies, University
of California, Berkeley)
  Includes index.
  1.  Regional planning—New York (State)  2.  New
York (N.Y.)—City planning.  3.  City planning—New
York (State)  4.  Urban renewal—New York (N.Y.)
5.  New York region—Politics and government.
I.  Doig, Jameson W.  II.  Title.  III.  Series: Publi-
cation of the Franklin K. Lane Memorial Fund,
Institute of Governmental Studies, University of
California, Berkeley.
HT393.N7D3      307.7′6      81-7480
ISBN 0-520-04371-5            AACR2

To the memory of
**Wallace S. Sayre**
and
**Richard T. Frost**
whose insights, enthusiasm and encouragement
shaped the education and future work
of their many students

# Contents

# Tables

# Maps

# Foreword

This volume is the fourth in the Franklin K. Lane series on the governance of major metropolitan regions. The series is sponsored by the Institute of Governmental Studies and the Institute of International Studies, University of California in Berkeley. Readers of these volumes and other relevant literature will no doubt agree with the authors of this book that similar patterns are found in New York, London, Toronto, Stockholm, and indeed in "every other major metropolitan region in the United States and in other advanced industrial societies." The presence of such common factors and trends, although they assume different configurations in various metropolitan regions, has been demonstrated by the work of many scholars, including Peter Hall, Brian Berry, Marion Clawson, Jean Gottmann, Larry Bourne and William Robson, as well as by the authors of the other Franklin K. Lane books—Donald Foley, Albert Rose and Thomas Anton.

In the present volume Michael Danielson and Jameson Doig have described and analyzed the cultural, economic, political and other social forces shaping development in the New York region. They present a picture of a region singular in its attractions, problems, geographic scope, magnitude of development, and complexity of the network of organizations involved in its governance.

## A Major Case Study

The book must be taken seriously as a major study of the nation's largest metropolitan region, and judged at least partly by its success in meeting the specifications and standards of the case study genre. We believe it does so magnificently. Readers are never allowed to forget that they are dealing with a specific region composed of identifiable urban and suburban communities, where individual public and private organizations are interacting to further or forestall specific outcomes. At the same time, the study is *comparative* in dealing with the many types of actors operating within the New York region.

The volume also offers much more than the standard empirical materials usually found in a case study. Danielson and Doig use the case approach analytically, subjecting the conclusions of other students to the test of congruence with the real world as they see it exemplified in the New York region. One of their major concerns is to reexamine the conclusions reached nearly two decades ago by Robert C. Wood and Raymond Vernon, also based on a landmark study of the New York region. Wood and Vernon contended that "public programs and public policies are of little consequence" in shaping the metropolis, and that governmental organizations "leave most of the important decisions for regional development to the private marketplace." But our two authors show how developmental decision-making is much more complex. They demonstrate that the Wood-Vernon thesis is inadequate to explain development because it fails to acknowledge the "close interconnection . . . in the United States and in other democratic societies . . . among individual attitudes, governmental policies, and the actions of economic organizations and individuals in the marketplace."

## Two Analytical Scales

Danielson and Doig trace the dynamics of this interconnection in their examination of municipal zoning and other local housing, urban renewal and land use policies; of local resistance to regional, state, and federal highway projects; and of the successes and failures of regional agencies in building bridges, tunnels, and airports and in operating rapid transit, buses and commuter railroads. The authors find a variety of relationships which they range along a spectrum from (1) the ratification of decisions made in the marketplace, to (2) a middle position where sensitivity to market forces is tempered with public policy goals, to (3) "the other end of the continuum" where "government actions have a critical initiating role in shaping development."

They have also devised another scale for describing the impact of governmental actions on urban development. Taken together, these two measures are represented in a matrix that can be used in any metropolitan region to identify, describe, and locate governmental units with respect to their degree of dependence on previous actions by economic units, as well as the impacts of the governments' own actions on urban development. The authors have thus supplied analytical tools and concepts that can help to provide an understanding of the role of government in shaping development in other metropolitan regions.

## Much More than a Case Study

For still other reasons, this book is much more than a case study of another large metropolis. Admittedly New York's scale and complexity are unique, but its striking features also exemplify important characteristics found elsewhere. Students, citizens and active participants in the governance of other regions can recognize New York as a *macrocosm* of their own regions: New York resembles other regions, but writ large. The New York region, with the central city and especially Manhattan Island as its major urban core, is certainly "one of the great unnatural wonders of the world," to use Robert C. Wood's phrase, quoted by the authors. Whether New York is accepted as unnatural, natural, or just inevitable, most Americans (and indeed probably most foreigners) love, hate, imitate, fear, embrace or avoid it.

In any event New York continues to be the major urban center of the United States, and indeed of North America. On the other hand New York has not dominated the life of its parent nation like London and Paris, perhaps because the country is continental in scale, as well as because New York is not the national capital. Moreover, the United States has thirty-four metropolitan planning regions of over a million population, and another forty with populations between 500,000 and 1,000,000. In the complexity of their developmental decisions, all these areas—even relatively new and rapidly growing ones in the Sun Belt—resemble the New York region, on a smaller but nevertheless impressive scale.

With development of automotive transportation and instantaneous communications, the regions of old and newer cities outside the United States are following the development patterns Danielson and Doig have outlined in the New York region. Toronto is an excellent example of a new fast-growing metropolis where, despite governmental reorganizations of major proportions, growth is spilling over the boundaries. Metropolitan Toronto and the Toronto-centered region are essentially a product of the last thirty-five years. During this time the inner suburbs of the Metropolitan Municipality that was created in 1953 have gone through the typical phase of rapid growth fed by migration from the old central city and elsewhere in Canada, as well as by immigration from abroad. Presently, however, Metro's growth is almost stationary (except for Scarborough), and the fast-growing suburbs are now outside Metro's political boundaries. Metro's inner municipalities are actually losing population.

Meanwhile the inner ring of suburbs has changed socially as well as demographically. According to a recent report of the Social Planning Council of Metropolitan Toronto:

> a growing majority of the people who live in the suburbs are tenants, working mothers, new immigrants, elderly struggling against inflation, solitary parents raising children alone, teenagers looking for things to do, unmarried couples living together and the unemployed. It is no longer possible to think of the suburbs as single family neighborhoods surrounding the more cosmopolitan and dangerous inner city. . . . All of Metropolitan Toronto has become a vast urbanized area.*

## Some Conventional Wisdom Undermined

Another reason why the Danielson and Doig book is not a typical case study is its richness in observations, interpretations, conclusions and generalizations. These should stimulate further intraregional as well as interregional and international comparative research. While any good case study ought to have such by-products, our two authors provide a profusion of intriguing leads and questions for exploration by authors of future volumes in this series, as well as by other students here and abroad.

As noted earlier, their principal purpose is to identify the variety of relationships among public and private actors in the development and redevelopment of the New York region. A central, recurring theme in their analysis is the importance of governmental organization, decisions and actions. In

---

*Social Planning Council of Metropolitan Toronto, *Metro's Suburbs in Transition*, Part II, *Policy Report: Planning Agenda for the Eighties* (Toronto, Ontario, September 1980), pp. 25–26.

the process of developing this theme, they seriously undermine some conventional wisdom that had seemed to be supported by the Wood-Vernon study of the New York region, noted earlier. Admittedly the interpretation that government serves largely in a secondary role—as contrasted with other prime movers that allegedly determine events—did not originate in the New York studies of Wood, Vernon and their colleagues. Such deterministic theses are, in fact, deeply rooted in the literature of economics. Wood's interpretation in his New York book, *1400 Governments*, stood for nearly twenty years without either comprehensive reexamination or a serious head-on challenge. The view of government as ineffective received a major impetus in the postwar era, especially when the big push for urban-metropolitan governmental reorganization of the 1950s and 1960s produced meager results, seeming to prompt the conclusion in some quarters, "oh well, it really doesn't matter anyway." In one form or another, the interpretation that government and public policy are largely incidental—or that government responds to social and economic factors far more than it shapes them—has been repeated by such influential political scientists as York Willbern, Norton Long, and Thomas Dye.

## Sorting Out Cause and Effect

Our two authors emphasize how the very complexity of forces shaping an urban region like New York makes it exceedingly difficult "to sort out the most important causes of urban change." Moreover they quote with approval these conclusions of a conference of scholars:

> It is always difficult and frequently impossible to isolate cause and effect relationships in any kind of social science research, and policy impact studies pose many particularly difficult, perhaps insoluble, methodological problems.

In fact, this fundamental difficulty in data interpretation has challenged philosophers and scientists at least since the time of David Hume: statistical association does not demonstrate causation. When events are seen to happen together or in familiar sequences, interpretation and inference must be employed in trying to distinguish cause from effect, or cause from incidental phenomena.*

Answering the question—"Does governmental policy at the local and metropolitan level make a significant difference?"—calls for such interpretations. We have noted how several writers seemed to doubt that it does. But we also see how Danielson and Doig vigorously—and we believe persuasively—contest the view that government and its activities are only incidental.

*The social sciences must constantly infer cause-and-effect relationships to help interpret data. In fact, to get beyond data collection and description of observations—which can be highly useful in their own right—the researcher *must* try to identify probable cause-and-effect relationships. Nearly always this means making assumptions that go beyond the evidence at hand: "only under very limited conditions can one unequivocally determine the underlying causal structure among the factors from the correlations among the observed variables. This fundamental indeterminancy . . . is due to the indeterminancy inherent in making *inferences* about the causal structure . . . [emphasis in original]. Jae-On Kim and Charles W. Mueller, *Introduction to Factor Analysis: What It Is and How to Do It* (Beverly Hills, Calif.: Sage Publications, 1978), p. 8.

## The Value-Laden Consequences of Structure

In fact, they convincingly argue that the very framework and structure of government can have important influences on the way governments make decisions and implement them, as well as on the substance of the decisions. Pointing out that organization and leadership in the New York region are more fragmented than in any of the nation's other regions, they go on to emphasize how such a structure can have value-laden consequences:

> Fragmentation makes it difficult for major officials in the region to analyze trade-offs, e.g., between environmental costs and job-creation benefits, and when the cost-benefit ratio is favorable, to press ahead vigorously with needed projects. Consequently . . . fragmentation tends to aid those who counsel delay and inaction in the use of government power to advance developmental projects.

At the beginning of the book, the authors had already emphasized how fragmented government helps determine the structure of politics, programs and interrelationships:

> The fragmented character of the governmental system both permits and encourages the region's citizenry to focus their attention on narrow and immediate problems. Businessmen, homeowners, parents, motorists and others concerned with particular policies and programs organize along the lines of the governments' geographic and functional divisions. . . . [B]oth public and private participants in the region's political system generally react to issues in terms of a territorial or functional frame of reference. . . .

## Long Time Spans for Policy Implementation

In attempting to interpret how governmental action can influence events we must recognize that—even without structural impediments like fragmentation—long time spans often elapse before the potentials of policies and program innovations can be fully realized. These long intervals no doubt contribute to the oft-expressed opinion that governmental actions do not produce the results intended, or are highly disappointing in their outcomes. But such criticisms tend to ignore or minimize the exceedingly important temporal factor in governmental efforts that are intended to effect significant social or economic change. Thus it usually takes a lot of time to achieve major innovations in governmental policy, still more time to put the innovations into effect, and yet more time to see substantial results, even when the policies are pursued with persistence and continuity.

Given this temporal factor, attempts to evaluate governmental policy impacts over comparatively short-run periods can sometimes grossly underestimate the role of governmental policies and programs. An example is the effort to evaluate the impact of San Francisco's three-county rapid transit system, BART. The crucial bond referendum that put BART into being was held in November 1962, and the system was largely built in the 1960s. Naturally eager to learn from the unique BART experience, the federal authorities sponsored BART-impact studies in the 1970s, when the system had been in operation only a few years. Impacts were found to be mostly minor, except of course for the obvious one of lots of people riding at the rush hour. But other major impacts, e.g., on land values, land uses, population densities and distribution, locations of employment, and journey-to-work patterns are likely to take decades to work themselves out, rather than a few short years. In fact, the 1990s may be a far better time than the 1970s to do meaningful impact studies of BART.

Unfortunately, policy research is often expected to evaluate the effectiveness of new initiatives on the basis of experience in much shorter time spans. It thus has to judge processes that are far from complete. This is likely to defeat the purpose of the experiments, especially if they are terminated or curtailed without a fair test of the results. It also underestimates the role and effectiveness of government, thus seeming to support one of the theses that Danielson and Doig challenge.

## A Look to the Future: No Drastic Consolidation

Danielson and Doig do not attempt to predict in detail future development in the New York region. Nor do they prescribe a specific restructuring of relationships among the many governmental actors. In fact, they foresee a continuation of the past and recent trends into the future:

> the variables that underlie the past behavior of the region's public officials will also be central to understanding their activities, their failures, and their successes in the next several decades. And we expect that the same themes and patterns underlie the political economies of other metropolitan regions.

In short, the modern metropolis is an "ecology of organizations"—public, private, and mixed. Each pursues its own interests, but with constant infringement from other organizations having different goals. These relationships are highly varied and complex, but are neither wholly random nor only reactive. Costs and benefits can be calculated, externalities can be identified and assessed, incremental adjustments can be made, and occasionally the system of relationships can be significantly rearranged.

The authors have carefully identified and developed typologies of inter-relationships among governmental organizations. These include organizations of limited scope, as well as more extensive geographic extent. They include organizations with single or limited purposes that are highly focused functionally and with substantial ability to concentrate resources in achieving their goals, as well as multiple-purpose governments having varied and often conflicting constituencies that may be constantly battling for shares of scarce resources.

Both limited-purpose and multiple-purpose agencies that are geographically small (e.g., small special districts and authorities, and small municipalities) are seriously limited in their ability to command and focus resources in achieving their goals, particularly when these require some kind of regional consensus and/or action. Even the large-scope multiple-purpose agencies that deal with extensive geographic areas (e.g., state and federal governments) have been successful with regional activities only when the state or federal agency involved is able to operate in relative isolation from the rest of the government—in other words, to act as if it were a special-purpose government. In short, the authors suggest that only *regional special-purpose agencies* will be able to surmount the divisive pursuit of constituency interests, and the consequent scattering of resources that is inherent in the current governmental fragmentation:

> In view of these constituency problems, which confront the national and state governments and most general-purpose governments in every region, there may of course be substantial advantages in looking. . . . [Thus] perhaps we need to create or find an engine of governmental power that can assemble the resources and overcome the difficulties, somewhat insulated from the buzzing confusion of constituent demands . . . [and perhaps] we need to apply to current and future efforts the advantages that the Port Authority brought to the George Washington Bridge project in the 1920s, and to the marine terminals in the postwar era, and which the carefully crafted alliances of the [Newark Housing Authority] brought to Newark's redevelopment in the 1950s. Indeed, this is the perspective that underlies the Port Authority's current initiatives in the region.

It is virtually certain that no drastic consolidation will integrate local governments and special-purpose agencies into a single regional government in the New York region. Even if the 1898 creation of Greater New York City—consolidating New York, Brooklyn, two other cities and all or parts of 21 towns—were repeated on a much grander scale, the region's governance would not be "consolidated across state boundaries." And even with a comprehensive metropolitan government, the governance of a large region like New York's would still comprise varied networks of intergovernmental, interagency and intergroup relationships involving units within and without the region. These of course include the national and state governments—themselves fragmented structurally and programatically—which also participate actively in the governance of metropolitan regions.

Given these complexities, the search continues for feasible, workable ways of structuring power and governmental relationships for greater effectiveness in achieving consensus and marshalling resources for regional endeavors. We can hope and anticipate that our two authors as well as other researchers will follow the unfolding story of this fascinating, frustrating and troubled, but also preeminently influential metropolis.

| | |
|---|---|
| *Stanley Scott* | *Victor Jones* |
| Editor, Lane Fund | Coeditor, Lane Studies in |
| Publications | Regional Government |
| | |
| Berkeley, California | January 1981 |

# Acknowledgments

We have incurred many debts during the years in which this study was conceived, nurtured, and completed. Our interest in metropolitan politics was originally stimulated by the two teachers and friends to whom this volume is dedicated, Richard T. Frost of Princeton University and Wallace S. Sayre of Columbia University. We have also learned much from Marver H. Bernstein, W. Duane Lockard, and the late John F. Sly, teachers and colleagues at Princeton. And a special note of thanks is due Robert C. Wood, who both encouraged our work and shaped the way a generation of political scientists have thought about the role of government in urban development.

Victor Jones and Stanley Scott of the Institute of Governmental Studies at the University of California, Berkeley, initially suggested that we undertake a study of the New York region as part of the Lane Studies in Regional Government. Over the years, they have been tolerant of our delays in completing the study, encouraging as to our approach, and lively commentators on the manuscript.

Others who read the manuscript in whole or in part, and offered helpful comments, include: Roger Gilman, Peter Goldmark, Harvey Sherman, John Brunner, and Robert Foote of the Port Authority of New York and New Jersey; William Shore and his associates at the Regional Plan Association of New York; John Harrigan of Hamline University; Stephen David of Fordham University; Charles Adrian at the University of California, Riverside; Erwin Bard, now retired from Brooklyn College; Annmarie Walsh of the Institute of Public Administration; Robert Curvin of the New York Times; Douglas Arnold, David Billington, and David Hammack at Princeton University; Chris Forbes of the Westway Coalition; Joan Aron and Mitchell Moss of New York University; Ellen Comisso at the University of California, San Diego; Jack Nagel at the University of Pennsylvania; and Charles Anderson of the U.S. Department of Transportation.

In addition, insights on particular development issues were offered by Arthur Gordon of the New York State Comptroller's Office; Jack Krauskopf, now in the New York City government; Chester Mattson of the Hackensack Meadowlands Development Commission; and Robert Moses.

Many former students gathered materials, wrote papers, and added to our understanding of pieces of the puzzle. These included William Bohnett, Andrés Gil, Lawrence Goldman, Duncan Grant, Sanford Greenberg, Norman Jacknis, Arthur Kent, David Kessler, Kate Levan, Melvin Masuda, Martin Murphy, Glenn Shafer, Lawrence Serra, and Joseph Taylor. And the graduate students in the Woodrow Wilson School's policy workshop on development issues in the New York region at Princeton University during the spring of

1980 helped sharpen our thinking on a number of issues.

We received assistance from numerous helpful people in identifying and locating photographs, correspondence, and other fugitive materials for the volume, including: Marion Ritz at the Triborough Bridge and Tunnel Authority; Louis Schlivek of the Regional Plan Association; Thomas Young and Steven Weissmann at the Port Authority; Barbara Reilly, NJ TRANSIT; Andrew Beresky at the College of Medicine and Dentistry of New Jersey; Wendy Shadwell and Helena Zinkham at the New York Historical Society; Susan Anisfield of the Hackensack Meadowlands Development Commission; and officials at the New Jersey Housing Finance Agency. To Charlotte Carlson and Elaine Seldner, we owe a special word of thanks for reproducing and constructing a fine set of maps.

The manuscript was typed and retyped through the collective efforts of Peg Anabel, Lucille Crooks, Betty Drotar, Jerri Kavanagh, Barbara Keller, Mary Leksa, Jean Nase, Nan Nash, Mary Robertson, and especially June DeRose, who combined organizing, typing, and research skills to keep our manuscript together and to locate the sources we needed in the final two years.

Generous research support from the Woodrow Wilson School of Public and International Affairs Princeton played an important part in providing us with the means to undertake this study. We appreciate the personal interest and institutional backing provided by Marver H. Bernstein, John P. Lewis, and Donald E. Stokes.

We are also grateful to the Lavanburg Foundation, whose officers, led by Oscar S. Straus and Ruth M. Glover, provided funds to underwrite the production of maps and photographs, and to assist in other elements of publishing and distributing this volume.

Books in process often disrupt the lives of those who live with authors, and this study has been around two households for more than a decade. Our children, who have grown much faster than the New York region during the years we worked on the book, were by and large tolerant. Our wives, Patricia R. F. Danielson and Joan N. Doig, helped us carry through to the finish, and with Jessica Danielson assisted in proofreading the volume.

As is always the case, many were helpful, but what follows is our responsibility.

*Michael N. Danielson*
*Jameson W. Doig*
Princeton, N. J.
May, 1981

# Abbreviations

| | |
|---|---|
| **CBD** | Central Business District (in Manhattan) |
| **H&M** | Hudson and Manhattan Railroad |
| **HUD** | Department of Housing and Urban Development (U.S.) |
| **ICC** | Interstate Commerce Commission |
| **LIRR** | Long Island Rail Road |
| **MCTA** | Metropolitan Commuter Transportation Authority |
| **MRC** | Metropolitan Regional Council |
| **MRTC** | Metropolitan Rapid Transit Commission |
| **MTA** | Metropolitan Transportation Authority |
| **NHA** | Newark Housing Authority |
| **PATH** | Port Authority Trans-Hudson Corporation |
| **RPA** | Regional Plan Association |
| **TBTA** | Triborough Bridge and Tunnel Authority |
| **THA** | Trenton Housing Authority |
| **TSRPC** | Tri-State Regional Planning Commission |
| **UDC** | Urban Development Corporation |
| **URA** | Urban Renewal Administration (U.S.) |

# Terms of Office

## Selected Political Executives in the New York Region, 1954–1981

### Governors

NEW YORK

| | |
|---|---|
| Thomas E. Dewey | January 1943–January 1955 |
| W. Averell Harriman | January 1955–January 1959 |
| Nelson A. Rockefeller | January 1959–December 1973 |
| Malcolm O. Wilson | December 1973–January 1975 |
| Hugh J. Carey | January 1975– |

NEW JERSEY

| | |
|---|---|
| Robert B. Meyner | January 1954–January 1962 |
| Richard J. Hughes | January 1962–January 1970 |
| William T. Cahill | January 1970–January 1974 |
| Brendan T. Byrne | January 1974– |

CONNECTICUT

| | |
|---|---|
| John Davis Lodge | January 1951–January 1955 |
| Abraham A. Ribicoff | January 1955–January 1961 |
| John N. Dempsey | January 1961–January 1971 |
| Thomas J. Meskill | January 1971–January 1975 |
| Ella T. Grasso | January 1975–December 1980 |
| William A. O'Neill | January 1981– |

### Mayors of Newark

| | |
|---|---|
| Leo P. Carlin | May 1953–July 1962 |
| Hugh J. Addonizio | July 1962–July 1970 |
| Kenneth A. Gibson | July 1970– |

### Mayors of New York City

| | |
|---|---|
| Robert F. Wagner | January 1954–January 1966 |
| John V. Lindsay | January 1966–January 1974 |
| Abraham D. Beame | January 1974–January 1978 |
| Edward I. Koch | January 1978– |

# 1

## Government and Urban Development

Cities grow and deteriorate, highways and houses spread across the urban landscape, racial and ethnic minorities cluster in ghettos, sources of water supply are polluted and reclaimed. These and other features of urban development are found in every major metropolitan region in the United States. And the basic elements differ little in other advanced industrial societies.[1] The patterns of development that characterize the modern metropolis are the product of the complex and continuing interactions of geographic, technological, economic, political, and other social factors which constantly mold and alter urban society.

Our central concern in this study is with the role of government in shaping urban development in modernized societies. More specifically: To what extent do the actions of governmental organizations have a significant independent influence on urban development, rather than having no significant role, or affecting development only by ratifying and supporting decisions previously made in other subsystems of the society, such as the private marketplace? By governmental organizations, we mean those organizations which authoritatively allocate values (i.e., make binding rules) for a society, and which are primarily oriented toward this function, together with subordinate units of such organizations.[2] The actions of governmental organizations must be examined in the context of the broader pattern of human relationships concerned with the authoritative allocation of values, i.e., the political system.[3]

The New York region is the focus of our study. Our immediate concern is the analysis of the role of government in shaping development within this metropolis, the largest and most complex in the United States. We also seek broader relevance. The approach used in this study should be helpful in understanding urban development in other areas; and our conclusions concerning the impact of city and suburban governments, public authorities, state and federal agencies, and other governmental units will suggest generalizations that apply in other regions, especially in the United States.

1. See, for example, Peter Hall, *The World Cities*, second edition (New York: McGraw-Hill, 1977).

2. Organizations that are not primarily oriented toward the rule-making function, such as the family or the church, may also make binding rules for a society; and in relatively nonmodernized societies this is frequently the case.

3. See Robert A. Dahl, *Modern Political Analysis*, third edition (Englewood Cliffs, N.J.: Prentice-Hall, 1976), p. 3 ff.; Marion J. Levy, Jr., *Modernization and the Structure of Societies: A Setting for International Affairs* (Princeton, N.J.: Princeton University Press, 1966), especially pp. 290–293, 333–336, 436 ff.

The difficulty in assessing the influence on urban development of any one set of organizations should be emphasized at the outset. There is, as York Willbern points out, a "chicken-and-egg" character to the question.[4] The many governmental and nongovernmental organizations operating in the metropolis influence each other continuously, making it very difficult to sort out the impact on development of any one factor. Moreover, the problem of determining cause and effect is particularly complex when one is analyzing causal factors related not to a clearly measurable outcome (such as the number of automobile accidents), but to a much broader set of outcomes comprising "urban development."

These difficulties have not prevented social scientists from assessing the impact of governmental organizations and other institutions on urban development. The most intensive analysis of this issue, certainly in terms of the New York region and perhaps for any modernized urban complex, was that conducted in the late 1950s by Raymond Vernon, Robert C. Wood, and their colleagues in the New York Metropolitan Region Study. Their conclusion is, to quote Wood, that "public programs and public policies are of little consequence" in shaping the metropolis. Governmental organizations "leave most of the important decisions for Regional development to the private marketplace."[5] Other observers such as York Willbern and Scott Greer have generally reached the same conclusion with regard to urban development in the United States.[6]

Our own position differs from that of Wood and Vernon and others who emphasize the dominance of economic factors. Admittedly, in some situations, governmental action appears to do little more than ratify decisions made in the private marketplace. On the basis of our review of the Wood and Vernon studies, however, together with additional evidence presented in the following chapters, we argue that governmental influence is frequently impor-

4. York Willbern, *The Withering Away of the City* (University, Ala.: University of Alabama Press, 1964), p. 30. Cf. Robert A. Dahl, *Democracy in the United States*, second edition (Chicago: Rand McNally, 1972), Chapter 21. On the general problem of analyzing causation in human affairs, see Robert MacIver, *Social Causation* (New York: Harper & Row, 1964).

5. Robert C. Wood, with Vladimir V. Almendinger, *1400 Governments: The Political Economy of the New York Region* (Cambridge, Mass.: Harvard University Press, 1961), pp. 173, 175; see also pp. 2–28, 110–113, 169–175, 190–199. Vernon's conclusions are set forth in the summary volume of the Metropolitan Region Study, *Metropolis 1985* (Cambridge, Mass.: Harvard University Press, 1960), especially chapters 10 and 11; see also Raymond Vernon, *The Myth and Reality of Our Urban Problems* (Cambridge, Mass.: Harvard University Press, 1966).

6. See York Willbern, *The Withering Away of the City*, especially pp. 29–32; Edward C. Banfield and James Q. Wilson, *City Politics* (New York: Vintage, 1963), p. 344; Scott Greer, *Urban Renewal and American Cities* (Indianapolis: Bobbs-Merrill, 1965), p. 164; Norton E. Long, *The Polity* (Chicago: Rand McNally, 1962), pp. 162–164; Martin Meyerson, "Five Functions for Planning," in Edward C. Banfield, ed., *Urban Government*, second edition (New York: Free Press, 1969), p. 589 (an article first published in 1956); Edward C. Banfield, *The Unheavenly City Revisited* (Boston: Little, Brown, 1974), chapter 2. Most of these authors rely heavily on the evidence and analysis provided in the volumes by Wood and Vernon. Conflicting conclusions, suggesting a more important role for government in urban development, are found in Benjamin Chinitz, "New York: A Metropolitan Region," in *Cities: A Scientific American Book* (New York: Knopf, 1965), pp. 113–121; Jameson W. Doig and Michael N. Danielson, "Politics and Urban Development," *International Journal of Comparative Sociology*, 7 (March 1966), pp. 76–95; and Michael N. Danielson, *The Politics of Exclusion* (New York: Columbia University Press, 1976).

tant. In many cases, public programs significantly modify or amplify developmental trends, and in some instances, governmental actions have a critical
initiating role in shaping urban development. These variations in governmental influence can be understood in terms of several factors—areal scope, functional scope, and the ability to concentrate resources. In this study, we define
these factors, and then use them to analyze the influence of various types of
governmental units.

Before examining the complex issue of cause and effect raised by the
question of what influence—if any—does government have on urban growth
and change, it is necessary to define what we mean by "urban development."
Some studies refer to "urban development" as the *process* of change in urban
areas; other discussions use the term to denote the *outcome* of the process at
any point in time. The latter definition is used in this volume. More specifically, our analysis focuses on the distribution of residences in urban regions,
in general and by income level and race; on the distribution of jobs; and on
the location of major transportation facilities. This focus is similar to that
used in the Vernon studies, although that analysis gave primary emphasis to
the distribution of jobs and residences.[7]

In our study, as in Vernon's, the main emphasis is on "physical" aspects
of urban society. The quality of education, police behavior, the welfare system, health care, and other service areas are not directly under scrutiny. It
may be that many of the forces—governmental and otherwise—which are
considered in our study also shape these aspects of urban life, but we leave
that exploration for another study.

We begin our analysis of the influence of government on urban development in the New York region by briefly examining the governmental system.
The remainder of the chapter explores in detail the general problem of evaluating governmental influence on urban development. This analysis provides
the framework which is used in the chapters that follow.

## Governments in the New York Region

As Robert Wood has commented, the tristate region centering on New
York City contains "one of the great unnatural wonders of the world"—an
interrelationship of governments "perhaps more complicated than any other
that mankind has yet contrived or allowed to happen."[8] The governments of
three states and the nation share responsibility in the metropolis with more
than two dozen county political units, over 700 municipalities, and several

7. See Edgar M. Hoover and Raymond Vernon, *Anatomy of a Metropolis: The Changing
Distribution of People and Jobs within the New York Metropolitan Region* (Cambridge, Mass.: Harvard University Press, 1959), p. 1; Vernon, *Metropolis 1985*, p. 215, and chapters 1 and 11; Wood,
*1400 Governments*, pp. vii, 169. At times, Wood gives transportation factors coequal status: "In
particular, we focus on the process for making those [governmental] decisions which most strongly
affect the private sector, that is, affect the location of firms and households or the transportation of
goods and people." Wood, *1400 Governments*, p. 3.

8. Wood, *1400 Governments*, p. 1.

hundred specialized functional districts.[9] The number of governmental units in the New York region in 1977 is shown in Table 1.

### Table 1—*Governmental Units in the New York Region: 1977*[a]

| | |
|---|---:|
| States | 3 |
| Counties | 31 |
| Municipalities | 780 |
| Special Districts | 716 |
| School Districts | 661 |
| TOTAL | 2,191 |

[a]Based on the 31-county definition of the New York region used by the Regional Plan Association. Wood's *1400 Governments* was based on a 22-county region. For a discussion of various definitions of the region, see Chapter Two.

*Source:* U.S. Bureau of the Census, *1977 Census of Governments*, Vol. 1, Governmental Organization (Washington: U.S. Government Printing Office).

Of nearly 2,200 nonnational units of government in the New York region, the three states possess the broadest array of powers. Each state has a wide range of policies that affect its portion of the metropolis, and all local government activity is subject to ultimate state control. But since New Jersey, New York, and Connecticut share these responsibilities, state policy in the New York region is far from uniform. Each state has distinct traditions of local government, and different policies for transportation, education, welfare, recreation, state aid to local governments, and other matters that affect the metropolis. These policies and programs are shaped not only by the needs and demands of residents of the New York region, but also in response to a variety of other urban and rural pressures in each state. Another important characteristic of state action is the fragmentation of programs among functional agencies within each state, many of which, such as highways and education, have considerable autonomy from the governor and legislature.

As in most metropolitan areas, local governments in the New York region vary greatly in size, governmental structure, policy goals, tax resources and expenditures, and political styles. One of these local governments, New York City, encompasses almost half of the region's population. Like the state governments, the complex governmental system of New York City is characterized by internal fragmentation and functional autonomy. In addition to New York, the region includes several large cities—Newark, with 329,000 residents in 1980, and Jersey City with 224,000, together with Paterson (138,000) and Elizabeth (106,000). Jersey City is itself the largest center in a

9. The numbers of governmental units vary, depending on whether the 22-, 25-, or 31-county definition of the region is used. (See Chapter Two for a discussion of the definition of the region.) In contrast with the other two states, the Connecticut counties no longer have any governmental powers.

cluster of older cities comprising Hudson County, with a total population of 557,000.[10]

The region also includes more than a dozen other cities with populations of over 50,000, many of which would be metropolitan centers if located outside the New York region. Interwoven with this complex of cities are suburban counties and municipalities, ranging from the placid local governments in the affluent enclaves of Westchester and Morris counties to the more intensively settled and financially hard-pressed suburbs of Middlesex and Nassau counties.

Finally, layered over this mosaic of governments are the special units, most of which have relatively narrow functional responsibilities. Most common are the school districts, which spend up to 75 percent of the local tax dollar in the region's newer residential suburbs. Most powerful are the regional public works enterprises, particularly the Port Authority of New York and New Jersey, with assets of over $3.6 billion in tunnels, bridges, airports, port facilities, a rail transit line, bus and truck terminals, and a world trade center. Until recently, great influence also was wielded by the cluster of specialized agencies long controlled by Robert Moses, a public entrepreneur without peer in urban America, whose monuments include bridges, tunnels, parks, parkways, garages, housing projects, and a coliseum. Two new regional organizations were added in the 1960s—the Metropolitan Transportation Authority, which now controls the Long Island Rail Road, the subways and toll bridges of New York City, and other transport facilities; and the Urban Development Corporation, created by New York State in 1968 to build housing and other projects without the encumbrance and inconvenience of local zoning and building restrictions.[11] Beyond the school districts and the regional authorities are several hundred other special districts concerned with such problems as water supply, sewage disposal, parking, and housing, and with jurisdictions ranging from several counties down to individual municipalities.

The impact of these governments on citizens varies greatly, depending on where they work and live. Tax burdens differ from state to state, from city to city, and from suburb to suburb. The per pupil expenditure for education, the amount and nature of public housing and downtown renewal, and other public services vary widely. Integrated regional policies for these and most other matters of public concern do not exist in the New York area.

These variations in effective demand and public policy in different parts of the region are readily illustrated by expenditures on education and on welfare-related services.[12] Some comparative data for New York City and suburban counties in the New York portion of the region are summarized in Table 2. These figures illustrate the relatively heavy per capita outlays for welfare and related services in the region's largest older city, compared with suburban areas.

---

10. Hudson County includes Bayonne (65,000), Union City (56,000), Hoboken (42,000), and several smaller municipalities. All population figures are for 1980.

11. The Urban Development Corporation's authority to override suburban zoning and building codes was severely restricted by the New York legislature in 1973; see Chapter Five.

12. For detailed analyses of local expenditures in the New York region, see Wood, *1400 Governments*, Chapters 2–3 and Appendix A; Regional Plan Association, *Public Services in Older Cities*, May 1968; and recent RPA and Tri-State Regional Planning Commission reports.

**Table 2–Per Capita Local Government Expenditures in the New York Sector of the Region: 1975**

|  | Total | Education | Health | Welfare | General Govt. |
|---|---|---|---|---|---|
| New York City | $1,912 | $366 | $330 | $263 | $149 |
| Suburban Counties | 1,074 | 515 | 90 | 70 | 117 |

*Source:* Regional Plan Association, *The Region's Money Flows* (New York: 1977), p. 13.

The wide variations among municipalities can also be indicated by comparing annual school expenditures per pupil within the New York region. At the upper end of the range are wealthier suburbs, while a number of older cities are concentrated toward the lower end of the scale. Table 3 gives a sample of the figures for the New Jersey portion of the region. Similar disparities are found in taxable valuation ("ratables") and tax burdens in the region. In the affluent suburb of Millburn, for example, ratables average $18,760 per resident, and the effective local tax rate (per $100 of actual value) is only $3.50. But in Elizabeth, only $8,495 in ratables stand behind each resident and the tax rate is $4.36; while in Jersey City, the ratables figure drops to $3,003 per capita, and the tax rate climbs to more than $7.50.[13]

**Table 3–Per Pupil Expenditures in Selected New Jersey Communities: 1975–1976**

| | |
|---|---|
| Princeton (Mercer County) | $2,204 |
| Millburn (Essex County) | 2,148 |
| Bedminster (Somerset County) | 2,088 |
| Ridgewood (Bergen County) | 1,981 |
| Newark | 1,541 |
| Elizabeth | 1,466 |
| Jersey City | 1,399 |
| Paterson | 1,096 |

*Source:* New Jersey, Department of Education, *Commissioner's Report for School Year 1975–1976* (Trenton, N.J.: 1976).

The fragmented character of the governmental system both permits and encourages the region's citizenry to focus their attention on narrow and immediate problems. Businessmen, homeowners, parents, motorists, and others concerned with particular policies and programs organize along the lines of governments' areal and functional divisions. In New York, as in other urban areas, both public and private participants in the region's political system generally react to issues in terms of a territorial or functional frame of reference. Consequently, as will become apparent in later chapters, municipal zoning policies and state highway plans are usually determined on the basis of a narrow calculation of costs and benefits. Affecting these calculations, in addition to financial considerations, are psychological factors, such as subur-

13. All ratables and tax rate figures are for 1976; see New Jersey Division of Local Government Service, *Annual Report, 1976* (Trenton, N.J.: 1976).

ban antagonism toward the older cities, racial and ethnic fears, and hostilities between those who would spend more for highways and those who would improve mass transportation.

Despite the localist and particularist bias of the region's political system, many problems cannot be dealt with adequately by individual local governments. As a result, networks of horizontal agreements have developed responding to such problems as traffic control, water supply, and refuse disposal. Such limited joint efforts are likely to develop "only when specific problems become acute and when the financial costs to be borne by each government can be clearly related to local benefits."[14] When benefits and costs cannot be readily identified and assigned—as in air pollution control and mass transportation—horizontal cooperation at the local level is unlikely to develop in the New York region.

In addition, a few program areas in the region have been characterized by a high degree of *vertical* functional cooperation. In highway construction and urban renewal, in particular, federal financing encouraged close relations among specialists at all three levels of the federal system. One example of vertical functional integration is the urban renewal programs of Newark and New York City, as they developed during the 1950s and early 1960s. Another is the regional highway program, where a complex alliance evolved over four decades, involving federal and state highway agencies, the Port Authority, the Triborough Bridge and Tunnel Authority, state toll road agencies, and most recently the Metropolitan Transportation Authority.[15]

As these functional alliances suggest, state and federal activities are important elements in the region's political system. During the postwar period, the dominant thrust of these activities has been to support and reinforce the areal and functional fragmentation of the region's political system. Financial assistance, particularly from the states to meet educational needs, has helped maintain the viability of the small-scale suburban municipalities and school districts. Most state and federal aid programs have been functionally specific, tending to weaken the integrative capabilities of general government. Where governmental action requires interstate cooperation, as in water and air pollution, conservation, recreation, and mass transportation, differing perspectives and priorities have made it difficult for state leaders to collaborate effectively. These characteristics of state and federal involvement in the region's political system reflect the localist and particularist perspectives that legislators elected from various parts of the New York region bring to the state capitals and to Washington.[16]

Since the early 1960s, increased efforts have been made, particularly by the federal government, to overcome this fragmentation. At the national level,

14. Jameson W. Doig, *Metropolitan Transportation Politics and the New York Region* (New York: Columbia University Press, 1966), p. 237.

15. See Harold Kaplan, *Urban Renewal Politics: Slum Clearance in Newark* (New York: Columbia University Press, 1963); Doig, *Metropolitan Transportation Politics*, Chapters 2 and 10; Wood, *1400 Governments*, Chapter 4.

16. See Michael N. Danielson, *Federal-Metropolitan Politics and the Commuter Crisis* (New York: Columbia University Press, 1965), Chapters 7 and 10; Harold Herman, *New York State and the Metropolitan Problem* (Philadelphia: University of Pennsylvania Press, 1965), Chapters 7–8; Doig, *Metropolitan Transportation Politics*, Chapters 5, 8–10.

formal requirements for interagency consultation have increased. For example, officials in the Department of Transportation and the Department of Housing and Urban Development must coordinate the development of transport plans in metropolitan areas; and a host of federal agencies were supposed to cooperate in planning, funding and implementing projects in Model Cities neighborhoods in the older cities. At the regional level, Washington has sought to foster the coordination of local, state, and federal planning across jurisdictional and functional lines by making federal aid in a number of program areas conditional on the existence of an areawide planning process. In the New York region, these responsibilities have been assumed by the Tri-State Regional Planning Commission, composed of federal, state, and local officials. To date, as indicated in later chapters, these efforts have had little significant impact on the traditionally separate funding and implementation of highway, housing, and other functional programs in the New York region.

## The Impact of Government on Development

In view of the profusion of governmental units pursuing different and often conflicting policies, and the clear influence of economic forces within every metropolis, the presumption readily emerges that government has little or no impact on urban development. In this section, we consider the approaches of Robert Wood and Raymond Vernon, whose pioneering analyses and conclusions emphasize this position. We then outline a contrasting approach, suggesting a far more significant governmental role in urban development.

### Government as Inconsequential: A Critique

In *1400 Governments*, Wood divides the governmental institutions of the New York region into two categories: agencies with "more or less Regional responsibilities"; and local governments together with "their satellites, the small special-purpose districts." In the first category, Wood concentrates on federal, state, and regional agencies concerned with transportation, water supply, and housing and urban renewal. These agencies "ride with" and "abet the economic forces already at work," rather than initiating new patterns of population settlement and economic growth. This occurs, Wood argues, because "conditions of institutional survival" make it difficult for these organizations to do otherwise. In seeking to maintain their economic and political power, the agencies favor private over public transportation, and support urban renewal in the central business district and suburban home construction, rather than improved housing in the ghettos. As a result, these regional agencies "support the present lines of development. They underwrite and accelerate the process of scatteration."

Local governments "arrive at their positions of negative influence" by a different route. Each community seeks to upgrade its own services and general environment locally, while maintaining its independence of action. However, because there are many units, each using land-use controls, building regulations, and other policies in trying to maximize local interests, the local governments "tend to cancel one another out." According to Wood, business-men and households are given a number of options from which to choose, and the pattern of development is determined mainly by their preferences, not by government policies.

The net result, in Wood's view, is that governmental activities are of "little consequence" in urban development. "Most of the important deci-sions" are left "to the private marketplace."[17] As noted earlier, this argument has been widely accepted by students of urban affairs as applicable not only to the New York region but also to urban America generally.

Wood's approach, however, oversimplifies the developmental process in two ways. First, his emphasis on a single generalization obscures the wide variations in governmental influence found in New York and other metropoli-tan regions. Consequently, he fails to explore the conditions under which governmental units are likely to play either greater or less important roles. Wood himself was aware of these variations, and the detailed materials in *1400 Governments* describe several exceptions to the generalization. Yet his concluding chapter emphasizes the major theme, and this thesis has predomi-nated in the writings of Vernon, York Willbern, and others who have relied upon Wood's research.[18]

The other difficulty in Wood's approach is his failure to give close consideration to individual and group preferences that underlie the actions of private economic and government units—preferences which result in a close intertwining of economic and political forces. In the New York region, as in any democratic political arena, governmental action is strongly influenced by the general values held by the voter, especially those values promoted by organized interest groups and public officials.[19] Underlying the region's eco-nomic system—which comprises the activities of producers, distributors, and consuming units operating in the marketplace—are general goals or values held by the ultimate consumer. Since the voter and consumer are largely the same, government and private economic organizations tend to respond to the preferences of the voter-consumer. To argue, then, that public policies "abet

17. Wood, *1400 Governments*, pp. 172–175; see also pp. 2–28, 110–113, 169–172, 190–199. Vernon's conclusions, which are similar, are set forth in *Metropolis 1985* (Cambridge, Mass.: Har-vard University Press, 1960), especially Chapters 10 and 11. As noted above, the analysis and conclusions in these two books are focused primarily on forces influencing the distribution of jobs and residences in the region.

18. To those familiar with the later work of Robert Wood and with his career in the public sector as a high official of the Department of Housing and Urban Development, president of the University of Massachusetts, and superintendent of schools in Boston, it is clear that Wood's views concerning the role of government in urban development have evolved since he wrote *1400 Govern-ments*. His public efforts and later writings, such as *The Necessary Majority* (New York: Columbia University Press, 1972), indicate a strong commitment to using governmental power to alter urban development—through such efforts as the model cities program and the creation of a major campus of the University of Massachusetts in Boston. Nonetheless, Wood's analysis in *1400 Governments* must be given serious attention. It resulted from a comprehensive scholarly examination of the central question of this study—the role of government in influencing urban development. And Wood's conclusions, combined with those of his colleague Vernon in *Metropolis 1985*, have been highly influential in the literature, as indicated above in note six.

19. Following Dahl, a democracy is defined as "a political system in which the opportunity to participate in decisions is widely shared among all adult citizens." Robert A. Dahl, *Modern Political Analysis*, third edition (Englewood Cliffs, N.J.: Prentice-Hall, 1976), p. 5.

the economic forces already at work" is to misinterpret the relationships. Generally, activities in both areas respond to the dominant configuration of underlying social values.[20]

These relationships can be illustrated by an aspect of urban development that is of particular concern to Wood and Vernon—the process of suburban growth or "scatteration." Privacy and open space are significant goals for a large proportion of Americans.[21] Increases in per capita wealth and advances in technology have made feasible widespread ownership of automobiles and single-family homes; and autos and houses both support the goals of privacy and open space. Therefore, in their role as consumers, Americans have bid for automobiles and houses—the latter largely in suburbia because of land availability and cost, as well as to achieve privacy—and these goods have been produced. Meanwhile, in their political role, Americans have provided support for federal mortgage programs and vast federal-state highway programs that make more feasible both home ownership and automobile access to suburban homes and jobs.

This process is complicated, of course, by a variety of feedback mechanisms and efforts of economic and political organizations to advance their own interests. For instance, while the quest for space and privacy is a fundamental goal, the desire to maximize these values has been further stimulated by the production of automobiles, highways, and suburban homes, together with the advertising campaigns and political activities of groups that benefit directly from the sale of suburban land, the construction of homes, the manufacture of automobiles, and the building of roads. These feedback mechanisms and institutional considerations illustrate the close interrelationships among political, economic, and other aspects of human behavior; they do not support the notion that private economic units have a prior or more basic role.[22]

20. The voter and consumer are not identical for several reasons. For example, the proportion of the poor who vote and are politically active is much less than that of the middle and upper classes; this relative political inactivity tends to reduce the impact of the poor on government policy. At the same time, of course, poverty reduces their influence as consumers. The impact of the voter also is shaped by the historical structure of government—e.g., in the United States, the allocation of seats in the United States Senate without regard to population, and the ability of small groups of voters to create insulated municipal enclaves, which tend to be responsive only to the narrow interests of their relatively homogeneous suburban populations.

21. Evidence on the importance of privacy and open space as social values in the United States is provided in John B. Lansing, "Residential Location and Urban Mobility: The Second Wave of Interviews," Survey Research Center, University of Michigan, 1966, and other SRC reports. The reports are also considered in William Michelson, "Most People Don't Want What Architects Want," Trans-action 5 (July/August 1968), pp. 37–44. Cf. Vernon, Metropolis 1985, Chapter 9. Privacy and open space are highly desired by most members of other industrialized societies as well; see Hall, The World Cities.

22. The use of "economic," "political" and "governmental" warrants a note of clarification, particularly since "economic" and "political" are terms that may refer either to concrete organizations or analytical categories. This study focuses on concrete organizations, called governmental units and private economic units (mainly private corporations and households), and on their relative influence in shaping urban development. As used in this volume, the phrases "economic forces" and "marketplace activities" refer to the actions of private economic units.

The "political aspect" of human behavior is not, however, the same as "the activities of governmental units"; nor is the "economic aspect" coextensive wih the activities of private economic units. "Political aspect" and "economic aspect" do not denote concrete organizations or people; they refer to different ways of looking at the same concrete organizations. The political aspect of any organization refers to the activities of its members as viewed in terms of power and

In general, the relationships among the various forces shaping urban regions can be summarized as follows. First, in the United States and in other democratic societies, there is a close interconnection among individual attitudes, governmental policies, and the actions of economic organizations and individuals in the marketplace. To be sure, consumer and voter preferences are in part shaped and constrained by the activities of large organizations—both governmental and economic—and by the choices they provide. In most instances, however, governmental and marketplace activities respond to values widely shared by the general public, and reinforce each other. The highway-housing example above illustrates these interrelationships.

Second, the extent to which the activities of economic organizations, or the actions of government (and of various levels of government), have a primary role in these interrelationships varies from society to society, depending on several factors. For example, in a nation with a tradition of governmental planning of economic and urban affairs, and with a history of public ownership of urban land—such as Sweden—public policies are more likely to have substantial influence on urban development than in a country without such traditions.[23] In the United States, the following factors are among the most important in relation to the development issue:

**1.** considerable emphasis on individualism and competitiveness in social relationships generally;

**2.** a system of vigorous private economic organizations;

**3.** historically, a low level of governmental involvement in economic affairs, in comparison with many other modernized societies;

**4.** substantial diffusion of governmental responsibility among semiautonomous local, state, and national units;

---

responsibility (within the organization, and in the broader society). Thus the role of General Motors and other private economic units can be fully understood only if such units are viewed from political as well as economic perspectives. Similarly, the economic aspect of any organization refers to the ways that its activities involve and affect the distribution of goods and services in a society. Thus, New York's Port Authority and other governmental units can be analyzed from economic as well as political perspectives.

As these comments suggest, it would be more accurate in most cases to denote an organization as "predominately politically oriented" or "predominately economically oriented." It is even possible that certain governmental units should, based on available evidence, be placed in the "predominately economically oriented" category—although we do not think the evidence on this point is persuasive for any of the governmental units considered in this volume. It is possible also that evidence would show that a particular private corporation acts primarily with reference to its power position, and thus belongs in the category of "predominately politically oriented" organizations. For purpose of this study, the benefits of redefining organizations in this way seem small. Thus we consider the issue of influence on urban development with reference to concrete units as they are commonly denoted—governmental units and private economic organizations.

Our discussion above draws primarily on Marion J. Levy, Jr., *Modernization and the Structure of Societies* (Princeton, N.J.: Princeton University Press, 1966); see especially pp. 290–293, 333–336, 436 ff., 503 ff. On the interdependence of social factors, see also the discussion of dynamic causation in Gunnar Myrdal, *An American Dilemma* (New York: Harper and Row, 1944), pp. 75 ff. and Appendix 3.

23. See Thomas J. Anton, *Governing Greater Stockholm: A Study of Policy Development and System Change* (Berkeley, Calif.: University of California Press, 1975); as well as Goran Sidenbladh, "Stockholm: A Planned City," in *Cities: A Scientific American Book* (New York: Knopf, 1966), pp. 75–87; Andrew Shonfield, *Modern Capitalism* (New York: Oxford University Press, 1965), pp. 199–211; and Thomas J. Anton, "Incrementalism in Utopia," *Urban Affairs Quarterly* 5 (September, 1969), pp. 59–82.

**5.** a continuing increase in governmental involvement in economic and other aspects of American society in recent decades, combined with closer relations among the several levels of government—thus modifying factors (3) and (4);

**6.** a tendency for significant governmental action to focus on specific problems, particularly as those problems reach a state of widely perceived "crisis";

**7.** governmental action, especially in noncrisis situations, that is responsive primarily to the concerns of organized and politically active interest groups; and

**8.** a greater emphasis (in governmental affairs and otherwise) on concrete, measurable goals and achievements than on esthetic and other less readily measured aspects.[24]

Third, the pattern of urban development is the result of a dynamic interplay of forces, some going beyond social preferences, government actions, and activities of economic organizations. Most prominent perhaps is the influence of technology. The impact of the railroad and the motor vehicle on the patterns of industrial and residential location are obvious examples.

Fourth, while it is sometimes convenient to refer simply to the activities of "government" and of "economic organizations," neither term refers to a cohesive group with a coherent set of development goals. On the contrary, different views on important issues generate wide divisions and conflict among public agencies and within the private sector. In highway and airport construction, state and regional public agencies are often in conflict with local governments and their constituents. To take another example, any new policy initiative involving abandonment, expansion, or added tax dollars for rail service in the region attracts widespread debate among political leaders—often pitting some cities, suburbs, and their state representatives against others, as they examine closely the proposed distribution of benefits and burdens.

Since our interest is mainly in understanding the role of government in shaping the New York region, we devote considerable attention to the great diversity of public agencies, and to the patterns of alliance and conflict among them. Indeed, the role of private actors occasionally fades into the background, as public entrepreneurs and opposing officials take center stage. Like public agencies, however, private interests also divide, often sharply, as we illustrate in the following chapters. Merchants in Newark resist mass-transit projects that may siphon off their shoppers to Manhattan, whose chambers of commerce applaud public action which would yield such benefits. Business leaders who see regional vitality and increased profits for their banks and other enterprises in the construction of new shopping malls, a world trade

---

24. On values and attitudes in the United States, see Dahl, *Democracy in the United States*, especially Chapter 22; Gabriel A. Almond and Sidney Verba, *The Civic Culture* (Princeton, N.J.: Princeton University Press, 1963); E. E. Schattschneider, *The Semi-Sovereign People* (New York: Holt, Rinehart and Winston, 1960). The impact on urban development of American attitudes toward private property and private enterprise is treated in Sam Bass Warner, *The Private City* (Philadelphia: University of Pennsylvania Press, 1968). For an interesting contrast between the emphasis on individualism and competition in the United States and the very different situation in Norway, see Harry Eckstein, *Division and Cohesion in Democracy: A Study of Norway* (Princeton, N.J.: Princeton University Press, 1966), especially pp. 80–89, 184.

center, or a new commercial complex in the New Jersey meadows, find themselves opposed by shopkeepers likely to be uprooted or drained of their customers. And both sides find ready allies among elected officials and public agencies whose own concerns—votes, highway expansion, environmentalism—seem likely to be aided or imperiled as a new project goes forward.

From the vantage point suggested by Wood, however, these divisions and intertwinings of public and private organizations can be considered relatively unimportant in assessing the role of government. The appropriate test for meaningful governmental influence in urban development, he argues, is "public direction of economic growth." More specifically,

> [this] would involve the establishment of a governmental structure which possessed the jurisdiction and the authority to make decisions about alternative forms of Regional development, more or less consciously and more or less comprehensively. . . . There would be some type of Regional organization empowered to set aside land for recreational purposes on the basis of a Regional plan. . . . There would be some type of Regional organization empowered to subsidize commuter transportation, if this were in accord with a general plan. . . . [25]

According to this view, government must be able to plan and act on a comprehensive basis for the entire region, in order to influence development in a significant fashion. If it lacks this capacity government is left in a position of "little consequence," while economic forces and other factors shape urban development.[26]

### Varieties of Influence

Government's role in urban development is far more varied than Wood's approach suggests. The major patterns of governmental influence can be expressed better in terms of a continuum than a dichotomy—as shown in Figure 1. At one end of the continuum, government officials merely ratify decisions made in the private marketplace. Typical are the actions of local officials in zoning vacant land to the specifications of developers who wish to construct

---

25. Wood, *1400 Governments*, pp. 174–175, 192. Cf. 171, 193 ff. Wood implies, especially on p. 192, that the standards for governmental action quoted in the text above are those advocated by reformers, and are not necessarily his own. In context, however, they appear to be the standards for a significant governmental role accepted in *1400 Governments*.

26. Wood's volume focused primarily on the nature of contemporary urban problems and programs, not on the reforms needed to alter current developmental trends. When advocates of reform approach urban problems with a lens similar to that used by Wood, the result is unrealistic and often confused proposals. That is, the reformer argues that regional development is shaped by two forces, the private market and government policy, the marketplace presently being the dominant force. He then tends to argue that existing urban problems (suburban sprawl, deterioration of the older cities, etc.) result from the dominant role of the market. The solution, then, is action by the other force—government—to counter market pressures and to substitute "rational" or "efficient" urban growth for the irrationality of the marketplace. Such public action, the reformer argues, is likely to be especially effective if undertaken by regional, state and federal agencies, with their broader perspectives (and perhaps broader powers and financial resources). If, as we argue, the actions of economic organizations and government are closely intertwined with underlying social preferences, the reformers' plea must be interpreted as an argument that the urban populace ought to substitute other values—presumably the "rationality" values of the urban planner—for the values that have previously guided economic and political behavior in the metropolis.

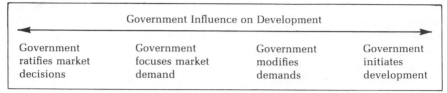

**Figure 1**

single-family homes on small lots, or the activities of local governments in facilitating private development of downtown parking lots that enhance the ability of main street merchants to compete with suburban shopping centers.

In the middle range of the continuum, a government unit is highly sensitive to economic and social forces, but contributes significantly to the specific content of the policy decision. Included here are the frequent situations in which demands for government action are relatively unfocused. Rapidly increasing automobile ownership creates the demand for new highways, but the appropriate government agencies must translate this unfocused demand into priorities and specific highway alignments. The same is true of demands for increased water supply or a new jetport. In each case, the specific content of the governmental decision will influence the subsequent pattern of development in the affected area. For instance, because a Garden State Parkway interchange was constructed in Paramus, that town became highly attractive for commercial development, and during the 1960s blossomed into one of the major shopping areas in northern New Jersey.

A more significant type of government influence on urban development occurs when a governmental unit's sensitivity to economic and social developments modifies or amplifies developmental trends. An example of this kind of governmental action is the use of restrictive zoning ordinances and building codes by suburban municipalities to prevent the construction of moderately priced, single-family housing. This type of zoning results from the awareness on the part of suburban officials and taxpayers that the private marketplace, if not restricted, will attempt to satisfy the lower-income family's quest for space and privacy with relatively inexpensive houses on small lots. Such homes threaten to cost the community more in services than they can generate in taxes, as do apartments priced for less affluent families. The use of minimum lot-size and other zoning restrictions to limit population—now an almost universal practice in the New York region—constrains the ability of real estate developers to maximize their investments through intensive development of suburban land. Such local government policies have significantly amplified the outward spread of residences and jobs in the region. The remaining land zoned for small houses, inexpensive apartments, and mobile homes tends to be located on the periphery of the region, where the local political systems are not yet sensitive to the costs of intensive suburbanization. These government policies also modify the effective demand for suburban housing, since many lower-income families are both dissuaded by the high cost of homes in suburbs situated close to the region's job centers, and discouraged by the journey-to-work associated with less expensive suburban housing forty miles or more from the core. In short, even in the middle range of this continuum, government decisions significantly influence development patterns.

*The interests and actions of public agencies such as the Port Authority determine when and where major public facilities are constructed, thus affecting the location and timing of development like that around the New Jersey end of the George Washington Bridge.*

Credit: Louis B. Schlivek, Regional Plan Association

Toward the other end of the continuum, government actions have a critical initiating role in shaping development. For example, early in the region's history New York State decided in 1816 to sell $8.5 million in bonds for a canal linking Lake Erie and the Hudson River. Completed in 1825, the 364-mile Erie Canal brought the old Northwest to New York's doorstep, giving the region a tremendous early competitive advantage. More recently, the redevelopment of Columbus Circle and the building of the Lincoln Center complex in Manhattan, the construction of the Verrazano-Narrows Bridge with its strong impact on development on Staten Island, the development of parks and beaches on Long Island, and the maintenance of much of northern Westchester County as a low-density, semirural enclave illustrate government acting as an important and relatively autonomous force in shaping the New York region.

Government's influence on urban development in the region thus appears to be considerably more significant than Wood's conclusions would lead one to believe. In general, we concur with Charles Abrams's view that "public policy for slum clearance, housing, race discrimination, zoning, road building, community facilities, transportation, suburban development, relief of poverty, and for spending and taxation is a main lever in manipulating the patterns of the society and the choices available to its members."[27] In a relatively responsive democratic political system such as that of the New York region, however, government's use of these levers is constrained by the developmental values which are widely shared or vigorously advanced. As a result, those who do not share the dominant social values, or have the resources to press their views, necessarily find it very difficult to employ government as an instrument to further their goals in urban development. But the situation is dynamic rather than static, because widely shared values and the capabilities to advance views change over time. As illustrated in the chapters that follow, public attitudes about the environment changed substantially in the 1970s, reducing consensus on the desirability of highway construction, while minority and lower-income groups in the region's older cities significantly increased their ability to persuade public development agencies to take account of their values.

### Varieties of Influence: A Further Look

The attentive reader will have noticed that Robert Wood's discussion of influence and our continuum both involve two variables—the *impact* of governmental action on urban development, and the *independence* of governmental action (particularly in relation to "private economic forces"). In the discussion above, these two variables have not been considered separately. Because of the interrelationships among social-political-economic factors, it is empirically difficult to sort out the "independence" variable. Also, our analysis in the following chapters devotes substantial attention to governmental activities that rank highly in both impact and independence, since these activities provide the clearest evidence with which to challenge the Wood-Vernon position.

Nevertheless, the chapters below do discuss some governmental units and activities—such as general governmental units in older cities—whose ranking in terms of the two variables may be quite disparate. In any event, exploring the relationship between "independence" and "impact" may help improve analytical clarity.

Our first step is to express each variable in terms of a continuum. Taking the Wood-Vernon perspective as a starting point, relative *"dependence"* of a governmental unit is measured by the extent to which the unit's actions are determined by (previous) actions taken by businesses, households, and other "economic units." This step is shown in Figure 2. Relative *impact* on urban development is measured by the extent to which the actions of any governmental unit shape the distribution of jobs, residences, and transportation facilities in the region, as shown in Figure 3.

27. Charles Abrams, *The City Is the Frontier* (New York: Harper and Row, 1965), p. 17.

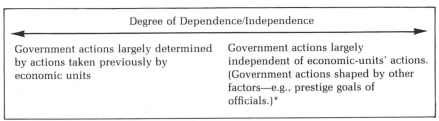

Degree of Dependence/Independence

| Government actions largely determined by actions taken previously by economic units | Government actions largely independent of economic-units' actions. (Government actions shaped by other factors—e.g., prestige goals of officials.)* |

[*In some situations, it might be asserted that officials of a government unit had decided "independently" that their actions should be largely directed toward facilitating the goals of certain economic units, without considering whether such facilitation would be helpful in meeting other goals. We would place such government actions/ units toward the dependence end of the continuum, by definition.]

**Figure 2**

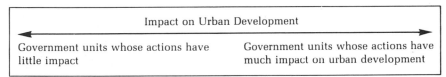

Impact on Urban Development

| Government units whose actions have little impact | Government units whose actions have much impact on urban development |

**Figure 3**

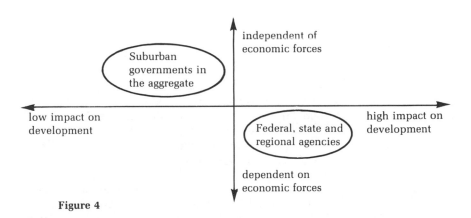

**Figure 4**

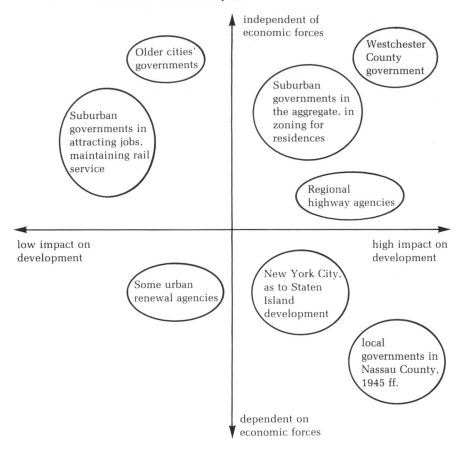

independent of
economic forces

Older cities'
governments

Westchester
County
government

Suburban
governments in
the aggregate, in
zoning for
residences

Suburban
governments in
attracting jobs,
maintaining rail
service

Regional
highway agencies

low impact on
development

high impact on
development

Some urban
renewal agencies

New York City,
as to Staten
Island
development

local
governments in
Nassau County,
1945 ff.

dependent on
economic forces

**Figure 5**

If the two continua are combined to form a matrix, Wood's conclusions regarding government units can be shown, as in Figure 4. That is, suburban governments act independently of the economic forces in the New York region, but their efforts "tend to cancel one another out," giving them little net impact on development. On the other hand, regional agencies do shape development in Wood's view, but only as responsive handmaidens to the "economic forces already at work."

Our contrasting conclusions, suggested in this chapter and amplified in later chapters, can be approximated in the same matrix, shown as Figure 5.

As visual representations of the differences between our conclusions and those of Vernon and Wood, these last two figures may be helpful. But the two variables can also be viewed as representing two different steps in the same causal chain. To take an example to be considered in a later chapter, the construction of the Narrows Bridge greatly increased the rate of population growth on Staten Island. Therefore, the actions of the two governmental agencies that planned and constructed the bridge (Triborough and the Port

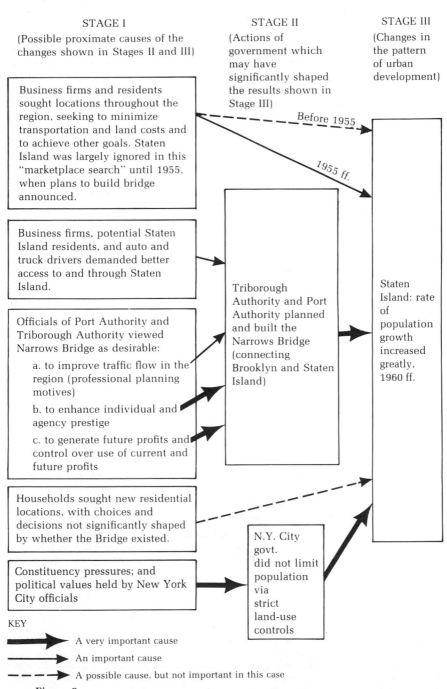

STAGE I
(Possible proximate causes of the changes shown in Stages II and III)

STAGE II
(Actions of government which may have significantly shaped the results shown in Stage III)

STAGE III
(Changes in the pattern of urban development)

Business firms and residents sought locations throughout the region, seeking to minimize transportation and land costs and to achieve other goals. Staten Island was largely ignored in this "marketplace search" until 1955, when plans to build bridge announced.

Before 1955

1955 ff.

Business firms, potential Staten Island residents, and auto and truck drivers demanded better access to and through Staten Island.

Officials of Port Authority and Triborough Authority viewed Narrows Bridge as desirable:

    a. to improve traffic flow in the region (professional planning motives)

    b. to enhance individual and agency prestige

    c. to generate future profits and control over use of current and future profits

Triborough Authority and Port Authority planned and built the Narrows Bridge (connecting Brooklyn and Staten Island)

Staten Island: rate of population growth increased greatly, 1960 ff.

Households sought new residential locations, with choices and decisions not significantly shaped by whether the Bridge existed.

Constituency pressures; and political values held by New York City officials

N.Y. City govt. did not limit population via strict land-use controls

KEY

    A very important cause

    An important cause

    A possible cause, but not important in this case

**Figure 6**

Authority) had an impact on development in a major sector of the New York region. The next step is to determine whether those governmental actions were taken primarily in response to economic forces, i.e., to determine the degree of independence of the two agencies in deciding to build the bridge. The proximate causal relationships are shown in Figure 6. The *independence* of various governmental units is suggested by the relative importance of the several arrows between Stage I and Stage II. The *impact* of various governments and other factors is suggested by the relative importance of various arrows entering Stage III.

The role of governmental action in shaping development is clearly significant in the Narrows Bridge case. The more difficult empirical problem is to determine the relative importance of the several causes (arrows) entering Stage II, i.e., to determine the degree of governmental independence of external economic forces. In other cases—for example, in analyzing the relative roles of suburban governments and of market forces in constraining housing choices in the suburbs—the main focus of the empirical problem shifts. The relative independence of local governmental action on land-use policies in many suburbs is fairly readily established, as we show in Chapter Three. Therefore, the main problem is to determine the importance of various factors in shaping housing choices and patterns (i.e., the relative strength of various causes or arrows entering Stage III).

The complexity of the causal linkages shown in Figure 6 underscores the point made earlier in the chapter—that the economic, governmental and other forces shaping urban development are closely intertwined, making it difficult to sort out the most important causes of urban change. As one conference of scholars concluded: "It is always difficult and frequently impossible to isolate cause and effect relationships in any kind of social science research, and policy impact studies pose many particularly difficult, perhaps insoluble, methodological problems."[28]

Despite these difficulties, some headway can be made. The first step, suggested by the Narrows Bridge example, is to state the interconnections among governmental and private economic units in ways that indicate their possible causal relationships.[29] Many (but not all) of the connections suggested by the Narrows Bridge illustration are power relationships. Consequently, we should briefly explore the problem of defining and measuring "power" or "influence." In his early, seminal essay on this problem, Herbert Simon defined the exercise of power as "affecting policies of others than the self."[30] That is, A has power or influence over B when B's choice among alternative behaviors is modified by the communicated preference of A. Building on Simon's approach, Jack Nagel provides a more rigorous and empiri-

---

28. Austin Ranney, "Studying the Impacts of Public Policies," *Social Science Research Council Items*, March 1972, p. 4. Cf. Paul Samuelson, "Some Notions on Causality and Teleology in Economics," in Daniel Lerner, ed., *Cause and Effect* (New York: Free Press, 1965), pp. 99 ff.

29. For a more detailed discussion of the issues surrounding the measurement of power and other forms of causation in urban affairs, see Jameson W. Doig and Michael N. Danielson, "From the Firm Ground of Result and Fact to the Tossing Sea of Cause and Theory: the Role of Government in Urban Development," *Policy Studies Journal* 8 (Summer 1980), pp. 852–861.

30. Herbert A. Simon, *Models of Man: Social and Rational* (New York: Wiley, 1957), p. 65. The terms power and influence will be used interchangeably in this volume, as they are in Simon's analysis.

cally more useful definition than previous studies: "A power relation . . . [is a] causal relation between the *preferences* of an actor regarding an outcome and the outcome itself."[31] This definition ensures that the search for power relationships will include both (1) situations in which A, acting on his or her own preferences, caused B to respond as A wished, and (2) those in which B anticipated that A would prefer B to do X (although A took no action) and B therefore did X.[32]

In some studies, various statistical techniques may be used to measure influence.[33] In assessing the pattern of power relationships in urban development, however, statistical methods do not appear to be very useful because there is little appropriate data in quantified form. For example, we have not found it useful to employ the quantitative approach developed by Thomas Dye and others in assessing the relative influence of various factors in shaping government action. The emphasis in these studies has been on statistical correlations among "economic development variables," political system characteristics, and quantifiable policy measures (such as annual expenditures for highways or education).[34] For some variables that are crucial to understanding urban development, such data are not available, or the available data provide a tenuous basis for analyzing the relevant actions of public or private institutions.[35]

Moreover, these studies have generally disregarded the complex arrangements through which various economic and political "inputs" are converted to "policy outputs"; as Douglas Arnold comments in a critical review, "nowhere is there a sense of the policy-making process at work."[36] If these political arrangements had no significant influence in determining which in-

31. Jack H. Nagel, *The Descriptive Analysis of Power* (New Haven: Yale University Press, 1975), p. 29; emphasis added. On the significance of Nagel's contribution, see R. Douglas Arnold, *Congress and the Bureaucracy: A Theory of Influence* (New Haven: Yale University Press, 1979), pp. 72–73, and Dahl, *Modern Political Analysis*, p. 30.

32. See Nagel, *The Descriptive Analysis of Power*, pp. 27 ff.

33. On the use of path analysis, see Nagel (ibid.), pp. 54 ff.; on probit analysis, see Arnold, *Congress and the Bureaucracy*, pp. 78 ff.

34. For example, Dye analyzed the relationships among four economic development variables (urbanization, industrialization, wealth and education), four political system characteristics (level of voter participation, degree of malapportionment, party control of state government, and level of interparty competition), and policy measures in health, welfare, highways and other areas. See Thomas R. Dye, *Politics, Economics, and the Public: Policy Outcomes in the American States* (Chicago: Rand McNally, 1966). For other examples of this approach, see Richard Dawson and James A. Robinson, "Inter-Party Competition, Economic Variables, and Welfare Policies in the American States", *Journal of Politics* 25 (May 1963), pp. 265–289; Ira Sharkansky and Richard Hofferbert, "Dimensions of State Politics, Economics, and Public Policy," *American Political Science Review* 63 (September 1969), 867–879; Virginia Gray, "Models of Comparative State Politics: A Comparison of Cross-Sectional and Time Series Analyses," *American Journal of Political Science* 20 (May 1976), pp. 235–256.

35. Robert Eyestone attempts, for example, to utilize quantitative analysis to examine planning and zoning policies in the San Francisco area, by using planning expeditures as the measure of policy output. Expenditure patterns, however, are a weak proxy for local land-use policies and for their impact on municipal development as it is shaped by these ordinances. See Robert Eyestone, *The Threads of Public Policy: A Study in Policy Leadership* (Indianapolis: Bobbs-Merrill, 1971), pp. 84 ff., 137 ff., and the review of Eyestone's volume by Michael N. Danielson in *Journal of Politics* 34 (May 1972), pp. 669–670.

36. Arnold, *Congress and the Bureaucracy*, p. 222. See also the review by David Cameron in *Policy Analysis* 5 (Summer 1979), pp. 405–407.

puts were used and how public powers were employed, such an omission might be pardonable. Even then the best way to determine which variables are influential would seem to be through analyzing actual causal patterns—as we attempt to do in the chapters below—rather than through the use of statistical correlations of inputs and outputs. In fact, some scholars who have emphasized the use of correlations have recently shown an interest in more direct measures of causation. Thus Thomas Dye and Virginia Gray urge that social scientists "move away from the associational reasoning" approach and devise causal models which "portray developmental and sequential ideas about *how* environmental and political forces and public policies interact." In their joint article Dye and Gray refer to the important role of politics in "the making of economic decisions which have enormous long-run consequences," and to the central role of such officials as Robert Moses in shaping American cities.[37]

In our own attempts to sort out the complex causal linkages involved in urban development, we have found two approaches to be particularly fruitful, and both are employed in the following chapters. The first is to identify cases, or preferably clusters of cases, where there is considerable evidence that identified governmental units and economic units prefer different outcomes, and act accordingly. Or, to state essentially the same point in a different way, one identifies situations in which the desires and actions of specified governmental units directly *conflict* with those of specified economic units. The outcome should indicate fairly clearly which set of units had more influence (in our study, more influence over the distribution of residences, job locations, and transportation facilities).[38] The analysis of suburban zoning in Chapter Three illustrates this approach.

Often, however, the preferences of important clusters of economic units and governmental agencies are not in conflict. Instead, they are directed toward actions that are similar or mutually reinforcing in shaping the urban region. In situations where such mutual efforts affect urban development, the question is whether the governmental role is merely to "abet the economic forces already at work"—which would imply that economic units are the initiating causes, operating directly, and also indirectly through the public agencies, as suggested by Figure 7.

In order to determine whether governmental units have more than a "merely facilitating" role, another approach can be used. The motives and perceptions of the relevant governmental officials are explored to determine what factors shape their decisions. Where other aims than that of facilitating

37. Thomas R. Dye and Virginia Gray, "Determinants of Public Policy: Cities, States, Nations," *Policy Studies Journal* 6 (Autumn 1977), pp. 86, 89. In a recent essay, Gray also suggests that we "move beyond" the previous efforts in order to examine "how the political system converts the demands of the population," and that we look for "determinants of public policy which can be manipulated by policymakers." She finds patterns of "substate delegation" of power and other organizational factors especially promising as explanatory variables. Virginia Gray, "The Determinants of Public Policy: A Reappraisal," in Thomas R. Dye and Virginia Gray, eds., *The Determinants of Public Policy* (Lexington, Mass.: Lexington-Heath, 1980), pp. 216–217, 220.

38. This research strategy is suggested by Max Weber's comment: "'Power' (*Macht*) is the probability that one actor within a social relationship will be in a position to carry out his own will despite resistance . . . " (quoted in Robert A. Dahl, "Power," in David Sills, ed., *International Encyclopedia of the Social Sciences*, vol. 12 (New York: Free Press, 1968), pp. 405 ff.; emphasis added).

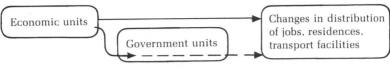

**Figure 7**

the goals of economic units become salient, one can speak with greater confidence of the "independent" initiating role of governmental action in shaping development. This approach is suggested in Figure 6 and used, for example, in analyzing highway decisions in the New York region in Chapter Six.

## The Sources of Governmental Influence

In a complex political system like that of the New York region, there are inevitably great differences in the ability of various governmental units to influence development. The extent to which an individual unit shapes the pattern of urban growth can be analyzed in terms of three sets of factors—its areal scope, its functional scope, and its ability to concentrate resources on specific developmental goals. The first two factors can be employed to distribute the region's governments in a matrix involving four categories, as shown in Figure 8. The third factor includes several elements used to analyze the actions and the impact of government within the limits defined by the first two factors.

### *Areal and Functional Scope: Toward a Classification of Governments*

Areal scope refers to the extent of the region in which a governmental unit has responsibility. In the New York region, this ranges from towns encompassing less than one square mile, such as Guttenberg in New Jersey and Hewlett Neck on Long Island, through New York City and the region's larger counties, to the three states and the national government.

Functional scope concerns the number of fields of activity with which the government institution is involved. At one end of the spectrum are single-purpose units, such as highway agencies and sewerage districts; at the other end are the governments of general jurisdiction in the region—the municipalities, counties, and state and federal governments—and more specifically the mayors, governors, legislators, and other officials within these units with broad multifunctional responsibilities.

When areal and functional scope are combined, the various governments in a region can be distributed in the matrix (Figure 8). Within the first quadrant (broad functional and narrow areal scope) are found the municipal and county governments of the region, and more specifically the mayors, county executives, planning and zoning agencies, and other central organs of local government.

The second quadrant (broad functional and broad areal scope) includes

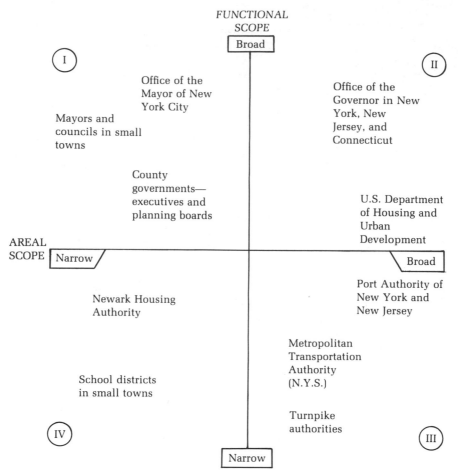

**Figure 8** *Governmental Units: Functional and Areal Scope (with examples)*

those components of the state and national governments concerned with general policy-making and coordination. At the state level, these include the governor's office, the legislature, and the agencies concerned with general planning and urban development. In Washington, integrative institutions with a role in urban development are the President and the Executive Office, Congress, the Department of Housing and Urban Development, the Department of Transportation, and the Environmental Protection Administration.

The third category (narrow functional and broad areal scope) includes the regional and subregional agencies with direct responsibility for carrying out specific programs in highways, housing, and other areas. Many of these agencies are line departments of federal and state governments. Others are semiautonomous public authorities and special districts, such as the Port Authority of New York and New Jersey and the Long Island Park Commission.

In the fourth quadrant (narrow functional and areal scope) are the special districts and other agencies with responsibilities in small portions of the region, such as the numerous school districts which are limited to one or two municipalities and specialized functional agencies within individual localities.

### Concentration of Resources

The third factor—the ability to concentrate resources—involves the focusing of public powers, funds, and skills in order to achieve specific developmental goals. The significance of this factor lies in the fact that urban development, especially in an industrialized, pluralistic society, results from a dynamic interplay of technological, political, economic and other forces. Consequently, government's efforts to shape development must overcome the dynamism of the other forces, and such efforts are likely to be more successful if governmental resources are focused on specific developmental areas and projects. Underlying the ability of a unit of government to concentrate resources for development purposes within its areal and functional jurisdiction are a number of elements. Particularly important are its formal independence of other governmental units, the variety and intensity of constituency demands on the unit, and five other kinds of resources available to the unit: funds; control over the use of land; leadership skills; control over subunits of the government; and planning capabilities. As the following discussion illustrates, these seven factors are interrelated, and clear boundaries around each cannot readily be drawn. The role of the various elements, especially in combination, becomes more evident in the following chapters as their relationships to the several categories of government are explored.[39]

**Formal independence.** Two of the factors concern political controls and pressures that are primarily external to the unit. The first is the extent to which a governmental body is formally independent of other governments in making policy, obtaining funds, and allocating funds for specific purposes. No governmental body in the United States is completely independent even in a formal sense, since all are subject to constitutional limitations and judicial oversight. But there are marked differences in the extent to which one unit or one set of officials is formally required to obtain the consent of others before acting.

Probably the greatest degree of formal independence is that permitted the President and his aides in foreign policy. Taken together, the central,

39. For discussion of these elements and of power resources generally, see Robert A. Dahl, *Who Governs?* (New Haven: Yale University Press, 1961), Books IV, V; Dahl, "Power," in *International Encyclopedia of the Social Sciences*, vol. 12, p. 409; Richard E. Neustadt, *Presidential Power* (New York: Wiley, 1960); Wallace S. Sayre and Herbert Kaufman, *Governing New York City* (New York: Russell Sage Foundation, 1960), chapters 8–9, 13, 15, 18; Eugene Bardach, *The Skill Factor in Politics* (Berkeley, Calif.: University of California Press, 1972), pp. 5 ff.

elective policymaking institutions at the national level (President and Congress) rank near the "independence" end of the continuum, as do their counterparts at the state level. Substantially less formal independence is given to the central policy institutions at the local level. Counties and municipalities are creations of the state government, and their activities in the urban field (as elsewhere) are restricted—often rather severely—by state constitutions and statutes, by state courts, and by the refusal of state legislators to enact particular laws requested by local officials.

Administrative departments and agencies, whether federal, state, or local, generally have no formal independence; funds obtained for their use, and the ways they can spend money or otherwise make policy, are under the control of elected officials. The normal arrangement through which funds are allocated for particular programs—the budgetary process—makes many line agencies highly vulnerable to a siphoning off of moneys which might be used for specific developmental projects. On the other hand, when funds are statutorily earmarked for a line agency, as is the case in many states with respect to road building, the agency has considerably more independence.

One other kind of government institution should be mentioned: the specialized functional unit generally referred to as a special district or public authority. This institution comes in a wide variety of sizes and types, ranging from the small-town school district with elected members and taxing power, to the mammoth port and highway authorities financed largely out of their own revenues and governed by officials appointed for fixed terms. Because of these wide variations, generalizations about the independence of districts and authorities are hazardous. Generally, they are less restricted than are regular line departments, and the authorities supported by tolls and other fees frequently have a degree of formal discretion substantially exceeding that of elected municipal officials.

**Variety and intensity of constituency demands.** Essentially every government unit is the object of close interest by a number of organized groups and clusters of individuals, each urging that the unit's officials use their funds and other resources to achieve goals favored by the particular constituency. The "variety" of different demands pressed upon the government may affect its ability to focus on specific developmental goals in several ways. First, the government may confront other kinds of demands. Pressures for governmental action to meet welfare, hospital, and law enforcement needs, for example, reduce the funds and leadership skills available for developmental purposes. These pressures are especially significant limitations in the older cities; they are much less important to the governments of the wealthier suburbs. Federal and state government efforts are also focused in part on welfare and other nondevelopmental needs of urban areas. Moreover, their resources are spread across a number of other substantive areas, most prominently foreign and military affairs, and agricultural and other rural concerns.

"Variety" also refers to the range of demands within developmental areas, but here the impact on governmental influence is more complex. The more narrowly focused the demands, the greater the ability of a governmental unit to affect the included area, whether parks or highways or schools. Yet the broader the range of functions with which the government is expected to deal, the wider the impact it can have on urban development as we have defined it—unless available resources are spread too thin to provide a significant counterweight to the economic, technological and other forces operating in various program areas. Perhaps the institution that best balances these competing considerations, at least in the New York region, is the Port Authority. Concerned with several functions, and possessing considerable resources, the Port Authority has been able to focus its funds and energies largely on significant developmental projects; thus it has had a substantial impact on urban development.

So far, variety of demands has been considered in terms of the number of distinct policy areas among which a government institution must allocate scarce resources. The "variety" factor has a somewhat different effect when the policy preferences of different constituencies directly conflict. Demands for parks or improved housing, for instance, may directly conflict with pressures for new highways, if proposed as alternative uses of the same land. Where one government must decide between such directly competing ends, vigorous government action is particularly difficult.

In the older cities, the conflicting interests of a heterogeneous population make it almost impossible for the mayor and other central government officials to pursue unambiguous developmental goals. Some of the conflicts are as obvious as the land use example just noted; others are more complex. For example, efforts to alleviate the disadvantages of the ghetto dweller through educational policies that encourage integration tend to hasten the exodus of the middle class to the suburbs, thus reducing the city's tax base and increasing the tendency for the older city to become predominately the home of the nonwhite poor. The homogeneous suburbs and functional authorities which are able to disregard these spillover effects find that clear goals and consistent action to shape "their" portions of the urban scene are far more readily attainable.

The ability of a governmental unit to concentrate resources on particular developmental problems depends not only on the variety of demands but on the relative intensity of different demands as well. "Government by crisis" is a phrase frequently (and pejoratively) applied to public action; and for those governments that confront many pressures, significant action is indeed far more likely when a widely perceived emergency exists. The substantial increases in state and federal action in mass transportation and air pollution in recent years have followed this route.

**Control over the use of land.** Although constrained by their constituencies and by other governmental units, public officials have a number of powers and other resources that can be used to shape urban development. Among the formal powers of government, land-use control is especially important to urban development. The extent of governmental control over land and the way this control is exercised affect the physical aspects of the urban scene directly. Control over land also has significant implications for the distribution of racial groups and for other social aspects of the metropolis.

Some land in the New York region is owned by governmental agencies. The overwhelming preponderance, however, is owned privately, and government shapes the development of this land through regulatory power. This power is exercised directly by local governments in the region, using zoning, subdivision, and building regulations. Federal and state planning standards generally are permissive guidelines for consideration (and adoption or rejection) by the municipalities, although more stringent state controls related to environmental goals in sensitive areas such as coastal zones emerged in the 1970s. Local land-use control also is subject to oversight by the courts, but prior to the 1970s judicial rulings almost always reinforced rather than diluted local self-determination in regulating land use.

Land-use control is a particularly significant tool for shaping the urban environment in those parts of the region with open land. Historically, the experience of Westchester County illustrates this particularly well. Early in this century, while much of the county was still undeveloped, political leaders in Westchester resolved that it would not become another Bronx—the densely settled borough of New York City that borders Westchester on the south. Planning and zoning policies were developed to ensure low residential densities and exclude industry from much of the county. During the past several decades, and in spite of the pressure of population expansion, these policies have been maintained, and much of northern Westchester remains a lightly developed sector of the region.

Once commercial and residential uses have replaced open space and agriculture, the economic, political and other social costs of significant governmental control over land use increase dramatically. Consequently, the strategy used by Westchester in the 1920s is available to Suffolk, Dutchess, and other outlying counties that still have substantial amounts of open space. This approach is much less useful in Nassau and other densely populated suburbs, and it is of very little significance in Newark, Jersey City, and most other older cities.

**Financial resources.** Financial strength is obviously important in determining the ability of any governmental unit to achieve developmental goals.[40] Yet it is also clear that this factor is closely intertwined with others considered above, especially the variety of demands impinging upon the government and the degree of formal independence of action. For money is likely to be diffused where multiple demands exist; and the ability to obtain funds through taxes may be severely limited by external controls, as state laws restricting New York City's taxing power amply demonstrate.

The problem of finance warrants separate emphasis because of a major characteristic of the region's fragmented governmental system: the tendency for local political units having the greatest per capita financial resources to be largely separate from those with the greatest financial needs. The nature of this separation between needs and resources, and its consequences, have been carefully analyzed by Robert Wood.[41] The process can be summarized as follows:

Certain kinds of urban land use yield a surplus of local tax revenue over

40. Of course, as Dahl and others have emphasized, the extent of actual influence will depend not only on the financial (and other) resources available, but also on willingness to use the resources to affect others' behavior. See Dahl, *Modern Political Analysis*, pp. 37 ff.

41. Wood, *1400 Governments*, chapters 2–3. Cf. Oliver P. Williams et al., *Suburban Differences and Metropolitan Policies: A Philadelphia Story* (Philadelphia: University of Pennsylvania Press, 1965).

expenditure. Industrial and commercial property, the homes of the wealthy, and more modest residences for adults without children are generally in this "surplus-revenue" category. Other property uses have the reverse impact, notably the residences of the poor and the aged, tax-exempt property, and homes for middle-income parents with young children. Typically, funds obtained from "surplus-revenue" properties are used to meet the relatively heavy needs for health, welfare, schools, and other services of these ("expenditure-generating") groups.

In general, the expenditure-generating population groups are concentrated in the older cities and in suburbs whose zoning regulations allow inexpensive housing. Some of the older cities, particularly New York City in and near its central business district, also have a strong concentration of surplus-revenue development. During the past three decades, however, the two kinds of development have tended to become increasingly segregated. Thus, businesses seek locations in towns without high expenditure-generating factors, in order to keep their taxes low. The wealthy seek a similar environment, in order to maximize privacy and social separation, and to minimize tax burdens. Local government officials maneuver to obtain these kinds of taxpayers in order to reduce tax burdens on other local land owners; but success generally accrues only to those localities that already have a relatively low level of expenditure-generating property use. Of course, the entire process is possible only because of the extensive fragmentation of municipal jurisdictions in the region. Moreover, the process is significant because of the substantial burden of locally financed governmental service in the metropolis.

If the segregation of needs from financial resources severely limits the ability of some governmental units to influence development—or even, as later chapters will show, to meet minimal local needs—it also induces heavy pressures for nonlocal financial support. The state governments of the region and the national government have greater financial resources, particularly in comparison with the older cities, and local officials and their constituents increasingly have sought and obtained funds from these sources to meet educational, welfare, health, transportation, and other needs. Use of their financial resources to meet urban-oriented problems has given state and federal governments substantial leverage in shaping urban development—especially in such important functional areas as transportation and urban renewal.

**Political skill.** The final three elements are less tangible than money or control over land use, but are no less important. The most general of the three is the political skill of governmental leaders; the others may be partly subsumed under this factor.

By political skill we mean the ability of governmental officials to identify goals clearly, within the constraints and opportunities outlined above, and to use resources efficiently in achieving these goals. The planning and zoning strategies of Westchester officials noted above illustrate this ability, in contrast to the relative lack of foresight by public officials in most other sectors with regard to the financial, aesthetic, and other implications of urban sprawl. The tactical skills and public relations talents of the Port Authority and Robert Moses provide other examples. Political skill was also a critical

factor in the ability of local officials and private interests to block the construction of a new jetport in suburban Morris County.

**Control over subordinate units.** The challenge of internal control is especially relevant to the mayors of larger cities, to county executives, to governors,
and to the White House. In larger governmental institutions, specialized units
in highways, education, urban renewal, and other functional areas tend to
define goals in terms of their own relatively narrow perspectives, to develop
strong ties with their clientele, and to create functional alliances with officials
at other levels of government. Frequently, these units are able to obtain semiautonomous legal status: many authorities and special districts are legally subordinate to general-government officials only to a very limited extent.

The ability of elected officials to achieve their preferred goals depends
substantially on their ability to control their line departments, and frequently
on their capacity to influence semi-independent authorities as well. The
power to appoint and remove leaders of these agencies is an important route
to control, as is the capacity to reorganize and combine executive agencies.

**Planning.** Many observers consider planning to be government's primary instrument in shaping urban development. However, the planning process must be examined in the context of the other resources and constraints
that shape governmental action.

Urban planning may be defined as "the application of foresight to
achieve certain preestablished goals in the growth and development of urban
areas." It involves a "continuous process of deriving, organizing and present-
ing a broad and comprehensive program for urban development and renewal," which should consider both "immediate needs and those of the
foreseeable future." According to professional planners, urban planning agencies—if they are to be really effective—should have broad areal and functional scope. Preferably, the planning process should embrace the entire
metropolitan area and be concerned with the interrelationships among all
relevant factors, rather than focusing on individual components such as
transportation or recreation. In addition, the planners' activities should be
influential: governmental action to shape urban development should be
based on the guidelines and detailed plans set forth by the professional
planner.[42] In its ideal form, urban planning is closely related to the regional
governmental structure that Wood argues is necessary if there is to be "public direction of economic growth."

Judged by this ideal, there is very little effective planning in the New
York region. Admittedly, a considerable amount of planning is done by municipal, county, subregional, and state general-planning units, and by the
wide variety of functional agencies in the metropolis. But the political leaders
of most of these units are not concerned primarily with the planners' ideal of

42. The quotations are from F. Stuart Chapin, Jr., "Foundations of Urban Planning," in
Werner A. Hirsch, ed., *Urban Life and Form* (New York: Holt, Rinehart and Winston, 1963), p. 218;
and Chapin, *Urban Land Use Planning*, second edition (Urbana, Ill.: University of Illinois Press,
1965), p. vi. See also T. J. Kent, *The Urban General Plan* (San Francisco: Chandler, 1964): Charles M.
Harr and Associates, "The Promise of Metropolitan Planning," in Michael N. Danielson, ed., *Metropolitan Politics*, second edition (Boston: Little, Brown, 1971), pp. 374–380.

balanced, long-range development of the region. Instead, they view planning, and more specifically their own planning staffs, as one of several instruments that can be used to maximize the interests of their own municipality, county, or functional agency. In other words, their planning units are important elements in the process of concentrating resources to attract certain kinds of industry, to insure that low-income groups do not invade the community in large numbers, or to calculate the profitability of a proposed new toll bridge or tunnel.

There are exceptions, of course. Some of the county, intercounty, and state planning agencies, as well as the New York City agency, are often able to operate with greater independence from immediate political pressures. Staffed by well-trained planners, these units draw up extensive plans that meet professional planning standards, and hold the promise of reshaping development in their segments of the region. But the actual power to act upon the proposals of the Westchester County planning agency, the New York City Planning Commission, or the New Jersey Division of Planning resides elsewhere in the governmental system. Almost invariably, the multiplicity of interests that must be reconciled to the plan soon strips it of consistency and long-range effect. A former executive director of the Nassau County Planning Commission laments:

> Achievement is not always the prime characteristic of a planner. Normally he must attune himself to the role of advocate . . . and content himself with whatever impact his advocacy might produce. If he is lucky, his recommendations will be discussed in committees and finally—after substantial modifications—acted upon. More often than not, however, the planner's labors of love become stymied by the numerous layers of bureaucracy which irrevocably stand between him and a sense of accomplishment. Occasionally, he may be frontally assaulted by vociferous opponents carrying "Save Our Homes" placards.[43]

Like many metropolitan areas, New York also has an official planning agency—the Tri-State Regional Planning Commission which dates from the early 1960s—that has carried out a number of studies of transportation, recreation, and general development on a regionwide basis. Although its membership includes the executives of state and federal transport and development agencies, the commission's studies have had relatively little influence on the numerous specific programs and projects carried out by the dozens of separate municipal and functional organizations in the region.

In summary, most planning in the New York region is far from the ideal. The planning staffs that are likely to have an impact on the region's development are those that are responsive to political forces as they are structured in the fragmented metropolis. In this role, the urban planner becomes an important instrument to assist the elected official, as he seeks ways to protect the interests of his own limited constituency.

43. Charles E. Stonier, "Planning in the Maturing Suburb," *Traffic Quarterly* 14 (April 1965), p. 285. On the political environment of urban planning, see Alan Altshuler, *The City Planning Process* (Ithaca, N.Y.: Cornell University Press, 1965); Francine Rabinowitz, *City Politics and Planning* (New York: Atherton Press, 1969); and Edward C. Banfield and James Q. Wilson, *City Politics* (Cambridge, Mass.: Harvard University Press, 1963), Chapter 14.

## Targets of Analysis

Our more detailed exploration of government's role in shaping the New York region's development occupies eight of the nine chapters that follow. To set the stage for this analysis, we explore in Chapter Two the general pattern of development in the older cities and suburbs of the metropolis. Then we focus on the interplay of government and suburban development in Chapters Three and Four, examining in detail local housing and land-use policies and the efforts of local interests to influence regional, state, and federal transportation agencies.

Government actors of regional scope are the subject of the next three chapters. In Chapter Five we examine in some detail the obstacles which stand in the way of "regional government" or even of modest regionwide cooperation, as well as the disparate resources and opportunities available to broader coordinating agencies like Tri-State and to narrower functional enterprises like the Port Authority. Transportation programs are central both in their influence on development patterns and in their need for a regional perspective, and we devote Chapters Six and Seven to the efforts of federal, state, and other regional actors in highway development and mass transportation.

Perhaps the governments facing the most complicated and difficult challenges are those which attempt to influence development in the older cities of the region. In Chapters Eight and Nine we turn to the many governmental actors that function in this complex arena, first examining their capabilities and strategies in New York City, Newark, and other older cities, and then in Chapter Nine looking more closely at urban renewal.

Finally, Chapter Ten pulls together the main threads of our analysis, with some attention to the implications of the rise of environmentalism and other values for the capacity of government to shape future urban development. We end where we began, emphasizing the importance of concentrating resources in shaping governmental influence on urban development.

Throughout, we have selected materials that illustrate the interplay between government and development, rather than attempting comprehensive treatment of land-use control, housing, highways, airport development, mass transportation, or urban renewal. Frequently, we examine issues for bounded periods of time, often in the context of particular cases and places. Some of our cases are indeed quite bounded, as in the treatment of the Port Authority bus terminal in Chapter Six or the competition to entice the New York Stock Exchange to leave Manhattan in Chapter Eight. Other cases take in longer spans of time and a wider range of actors, but still without comprehensive coverage and often without bringing each strand of activity up to date through the 1970s. Thus, in Chapter Six we concentrate on highway development from the 1920s to the 1960s, the era in which the highway coalition secured the resources to build the major bridges and roads that now shape the region. In Chapter Seven we frame much of the analysis of recent mass transit programs in terms of New York's Metropolitan Transportation Authority, with less attention to efforts in New Jersey. And we devote the bulk of our examination of urban renewal in Chapter Nine to redevelopment efforts in Newark.

Our selective approach necessarily means that we omit or treat briefly many issues, problems, and programs. For example, while urban renewal is examined in some detail, little attention is given to the model cities program, or to the community development block grant and urban development action grant programs that have provided funds for urban redevelopment in recent years. All of these programs are important and could have provided interesting case materials. All tend to illustrate points regarding government efforts in older cities similar to those illuminated by urban renewal and other programs that we do examine.

Our principal concern is with government—but not with all governments in the region in all of their activities. Instead, we focus on governmental agencies that seek to affect the region's development pattern. Thus, we do not treat government in the comprehensive fashion of Sayre and Kaufman's classic examination of New York City.[44] Nor do we organize the volume along traditional government lines, with chapters on local, regional, state, and federal governments. Instead, each of these kinds of government is examined in the context of various development issues. In Chapter Three, for example, we focus on local governments in suburbia because they are the prime public agents regulating land use and housing, but we also treat the role of the three state governments in shaping local government activities in the region's far-flung suburbs. While Chapter Four also deals with suburbia, much of the analysis concerns public agencies that plan and build major transportation facilities affecting development in the suburbs. By the same token, the discussion of the older cities in Chapters Eight and Nine explores the capabilities of a wide range of governmental actors—the general governments of older cities, functional agencies at various levels of government, and a host of state and federal participants in the politics of development in the region.

Our substantial emphasis on local and regional units may surprise those who see the state and particularly the federal role in urban development as crucial. As we indicate frequently in the pages that follow, state and federal actors play important parts in whatever happens or does not happen with respect to development in the New York region. Many state agencies are directly involved in the New York region. Moreover, all local and regional units are the creatures of state government, deriving their legal powers and financial resources from the state. Federal money is clearly a prime engine of urban development—fueling highway and mass transportation, subsidized housing, urban revitalization, water and sewer projects, and a variety of other public activities. And there is no question that federal policies which promoted home ownership, residential segregation, and highway development helped stimulate the rapid outward growth of metropolitan areas.

Recognizing the importance of the states and the federal government, however, does not provide satisfactory answers to the basic questions this study poses concerning the relative importance of governmental influences in the urban development process, and the nature of the factors that explain the varying capabilities of governmental units to affect urban patterns. Neither the federal government nor the states are monolithic entities confronting the urban landscape in a cohesive and coherent fashion. Instead, many different state and federal agencies, policies, and programs have impacts on the location of activities and facilities in urban areas. None operates in isolation from

44. Sayre and Kaufman, *Governing New York City.*

other governmental units. State programs are shaped by local governments and interests, by regional agencies such as the Port Authority, and by the sensitivity of governors and state legislators to the views of organized interests and local constituents. Federal programs are subject to the same constraints, and depend even more heavily on other units for implementation. Federal highway dollars are turned into actual routes by state officials; money for the various federal urban programs is spent by city and state agencies. Intervention from the state capitals and Washington follows no simple and predictable patterns, because neither the states nor the federal government has a coherent set of urban development policies, because agency goals and programs are in conflict, and because local pressures differ from case to case.

Our plan is to examine the wide range of governmental units that seek to influence development in the nation's largest urban area—from small suburban governments to large city, regional, state, and federal agencies. We look carefully at local and regional actors because the decentralized system of government in the United States continues to provide the grass roots with the power to make or veto important decisions on urban development. In a complex decentralized political system like that of the New York region, there are many avenues to influence, and in the following pages we explore a number of these roads in the belief that they will lead to a better understanding of the interplay between political institutions and the other forces which shape our urban society.

# 2

# Development in the New York Region

To argue that governmental officials can and often do shape urban development is not, of course, to argue that other factors are unimportant. As noted in Chapter One, economic forces, technology, and other factors have combined with governmental activities to produce the patterns of development found in urban regions. And the interactions of these forces have been continuous and cumulative—laying down in each decade a further layer of transportation routes, housing, industrial and commercial structures, habits and traditions which constrain and help to direct future development.

In this chapter, we outline the main features of those interactions in the New York region as they have evolved historically. We permit the role of government to recede temporarily into the background, in order to direct attention to the crucial importance of topography, economic aspects, and other factors that have shaped this region—as they shape all urban complexes. We then turn in subsequent chapters to the strategies, successes, and failures of governmental agencies as they have attempted to use—or overcome—these forces to achieve their own purposes.

## Size and Complexity

New York is a region of superlatives. Within its 12,000 square miles, more than nineteen million people have come together to form one of the largest urban concentrations in the world. Its eight-million-person work force produces a greater variety and volume of goods and services than any other region, and accumulates and spends more wealth than is found in any other metropolitan area. Almost 40 percent of its residents live in New York City, a city so huge that its public housing alone shelters more people than live in New Orleans. The remaining residents of the region are spread over 550 municipalities in two-score counties in parts of three states, which together with New York City form the most complex urban governmental system on the globe.

In fact, the New York region is so large and has grown so rapidly at its periphery in recent years that no consensus exists on its precise scope. For the past three decades, one commonly used definition has been the 22-county, 6,900 square-mile New York Metropolitan Region outlined by the Regional Plan Association (RPA) in 1947. RPA's 22-county region includes (1) the five counties comprising New York City (Bronx, Kings [Brooklyn],

## Table 4—*The Scope of the New York Region: 1980*

|  | Population | Area | Population Density (sq. miles) |
|---|---|---|---|
| 20-County Census Bureau Consolidated Area | 16,114,045 | 5,270 | 3,058 |
| 22-County RPA Metropolitan Region | 17,100,300 | 6,924 | 2,470 |
| 24-County Tri-State Region | 17,913,000 | 7,634 | 2,346 |
| 31-County RPA Study Area | 19,178,700 | 12,757 | 1,503 |

New York [Manhattan], Queens, and Richmond [Staten Island]); (2) seven additional counties in New York State (Dutchess, Nassau, Orange, Putnam, Rockland, Suffolk, and Westchester); (3) nine counties in New Jersey (Bergen, Essex, Hudson, Middlesex, Monmouth, Morris, Passaic, Somerset, and Union); and (4) Fairfield County in Connecticut. The Tri-State Regional Planning Commission, the official planning agency for the New York metropolitan complex, adds New Haven and part of Litchfield in Connecticut to produce a 24-county, 7,600 square-mile Tri-State Region. To complicate the definitional question further, the Regional Plan Association's Second Regional Plan of 1968 is based on a 31-county, 12,700 square-mile Study Area, which encompasses the Tri-State Region plus Ocean, Mercer, Hunterdon, Warren, and Sussex counties in New Jersey and Sullivan and Ulster in New York. And the Census Bureau uses yet another approach based on 20 counties.[1] The various regions are shown in Map 1. (See also Table 4.) Regardless of the definition employed, however, it should be remembered that the overwhelming majority of the region's population and jobs are located in the 3,600 square miles in and around the heart of the region and along the coastal plains and valleys. This intensely developed area encompasses about sixteen million of the region's inhabitants and over six million of its jobs.

1. The U. S. Census Bureau's New York-Newark-Jersey City Standard Consolidated Statistical Area includes all of the counties in RPA's twenty-two-county New York Metropolitan Region except Dutchess, Orange, and part of Fairfield. Within the New York-Newark-Jersey City Standard Consolidated Statistical Area, the federal government further defines nine Standard Metropolitan Statistical Areas (SMSA) as follows:
   1. New York SMSA—New York City's five counties, Bergen, Putnam, Rockland, and Westchester Counties;
   2. Nassau-Suffolk SMSA—Nassau and Suffolk Counties;
   3. Newark SMSA—Essex, Morris, Somerset, and Union Counties;
   4. Jersey City SMSA—Hudson County;
   5. New Brunswick-Perth Amboy-Sayreville SMSA—Middlesex County;
   6. Paterson-Clifton-Passaic SMSA—Passaic County;
   7. Long Branch-Asbury Park SMSA—Monmouth County;
   8. Stamford SMSA—part of Fairfield County;
   9. Norwalk SMSA—part of Fairfield County.
See U.S. Executive Office of the President, Office of Management and Budget, *Standard Metropolitan Statistical Areas 1975*, revised edition, prepared by the Statistical Policy Division (Washington: U.S. Government Printing Office, 1976).
   For a useful discussion of the advantages and disadvantages of these various definitions of the New York area, see Dennis R. Young, "Towards a Regional Perspective," *New York Affairs* 5(1978), pp. 8–11.

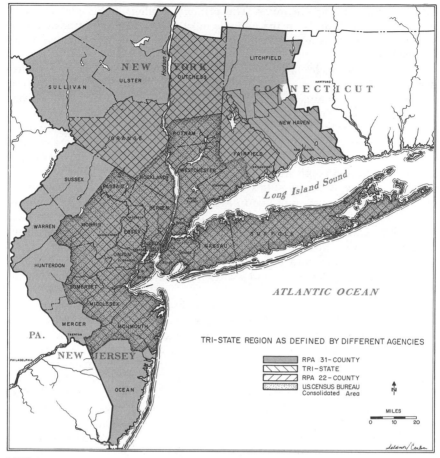

**MAP 1**

Beyond its gargantuan proportions, the most striking feature of the New York region is its unique central business district. Manhattan south of 6oth Street is the financial heart, corporate headquarters, and communications center of the United States. About three-quarters of all stock transfers take place in the New York exchanges; 61 of the 500 largest corporations have their home offices in the city; and the lion's share of the nation's books and magazines are published in mid-Manhattan. To house New York's headquarters functions, 289 new office buildings were constructed in Manhattan between 1947 and 1980. Manhattan is also America's cultural and intellectual capital—a magnet for artists and writers, the national home of the legitimate theater and the other performing arts, and the operating base of the twentieth-century counterparts of the Renaissance patrons of the arts and sciences, the foundations of Ford, Carnegie, and Rockefeller. New York also houses the United Nations and its steadily growing diplomatic corps. These headquarters' functions and the myriad other activities of the Manhattan central business district require the daily concentration of almost two million people into less than 10 square miles. The primary burden of this massive daily influx and exodus falls on the nation's most extensive public transportation system, whose trains and buses carry three out of every four travelers to the Manhattan hub.

Despite the scale of the New York region and its singular central business district, the patterns of urban development in the region are far from unique. The economic, social, technological forces of urban growth and change are transforming the New York region in much the same way as they are other metropolitan areas from coast to coast. Most of the region's inhabitants live in city neighborhoods or suburban communities that have counterparts in almost every major metropolitan area. While the ghettos of Harlem and Bedford-Stuyvesant are bigger and more densely populated than most, they differ little from the slums of Philadelphia or Chicago. Except for the relatively high proportion of Puerto Ricans, there is nothing unique about the steady influx of rural migrants into the older cities of the New York region, or about the parallel migration of whites to the suburbs. Nor does the region differ much from other metropolitan areas in the Northeast in terms of economic decay in the core cities, a dramatic slowing of the overall rate of regional growth in the 1970s, and a concentration of growth along and beyond the region's periphery.

As in every large metropolitan area, suburbs in the tristate region come in all sizes, shapes, ages, and prices, ranging from exclusive preserves like Westchester's Scarsdale and Essex's Short Hills to the mass-produced Levittowns of Nassau and Middlesex counties. And perhaps most significant, despite the great centripetal pull of its massive central business district, the New York region, like all of urban America, spreads inexorably outward. Beyond the Manhattan hub, the ghettos and gray areas, the older industrial districts, and the established suburbs, the New York region loses its distinctive identity almost completely. Aside from minor differences in design, terrain, and foliage, the subdevelopments, shopping centers, sleek new schools, industrial parks, and superhighways of Monmouth, Rockland, and Suffolk counties are identical to those spreading outward from Rochester, Atlanta, Omaha, Spokane, or San Diego.

As a result, the overall pattern of development in the New York region— and the problems and public issues posed by the forces of urban growth and change—are not greatly different from those found in other large metropolitan areas in the United States. Within the constraints imposed by topography and transportation corridors, development has occurred in a set of concentric rings, with the oldest and most concentrated development at the center and the newest and least intensive at the periphery, as indicated in Map 2. Along with a lion's share of the region's pre-twentieth century development, its most serious social and economic problems are focused in the intensively settled core, composed of New York City (less Staten Island), Hudson County, and the city of Newark in Essex County. Increasingly the problems of the core spill over into the older suburbs of the inner ring—composed of Nassau, southern Westchester, Bergen, southern Passaic, suburban Essex, Union, and Staten Island. Since 1960, new development in the region has been concentrated in the rapidly growing suburbs of the intermediate ring—western Suffolk, northern Westchester, southern Fairfield, New Haven, Rockland, northern Passaic,

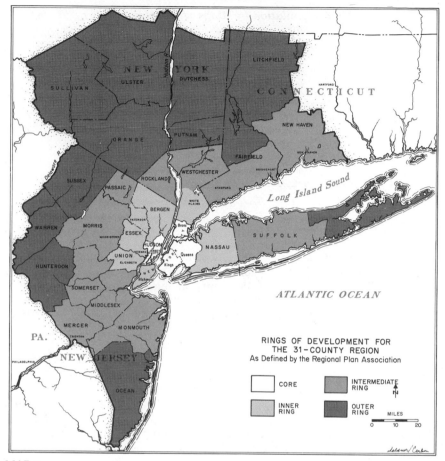

RINGS OF DEVELOPMENT FOR
THE 31-COUNTY REGION
As Defined by the Regional Plan Association

CORE  INTERMEDIATE RING

INNER RING  OUTER RING

MILES
0   10   20

**MAP 2**

Morris, Somerset, Middlesex, Monmouth, and Mercer—and increasingly spills over into the sparsely settled counties of the outer ring.[2] Population figures for 1980 are shown in Table 5.

    2. The Regional Plan Association divides communities in Westchester County in the inner and intermediate rings as follows: *Inner Ring*—Eastchester, Greenburgh, Harrison, Mamaroneck, Mt. Vernon, New Rochelle, Pelham, Rye City, Rye Town, Scarsdale, White Plains, Yonkers; *Intermediate Ring*—Bedford, Cortlandt, Lewisboro, Mt. Pleasant, New Castle, North Castle, North Salem, Ossining, Peekskill, Pound Ridge, Somers, Yorktown.

    Communities in Passaic County are divided between the inner and intermediate rings as follows: *Inner Ring*—Clifton, Haledon, Hawthorne, Little Falls, North Haledon, Passaic, Paterson, Pompton Lakes, Prospect Park, Totowa, Wayne, West Paterson; *Intermediate Ring*—Bloomingdale, Ringwood, Wanaque, West Milford.

    Communities in Suffolk County are divided between the intermediate and outer rings as follows: *Intermediate Ring*—Babylon, Brookhaven, Huntingdon, Islip, Smithtown; *Outer Ring*—East Hampton, Riverhead, Shelter Island, Southampton, Southold, Shinnecock Indian Reservation.

    Communities in Fairfield County are divided between the intermediate and outer rings as follows: *Intermediate Ring*—Bridgeport, Darien, Easton, Fairfield, Greenwich, Monroe, New Canaan, Norwalk, Shelton, Stamford, Stratford, Trumbull, Weston, Westport, Wilton; *Outer Ring*—Bethel, Brookfield, Danbury, New Fairfield, Newton, Redding, Ridgefield, Sherman.

## Table 5—*Population by Rings of Development: 1980*

|  | Population | Percentage of Total |
|---|---|---|
| Core | 7,605,000 | 39.7 |
| Inner Ring | 4,571,000 | 23.8 |
| Intermediate Ring | 5,161,000 | 26.9 |
| Outer Ring | 1,842,000 | 9.6 |
|  | 19,179,000 | 100.0 |

*Note:* Unless otherwise indicated, population data in the tables in this and subsequent chapters are derived from publications of the U.S. Bureau of the Census.

## The Physical Setting

The configuration of the land and water in the vicinity of latitude 40° 45'N and longitude 74°W has shaped all of man's efforts to develop what has become the New York region.[3] Proximity to the sea and the great natural harbor first attracted Europeans to New York. The Hudson River, navigable for more than 150 miles, drew trade to the fledgling port from the north and west. The Hudson's broad expanse also divides the region physically and politically. Separated by the Hudson barrier from the major job markets of the metropolis, the New Jersey half of the region has not grown as fast as the New York side. The states on the opposite banks of the Hudson have very different political styles, philosophies of taxation, and traditions of local government. Moreover, the problems and opportunities posed by the Hudson River created the need for a governmental agency with a bistate jurisdiction, a need filled in 1921 by the creation of the Port of New York Authority, which in the ensuing half century has become the most influential public developmental institution in the New York region.

Near the waters of New York harbor, Long Island Sound, and the Atlantic Ocean, the land is flat, sandy, and easily developed, as indicated by the surge of settlement after World War II eastward on Long Island and southward

---

3. The most comprehensive general discussion of the development of the region is Raymond Vernon's *Metropolis 1985* (Cambridge, Mass.: Harvard University Press, 1960); also available in a 1963 Anchor Books edition. As noted in Chapter One, Vernon's study is a summary and interpretation of the New York Metropolitan Region Study which he directed for the Regional Plan Association. A more detailed treatment of the general pattern of development in the region is found in the first volume of the New York Metropolitan Region Study, Edgar M. Hoover and Raymond Vernon, *Anatomy of a Metropolis* (Cambridge, Mass.: Harvard University Press, 1959), which is also available in an Anchor edition. Also useful are: Eli Ginzberg, ed., *New York Is Very Much Alive* (New York: McGraw-Hill, 1973); Louis B. Schlivek, *Man in Metropolis* (Garden City, N.Y.: Doubleday, 1965); Regional Plan Association, *Spread City*, RPA Bulletin No. 100 (New York, 1962); Port of New York Authority, *Metropolitan Transportation—1980* (New York, 1963); Tri-State Transportation Commission, *Measure of a Region* (May, 1967); Regional Plan Association, *The Region's Growth* (May 1967); Tri-State Regional Planning Commission, *Metromonitor: A Regional Review of Social and Economic Trends* (May 1977); Regional Plan Association, "State of the New York Region: Selected Trends of the Last Quarter Century," (January, 1975); Port Authority of New York and New Jersey, *People & Jobs* (May 1974).

through Middlesex and Monmouth counties in New Jersey. To the north and west of the sea are the hills of the Watchung and Ramapo ranges, which mark the southernmost extension of the last Ice Age. From the beginning, development has been channeled into the gentle terrain of the corridor that runs through the region from the northeast to the southwest between the hills and the ocean. This narrow shelf of coastal plain is the backbone of the Boston-to-Washington urban belt, and one of the most heavily traveled transportation corridors in the world. Growth along the northeast-southwest axis has brought into the region's orbit a procession of fairly large cities—Newark, Elizabeth, New Brunswick, and now Trenton to the southwest and Stamford, Bridgeport, and New Haven to the northeast. The presence of these cities in the New York region has reduced the region's economic focus and increased its political complexity.

### Genesis from the Sea

Of the various physical factors influencing the development of the region, none has been more important than the magnificent harbor that lies within the portals of the Narrows. As one observer notes, "the preeminence of New York as a city, and now as a Metropolitan Region, rests first of all upon the preeminence of New York as a port."[4]

Despite its natural advantages, preeminence did not come automatically to the port of New York. During the eighteenth century, New York trailed far behind its chief rivals, Boston and Philadelphia; in 1790, the port handled less than 6 percent of the young nation's foreign trade. Early in the nineteenth century, two governmental actions, one by a foreign power, the other by the state of New York, played an important part in the port's rise to the top. At the end of the War of 1812, the British sold their surplus textiles through New York merchants, which helped the port become the nation's leading market for textiles—a product which accounted for approximately one-third of all American imports between 1820 and 1850.

Even more important for the future of the port and the region was the financing in 1816 of the Erie Canal by New York state, which as noted in Chapter One gave the New York region a significant advantage over other eastern cities. Five years after the completion of the canal, the port had nearly 40 percent of the United States' foreign trade, a fourfold increase in thirty years. Now, as Vernon points out, "growth fed on growth."[5] As it grew, New York was able to offer the shipper more sailings, more brokers, more wholesalers, and more specialized services than its rivals. The external economies that resulted from size and specialization meant lower costs and more business.

By the middle of the nineteenth century, the American economy's dependence upon foreign trade was easing as the frontier pushed westward and the northeast industrialized. But the solid economic base of the port enabled New York to secure a commanding position in the rapidly expanding domestic economy. Drawn by the magnet of New York's foreign trade were all the

4. Schlivek, *Man in Metropolis*, p. 59.
5. Vernon, *Metropolis 1985*, p. 31.

***Ships and cargoes crowd the South Street Manhattan docks in the
booming port of the 1860s.***

Credit: The New York Historical Society, New York City

major eastern railroads, making the region the nation's largest rail terminal.
Commercial enterprises spawned in the port reached out to corner a major
share of the burgeoning domestic market in wholesaling, insurance, banking,
and a host of lesser activities. These enterprises enabled New York to capitalize on the shift from plant-based manufacturing to office-based finance and
management. By the second half of the nineteenth century, the city's role as
the nation's financial capital and business center was unquestioned; and its
economic growth was increasingly independent of the port that had given the
city and the region its initial comparative advantage.

    Over the next hundred years, New York's share of the nation's ocean-going foreign trade steadily declined. Underlying this development was the westward movement of the nation's population and the growing importance of non-European trading partners served by ports such as Miami, New Orleans, and San Francisco. The growth of bulk cargo shipments also damaged the relative position of the port. The external economies of doing business in New York—more sailings, specialized insurance and brokerage services, and a wide variety of packaging and forwarding services—mean little to the bulk shipper.

Another adverse factor has been advances in transportation technology. In the railroad era, the advantages of New York's multiplicity of connections outweighed the disadvantages of its relatively high rates. Much of this comparative advantage was lost in the age of the combustion engine. The flexibility of the truck traveling on the public highway, with a rate structure far more sensitive to distance than that of the railroads, has shifted a good deal of freight to ports closer to the cargo's origin or destination. The policies of the national government also increased the competitive advantage of other ports. The St. Lawrence Seaway (whose creation was heavily subsidized by Washington) offers cheaper rates to the shippers who handle 20 percent of the cargoes that have traditionally passed through the port of New York. And the need for political support in Congress for the continuation of federal merchant marine subsidies has prompted steamship operators to divert sailings from New York to Philadelphia, Baltimore, and other East Coast ports.

These changes in the port's national role have been reflected in the relative decline in its importance within the region. By 1975, less than three percent of the New York region's jobs were directly tied to the activities of the port. Nonetheless, its impact on the region's economy is indelible. Because of the harbor, the region prospered despite its lack of raw materials and its growing distance from the nation's markets. The development of the port triggered the chain reaction that gave the region its vast cluster of wholesalers and jobbers, its financial and insurance complexes, the headquarters of most of the great industrial empires, and Madison Avenue's world of make-believe. Consequently, the region has a distinctive office-based economy heavily dependent upon face-to-face communication—in banking, securities, corporate management, advertising, mass communications, and publishing.

The port's heritage is equally significant for manufacturing, which accounts for two out of every three national market jobs in the region. As Vernon indicates, the start provided by the port gave the region a competitive advantage over other areas with respect to the location of manufacturing. "Within its borders a manufacturer could find an enormous amount of rentable space; an amazingly varied group of suppliers of industrial materials and services; an extremely diversified labor force; and extensive transportation facilities."[6]

The port also continually replenished the labor force. New York was the chief gateway for the thirty-six million immigrants who arrived during the century preceding the passage of the restrictive immigration legislation of 1924. Many stayed—in 1890 four out of five residents of Manhattan were first- or second-generation immigrants—to provide the region with cheap and fre-

6. Ibid., p. 100.

**The towers of the financial district loom above older waterfront buildings in lower Manhattan.**    Credit: Louis B. Schlivek, Regional Plan Association

quently skilled labor, as well as a cosmopolitan ethnic character that in turn attracted new immigrants.

Given a plentiful labor supply and a relatively disadvantageous location with respect to national markets, the region tends to specialize in products like clothing with a high value per pound. Attracted to the region are industries which require proximity to a large pool of specialized services such as brokerage and insurance—specialization that originally developed in the harbor. Thus, among the preeminent industries are women's clothing, electronics, toys, and job printing. As a result of their need for face-to-face communication and specialized services, the region's distinctive industries tend to cluster. Typically they are relatively small establishments, frequently located in a single plant, and rarely employing heavy capital equipment. As Vernon puts it, the producers of the New York region "accept the handicaps of high labor costs, traffic congestion, urban rents, and urban taxes, while exploiting the advantages of speed, flexibility, and external economies."[7]

## The Unique Central Business District

Almost two million jobs, one-fourth of the region's total, are located within the nine square miles of Manhattan south of 60th Street, a concentration of economic activity unequalled anywhere in the world. The Manhattan central business district (CBD) employs more people than are found in the total labor force of all but two metropolitan areas in the United States—Chicago and Los Angeles.

To a substantial degree, the sheer size of the Manhattan CBD accounts for the region's scale and affluence. Historically, because of the CBD's major role in the national and international economies, the region has been considerably less dependent for its economic health upon the regional sales and service functions that preoccupy most metropolitan areas.

### External Economies and White-Collar Jobs

The unparalleled concentration of activity within the Manhattan CBD is a product of the nature of the region's major industries. In New York, almost every economic activity in which the region specializes requires a location that facilitates personal interaction and rapid communication, as well as provides access to a wide range of supporting services. The needs of these industries—banking, securities, insurance, corporate management, legal and business services, radio and television, publishing, wholesaling, shipping, printing, and apparel—have been best satisfied in the congested heart of the region.

Since World War II, the activities most dependent upon the external economies of a location in Manhattan have steadily increased their share of CBD jobs. While manufacturing and wholesaling employment have declined, offsetting increases have been registered in finance, insurance, government, and business and professional services. Managerial functions remain strongly tied to the complex CBD marketplace of goods and services. These executive jobs have been growing more rapidly than any other major component of CBD employment. Here technology has fostered concentration, since "recent advances in air transportation and in communications and computer technology have made it increasingly possible to centralize control and management functions at one point in space, making major commercial, financial, and office centers more attractive for these activities than locations in lesser cities."[8]

Because of the strong centripetal force exerted by the Manhattan hub, a majority of the headquarters of major corporations in the region are located in

7. Ibid., p. 107.
8. Regional Plan Association, *The Region's Growth*, p. 117.

the CBD. Some large firms, notably International Business Machines, General Foods, American Cyanamid, Pepsico, American Can, General Telephone and Electronics, and General Precision Equipment, have followed their work force out to the suburbs during the postwar period in order to escape congestion, high rents, crime, pollution, and increasing taxes.[9] As an official of one departing firm explained: "We find it difficult to get people to come to work here. Most of our employees live in New Jersey, Long Island, Westchester or Connecticut, and commuting is a burden for them. In addition, some of us often have to work overtime and we don't consider the streets downtown safe at night."[10] But many corporations find the benefits of a CBD location continue to outweigh the costs. And even those corporations that have moved their headquarters from Manhattan frequently maintain substantial establishments in the CBD. For example, IBM now uses more office space in Manhattan than it did before its corporate headquarters was moved to suburban Yorktown.

The growing specialization of office employment in the CBD has steadily increased the proportion of managerial and professional positions. Since executives require a good deal more office space than clerks, specialization in the decision functions has fed the prolonged postwar boom in office-building construction, which added 145 million square feet of rentable space to the Manhattan office inventory between 1947 and 1980. In recent years, the average office space per employee has increased from 100 to 150 square feet, and 200 square feet is common in the newest glass towers of Park Avenue and the Avenue of the Americas.

Another important aspect of growth and change in the Manhattan CBD is the spectacular postwar development of the midtown area. In the late nineteenth century, the railroads and trusts began choosing "prestige" midtown locations for their headquarters, away from the congested downtown financial and port district. By the first decade of this century, commuters from Westchester, Fairfield, Long Island, and parts of New Jersey were delivered directly to the midtown rail terminals, while jobs downtown required an additional three- or four-mile subway trip. After World War II, the steady northward movement, particularly of corporate headquarters and communications activities, became a stampede. More than two-thirds of the office space built in the CBD after 1945 went into the area between 32nd and 60th Streets. Much of this development in the 1950s was concentrated on the east side of the island, but more recently the office builders have moved westward in their search for suitable sites.

9. IBM moved to Yorktown in Westchester, General Foods to White Plains in Westchester, American Cyanamid to Wayne in Passaic, Pepsico to Purchase in Westchester, American Can to Greenwich in Fairfield, Olin and General Telephone to Stamford in Fairfield, and General Precision Equipment to Tarrytown in Westchester.

10. W.J. Heinz, executive vice president of Ingersoll-Rand Company, quoted in "Ingersoll-Rand Is Leaving the City for a Jersey Site," *New York Times*, July 20, 1971. Ingersoll-Rand moved to a site adjacent to the Garden State Parkway in Woodcliff Lake in Bergen County. It is also worth noting that an overwhelming proportion of top executives of major corporations in the region live in the suburbs. A 1977 survey of chairmen, vice chairmen, presidents, and vice presidents of 188 corporations found that over 80 percent lived in suburban locations outside New York City; see Michael Sterne, "Corporate Moves: New York Region Holds Its Own," *New York Times*, August 14, 1977.

While commercial banking and other traditional downtown activities have followed their corporate customers uptown, the sustained growth of the midtown area has not turned lower Manhattan into a depressed area. In fact, since the decision of the Rockefellers in the late 1950s to build the sixty-story Chase Manhattan Building on lower Broadway, the old financial district has been booming. However, in contrast to midtown where all the new office development has been private, more than one-half of the new downtown office space has been in a public project, the Port Authority's World Trade Center, whose twin 110-story towers cap the largest office complex ever constructed.

### Benefits and Costs of the Central Business District

From the perspective of the private marketplace, the Manhattan CBD, with its dynamic headquarters economy and unparalleled external economies, is an unalloyed benefit to the city and the region. The tremendous concentration of economic activity draws three million people into the Manhattan hub on an average business day. Almost every form of economic activity benefits from this huge daytime population and the perpetual horde of visitors, most of whom are members of the affluent classes. Despite the tremendous growth of retail outlets in the suburbs, Manhattan continues to account for more than 20 percent of the region's retail sales, primarily because of the strength of CBD-oriented retail activities such as clothing, luggage, books, jewelry, cameras and optical goods, food, and drinks. The CBD also supports the nation's largest hotel center, and the vitality of the CBD is an essential condition for the survival of many of Manhattan's cultural activities, restaurants and night clubs, and the booming art galleries and antique shops of the upper East Side.

Also sustained by the headquarters economy is the forest of luxury apartment buildings that have risen in and around the CBD in the postwar years. Almost half of all the apartments built in Manhattan during the postwar period have been developed privately for upper income residents willing to pay monthly rents of $150 or more per room for accommodations close to their offices and the other attractions of the CBD.

These CBD facilities constitute a sizable benefit to the governmental system as well as the private entrepreneur. Manhattan's office buildings account for about one-eighth of New York City's total assessed valuation. Both the city and New York State collect income taxes from New Jersey and Connecticut commuters. City and state governments also benefit more generally from the fact that the CBD employs half of New York City's job-holding residents. Another beneficiary is the suburban political economy, since over 300,000 commuters are employed in the CBD. These jobs are particularly valuable to the upper-income suburbs along the rail lines of Fairfield, Westchester, Nassau, Bergen, Essex, and Morris counties, where most of the CBD's executive and professional commuters live.

But there is another side to the ledger: inevitably the massive CBD means substantial costs for the city and the region. As Roscoe Martin and Douglas Price indicate, relatively little attention has been given to the "external diseconomies created by extreme congestion and interdependence. This may be due to the tendency of economic studies [which make extensive use of the external economies concept] to concentrate on the private sector of a region, whereas most of the 'problems' (i.e., external diseconomies) affect primarily the public sector."[11] Vernon, for example, argues that "the office district's external economies . . . help to overcome the disadvantages of high land costs. The fact that office space can be piled up layer on layer over a costly building site without any loss in efficiency—indeed, with some gains— contributes to the same ends."[12]

If the frame of reference is broadened, however, how "efficient" is, say the Pan Am Building? In constructing an enormous office structure next to Grand Central Terminal, its builders certainly sought to maximize the external economies of a mid-Manhattan location. But to realize this "efficient" use of land, the fifty-nine-story Pan Am Building squeezes 25,000 more people into the heart of the CBD's booming midtown office district. On the debit side are the increased peak-hour loads on the subways, buses, and commuter trains, the incremental traffic on the crowded sidewalks and congested streets, and the discomfort of overtaxed luncheon facilities, to say nothing of the esthetic loss suffered because "the south end of Park Avenue is walled up" by a building "which bulks brutally over Grand Central Terminal."[13] Similar congestion costs are now being generated by the World Trade Center, which crams 50,000 office workers on 16 acres of crowded lower Manhattan and is stimulating intensive development in the surrounding area.

Nothing more graphically illustrates the costs and diseconomies for the public sector of the Manhattan CBD than the plight of the region's mass transportation systems. Without mass transportation, the CBD could not perform its essential concentrating and communicating functions. Public transportation accounts for almost 90 percent of trips to the CBD made during the peak hours. Over 90 percent of this public transportation service is provided by rail—the 237-mile New York City subway system, the 8.5-mile Port Authority Trans-Hudson (PATH) system (formerly the Hudson and Manhattan tubes), and the 800-odd miles of commuter rail service that links much of the region to the CBD. No other mass transportation system in the nation and few in the world approach New York's in extent or number of passengers hauled.

Despite its gargantuan proportions, the public transportation system of the New York area has not fared well at the hands of the forces of change at work in the CBD and the region. The public transport network primarily serves the travel needs of those who work in the CBD, needs that are compressed into peak periods each weekday morning and evening. Throughout the postwar period, the healthy economy of the CBD has kept peak hour ridership relatively constant. But off-peak weekday ridership on subways, commuter railroads, buses, and ferries declined continuously as fewer people used these modes for shopping and recreational travel. Weekend and non-CBD journey-to-work usage of public transportation also has been shrinking. Since the equipment and manpower requirements of a public transportation operation are set by the peak-hour demand, the growing concentration of

11. Roscoe C. Martin and Douglas Price, *The Metropolis and Its Problems* (Syracuse, Maxwell Graduate School of Citizenship and Public Affairs, 1959), p. 14; reprinted in Michael N. Danielson, ed., *Metropolitan Politics* (Boston: Little Brown, 1966), pp. 135–142.

12. Vernon, *Metropolis 1985*, p. 159.

13. Richard J. Whalen, *A City Destroying Itself* (New York: William Morrow, 1965), pp. 52, 50.

ridership in the rush hours has steadily reduced the efficiency with which the carriers can use their resources. Compounding the problem, particularly for the rail systems, has been the reluctance of governmental institutions—sensitive to constituency pressures—to permit fare increases. As a result of the peak-hour drain on resources and the shortage of revenues, deficits in all components of the system have steadily increased.

Of the various modes of public transportation, the commuter railroads have been the most adversely affected. During the past three decades, the suburban railroads have become an almost exclusively CBD rush-hour operation and more than three-quarters of all commuter railroad trips to the Manhattan hub are now made during the peak hours. The commuter-rail problem is further compounded by the region's jurisdictional complexity. Almost every line crosses state boundaries, which subjected the rail lines to often-conflicting regulation by both state agencies and the Interstate Commerce Commission. In addition, until recently the railroads were taxed by state and local governments in both New Jersey and New York at the highest rates in the nation. Little wonder that the railroads have doggedly sought to divest themselves of the expensive burden of commuter rail service. Or that by the mid-1950s the suburban railroads had become the most vexing regional problem in the New York area. Or that two decades of complicated political activity has now produced significant financial and policy involvement by all three states, the Port Authority, and the federal government—without producing any long-range program capable of resolving the underlying difficulties of this unprofitable but critical adjunct of the Manhattan CBD.

The growing proportion of managers and professionals in the CBD work force also increases the burdens on the public transportation system. Manhattan's executive corps tends to live further and further from the CBD, and the average journey-to-work trip to the center steadily lengthens. The lengthening trip has had a mildly depressing effect on the revenues of some commuting railroads, whose mileage rates decrease with distance. Longer trips have had an even greater impact on the finances of the New York City subway system, which uses a flat nonzoned fare. With many suburbanites driving or taking buses to subway stations in the outer reaches of the Bronx, Brooklyn, and Queens, operating costs have increased without commensurate increases in revenue. Since most of the funds to cover the transit system's mounting losses come from the city budget, New York City's taxpayers are underwriting the movement of CBD workers to the far corners of the city and even beyond its boundaries.

The shift in CBD growth to the north and east has also left its mark on the public transportation system. It has hastened the decline of the New Jersey commuter railroads. Except for the former Pennsylvania Railroad mainline, none of the New Jersey routes has a direct connection to Manhattan. The Jersey lines were oriented to the financial district in downtown Manhattan, which their commuters reached by ferry or the Hudson Tubes. The increase in uptown jobs and the growth of direct bus and automobile access to midtown have been major factors in the sharp drop in rail commuting from New Jersey. On the other hand, the location of Grand Central Terminal in the middle of the booming upper east side of the CBD, combined with the lack of attractive bus service from Westchester and Fairfield Counties, gave a fairly stable share of the commuter markets to the New York Central and the New Haven (both now part of Conrail—along with the Pennsylvania and other railroads in the region). But since this business was concentrated in the peak hours, the railroads derived little benefit from it. The growth of midtown Manhattan also has generated pressures on the city, state, and federal governments for the funds to embark on major capital improvements in the rail system, including a subway tunnel between East 61st Street and Queens, an east side station for Long Island and Pennsylvania commuters, and direct access to midtown for New Jersey suburbanites whose rail service terminates on the west shore of the Hudson. The political response to these pressures is treated in later chapters.

## The Decline of the Older Cities

New York, Jersey City, Hoboken, and most of the region's other older cities derived their initial developmental advantages from their locations along the waterfront. During the nineteenth century, the major economic activities of the New York region were clustered around the port. The rudimentary transportation system compelled most people to live near their places of work. As a consequence, the inner neighborhoods of the older cities were intensively developed, with residential densities reaching 300,000 per square mile in lower Manhattan. As long as economic and technological factors required the concentration of industrial, residential, and commercial activities in and around the port, the older cities thrived. Between 1850 and 1910, Manhattan's population more than quadrupled (from 516,000 to 2.3 million) while that of Brooklyn soared from 139,000 to 1.6 million. During the same period, Newark grew from a town of 40,000 to a city of 347,000; and Jersey City was transformed from a small port of 7,000 into the region's most important rail terminus with a population of 268,000.

For more than sixty years, however, the economic, technological, social, and political tides have been running against the older cities. Many of the advantages the intensively developed cities enjoyed during the age of steam have become liabilities in the era of the internal combustion engine. Like the inner districts of metropolitan areas across the nation, New York's older cities have been losing both people and jobs to the suburbs, particularly in the years since World War II.

In the late nineteenth century, improvements in the transportation system began to free residential development from its ties to the inner section of the New York region. Subway construction in New York City began in 1900; within a decade Manhattan's teeming lower east side was losing population. By 1920, overcrowded Manhattan itself registered an absolute decline. Decentralization was speeded in the 1920s as automobile usage increased rapidly, coupled with the growth of a regional highway network which spanned the major water barriers. In 1920, 72 percent of the 22-county region's population lived in the core. By 1950, the core's share had dropped to 63 percent. During these three decades, the population losses in the older sections of the core were balanced by continued growth in the cities' outer neighborhoods. As a result, the core as a whole gained 1.4 million residents between 1920 and

1930. By the 1940s, however, the core's rate of growth was less than a fifth of that of the suburbs.

During the 1950s, these trends rapidly accelerated. Five of the region's seven largest cities failed to grow. New York City lost 110,000 residents during the decade; and in the three oldest boroughs—Manhattan, Brooklyn, and the Bronx—the decline totaled close to 400,000. Across the river in crowded Hudson County, which had been losing residents steadily since 1930, all but two of the county's twelve municipalities declined. During the 1950s, the core lost 210,000 residents while the suburbs were gaining 2.4 million. By 1980, the population of the core had declined to 7.6 million, and accounted for only 40 percent of the inhabitants of the 31-county region. These figures are shown in Table 6.

### Table 6—*Population Change in the Core: 1950–1980*

|  | 1950 (000) | 1960 (000) | 1970 (000) | 1980 (000) | 1950–1980 (000) | *Percentage Change 1950–1980* |
|---|---|---|---|---|---|---|
| Bronx | 1,451 | 1,425 | 1,472 | 1,169 | −282 | −19.4 |
| Brooklyn | 2,738 | 2,627 | 2,602 | 2,231 | −507 | −18.5 |
| Manhattan | 1,960 | 1,698 | 1,539 | 1,428 | −532 | −27.1 |
| Queens | 1,551 | 1,810 | 1,987 | 1,891 | +340 | +21.9 |
| Hudson County | 647 | 611 | 609 | 557 | −90 | −13.9 |
| Newark | 439 | 405 | 382 | 329 | −110 | −25.0 |
| Total Core | 8,787 | 8,576 | 8,590 | 7,605 | −1182 | −13.5 |

*Note:* Columns may not add up to totals shown due to rounding.

### *The Departure of Middle-Class Whites*

Underlying postwar population change in the core has been the massive exodus of white families from the region's older cities. Throughout the twentieth century, the outward flow from the older neighborhoods has been composed primarily of white middle-class families with children in search of more space, better schools, fresh air, and "the good life." In recent years, rapidly rising wages for skilled workers have combined with the decentralization of manufacturing to add large numbers of middle-income blue-collar workers to the ranks of those moving outward. Except for sprawling Queens, which gained 340,000 inhabitants between 1950 and 1980, little land has been available in the core for single-family housing or garden apartments. The more attractive housing in the older cities tends to be too expensive or too cramped for middle-income families with children. But most of the core's available housing is obsolete, deteriorating, and located in crime-ridden neighborhoods. Also, city schools suffer by comparison with those in most suburbs. Nor can the crowded neighborhoods of the older cities compete effectively with the suburbs in the provision of play space for children, recreational opportunities for the entire family, or off-street parking facilities for the ubiquitous automobile. For the citizen interested in influencing local school, tax, or land-use policies, the small-scale governments of suburbia appear to offer greater opportunities for effective participation than the massive, inertial bureaucratic system of New York City, or the machine politics of places such as Jersey City.

For these and other reasons hardly unique to the New York region—not the least of which is the fact that the postwar version of the American dream for most has been a *suburban* dream—the core experienced a net decrease of 1.25 million whites between 1950 and 1970, as shown in Table 7. These data, however, understate the total number of whites who actually left the core, since natural increase (births minus deaths) compensated for some of the out-migration. The vast majority of the whites who deserted the core settled in one of the region's 500-odd suburbs, which added 3.8 million whites to their population during the 1950s and 1960s.

**Table 7–*White Population Change in the Core: 1950–1970***

|  | 1950 (000) | 1970 (000) | 1950–1970 (000) | Percentage Change |
|---|---|---|---|---|
| Bronx | 1,352 | 1,114 | −238 | −17.6 |
| Brooklyn | 2,525 | 1,946 | −579 | −22.9 |
| Manhattan | 1,557 | 1,159 | −398 | −25.6 |
| Queens | 1,497 | 1,729 | +232 | +15.5 |
| Hudson County | 624 | 547 | −77 | −12.3 |
| Newark | 364 | 175 | −189 | −51.9 |
| Total Core | 7,919 | 6,670 | −1,249 | −15.8 |

In recent years, these general trends have been slowed in a few core neighborhoods. Rapidly rising housing costs in the suburbs have increased the attractiveness for some whites of older housing in parts of the core. Changing life styles—which have dramatically increased the number of single individuals and childless couples—have decreased the importance of schools for many younger white adults, and thus enhanced the attractiveness of housing bargains and convenient locations in sections such as Cobble Hill in Brooklyn and Hoboken in Hudson County. But these developments have affected overall population trends only slightly. Between 1970 and 1975, 700,000 more whites left New York City than moved in, and the net loss of white residents was more than 450,000.

### The Growth of Black and Hispanic Ghettos

Most of the whites who left the core during the past quarter-century were replaced by blacks or Hispanics. In comparison with other large metropolitan areas, the most striking feature of this influx has been the number of Hispanics, primarily Puerto Ricans, who accounted for 21 percent of the population of the core in 1980. Between 1950 and 1980, the core's Hispanic population increased more than sevenfold to nearly 1.6 million, with substantial numbers of Cubans, Dominicans, and other Latin Americans joining Puerto Ricans in the older neighborhoods of the region's core. Over the same three decades, the black population more than doubled, from 876,000 in 1950 to 2.0 million in 1980.[14] Each of the core's six components shared in this massive influx. (See Table 8.) By 1980, Brooklyn had the largest number of blacks, while the largest concentration was in Newark, where 58 percent of the population was black and 18 percent Hispanic. Altogether blacks and

14. Census data for 1980 enumerated blacks of Hispanic origin in both categories.

**Table 8—*Blacks and Hispanics in the Core: 1980***

|  | Total Population (000) | Blacks (000) | Percentage Blacks | Hispanics (000) | Percentage Hispanics |
|---|---|---|---|---|---|
| Bronx | 1,169 | 372 | 31.8 | 397 | 34.0 |
| Brooklyn | 2,231 | 723 | 32.4 | 392 | 17.6 |
| Manhattan | 1,428 | 310 | 21.7 | 336 | 23.5 |
| Queens | 1,891 | 354 | 18.7 | 262 | 13.9 |
| Hudson County | 557 | 70 | 12.6 | 145 | 26.0 |
| Newark | 329 | 192 | 58.4 | 61 | 18.5 |
| Total Core | 7,605 | 2,020 | 26.6 | 1,593 | 20.9 |

*Note:* Spanish-speaking blacks were enumerated in both categories in the 1980 Census.

Hispanics accounted for more than 40 percent of the population of the core by 1980.

Like the earlier immigrants, most blacks and Hispanics arrive in the New York region poor and unskilled. As their predecessors did, they occupy the region's oldest and least desirable housing. Since most of this housing is in the core, these groups are captives of the decaying neighborhoods of the older cities. In 1970, 73 percent of the region's 2.6 million nonwhites and 87 percent of its 993,000 Puerto Ricans lived in the core. To date, relatively few of these newcomers have had sufficient income to follow the trail of the earlier immigrants, who have moved out from the slums and obsolete gray areas of the core. Those having the income to command better housing in the outer neighborhoods of the cities or in suburbia must contend with ethnic and, more important, racial prejudice, which is reinforced by the policies of local banks, real estate brokers, suburban governments, and school boards.

For the blacks and Puerto Ricans, as for the Irish, Italians, and Jews before them, New York was the land of opportunity. As Harlem-born Claude Brown puts it: "These migrants were told that unlimited opportunities for prosperity existed in New York and that there was no 'color problem' there. They were told that Negroes lived in houses with bathrooms, electricity, running water, and indoor toilets. To them, this was the 'promised land' that Mammy had been singing about in the cotton fields for many years."[15] But in New York, as in every metropolitan area, the promised land turned out to be a squalid slum in a segregated ghetto of a racially divided metropolis.

Central Harlem is the core's oldest black ghetto; but it differs little from the region's other concentrations of low-income blacks and Hispanics, such as East Harlem and the lower east side in Manhattan, Morrisania in the Bronx, Bedford-Stuyvesant and Brownsville in Brooklyn, Corona in Queens, or Newark's central ward. Almost all of central Harlem's 80,000-odd residents are black. More than half of its housing is deteriorated or dilapidated. The unemployment rate is twice that of the rest of New York City. Family income is one-third that of the rest of New York City. Children are disadvantaged at every turn in Harlem and the core's other ghettos. Harlem's infant mortality rate is almost twice that of New York City as a whole. The lack of recreational areas other than the streets helps account for the fact that children in Harlem

15. Claude Brown, *Manchild in the Promised Land* (New York, Macmillan, 1965), p. 7.

are far more likely to be killed by automobiles than elsewhere in the city. Almost all of Central Harlem's school-age children attend de facto segregated schools, where, as Kenneth Clark shows, "the basic story . . . is one of inefficiency, inferiority, and massive deterioration. The further these students progress in school, the larger the proportion who are retarded and the greater is the discrepancy between their achievement and the achievement of other children in the city."[16]

### The Dispersal of Blue-Collar Jobs

Adding to the plight of the newcomers has been the steady erosion of employment opportunities in the core for those lacking education and white-collar skills. Except for the small minority with the talents in demand in the CBD, the job prospects for blacks and Puerto Ricans in the older cities have grown progressively worse in the postwar years. Between 1947 and 1976, factory jobs in New York City were more than halved, dropping from 1.12 million to 543,000. In 1975 alone, the city lost 65,200 blue-collar jobs.

Jobs, like people, have been leaving the inner sections of the New York region for a long time. Economic and technological changes have slowly eroded the competitive position of large portions of the core. Before the advent of the railroads, the island of Manhattan was a highly preferred industrial location, as entrepreneurs sought to gain the advantage of cheap water transportation. This comparative advantage disappeared because most of the railroads serving the region stopped at the west side of the Hudson. As a result, as Vernon points out, "plants with major freight-moving requirements . . . increasingly [favored] the New Jersey side of the Region. At first, this preference retarded growth in Manhattan only, but later its effects were felt in Brooklyn and Queens as well."[17] By freeing many industrial operations from their dependence on the railroads, the development of the truck and the public highway speeded the decentralization of manufacturing operations in the region.

Equally important in pushing industry out from the intensively developed sections of the core has been industry's quest for space. By the end of the nineteenth century, most of the region's noxious industries had left their original locations in Manhattan. The slaughterhouses, chemical plants, and refineries sought space for their operations and wastes in less-developed parts of the core and beyond, in areas such as Brooklyn's Newton Creek, Hunts Point in the Bronx, the Jersey Meadows, and the shores of the waterway separating Staten Island and New Jersey. Manufacturers, particularly those with large plants and growing employment, joined the exodus in the twentieth century.

Space and transportation also underlie the postwar decentralization of industry. Modern industrial processes require large tracts of land that are extremely difficult to assemble in the crowded core with its rectangular street grid and small blocks. Unable to adapt its Manhattan plant to modern continuous flow operations, the National Biscuit Company moved to Fair Lawn, New Jersey, where it built a quarter-mile-long automatic bakery. Another rea-

16. Kenneth B. Clark, *Dark Ghetto* (New York, Harper & Row, 1965), pp. 119–120.
17. Vernon, *Metropolis 1985*, p. 38.

*The increasing space requirements of industry moved factories out-ward from the center, initially along the region's waterways, as in the case of this large plant located near Newark.* Credit: Michael N. Danielson

son Nabisco left the city was the heavy toll placed on its distribution opera-tions by traffic congestion on the narrow streets of lower Manhattan. Lack of room for expansion, the inadequacy of city factories and lofts for modern operations, and the high costs of congestion also push much smaller concerns out of the core. Typical is the paper jobbing firm that left an old four-story building in Brooklyn for an industrial park in Syosset where a modern con-veyor system could be employed; or the paint wholesaler who would not have abandoned Brooklyn for Farmingdale "if we had had a plant in New York with adequate facilities for future expansion . . . and where we wouldn't have had to fight traffic and parking problems every day . . ."[18]

Many of the industries that remain in the core's older manufacturing districts are small firms reliant on external economies. Of the factories re-maining in New York City, two-thirds employ fewer than twenty people. Most of these small firms depend on outside contractors and suppliers. These small, frequently marginal, concerns also are attracted to the core by the cheap space available in the loft districts and the new low-wage labor pool provided by the spreading ghettos. As Schlivek observes, "the arrival of the latest group of newcomers—and especially the women among them—has acted as a brake to slow down [the flight of industry]. If they were not here to supply a cheap bank of labor it is unlikely that many of the more routine jobs still carried on in the city, e.g., the assembling of electrical fixtures, toys, and

18. Emanuel Cantor, president of Cantor Brothers, Inc., quoted in Dudley Dalton, "Space Not Taxes, Prompts Moves," *New York Times,* August 9, 1964.

*Abandoned industrial buildings in Brooklyn, typical of thousands of obsolete facilities which no longer provide employment for unskilled newcomers to the region's core.*          Credit: Michael N. Danielson

other low-priced gadgets—would have remained this long."[19] Indicative of the core's serious plight is the fact that the ghettos of the low-skilled are one of the older cities' remaining attractions for industry. It is questionable whether these low-wage, marginal industries can contribute much to the economic and social revitalization of the inner city. In many of these jobs, blacks and Puerto Ricans fail either to advance or to acquire transferable skills. Their earnings are low, while their prospects for technological unemployment are high.

### The Burdens of the Cities

The flight of the white middle class, the influx of blacks and Hispanics, and the erosion of the economic base (outside the still-thriving CBD) have concentrated social and economic dislocations in the older cities of the New York region. As in every other major metropolitan area in the United States, the inner areas have the lion's share of the region's unemployment, poverty, slums, crime, and other social welfare problems. The adverse consequences of urban growth and change constantly threaten to overwhelm the public services of the older cities.

All these developments trouble the majority of the residents of the core, who are not poor, do not live in slums, are not on the welfare rolls, and do not commit crimes. Large numbers who live there prefer to remain in the core. Residents of Manhattan's luxury apartments and the core's other oases have combined gracious living with convenient access to jobs, entertainment and

19. Schlivek, *Man in the Metropolis*, p. 164.

cultural activities. The vast horde of office, factory, and other moderate-income workers in Brooklyn, Queens, the Bronx, and Hudson County have housing they can afford, and relatively inexpensive rapid transit connections to their jobs in or near the CBD. And for many others, the older neighborhoods of the core offer family and ethnic ties that are not easily severed. Nonetheless, for more and more of these people, the costs of living in the core have outrun the benefits. Fear and dislike of newcomers, congestion, pollution, noise, mediocre schools, and inadequate housing turn the thoughts of the most dedicated city dweller to suburbia. Even in a quiet middle-class backwater of the core like Brooklyn's Sheepshead Bay, "Long Island [is] the thing." As Myra Gershowitz, an accountant's wife, wistfully notes: "Everyone's moving to the island. You think you're missing something if you don't move out there."[20]

## The Spreading Metropolis

As more and more people from Brooklyn and elsewhere in the core decided to "move out there"—to Nassau, Westchester, Fairfield, Rockland, Bergen, Morris, Middlesex, Monmouth, and beyond—the New York region spread at an accelerating rate. In the three centuries before 1929, approximately 700 square miles were settled in the region. During the next three decades, over 1,100 additional square miles were developed. As the region has pushed outward, development has been progressively less intensive. At the end of World War II, Levittown on Long Island was developed at seven households to the acre. Lots of roughly that size characterized much of the region's inner ring during the first postwar decade. Twenty years later, development focused on the region's intermediate ring, where the average lot available for single-family housing was nearly three-quarters of an acre. During the 1970s, residential densities of less than one family per acre were common, as a growing proportion of the land available for development in the intermediate and outer rings was zoned by local governments for one-acre lots or larger, resulting in low population in these areas. (See Table 9.)

### Table 9—*Population Density by Ring: 1980*

|  | Population (per sq. mile) |
| --- | --- |
| Core | 24,477 |
| Inner Ring | 4,603 |
| Intermediate Ring | 1,311 |
| Outer Ring | 245 |

As in every metropolitan area, a primary force behind the spread of the New York region is the family with children. Vernon points out: "The higher the proportion of children in the household, the stronger is the incentive for a family to seek lower-density single-family housing with agreeable neighborhood conditions and good schools. This drive seems to permeate every in-

20. Quoted in Richard Weinraub, "Boon in Brooklyn," *New York Times*, February 8, 1966.

come level and racial group in the Region."[21] In Suffolk County, whose population grew by more than 300 percent during the 1950s and 1960s, almost 40 percent of the population was under 18 years of age in 1970, and there were 3.7 persons per household. By contrast, only 22 percent of Manhattan's population was under 18 in 1970 and the average household had 2.2 persons.

## The Impact of Transportation

In encouraging the outward movement of families who seek space, status, good schools, and accessible governments, transportation has played a crucial role in the New York region as in other urban areas. Commuter railroads fostered the region's early suburbs; and the massive postwar decentralization of the region was made possible by widespread automobile ownership and the development of the nation's most extensive urban highway system, composed of over 1,500 miles of limited access expressways, parkways, and turnpikes, as well as over 5,000 arterial highways. By freeing the region's development from the constraints imposed by the fixed-rail systems, the automobile and the highway opened up vast new territories for development and "made possible a more lavish use of the land by adding so much to the urban supply."[22]

The scale of the New York region, its immense central business district, and the extensive rail network produced considerable suburbanization before the advent of the automobile. Located primarily in the inner ring along the commuter rail lines that radiate out from the core, most of these older suburbs were settled in the late nineteenth century and first three decades of the twentieth century. Their development patterns were strongly influenced by the rail system. Since most of their residents wanted to be within walking distance of the station, land use was fairly intensive in suburbs like Great Neck on the Long Island Rail Road, Larchmont on the New Haven, Scarsdale on the New York Central, Ridgewood on the Erie, and Montclair on the Lackawanna.

Large homes on relatively small lots predominate in these and a score of similar communities, together with extensive apartment house development in the vicinity of some local stations. Most of the commuters who originally settled in these communities had white-collar jobs in the CBD and above-average incomes. With their superior school systems, spacious and expensive housing, high social status, and relative proximity to Manhattan, many of the older suburbs have continued to attract upper-income CBD executives and professionals. Others in the higher-income levels have exchanged the convenience of the close-in commuter rail towns for the more spacious exurbs of the intermediate and outer rings. Although the ride is longer and the plots considerably larger, suburbs like Pound Ridge, Westport, Rumson, and Bernardsville have been almost as dependent on the commuter railroads for their development as the older suburbs.

The new suburbs of the automobile age differ in several important respects from the older suburban communities along the commuter rail lines. Initial development in the postwar towns has been almost exclusively in single-family homes. In Suffolk and Monmouth, two of the suburban counties that grew most rapidly, 95 percent of the housing built during the 1960s was

21. Vernon, *Metropolis 1985*, p. 191.
22. Ibid., p. 199.

*Shopping malls proliferated in the region's suburbs throughout the 1960s and 1970s, typically at the intersection of major highways, as in the case of the Garden State Plaza in Paramus, New Jersey.*
Credit: Louis B. Schlivek, Regional Plan Association

single-family. In the newer suburbs, lots have been a good deal larger, with correspondingly lower residential densities than those found in the suburban areas settled before World War II.

Unlike the pioneer suburbanite who generally commuted to the CBD, most of the residents of the new automobile-oriented suburbs work outside Manhattan. Between 1950 and 1970, the number of employed people in the outlying counties increased by 500,000, but less than 100,000 new commuters were added to the CBD work force during the same period. Relatively few residents of the new suburbs use public transportation for their journey to work, or for any other travel. Another contrast with the older suburbs is the much higher proportion of working-class residents. Upwards of 40 percent of the residents of the postwar suburbs are blue-collar workers, almost all of whom drive to their jobs. These people live in what the Regional Plan Association calls "spread city," a rapidly growing area encompassing the outer reaches of the region's inner ring and everything beyond in which residences, stores, factories, schools, churches, roads, and every other facility requires more and more space.

Speaking of this rubber-borne revolution, Louis Schlivek notes that it is "changing the face of the region more rapidly and extensively than any other phenomenon in three hundred years of history."[23] In 1950, there were fewer than 2,000 residents in Plainview, a truck farm community astride the path of the Long Island Expressway on the Nassau-Suffolk line. By 1960, almost 28,000 people lived in Plainview, which also acquired shopping centers, industrial parks with ninety-five industrial facilities employing 7,000 people, and a phalanx of restaurants and hotels along the expressway. The transformation of Waldwick in northwestern Bergen County also is typical. Waldwick had less than 3,000 residents when the developers arrived in 1946. Fourteen years later, 10,500 people lived in the community, 44 percent of whom were of school age. Between 1950 and 1960, school enrollment increased 500 percent, requiring 1,340 new places in the borough's elementary schools, the construction of a new high school, and a threefold increase in local taxes. Elsewhere along the region's rapidly advancing frontier, the story was similar as people and automobiles combined to produce explosive growth.

The new suburbs' low residential densities mean that almost everyone lives beyond walking distance of stores, schools, churches, commuter railroad stations, and bus stops. In addition, an increasing proportion of the new suburbs' residents work outside the core; for most there is no alternative to the automobile even if they sought one. Thus, the average suburbanite portrayed in a recent Nassau County advertisement was not the stereotyped CBD-bound commuter, but "the man who works minutes from home," who "gets into his car in the morning to drive the few miles to work."

These developments, as the Port Authority points out, have produced a "pattern of regional travel [that] is becoming more diffuse, less distinct. More points of origin are becoming linked with more points of destination, but the links do not form any continuous linear arrangement. Travel paths are growing in number and channelization is being eroded by dispersal. The opportunities for group travel diminish, the demands for individual travel increase."[24] The result has been a phenomenal increase in automobile use in the newer suburbs. Morris and Suffolk counties have more than 1.5 autos per household, compared with one for every two households in Brooklyn and one for every four in Manhattan. Despite the heavy use of mass transportation, the automobile accounts for two-thirds of the weekday trips made in the region's intensively developed 3,600 square miles. Because of the growing diffusion of origins and destinations in the new suburbs, the focus of highway development shifted in the 1960s from radial to circumferential roads.[25]

### The Movement of Jobs and Homes

Closely related to these developments has been the steady decentralization of employment in the New York region. Three out of every five jobs in the region involve servicing local populations. Even with the unique CBD, about half of the region's white-collar workers are engaged in decentralized activities

23. Schlivek, *Man in Metropolis*, p. 270.

24. Port of New York Authority, *Metropolitan Transportation—1980*, p. 285.

25. See, for example, Tri-State Transportation Commission, *Tri-State Transportation—1985, An Interim Plan* (May 1966), pp. 24–35.

*Jobs inevitably follow residents as the metropolis spreads outward,
and the relationship is nicely underscored by the sign on a department
store under construction in a Bergen County suburb.*
Credit: Louis B. Schlivek, Regional Plan Association

such as banking, insurance, real estate, and government. These consumer-oriented trades and services are tied to their markets. As people have moved outward from the core, jobs in retailing, local services, banking, and scores of other fields have not been far behind. For example, retail employment outside the core rose from 349,000 to 529,000 between 1950 and 1976, while within the core it dropped from 636,000 to 520,000. Another sign of the times is the suburban boom in low-rise office buildings, complete with landscaping and parking lots. A Long Island planner explains: "The upsurge in office building is related to the tremendous growth in population and influx of industry. As we have become older in suburban development, the white-collar work force has started increasing faster than any other."[26]

As noted previously, industrial jobs also have been moving outward from the region's core. In 1965, for example, while New York City was losing 12,000 manufacturing jobs, Nassau County was adding 1.6 million square feet of plant space to its industrial inventory. During the same year, $9.5 million in investments by 106 concerns provided a million square feet of new industrial space in Morris County, largely in the vicinity of Interstate Routes 80 and

26. Lee E. Koppelman, executive director of the Nassau-Suffolk Planning Board, quoted in Byron Potterfield, "L.I. Skyscrapers Mark New Trend," *New York Times*, February 27, 1966.

*The sign at an industrial park on Long Island illustrates the movement of blue-collar jobs to the suburbs.*

Credit: Louis B. Schlivek, Regional Plan Association

287. The reasons for this industrial decentralization are hardly unique to the New York region: trucks and highways permitted industry to take advantage of suburbia's space for development, relative freedom from congestion, and what an official at Nabisco's Fair Lawn plant calls "a congenial atmosphere for doing business."[27] In skilled industries, a suburban location puts a firm closer to the residences of a growing proportion of its employees. For the research and electronics concern, a location in or near an affluent community with attractive homes and excellent schools can be a powerful inducement in attracting scientific and engineering personnel. Industry, on the other hand, offers suburbia tax revenues to offset the spiraling costs of new schools, streets, sewers, and other public facilities, inducements all but the wealthiest residential enclaves find hard to resist.

Despite the forces of decentralization, jobs have not been spreading outward in the New York region as rapidly as residences. Almost half of the

27. Quoted by Schlivek, *Man in Metropolis,* p. 326.

region's jobs are still within five miles of Times Square, while a circle more than twice that radius is required to encompass one-half the region's population. In part, this disparity reflects the tremendous concentration of jobs in the Manhattan CBD. Equally important, despite the strength of industrial decentralization in the region, manufacturing jobs have not been moving as far away from the core as people. During the 1960s, the largest gains in industrial jobs were registered in the inner ring of suburban counties, while population increased most rapidly in the communities of the intermediate ring. Finally, suburban office jobs, an increasingly important component of the region's economy, have tended to cluster. Whether in the CBD or the suburbs, office development "implies a tighter pattern of employment location" because of the "need for physical proximity to related functions carried on by other firms" and the fact that office work permits higher floor-space densities and taller structures, thus reducing land rent per employee.[28] The growing separation of suburban homes and jobs, as well as the sheer size of the region's outer sections, has lengthened the drive to work for an increasing number of new suburbanites.

Home-to-work linkages in suburbia have been further lengthened, particularly for blue-collar workers, by the acceleration of residential dispersion caused by rising land costs in the intermediate and outer rings, and by the growth of restrictions against lower-cost housing. The widespread adoption of restrictive land-use ordinances has zoned almost all of the undeveloped land in the inner and intermediate rings for lots of more than a quarter-acre. Increasingly, families with moderate incomes in search of suburban housing find it necessary to buy in the periphery of the intermediate ring—thirty to fifty miles from Manhattan—or beyond in the outer ring where some land is still available in smaller plots.

The growing scarcity of land for moderately-priced housing, combined with a decline in the size of households, has produced a sharp increase in apartment building in the region's suburbs. In 1960, 14 percent of all the new housing units in the intermediate ring were apartments. By the early 1970s, the proportion had more than tripled to 44 percent. During the 1950s 98 percent of Middlesex's new housing was single-family; two decades later, over 40 percent of construction was in apartments. Below Middlesex in Monmouth County, apartment building increased 86 percent between 1960 and 1966, when multifamily units accounted for one-third of all housing starts in the county. During the early 1970s, half or more of the new housing in Bergen, Dutchess, Essex, Nassau, Union, and Westchester counties were apartments.

Despite the massive CBD, the new suburban apartments, and the tendency for jobs to remain closer to the core than residences, the New York region continued to spread in the 1960s and 1970s. Analysis of the many factors influencing development in the New York region reinforces the conclusion reached by Vernon and his colleagues in 1960 that the "basic technological developments in transportation and deep-seated changes in consumer wants" which have moved people and jobs outward "seem near-inexorable."[29] These conclusions were received with considerable dismay by the study's

28. Regional Plan Association, *The Region's Growth*, p. 117.
29. Vernon, *Metropolis 1985*, pp. 211–212.

sponsor, the Regional Plan Association (RPA), which finds many cracks in the picture window. Like critics of suburbia across the nation, RPA scores the spreading metropolis for its lack of variety, the restricted range of housing choices, the rising cost of housing in the monolithic residential community, and the vast highway investments required by the new suburbs' almost complete dependence on the automobile.[30]

Nor do blacks and Hispanics fare very well in the spreading metropolis. Relatively few members of these minority groups have been able to penetrate the economic, racial, and ethnic barriers that surround most of the region's new or desirable suburban housing. Most of the 950,000 blacks and 500,000 Hispanics living outside the core in 1980 were in older cities such as Paterson, Elizabeth, New Brunswick, or Stamford—living in slums which are smaller but otherwise differ little from the sprawling ghettos of the core—or were concentrated in older suburbs like Mount Vernon, New Rochelle, Englewood, and East Orange. In these towns, few blacks have been able to purchase attractive housing outside the segregated and deteriorating neighborhoods settled by those who first came to these communities a generation or more ago to work as domestics. In the older suburbs, as in the other concentrations of minorities in the region, most blacks occupy the least desirable housing, and their children attend the poorest schools, where almost all of their classmates are black.

Neither the plaints of the critics who yearn for the rebirth of the core, nor the plight of black and Hispanic citizens, however, have much impact on the hundreds of thousands of New Yorkers who during the 1950s and 1960s voted with their feet (and their automobiles) for the spreading metropolis. An overwhelming majority of those with the means to do so have chosen the new over the old in the New York region, or, as Schlivek puts it, have decided to "swim . . . in the mainstream of American culture—a middle-class culture which in its day-in and day-out living arrangements has shown a marked preference for quiet and privacy over visible excitement; for freedom of movement and space (no matter how monotonous) over confinement and crowding (no matter how colorful the neighborhood setting)."[31]

### The Slowing of the Region's Growth

During the 1970s, the region continued to grow along its expanding periphery. Between 1970 and 1980, over 642,000 people were added to the populations of the counties of the intermediate and outer rings. (See Table 10.) Almost 60 percent of this growth was registered in the distant outer ring, with the largest increases in Ocean, Orange, and Sussex counties. Growth in the developing suburbs, however, was no longer sufficient to offset population losses in the region's older sections. The core alone lost 985,000 residents during the decade. And the population of the inner ring dropped by 250,000, ending a period of vigorous growth that had increased its population from 3.1 million in 1950 to 4.8 million in 1970. As a result, the region as a whole lost 573,800 residents between 1970 and 1980. Even areas that continued to increase their populations were growing less rapidly than in the preceding

30. See Regional Plan Association, *Spread City*, pp. 32–33.
31. Schlivek, *Man in Metropolis*, p. 288.

decade. Thus, the annual rate of growth in the intermediate ring was less than one percent in the 1970s, compared with over 3 percent in the 1960s, while in the outer ring the annual rate dropped from 3 percent to 2.3 percent.

Table 10–*Population Change by Ring: 1970–1980*

|  | Population | | Population Change | |
|---|---|---|---|---|
|  | 1970 | 1980 | Net | Percentage |
| Core | 8,590,400 | 7,605,100 | −985,300 | −11.5 |
| Inner Ring | 4,801,400 | 4,570,800 | −230,600 | −4.8 |
| Intermediate Ring | 4,887,300 | 5,161,200 | +273,900 | +5.6 |
| Outer Ring | 1,473,300 | 1,841,500 | +368,200 | +25.0 |
|  | 19,752,400 | 19,178,600 | −573,800 | −5.0 |

The region's population stopped growing in the 1970s because of far-reaching demographic and economic changes. As in the nation as a whole, birth rates declined sharply, with the number of births per 1,000 women of childbearing age falling from 20.3 in 1963 to 12.5 in 1973. While fewer people were being added through natural increase, more individuals began leaving the region than were migrating into the tri-state area. Sixteen of the region's 31 counties lost more migrants than they gained between 1970 and 1975; and the region's net out-migration was over 570,000. Only four outer-ring counties—Ocean, Putnam, Sullivan, and Sussex—had net in-migration rates of more than 10 percent during the first half of the 1970s. Outward migration also was part of a larger national trend, the accelerating movement of Americans away from the northeast and midwest to the south and west.

Interacting with these demographic changes has been a regional economy which ceased growing in the 1970s. After adding more than 800,000 jobs during the previous decade, regional employment leveled off in the early 1970s at around eight million. The weakest link in the region's economy has been manufacturing, with factory jobs leaving the older sectors much more rapidly in recent years than they have been added in suburban industrial developments. As is the case with other northeastern and midwestern areas, the New York region lost most of these jobs to the south or west where manufacturers were offered less expensive land, cheaper labor, lower taxes, and less stringent environmental regulation. The steady decline in the region's industrial sector was accelerated by the severe national recession of 1970, with 255,000 manufacturing jobs being lost between 1970 and 1972 alone. The westward and southern movement of both people and jobs also lessened the region's attraction for corporate headquarters and related business functions, with the primary impact in the Manhattan CBD which lost over 200,000 jobs between 1969 and 1973.[32]

The ebbing of growth in the region as a whole, of course, *does not mean* that all parts of the region have stopped developing. The intermediate and outer rings continue to expand, as new housing development, shopping centers, and industrial parks spread across the suburban landscape. Even

32. The data in this paragraph and elsewhere in this chapter dealing with employment trends are derived from publications of the U.S. Bureau of Labor Statistics.

without future net in-migration, about a million households will be added to the region between 1980 and 1990, most of which are likely to settle along the region's developing periphery. In the process, these newly settled areas will experience many of the same problems and conflicts that have characterized past suburban development in the region. Moreover, the slowing of growth does not end concern with development. On the contrary, as the following chapters amply illustrate, the aging process usually intensifies conflict over development as localities seek to retain residents, bolster tax bases, and attract jobs.

# 3

# Maximizing Internal Benefits

"There are 10 million people up there," the Southampton homeowner warned, pointing to New York City 85 miles to the west, "and make no mistake about it, they're on their way here."[1] As in many suburbs in the New York region during the 1960s and 1970s, the cause for concern in affluent Southampton was a proposed garden apartment project. And like communities throughout the region faced with growing demands for more intensive land use, Southampton responded negatively, in this case with an amendment to the zoning ordinance which made the cost of garden-apartment development prohibitive.

Growth has been the basic influence on the politics of development beyond the inner ring of the New York region. Few communities can insulate themselves from the pressures for new homes, shopping centers, offices and factories, and from the changes that follow in the wake of these developments. With growth comes mushrooming demands on the newer suburbs for schools, roads, and sewers. In older suburbs, growth and change frequently produce increased residential densities, an influx of lower-income families and ethnic minorities, and commercial decline. Nor can any suburb escape the general rise in demand for increasingly expensive public goods and services. And all must grapple with the crucial questions of who will settle where under what kinds of restrictions, questions whose answers shape the political economy of each of the region's 775 suburban jurisdictions.[2]

From the regional perspective of many planners and urban specialists, development in suburbia represents a massive lost opportunity. As a consequence of local control of land use, hundreds of small-scale governments employ zoning codes and other regulatory devices to pursue parochial development goals. In the view of the critics, the uncoordinated and often contradictory development strategies that emerge from the suburban mosaic ignore sound planning principles and broad regional needs. The result, in the eyes of the Regional Plan Association, environmentalists, and like-minded groups and individuals, is a recurring pattern of inefficient development and disor-

1. Quoted in Francis X. Clines, "Housing Curbed in Southampton," *New York Times*, March 6, 1966.
2. The term "suburbs" as used in this volume refers to the municipalities of the New York region, minus the large older cities (New York City, Elizabeth, Jersey City, Newark, Passaic, Paterson, and Trenton in New Jersey, White Plains and Yonkers in New York, and Bridgeport, New Haven, Stamford, and Waterbury in Connecticut). Under this definition, a number of smaller cities such as New Brunswick, N.J. and Mt. Vernon, N.Y. are considered suburbs in the discussion in Chapter Three and Chapter Four.

derly growth, characterized by monotonous housing tracts, highly limited residential options for the lower and middle classes, vanishing open spaces, misplaced industry, overcrowded schools, congested highways, polluted air and water, overburdened utility systems, and spiraling taxes. In the absence of fundamental change in the system of land-use control and perhaps broader governmental reorganization as well, regional planners foresee more of the same in the spreading metropolis, as well as even greater inequalities in the distribution of costs and benefits among the residents of the tristate area.[3]

Most suburbanites perceive development politics in a different light. At the grass roots, development issues tend to be viewed in a narrow frame of reference focused largely on home, family, and local taxes. The typical suburban homeowner sees little need for change in local political institutions, since small-scale government usually provides a political system relatively responsive to homeowner interest in maintaining property values, preserving the residential character of the community, stabilizing local taxes, and providing adequate public education. This broad base of shared values among homeowners does not, however, always produce consensus on development issues. Thus, some in a residential suburb will favor new commercial or industrial development as a means of stabilizing local property taxes, while others will oppose such development as undermining the community's residential character. Moreover, not everyone in suburbia shares the values of the homeowning majority. Apartment dwellers are less sensitive than homeowners to the impact of locally financed public services on property taxes. Large-scale landowners and developers are primarily interested in maximizing the return on their investments. Managers of commercial and industrial establishments are more concerned with providing adequate access to their facilities and with the availability of labor and customers than with maintaining the residential character of a particular suburb. And a growing number of less fortunate residents of suburbia enter the political arena to seek low-income housing, access to jobs, and public schools more responsive to their needs.

Despite these crosscurrents, the development policies of the vast majority of suburban governments in the New York region have reflected the overriding interest of most of their constituents in protecting an investment in a home and its environs. As a result, most suburbs seek to control changes within their boundaries in order to maximize the benefits and minimize the costs of any new development to existing residents. They also try to minimize adverse effects within their jurisdiction of the activities of other public agencies, such as the state highway departments and planning agencies.

This chapter and the next analyze the efforts of suburban governments as they pursue these often elusive goals. Maximizing internal benefits is the primary concern of this chapter, while Chapter Four explores the suburbs' efforts to minimize the intervention of outside agencies. Before turning to this analysis, we examine briefly the capabilities which suburban governments in the New York region bring to the task of concentrating resources effectively to influence urban development.

3. See, for example, Regional Plan Association, *Spread City*, RPA Bulletin No. 100 (New York: 1962); and Tri-State Regional Planning Commission, *Proceedings: Tri-State Regional Conference* (New York: 1976).

## Suburban Capabilities

Almost all of the region's suburbs bring similar advantages to the complex task of shaping development along desired lines. These developmental assets are formal independence, control over the use of land, and a relative lack of conflicting constituency demands. Each faces the same basic set of constraints: limited areal scope, limited political skills, reliance on the property tax, and at least formal dependence upon the state government. Moreover, location, topography, socioeconomic composition, and the pattern of previous development strongly influence the ability of any particular unit to overcome its inherent shortcomings and to concentrate its resources effectively. As the discussion in this and the next chapter indicates, great variations exist in the ability of suburban jurisdictions to shape development. Equally important, given the nature of suburban capabilities, some kinds of development decisions are far more susceptible to suburban influence than others.

### The Constraint of Size

Most suburbs in the New York region are small. More than half of the 775 suburban jurisdictions encompass less than five square miles. In 1970, the average suburb had approximately 14,000 residents. But almost 10 percent of the suburban units had fewer than 1,000 inhabitants. And only eight had 100,000 or more residents, all of which were two-level local jurisdictions in Nassau and Suffolk counties.[4] (See Table 11.)

Table 11 – *Suburban Governments: Area and Population: 1970*

| Area (sq. miles) | Number of Units | Average Population |
|---|---|---|
| less than 5 | 408 | 8,063 |
| 5 to 10 | 63 | 19,004 |
| 10 to 25 | 106 | 15,885 |
| 25 to 50 | 143 | 12,543 |
| 50 or more | 55 | 53,555 |

The limited areal scope and small population of the typical suburb shapes to a considerable degree its role in the politics of urban development. Small size means limited financial resources and, perhaps more important, limited political skills. Because of the resource constraints imposed by size and reliance on the property tax and state assistance, most suburbs are rarely able to use their construction and other investment decisions to influence development. Instead, they rely primarily on zoning and other regulatory devices in their efforts to shape development along desired lines. Limited financial resources also combine with restricted area to increase the reliance of suburban jurisdictions on special agencies to provide water, sewage dis-

4. The suburban jurisdictions with populations over 100,000 in 1970 were the towns of Hempstead, North Hempstead, and Oyster Bay in Nassau County and the towns of Babylon, Brookhaven, Huntington, Islip, and Smithtown in Suffolk County. All of these large towns encompassed villages, as discussed below and indicated in Table 12.

BERGEN COUNTY'S
78 MUNICIPALITIES
MAP 3

posal, and other public services that are beyond the fiscal and territorial capacity of the individual municipality. As for political skill, few suburbs are large enough to support full-time elected officials, specialized bureaucracies, or professional planning agencies; and many are so small as to have no effective administrative capacities at all. Nor is the average suburb large enough by itself to have much influence in the political arenas of the region, state, and nation. To some degree, however, these political weaknesses are offset by common interests among suburbs·on many development issues, the responsiveness of state legislatures to widely shared suburban interests, and the availability of financial and technical assistance from the states and the federal government. A good example of the latter is the federal 701 program, which has provided funds to many suburbs for professional planning assistance they could not otherwise afford.

Limited areal scope also greatly restricts a suburb's sphere of action. For the typical suburban unit, the small amount of territory under local control makes it highly vulnerable. The decision of one of New York City's neighbors to change the character of territory adjacent to the city may adversely affect the fortunes of one or two neighborhoods, but it will not disrupt the city as a whole. Similarly, construction of the Cross-Bronx Expressway cut a wide swath through a section of New York City, but had little impact on the overall pattern of development in the city. This is not the case with small suburban jurisdictions. A six-lane expressway may take a sizable proportion of the taxable property in a three-square-mile municipality, as well as permanently bifurcate a residential community. The efforts of a small suburb to exclude garden apartments or industry may be undermined by a neighboring community's decision to accept such development in order to increase the amount of taxable property (or tax ratables). Because the suburb in question is small, the actions of adjacent municipalities can have as much effect on the character of the community as its own land-use controls.

Illustrative of suburban vulnerability is the impact of large shopping centers on surrounding areas. One of the attractions for local officials in Wayne Township of the massive Willowbrook shopping center located on Wayne's border has been that neighboring Little Falls gets "all the traffic and harassment. We get all the taxes."[5] Given this kind of mismatch between costs and benefits, residents of adjacent communities typically oppose such developments. Plans for the construction of a large shopping center in Yonkers adjacent to its boundary with Hastings-on-Hudson were vigorously denounced in Hastings. "We would not benefit from the shopping center but it would cost us a lot," argued the opponents. "Tax revenues would all go to Yonkers while our shops would be wiped out. We would need more police and wider roads. Our property values would drop too."[6] Increasing the vulnerability of suburbs such as Hastings-on-Hudson is their lack of any direct role in the decisionmaking processes of neighboring communities.

### Variations Among Suburbs

One of the most striking features of the New York region—another product of its size and scope—is the great variation among the 775 units of general government in suburbia. In addition to differences in size that affect suburban development capabilities, important variations in the structure and function of local government result from the tristate nature of the New York region. The most complex local governmental arrangements are found in New York

5. Harry Butler, former mayor of Wayne, N.J., quoted in Jack Rosenthal, "Suburbs Abandoning Dependence on City," *New York Times*, August 16, 1971.
6. Mrs. Richard Evans, Hastings-on-Hudson, N.Y., quoted in James Feron, "Huge Shopping-Mall Plan Stirs a Battle in Yonkers," *New York Times*, June 18, 1973.

State where, as Robert C. Wood points out, "no hard and fast rules exist with respect to the division of functions among . . . governments."[7] In suburban New York, the primary units of local government—cities, towns, and villages—have varying degrees of independence, although all have power to control land use. Cities have more autonomy than towns, which depend on county government for a number of important functions. Villages are subdivisions of towns, empowered to control land use and other local functions within their boundaries. Towns are particularly important on Long Island since large portions of Nassau and Suffolk counties have not been subdivided into villages. As indicated in Table 12, only 23 percent of the population of the eight largest towns on Long Island lived in villages in 1970.

**Table 12–*Proportion of the Residents of the Largest Towns on Long Island Living in Villages: 1970***

| County and Town | 1970 Population | Number of Villages | Population of Villages | Percentage of Pop. in Villages |
|---|---|---|---|---|
| Nassau | | | | |
| Hempstead | 801,110 | 21 | 266,870 | 33.3 |
| North Hempstead | 234,984 | 30 | 130,767 | 55.6 |
| Oyster Bay | 333,089 | 18 | 59,804 | 18.0 |
| Suffolk | | | | |
| Babylon | 203,570 | 3 | 51,050 | 25.1 |
| Brookhaven | 243,915 | 8 | 30,717 | 12.6 |
| Huntington | 200,571 | 4 | 13,140 | 6.6 |
| Islip | 278,399 | 3 | 3,954 | 1.4 |
| Smithtown | 114,004 | 3 | 3,738 | 3.3 |

Further complicating the picture in New York is the widespread use of local special districts in suburban counties. (See Table 13.) In addition to six cities, eighteen towns, and twenty-two villages, Westchester had ninety special districts in 1977 empowered to raise local taxes to finance education, fire protection, garbage collection, street lighting, water supply, and other public services. Another important feature of the New York system for the politics of development is the subdivision of the towns for the provision of public education. In Suffolk, for example, the county's ten towns contain seventy-five school districts, each with its own local tax base. This means there are substantial tax differentials among school districts within a town, as well as competition within a town for development that will contribute to the financing of public education.

**Table 13–*Local Governments in Suburban Counties by State: 1977***

| | General Purpose | School Districts | Special Districts |
|---|---|---|---|
| Connecticut | 106 | 39 | 113 |
| New Jersey | 313 | 303 | 225 |
| New York | 364 | 319 | 351 |

7. Robert C. Wood, *1400 Governments* (Cambridge, Mass.: Harvard University Press, 1961), p. 24.

County government plays a more significant role in New York than in New Jersey (or in Connecticut, where county governments were abolished in 1960). The three large New York suburban counties—Westchester, Nassau, and Suffolk—have developed strong county-government units. Each has a full-time elected political executive, a substantial budget, an active and professional planning agency, and major responsibilities that affect development policies, including highways, water supply, sewage disposal, and recreation. A counterweight to these centralizing forces was provided prior to 1970 by the direct representation of towns (and cities in the core of Westchester) in the county legislature, which tended to make the New York counties particularly responsive to the interests of their component local governments.[8]

In New Jersey, all general purpose local units—cities, boroughs, villages, towns, and townships—have been delegated approximately the same functions by the state legislature. These primary units of local government share few powers with county governments, which have considerably less responsibility than in New York. Also in contrast with New York, school-district boundaries in New Jersey generally coincide with those of municipalities. And local special districts are relied on less than in the New York suburbs. In the Connecticut corner of the region, cities and towns function in the absence of county government, and independent school districts are less numerous than elsewhere in the region, but special districts for other functions are extensively used.

As indicated in Chapters One and Two, suburbs in the New York region also vary in terms of their pattern and time of settlement, state of development, socioeconomic composition, and property tax revenues per capita. All these factors influence an individual suburb's development goals and capabilities. Most of Bergen County's seventy municipalities are residential communities whose development interests and resources differ from those of "atypical" Bergen municipalities like Teterboro, a completely industrial borough, or Hackensack, the county seat and an older commercial center, or Paramus, a booming industrial, commercial, and residential community at the juncture of several major highways. But just as significant for the politics of development are the differences among Bergen's many bedroom communities. Lower-middle-class Waldwick, slowly recovering from the trauma of rapid expansion in the automobile age, inevitably views development strategies such as the attraction of industry more favorably than neighboring Ridgewood, a stable upper-middle-class municipality settled more than a generation ago by rail commuters whose principal development goal was the maintenance of a comfortable status quo. A different set of development problems preoccupy Englewood—an older suburb of large homes a few miles to the east of Waldwick and Ridgewood—because Englewood includes an increasingly militant low-income black neighborhood. And along the urban frontier, in northwest Bergen's Oakland, the politics of development are framed in terms

8. The county legislatures, which were known as boards of supervisors, were reorganized after a court suit overturning the apportionment of seats on the basis of local governmental units rather than population. Suffolk and Westchester replaced their boards with county legislatures based on single-member districts, thus eliminating the direct representation of local governments and their officials. Nassau retained direct representation of local units by providing each of its town supervisors with a vote on the board of supervisors weighted according to population.

of larger-lot zoning designed to insulate the town's affluent suburbanites from the adverse consequences of urban growth and change.

### Homogeneity and Heterogeneity

The differences among communities like Waldwick, Ridgewood, Oakland, Englewood, Paramus, Hackensack, and Teterboro make Bergen County as a whole—or for that matter, almost any other suburban county in the New York region—a varied aggregation of people and jobs. During the past quarter-century, the overall heterogeneity of suburbia has been enhanced, as large numbers of blue-collar workers and an increasing number of low-income families have followed the middle class into the suburbs. Because of the aging process in the inner suburbs, the growth of apartment living outside the cities, and the influx of blacks and Puerto Ricans into many areas, a growing number of municipalities in the suburbs have more in common with the older cities than with the newer suburban areas. Almost 62,000 of Nassau County's 1.4 million residents were below the poverty line in 1970; and one-third of the county's $270-million budget was devoted to welfare. Almost one-half of Westchester's population lives in four older suburban cities—Yonkers, Mount Vernon, New Rochelle, and White Plains. Thus, from the regional perspective, suburbia increasingly shares the socioeconomic diversity of the older cities, leading some observers to speak of "the City of New Jersey," and to comment that "Long Island Is Becoming Long City."[9]

But suburbia certainly is not a city in the political sense of being a single heterogeneous municipality. Upper-income families cluster in a few suburban jurisdictions, middle-income families predominate in a large number of suburbs, others are populated mainly by blue-collar suburbanites, and blacks and other low-income groups are concentrated in the municipalities which contain suburbia's older and less desirable housing. Thus it is not surprising that most suburbanites do not perceive their communities as becoming more city-like. In a 1978 survey, 63 percent of the suburban dwellers responded negatively to a question which asked whether their area was becoming more like a big city.[10]

In general, the socioeconomic variations among suburbs tend to be substantially greater than the variations within any one community. The relative homogeneity of the individual suburb results from superimposing the typical urban pattern of neighborhood differences along income, ethnic, and racial lines on the small scale of the average suburban municipality. Reinforcing this tendency has been the uniform pricing of large-scale housing developments and local land-use policies, which tend to set similar housing patterns within a town, thus homogenizing income levels within any one community. Consequently, the growing heterogeneity of suburbia as a whole rarely is reproduced in individual suburbs.

The socioeconomic homogeneity of the typical suburb has important consequences for development politics in the New York region. Compared

9. See Joe McCarthy, "Long Island Is Becoming Long City," *New York Times Magazine* (August 30, 1964), pp. 17, 65–67; and John E. Bebout and Ronald J. Grele, *Where Cities Meet: The Urbanization of New Jersey* (Princeton: Van Nostrand, 1964), pp. 91–111.

10. *New York Times*, "1978 Suburban Poll" (1978), p. 8.

with the older cities, the residents of any one suburb exhibit greater consensus on development goals, and generate fewer conflicting pressures on local policymakers. Internal consensus on goals helps many suburbs overcome some of the constraints imposed by restricted areal scope, limited resources, and the internal fragmentation of formal governmental authority among general-purpose units, semiautonomous planning boards, school districts, and other special-purpose agencies. When, as is often the case, these agencies share the same constituency, and the constituency largely agrees on community goals, policy determinations in each agency tend to be consistent and mutually reinforcing.

The importance of homogeneity in suburban politics also is illustrated by the fact that goal conflict is most common in the more extensive jurisdictions and the older suburbs, both of which typically encompass more varied populations. Finally, limited areal scope and homogeneity tend to structure many development issues along "external" rather than "internal" lines. More often than not, development contests involve conflict with outside parties—other municipalities, state highway agencies, garden-apartment developers, or blacks who desire to purchase homes—rather than conflict among groups and individuals within a particular suburb.

### The Central Fact of Autonomy

All of the distinguishing features of the suburban political arena—fragmentation, small-scale government, variation among suburbs, and homogeneity within them—are rooted in the considerable autonomy delegated to the primary units of local government by the states of Connecticut, New Jersey, and New York. Independence is the most significant political resource of most suburbs in the struggle to shape development along lines desired by residents, to maintain freedom of action in the competition for revenue sources and desirable development, and to avoid situations in which the costs to a community outweigh the benefits. Through incorporation and other forms of state delegation, local communities in the region are protected from the territorial ambitions of other jurisdictions, are shielded from unattractive joint ventures, and are given varying degrees of control over local services, expenditures, taxes, and land use.

Suburban independence is, of course, limited rather than absolute. As is the case with the older cities, suburban municipalities are creatures of state government. Although the patterns vary from state to state, local autonomy is limited by the setting of state standards, the mandating of local expenditures by the state legislature, the assignment of responsibilities to counties and special districts, and the retention of activities by the state itself. The state agencies that build highways, colleges, parks, and other public facilities are not subject to local land-use controls. And the state courts are the principal arbiters of disputes that arise over the actions of state agencies within suburbia and over the use by local governments of state-delegated powers.

Local control, however, is practically complete with respect to the regulation of land use, the most significant aspect of suburban autonomy for the politics of development. Like all local powers, control over land use is derived from the state government. But state legislatures, responsive to suburban interests, have been reluctant to interfere with local prerogatives in this extremely sensitive area of public policy. With only a few exceptions, state agencies have no active policymaking role in land-use regulation. Moreover, the courts in the three states traditionally have been wary of substantive challenges to local land-use regulations, confining themselves instead until recently to procedural issues.[11] As a result, over the past quarter-century suburban regulatory bodies in the New York region have enjoyed great freedom in using zoning and building codes, subdivision regulations, and other devices to control lot size, the area and height of structures, and the location and use of buildings for specific purposes. Through their ability to regulate land use, suburban governments strongly influence population densities, settlement patterns, the location of commerce and industry, tax rates, and the overall quality of life.

Local regulation of land is hardly an accidental consequence of political independence. On the contrary, the desire for local autonomy in the development process has been a primary cause of the fragmentation of the New York region into independent small-scale jurisdictions during the past century. Between 1860 and 1930, 450 municipalities were created in New Jersey largely in response to the desire of land owners, real estate agents, and residents for local control over land use and public services. In 1894 alone, twenty-six local government units were organized in Bergen County, whose seventy municipalities in the words of a recent chairman of the county planning board "are mostly the handiwork of politicians, lawyers, and real estate agents who each had his own interest to look after."[12]

The benefits promised by community control continue to generate pressures for the creation of new primary units of local government, particularly in the unincorporated villages of New York's sprawling towns. For example, in 1963 demands for autonomy over local land use led tiny Hampton Bays (population 1,512) to consider breaking away from the town of Southampton in Suffolk County. A few years later, residents of Strathmore, a Levitt development, sought political independence as a way to escape the zoning and planning controls of Brookhaven, Suffolk's largest town. In Rockland County, the prospect of a $75 million garden apartment complex prompted homeowners to incorporate Pomona in 1967 to protect their neighborhood against development decisions by town governments they considered unresponsive to their interests.[13] During the same year, estate owners in Purchase attempted unsuccessfully to secure local land-use control through incorporation as a village, in order to prevent the development of a $12 million corporate headquarters in

11. Of the three states, New Jersey's courts were most active during the 1970s in restricting local freedom of action in controlling land use, particularly when housing for lower-income families has been at issue. The most important ruling was handed down by the New Jersey Supreme Court in *Southern Burlington County N.A.A.C.P. v. Township of Mount Laurel*, 67 N.J. (1975). The Supreme Court concluded that "developing municipalities" like Mount Laurel—which is located outside the New York region in Burlington County, one of the most rapidly developing parts of the Philadelphia region—have an obligation to consider the housing needs of all categories of people in devising and applying local land-use regulations.

12. Edward Emrich, quoted by Robert Houriet, "Many Motives Created State's Small Municipalities," *Newark Sunday News*, August 28, 1966.

13. The area incorporated as Pomona was located in the towns of Haverstraw and Ramapo. In 1970, Pomona's population was 1,792, while Haverstraw had 25,311 residents and Ramapo 76,702.

their unincorporated section of the sprawling town of Harrison. In 1979, voters in North Tarrytown and Pleasantville in Westchester County over- whelmingly approved referenda directing local officials to seek indepen- dence. In the case of North Tarrytown, local autonomy promised $220,000 in tax savings and $90,000 in additional federal and state aid, at the cost of only $43,000 in new expenditures.[14] The fact that almost all of these efforts failed indicates that the political geography of the region is far less malleable than in the past, largely because existing suburban jurisdictions are increasingly un- willing to lose control over areas whose development promises tax or other advantages to the community as a whole.

### The Pervasive Influence of the Property Tax

Local dependence on the real property tax also plays a crucial role in the suburban quest for political autonomy and community control over land use. More than 60 percent of all suburban revenues in the New York region are derived from local property taxes, state assistance providing the only other major revenue source for most municipalities. Since property tax revenues are a function of the way land is used, as are the public expenditures necessitated by development, the power to regulate land use is the key to fiscal planning in most suburban jurisdictions. Commercial and industrial development nor- mally generates more property tax revenues than local expenditures, and thus is considered profitable by most suburbs. Some kinds of housing—expensive single-family dwellings on large lots and apartments that are too small to accommodate families with school-age children—also generally produce local "profits." On the other hand, apartments with two or more bedrooms, most single-family housing developments, mobile homes, and subsidized housing projects almost invariably involve local expenditures that are substantially greater than the local taxes paid by these forms of housing.

As the New York region developed, suburban communities sought with considerable success to stake out local boundaries that would maximize prop- erty-tax revenues and minimize high-expenditure development. Discussing the creation of sixty-four new municipalities in New Jersey during the 1920s, John E. Bebout and Ronald J. Grele observe: "Tax avoidance was a main reason for setting up new municipalities . . . both newcomers and old settlers tried to escape social responsibility and higher taxes."[15] Similar objectives motivated the more recent efforts to incorporate villages in New York, already noted. The wealthy residents of Purchase in Westchester hoped to lower their property taxes by fencing themselves off from more intensely developed sec- tions of Harrison. In Suffolk, the advocates of Strathmore's incorporation sought residential tax relief by folding most of the area's industrial develop- ment into their proposed municipality.

The significance of political autonomy and fiscal zoning grows as the spiraling costs of suburban government produce steady increases in property taxes. Especially important is the fact that educational costs, the principal component of suburban expenditures, have been rising much faster than other

14. See Ronald Smothers, " 'Breakaway' Villages Worry Albany," *New York Times*, May 13, 1979.

15. Bebout and Grele, *Where Cities Meet: The Urbanization of New Jersey*, pp. 61–62.

outlays. Restrictions on development designed to limit the size of the school-age population are the most effective means of controlling education costs. Although school-district budgets are frequently rejected by the public in referenda, particularly in the rapidly developing suburbs, these expressions of voter discontent rarely produce significant cuts in educational expenditures, and have little effect on the upward climb of school taxes. While state assistance underwrites a growing proportion of local school costs, state aid to date has not been sufficient to reduce significantly suburban efforts to employ land-use regulation as a means of limiting families with school-age children.

Political fragmentation, the property tax base, fiscal zoning, and rising educational costs combine with neighborhood differentiation and the locational decisions of commerce and industry to produce a significant mismatch of resources and needs in the region's suburbs. Consider the impact of land-use regulation and settlement patterns on two of Harrison's four school districts. The district encompassing Purchase, largely composed of estates and four-acre minimum lots, had $99,000 in property for each of 204 pupils in 1967, while the district embracing the more intensively settled section of Harrison backed each of its 2,450 students with only $19,000 worth of real estate. Moreover, the municipal beneficiary of a major commercial or industrial facility rarely has to bear anything approaching the full costs of educating the employees' children or providing other public services. For example, one of IBM's Westchester plants happens to be located in the Ossining school district, while most of the school costs generated by the IBM development fall upon the neighboring Yorktown school district. A beleaguered local school official complains: "The wealthier get wealthier and we get the additional children to educate. Now people perhaps will understand why I want the four districts to merge."[16]

Of course mergers, zoning changes, and other schemes designed to bring suburban resources into line with needs are strenuously resisted by jurisdictions that benefit from the existing system. A typical example of the response of the "haves" to the needs of the "have-nots" is provided on Long Island's North Shore, where the New York State Department of Education pressed for a merger of a number of school districts with varying tax bases into a single district. The ironic response was a merger of the two wealthiest districts, Stony Brook and Setauket, in order to foreclose consolidation with the poorer districts.

## The Logic of Exclusion

Throughout the region, the developmental and fiscal pressures generated by the outward movement of people and jobs have produced increasingly restrictive zoning ordinances and building codes, outright bans on multiple-family housing or severe limitations on the size of apartment units, prohibitions on cluster developments and mobile homes, and highly selective strategies to attract industrial and commercial taxable property. The primary goal of

16. Louis Klein, Superintendent of Schools, Harrison, N.Y., quoted in Merrill Folsom, "Westchester Finds Influx of Business a Worry," *New York Times*, August 18, 1967.

these suburban strategies is to maintain or achieve favorable ratios of property-tax revenues to demands for public services, while preserving or upgrading the residential amenities.

In a suburban political economy where local taxes are highly sensitive to land-use decisions, and where constituency concerns tend to be localistic and conservative, efforts to maximize the internal benefits of development constitute a rational course of action for the local policymaker. As Paul Davidoff points out, "they act perfectly rationally to protect their interests by keeping everybody else out. And you can see their success by looking at the number of development projects turned down by any suburban government. They only change zoning if they desperately need industry to help pay the tax bills."[17] Of course, what is rational for a local community may be highly disadvantageous for individuals whose housing opportunities are limited by the actions of suburban governments, or for developers whose prospects for profits are diminished, or for those who seek a more regionally oriented "rational" pattern of development.

Nor is a rational local strategy necessarily effective, even for the individual community. The patterns of past development and topography play a role in determining the relevance and effectiveness of particular strategies for maximizing internal benefits, as do political and technical skills used in devising and implementing policies suited to the particular circumstances. The influence of local land owners, developers, and corrupt officials can undermine local plans and zoning ordinances. But perhaps the most important factor of all is foresight. As Wood emphasizes, "the real effectiveness of land-use policies hinges on their timing: the date when comprehensive programs are applied."[18]

### The Westchester Approach

Certainly foresight accounts for much of Westchester County's success in developing and applying public policies designed to maximize internal benefits and minimize the impact of the forces of regional growth and change. In 1912, the Bronx Parkway Commissioners forecast that "Westchester would rapidly become no more than an extension of the Bronx."[19] But Westchester's leadership, as pointed out in Chapter One, was determined to prevent the "Bronxification" of their largely unsettled county. The basic strategy was devised under the guidance of county Republican leader William L. Ward, whose goal was to attract "class" rather than "mass" to Westchester. Instead of rapid transit or typical highways, the county built parkways that restricted

17. Quoted in Richard Reeves, "Land Is Prize in Battle for Control of Suburbs," *New York Times*, August 17, 1971. Davidoff was one of the founders of the Suburban Action Institute, a public interest advocacy organization that has brought court actions against a number of exclusionary suburbs in the New York region, and has pressed the Tri-State Regional Planning Commission to play a more assertive role in expanding housing opportunities for lower-income and minority families in the region's suburbs. For Suburban Action's view of its mission, see Linda Davidoff, Paul Davidoff, and Neil N. Gold, "The Suburbs Have to Open Their Gates," *New York Times Magazine*, November 7, 1971, pp. 40–50, 55–60.

18. Wood, *1400 Governments*, p. 111.

19. See Robert Daland, "A Political System in Suburbia" (typescript, 1960), pp. 111–115. The discussion in this and the following paragraph draw heavily on Daland's excellent case study.

commercial traffic and strip development while preserving a rural atmosphere. Land use was controlled by autonomous suburban jurisdictions that
jealously guarded the integrity and residential image of individual communities far more than would have been possible if zoning had been in the hands
of a large-scale countywide jurisdiction with a heterogeneous constituency.
With the encouragement of a talented county planning agency and the assistance of professional consultants, Westchester's local governments developed
and applied sophisticated regulatory techniques in advance of major development pressures, and long before most other suburbs in the region.

Because of the timely and skillful application of appropriate policies,
along with a powerful assist from topography, what Robert Daland calls "the
image of Westchester" has been substantially preserved. Outside of Yonkers,
New Rochelle, Mount Vernon, and White Plains, contemporary Westchester is
characterized by "rural appearance, low population density, a high standard
of amenities for the good life, and an elite citizenry."[20] Low-density development has given many Westchester communities a favorable balance of property tax revenues over demands on the public exchequer. Consequently, high
levels of service have been maintained without undue burdens on the local
taxpayer. Under these conditions, indiscriminate pressures for industrial and
commercial development to relieve local tax burdens have been rare. The
most successful and affluent communities, like Scarsdale and Bronxville,
want no industry or large-scale commerce at all. Elsewhere in the county,
highly selective industrial and commercial strategies have been pursued in
recent years with considerable success.

In no other suburban county in the New York region have so many
municipalities successfully pursued the goal of maximizing internal benefits.
At the other end of the scale in terms of overall success in moderating the
forces of suburban growth is Nassau County, where primitive land-use controls in most municipalities were overrun by the postwar surge of development eastward. Nassau's governmental structure was much like that of Westchester, but its political leaders and their constituents showed little of the
foresight and interest in controlling development found in Westchester. The
early suburbanites in Westchester were more affluent than those in Nassau;
most tended to define their interests in terms of the preservation of an attractive residential locale for themselves, and the county's political system reflected these interests. In Nassau, on the other hand, the pressures for mass
development represented an opportunity for profits rather than a threat to a
way of life for most potato farmers and other land owners. Moreover, even if
Nassau had used sophisticated planning techniques in advance of development pressures, its topography would have reduced the prospects for success
in comparison with Westchester. With much of its terrain flat and treeless,
Nassau inevitably was far more susceptible to mass development, and considerably less attractive to the affluent than hilly, wooded Westchester.

On the other hand, a few communities within Nassau, particularly those
along the scenic North Shore of Long Island, have followed the Westchester

20. Ibid., pp. 111–114. The diversity of Westchester's various communities and the implications of this diversity for contemporary housing are examined in John Levy, "The Politics of Housing in Westchester," *New York Affairs* 5(1979), pp. 95–102.

strategy with considerable success. Other municipalities that have emulated Westchester are scattered throughout the region, and their ranks are growing as development pressures encompass more and more communities. Within their boundaries, timely application of land-use controls has combined with other factors—topography, convenient access to the Manhattan central business district, or the pattern of past development—to produce upper-income sanctuaries effectively insulated from many of the pressures and costs of regional growth. For these communities, like Short Hills in Morris County and Princeton Township in Mercer County, the key to the good life is the use of governmental powers to ensure the maintenance of a "single-family residential area of high-quality amenity and visual attractiveness."[21]

### Planning for Fewer People

In all suburban areas, the power to regulate land use is the primary means available to direct growth, protect the tax base and property values, and preserve amenity and community character. Throughout the New York region, more restrictive zoning and building codes have been the typical suburban response to population growth. A large developer explores possibilities for tract housing in Cranbury in southern Middlesex, and quickly is faced with the rezoning of most of the township's vacant land upward to one-acre parcels. In Millburn, in Essex County, the local government examines development trends and responds with two-acre and five-acre zoning in order to "make sure that the type of township we have now will be preserved in the future."[22] In addition to increases in minimum lot sizes, suburbs seek to limit intensive and inexpensive development by requiring minimum house sizes, forbidding mass-produced housing through such devices as "no look-alike" provisions in local zoning ordinances, enacting building codes that drive up the costs of housing construction, prohibiting the construction of multiple-family dwellings, restricting the number of bedrooms in apartment units, and forbidding mobile homes.[23]

The region's richer suburbs have the most restrictive codes and the most successful development policies, but almost every suburb with vacant land has sought to maximize internal benefits by zoning for fewer people. Over the past quarter-century local planning throughout the region has become far more sensitive to the costs and benefits of residential development, in part because state and especially federal planning assistance have provided resources for professional staff and consultants. Along the region's frontier, planners teach the contrasting lessons of Westchester and Nassau to those who still harbor the "misconception that the more houses you build, the more ratables you have, and the lower your tax burden."[24] Sophisticated plans are developed to limit population, with increasing attention given to environmen-

21. Princeton Township Planning Board, *1967 Annual Report* (Princeton, 1968), p. A–3.

22. Mayor Ralph F. Batch, quoted in the *Newark News*, December 21, 1965.

23. See Michael N. Danielson, *The Politics of Exclusion* (New York: Columbia University Press, 1976), especially pp. 50–74; Mary Brooks, *Exclusionary Zoning* (Chicago: American Society of Planning Officials, 1970); and Norman Williams, Jr., and Thomas Norman, "Exclusionary Land Use Controls: The Case of Northeastern New Jersey," *Syracuse Law Review* 22 (1971), pp. 475–507.

24. Donald McCoy, planning board secretary, Hopewell Borough (Mercer County), quoted in *Trenton Times*, August 15, 1967.

tal factors that are seen as severely constraining future development. In intensively settled suburbs like Madison Township in Middlesex, new homeowners in their tract houses soon grasped the rudiments of suburban political economy. Faced with rapidly mounting costs caused by mass development on 50-by-100-foot lots with no offsetting industrial or commercial property, Madison residents sought relief by rezoning undeveloped land for one-half and one-acre lots, so that people like themselves would no longer be able to settle in the municipality.[25]

Largely as a result of these pressures in suburbs rich and poor, the average lot size in five inner- and intermediate-ring counties—Fairfield, Bergen, Middlesex, Passaic, and Westchester—more than doubled between 1950 and 1960. In 1952, Westchester was zoned for 3.2 million people; nineteen years later upzoning had reduced the county's residential capacity to 1.8 million. By 1962, two-thirds of all the vacant land in the New York region was zoned for one-half-acre or larger lots, while two-fifths of the total was reserved for parcels of one acre or more. Over half of all the land in Westchester's towns—which encompass most of the county's undeveloped acreage—was zoned for lots of two acres or more by 1968. (See Map 4.) By 1970, in the New Jersey suburban belt which encompasses Morris, Somerset, Middlesex, and Monmouth counties, over three-quarters of the undeveloped residential land was zoned for one acre or more, and houses of at least 1,200 square feet were required on 77 percent of the total acreage available for single-family dwellings.[26]

The trend toward more restrictive land-use controls in the New York region drew increasing fire in the late 1960s. Civil rights groups, fair housing organizations, labor unions, and other critics attacked the exclusion of blacks, lower-income groups, and blue-collar families from housing opportunities in the suburbs. Among the more vocal opponents of restrictive zoning are institutions with a regional perspective, such as the Regional Plan Association and the *New York Times*. The RPA's report on "Spread City" scores suburban land-use policies for promoting social irresponsibility, exporting costs and problems to others, wasting land, increasing the costs of public-utility systems, and undermining public transportation.[27] Similar concerns have been voiced by state officials in New Jersey, who have advocated a reversal of municipal land-use trends in the face of the state's growing housing crisis.[28]

---

25. Madison Township's zoning restrictions were successfully challenged in state court in 1971 by a developer and Suburban Action Institute; see *Oakwood at Madison, Inc. v. Township of Madison*, 117 N.J. Super 11 (1971) and *Oakwood at Madison, Inc. v. Township of Madison*, 128 N.J. Super 438 (1974). During the course of the extended court fight, Madison Township changed its name to Old Bridge Township.

26. See Regional Plan Association, *Spread City*, RPA Bulletin No. 100 (New York: 1962); Economic Consultants Organization, *Zoning Ordinances and Administration* (New York: 1970); Westchester County Department of Planning, *Interim Report 6, Residential Analysis for Westchester County, New York* (White Plains, N.Y.: 1970), pp. 8–15; and State of New Jersey, Department of Community Affairs, Division of State and Regional Planning, *Land Use Regulation: The Residential Land Supply* (Trenton: 1972), pp. 14–16.

27. See Regional Plan Association, *Spread City*, passim.

28. See State of New Jersey, Department of Conservation and Economic Development, Division of State and Regional Planning, *The Residential Development of New Jersey: A Regional Approach* (Trenton: 1964); State of New Jersey, Governor, *A Blueprint for Housing in New Jersey*, A Special Message to the Legislature by William T. Cahill, Governor of New Jersey (December 7, 1970); and State of New Jersey, Governor, *First Annual Message to the Legislature*, Brendan Byrne, Gover-

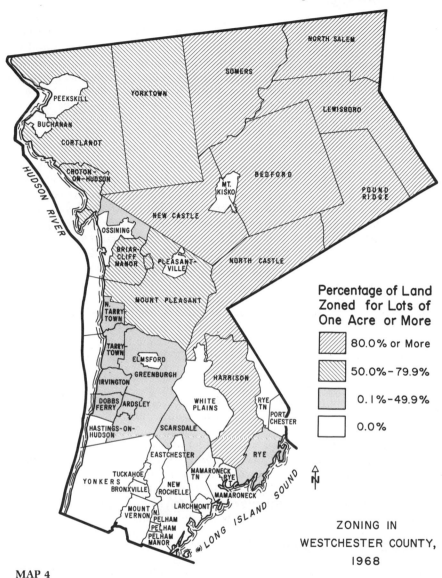

Percentage of Land
Zoned for Lots of
One Acre or More

80.0% or More

50.0% – 79.9%

0.1% – 49.9%

0.0%

ZONING IN
WESTCHESTER COUNTY,
1968

MAP 4

Vigorous support for these proposals comes from most of the region's residential developers, who have little love for the land-use practices of the "tight little islands with a stay-out sign for home builders [and which] are unconcerned about the population explosion."[29]

nor of New Jersey (January 14, 1975). Efforts by the Cahill and Byrne administrations to ease suburban zoning restrictions are discussed in Chapter Five, as are earlier proposals made during the administration of Governor Richard J. Hughes.

29. John B. O'Hara, President, New Jersey State Home Builders Association, quoted in John W. Kempson, "Zoning Called Bar to Full Land Use," *Newark News*, March 4, 1965.

But this criticism has little direct impact on the policies of suburban governments. While pockets of local opposition to fiscal zoning are found in the region, particularly in suburbs with more heterogeneous populations, those who favor liberalization rarely succeed in their encounters with local planning or government bodies. In Princeton Township, for instance, liberal Democrats, civil rights groups, teachers, and moderate-income members of the Italian-American Federation sought in vain during the 1960s to alter restrictive land-use policies in order to foster a balanced and diversified community. Among the opponents of liberalized zoning in 1966 were two successful candidates for local office, one of whom did "not see the point of providing housing for anybody and everybody," while the other "certainly [didn't] want this Statue of Liberty in Princeton."[30] During the same year, a campaign to rezone a large area of Greenwich downward to one-half-acre lots failed, despite the support of local firemen, nurses, post-office employees, and some owners of large parcels of undeveloped land. Defenders of four-acre zoning insisted that their resistance to change had "nothing to do with racial or religious factors. It's just economics. It's like going into Tiffany and demanding a ring for $12.50. Tiffany doesn't have rings for $12.50. Well, Greenwich is like Tiffany."[31]

Local government agencies like Princeton's planning board and Greenwich's zoning commission successfully resist pressures for more intensive land use because they are responsive to the desires of the majority of their constituents. Opposed to rezoning in Greenwich in 1966 were thirty-four local organizations, ranging from taxpayer groups and neighborhood associations to garden clubs. "In Greenwich," observed a landowner who favored change in local four-acre zoning, "no one can get elected unless he swears on the Bible, under the tree at midnight, and with a blood oath to uphold zoning."[32] Once in office, such officials are strongly guided by community sentiment and local self-interest. As the chairman of Princeton's planning board explained in 1966: "Unless there is a groundswell or sentiment for high-density zoning, or through court action, Princeton will remain a residential town of relatively large home lots. . . . [The people of Princeton] would rather live in a low-density suburban area than in a town or city. . . ."[33] As the 1970s came to a close, no groundswell had yet appeared in the vast majority of the region's newer and richer suburbs, most of whose residents continued to prefer spacious zoning.

### The Dilemma of Apartments

Zoning for fewer people in single-family residences has accelerated demand for apartments in the suburbs. The rapid rise in apartment construction in the region results both from the growing unavailability of moderately

30. John D. Wallace and David Thomson, Republican candidates for Township Committee, quoted in Jacqueline Pellaton, "Issue of Low-Cost Housing Divides Princeton Candidates," *Trenton Times,* October 27, 1966.

31. Everett Smith, Jr., quoted in Ralph Blumenthal, "Pressures of Growth Stir Zoning Battles in the Suburbs," *New York Times,* May 29, 1967.

32. Williams H. Hernstadt, quoted in the above article.

33. Hans K. Sander, quoted in "Planners Set Forth Objectives," *Princeton Packet,* March 2, 1966. A few years later, local advocates of lower-income housing were able to prevail over bitter local opposition to secure approval of two small federally subsidized moderate-income housing projects in Princeton Township.

*Garden apartments developed in the mid-1960s in Middlesex County,*
*adjacent to single-family housing on the small lots typical of suburban*
*development in the 1950s.*

Credit: Louis B. Schlivek, Regional Plan Association

priced single-family homes and changes in the age and income structure of
the suburban population. The planning process in suburbia, however, gives
relatively little consideration to the role of apartments in meeting the housing
needs of the newly married, the elderly, single individuals, and moderate-
income families. Instead, as is the case with single-family residences, the
realities of the suburban political economy dictate that local officials consider
apartment proposals in the context of localized values, with a narrow calculus
of costs and benefits.

Apartment construction, however, raises more complex issues within
suburban jurisdictions than those posed by moderately priced homes on
small lots. Some suburbanites, including local officials who must balance
municipal budgets, see apartments as valuable tax ratables whose development can be regulated to produce a net contribution to the local treasury.
Others, usually in the majority, consider apartments a threat both to municipal solvency and to community or neighborhood character. As a planner comments concerning the opposition of a Bergen County suburb to

high-rise apartments: "The residents feel they have a sanctuary in Tenafly and they're literally afraid of people moving in. They feel that they have successfully escaped from the central city and they don't want the central city to pursue them."[34] Most suburbanites polled in a 1978 survey opposed new apartment construction, with 76 percent responding negatively to the question "would you approve of more apartment buildings being built in your area?"[35]

Because of these different perceptions within individual suburbs, apartment proposals often become highly contentious issues, at least in comparison with single-family housing questions where internal consensus usually is high, and where conflict tends to be external rather than internal. And because the question of apartments poses a choice between two key suburban development goals—maximizing internal benefits and maintaining the suburban residential image—conflict often is intense and bitter.

The issues and conflicts generated by apartments have produced a common scenario in a number of the region's suburbs during the past decade. The action begins when a developer seeks a building permit or a zoning variance, in order to construct a garden-apartment project in a suburb dominated by single-family residences. Mayors, councilmen, and school-board members often find the proposal attractive because it promises to stabilize or lower the tax rate. But many of their constituents think otherwise, and groups like the Livingston Citizens Against Apartments, the Hillside Homeowners Action Association, and the Madison Township Political Action Group Against More Apartments, are quickly organized. The chief complaints are that school costs and other public expenditures will skyrocket, that traffic congestion and parking problems will intensify, that the character of the community will be changed, and that apartments will attract blacks and soon become slums.[36] The most vehement reaction comes from those in the immediate vicinity of the proposed project who fear that apartments will depreciate the value of their homes. In most jurisdictions, as a Long Island builder notes, "public opposition is unbelievable. There's a desperate need for this kind of housing, but people just go crazy when you talk about building in their town. Four out of five projects I've started have been stopped—people scream that they'll increase traffic, put more kids in the schools, change the neighborhood. They're afraid of any kind of change out here."[37]

In many instances, adverse public reaction kills the initial apartment proposal. Sometimes opposition also sweeps an incumbent administration out of office, as in East Brunswick in Middlesex County and Clark in Union

34. Isadore Candeub, Candeub-Fleissig and Associates, Newark, N.J., quoted in Gary Rosenblatt, "1962 Dispute Still Persists on Tenafly High-Rise Plan," *New York Times*, March 19, 1972. The Candeub firm prepared a plan for a New York developer involving the construction of 4,000 apartments and 2.8 million square feet of office space in high-rise buildings on a 274-acre tract in Tenafly. Local opposition prevented the rezoning needed for the project, and led to an effort by Tenafly to acquire the land through condemnation for use as a park.

35. *New York Times*, "1978 Suburban Poll" (1978), p. 9.

36. See State of New Jersey, County and Municipal Government Study Commission, *Housing & Suburbs: Fiscal and Social Impact of Multifamily Development*, Ninth Report, October, 1974 (Trenton: 1974).

37. Alvin Benjamin, quoted in Richard Reeves, "A Changing L.I. Is Opposed to Change," *New York Times*, June 3, 1971.

County. Often public antipathy to apartments and the kinds of people who live in them produces prohibitions on future apartment construction. In the 1960s, only 1 percent of the residential land in the region's suburbs was zoned for multiple dwellings, and much of this was located in the older suburban jurisdictions. In Westchester, apartments could be built on almost 5 percent of the 55,000 acres of all land zoned for residential use in cities and villages, but on less than ½ of 1 percent of the 198,000 acres assigned to residential use in the less-intensely settled towns where most future development would occur. Only 2,000 of the 400,000 acres of undeveloped residential land in Morris, Somerset, Middlesex, and Monmouth counties were zoned for multiple dwellings in 1970.[38]

In many communities, prohibitions on multiple dwellings are only a prelude to the second act of the apartment drama. This phase often starts when a developer or landowner brings suit after his application to build apartments has been rejected. Court orders sometimes result which force a locality to rezone for apartments or remove a moratorium on apartment construction. In other suburbs, rising municipal burdens produced by intensive single-family development lead to renewed interest in apartments on the part of local officials, who seek to demonstrate to their constituents that under the proper conditions apartments will provide a favorable ratio of local property-tax revenues to public costs, especially for education. One source of reassurance is a study by George Sternlieb which found that a community can profit from one-bedroom and efficiency apartments, but must severely limit the number of multiple-bedroom units if it does not want school costs to exceed property tax revenues from the project.[39] These and similar findings are reflected in the garden apartment regulations drafted by suburban planners and their private consultants. A typical ordinance, like that of Hillside or East Brunswick, requires 80 percent of the apartments to have one bedroom or less. Table 14 shows the pattern of restrictions in Middlesex County in 1970.

**Table 14—*Restrictions on Apartments in Middlesex County, N.J.: 1970***

| Nature of Restriction | Number of Municipalities |
|---|---|
| Apartments Excluded | 7 |
| 90% one-bedroom, 10% two-bedrooms | 2 |
| 85% one-bedroom, 15% two-bedrooms | 1 |
| 80% one-bedroom, 20% two-bedrooms | 6 |
| 80% one-bedroom, 15% two-bedrooms, 5% two-plus-bedrooms | 1 |
| 75% one-bedroom, 25% two-bedrooms | 1 |
| 75% one-bedroom, 20% two-bedrooms, 5% two-plus-bedrooms | 1 |
| 70% one-bedroom, 30% two-bedrooms | 1 |
| 50% one-bedroom, 30% two-bedrooms, 20% two-plus-bedrooms | 1 |
| No restrictions | 4 |

*Source:* Middlesex County Planning Board.

38. See Economic Consultants Organization, *Zoning Ordinances and Administration*, p. 16; and Williams and Norman, "Exclusionary Land-Use Controls: The Case of Northeastern New Jersey."

39. See George Sternlieb, *The Garden Apartment Development: A Municipal Cost-Revenue Analysis* (New Brunswick: Bureau of Economic Research, Rutgers—The State University, 1964), p. 14.

Once an apartment ordinance is proposed, another battle ensues, with the threatened neighborhood leading the opposition, frequently taking the conflict to the courts. Nor does the controversy end with the construction of an initial apartment project, since pressures often develop for a moratorium on further apartment development so that the local government may evaluate the impact on taxes and municipal services of those that have been built.

In a few suburbs, high-rise apartments produce a third act, replete with renditions of many familiar themes from earlier conflicts over tax ratables, school costs, and community character. Given the limited amount of land available for multiple dwellings in the region's suburbs, the issue of high-rise apartments may follow hard on the heels of garden-apartment settlements. This was the case in Cedar Grove in Essex County, where acceptance of garden apartments was followed by a developer's proposal to build high-rise apartments on the crest of First Mountain. And when high-rise controversies are resolved, the zoning regulations closely resemble those designed to maximize suburban revenues from garden-apartment development. In Port Chester in Westchester County, for example, only 253 of 981 units in three apartment towers have as many as two bedrooms.

Of course, many variations in this scenario are found in a region as large and complex as New York. Prohibitions on apartments have been maintained successfully by some communities, typically those that can afford to value their single-family residential character more highly than the municipal profit promised by one-bedroom apartments. Others have demonstrated skill and foresight in adopting restrictive apartment regulations that effectively foreclose the typical garden apartment, with its monotonous box-like buildings, crowded acreage, and unattractive site planning. At the other end of the spectrum are less sophisticated suburbs whose initial response to apartments has been highly permissive. These communities typically already had severe fiscal problems arising from intensive single-family development, so indiscriminate apartment construction threatens municipal disaster. In Parsippany-Troy Hills, minimal controls on garden apartments led to explosive growth that doubled both the population of the Morris County community (from 25,000 to 50,000) and many municipal costs between 1960 and 1967. This led the hard-pressed local government to adopt a two-year moratorium on new apartment development in 1966.

For many suburbs, however, the scenario has been shortened, as knowledge about the costs and benefits of apartments is spread through the region by planning consultants, county planning agencies, and professional journals, as well as by the well-publicized experiences of Parsippany-Troy Hills and other unfortunate suburbs that failed to adopt apartment controls designed to maximize internal benefits before the arrival of the developers. Almost every suburban jurisdiction that permits multiple dwellings has by now adopted bedroom restrictions. And for most, garden apartments constructed under these constraints have proved to be profitable in terms of tax revenues. Madison—a Middlesex County suburb that limited two-bedroom apartments to 20 percent of the total in a development—collected 13.5 percent of its 1970 school taxes from its ten garden-apartment developments, which housed only 5.8 percent of the school population. As a result, apartments contributed $326 per unit to school taxes each year while generating educational outlays of only $135 per unit, for a school surplus of $191 for each

*The quest for additional tax revenues stimulates aggressive efforts to*
*lure industrial development to the suburbs.*

Credit: Louis B. Schlivek, Regional Plan Association

apartment. By contrast, an average of $675 in school taxes was collected from single-family homes in Madison, while $955 was spent to educate the children housed in the typical single-family dwelling.[40]

### The Right Kind of Industry

In the great suburban game of increasing taxable property without assuming responsibilities for the education of large numbers of children, the most dramatic opportunities for the maximization of internal benefits are provided by industrial and commercial decentralization. As indicated in Chapter Two, such opportunities are increasingly numerous, since almost every form of economic activity in the region has been moving outward. To be sure, a few suburbs continue to value their residential character above the potential benefits of industrial parks, corporate headquarters, research laboratories, and shopping centers. But most cannot resist the lure of valuable properties that by themselves add no pupils to the local school rolls. As the mayor of a suburb that attracted a major office facility in 1971 explains: "With rising costs, a town can't survive anymore strictly on residential property taxes. I.B.M.'s coming was very timely. While it hasn't lowered our tax rate, it certainly has stabilized it."[41]

40. See Marshall R. Burack, "Apartment Zoning in Suburbia," Senior Thesis (Princeton University, 1971), pp. 112–114.

41. Mayor Thomas Pawelko, Franklin Lakes, N.J., quoted in "I.B.M. Is Proving a Good Neighbor in Affluent Bergen Town," *New York Times*, May 20, 1973.

Because of these considerations, large amounts of vacant land in the suburbs have been zoned for industrial development—far more, in fact, than industry is ever likely to need, especially considering the inaccessibility of some suburban "industrial" zones. For many suburbs, however, zoning land for industry that will never materialize is also an attractive strategy, since it serves as an effective way to prevent or forestall unwanted residential development.

Because the objective of attracting industry is to maximize internal benefits to the particular community rather than to serve the interests of employers or employees, suburbs that zone land for industrial purposes rarely make provision for housing those who will work in the community. In 1970, for example, in the area around Princeton, local governments had reserved enough land for business uses to support 1.17 million jobs. But under existing zoning, housing could be constructed for only 144,000 families, and almost all of it would be priced far beyond the reach of the average industrial wage-earner.[42]

Furthermore, most suburbs want only certain kinds of industrial or commercial development. The typical suburban goal is to attract industry that will provide tax revenue without compromising the community's residential character. Under these circumstances, the ideal industry, as a Westchester planner wryly notes, "is a new campus-type headquarters that smells like Chanel No. 5, sounds like a Stradivarius, has the visual attributes of Sophia Loren, employs only executives with no children and produces items that can be transported away in white station wagons once a month."[43] The trouble with this kind of industry, of course, is that the supply falls far short of the demand. Moreover, the most desirable industrial and commercial facilities seek the most attractive locations. Consequently, factors such as favorable topography, high-quality residential development, and good transportation facilities tend to overshadow local industrial strategies in decisions concerning the location of suburban office and research facilities. In the process—as with other aspects of suburban development politics—the wealthier communities tend to secure the most desirable development, while the poorer suburbs have great difficulty in maximizing internal economic benefits without seriously compromising residential goals.

At the other end of the scale in terms of suburban desirability is heavy industry, with its pollutants, heavy transport requirements, and unskilled work force. Given the inhospitality of the suburban value structure and political economy to lower-income residents, the latter factor is particularly important. As former Westchester County Executive Edwin J. Michaelian explained: "We do not have a pool of personnel available for heavy industry . . . [we] wouldn't know where to put, where to house a large group of people who were to come in with a manufacturing industry. . . ."[44]

Occasionally, however, geography and restrictive zoning permit a residential suburb to obtain the benefits of heavy industry without sacrificing

42. See Middlesex-Somerset-Mercer Regional Study Council, *Housing and the Quality of our Environment* (Princeton, N.J.: 1970).

43. Sy J. Schulman, Westchester County Planning Commissioner, quoted in Merrill Folsom, "Westchester Finds Influx of Business a Worry," *New York Times*, April 18, 1967.

44. Quoted in Martin Arnold, "Westchester Cites Industrial Goals," *New York Times*, February 20, 1967.

residential amenities or incurring the burdens of servicing blue-collar residents. This is the case in Mahwah in northwest Bergen County, whose major source of revenue has been a Ford Motor plant that is isolated from the remainder of the residential suburb by the Erie-Lackawanna Railroad and a major highway. Within Mahwah, land-use restrictions ensured that local housing would be beyond the means of Ford's 5,200 workers. Confronting similar restrictions in neighboring communities, most of the Ford workers had to travel long distances to their jobs. On the other hand, the factory's presence helped provide Mahwah's middle-income residents with high-quality public services at relatively low property tax rates compared with neighboring communities.

For their part, business firms are just as eager as suburban officials to avoid the tax burdens imposed by a surfeit of families with school-age children. When space, market, transportation, and labor-force requirements offer business a choice of sites—as they frequently do in a region as large as New York—lower taxes are often the determining factor in industrial and commercial locational decisionmaking. A study of the effects of local taxes on the location of business by the U.S. Advisory Commission on Intergovernmental Relations concludes:

> among local governments within a State and especially within a metropolitan area, tax differentials exert discernible plant location pull—the industrial tax haven stands out as the most conspicuous example. In almost every metropolitan area there exist wide local property tax differentials—a cost consideration that can become a "swing" factor in the final selection of a particular plant location.[45]

As a consequence, lower-tax suburbs enjoy an initial advantage in the quest for attractive industry and commerce. Moreover, municipal success in securing industrial and commercial development tends to be cumulative, since the lower taxes made possible by the initial successes help attract additional industry. Finally, taxes combine with transport, topography, and other factors to produce clusters of suburban industry and commerce, which in turn contribute to the mismatch between resources and needs discussed earlier in this chapter.

From industry's perspective, of course, the ideal suburb would have no residents at all. In the New York region, a number of companies enjoy the manifest benefits of such a location in Teterboro in Bergen County. Teterboro was the brainchild of Alexander Summer, a real-estate developer who reasoned correctly that business would be eager to buy land in a municipality whose lack of residents would ensure a low and stable tax rate. Summer's thesis was that if he and his associates purchased most of the homes in sparsely settled Teterboro, "along with all the remaining undeveloped land in the borough, we could reasonably expect full municipal cooperation instead of the bickering and frustrations that a developer usually encounters in dealing with the governing bodies of small communities." Once the homes were

---

45. Advisory Commission on Intergovernmental Relations, *State-Local Taxation and Industrial Location* (Washington: U.S. Government Printing Office, 1967), pp. 78–79. Italics in original omitted.

purchased, rents were drastically reduced to secure the support of the tenants, who included the mayor, most of the councilmen, and a majority of the municipality's residents. After Summer and his associates acquired the land, "the first official action of the mayor and council (at our request) was to zone the whole community against residential use."[46] In 1977, two dozen people lived in Teterboro, which has no schools, one of the lowest municipal tax rates in New Jersey, and public services devoted almost exclusively to servicing the needs of its thirty-five major industries, which employ 24,000 nonresidents.[47] For an official of the Bendix Corporation, Teterboro's largest employer and major landowner, the borough was not "a tax haven," but rather "a community designed for industry."[48]

Not the least of the advantages offered by a municipality like Teterboro is the absence of residents worried about the encroachment of industry on residential values. When industry comes to a suburb with people, on the other hand, opposition is common and conflict often intense. The prospect of industrial and commercial development, like apartments, forces suburbanites to choose between maximizing tax revenues and preserving the residential character of their community. "We realize that there are a lot of problems in living with industry," acknowledges the mayor of a suburb that has attracted a number of major firms, "but we were willing to do it because of the tax benefits to residents of the community."[49] Also resembling the apartment controversies is the conflict engendered by industry between the interests of the community as a whole and the particular neighborhood most affected by industrial or commercial development. The result, as illustrated by the recent experiences of Pepsico, Inc., E. R. Squibb & Company, and the Western Electric Company in the New York region, is that even the most desirable industrial property rarely receives a unanimous welcome in the suburbs. In each of these cases, the corporation sought an attractive location in a high-quality residential area, and was strongly opposed by affluent local residents determined to preserve the character of their neighborhood.

For the estate owners in Purchase, in Westchester County, Pepsico's plan for a $12 million office building for 1,000 employees on a 112-acre site zoned for 2.5-acre residences was "progress with desecration."[50] For the rest of the town of Harrison, however, Pepsico was a prize that would generate four times as much local revenue as residential development on the same site,

46. Quoted in John R. Lancelotti, "Albanese Demands End of Teterboro," *Newark News,* January 3, 1966.

47. In 1976 Teterboro's tax rate was 65¢ per $100 of property, the second lowest rate in northern New Jersey. All 24 of Teterboro's residents lived in housing owned by the Bendix Corporation, including the mayor, all the members of the borough council, and a number of municipal employees. Teterboro's one school-age child in 1977 was enrolled in nearby Hackensack, at a cost of $4,400 for the community's industrial taxpayers.

48. Martin Paskoff, northeast regional counsel, Bendix Corporation, quoted in William Tucker, "A Taxpayer's Camelot in New Jersey," *New York Times,* February 20, 1977.

49. Mayor Frederick Knox, East Hanover, N.J. Located in Morris County near the junction of I-80 and I-280, East Hanover was the site of major facilities of Sandoz Chemicals, Norda Chemicals, and Tempco, as well as the international headquarters of Nabisco Corporation. As a result of its substantial business tax base, East Hanover had the lowest tax rate in Morris County in 1976.

50. Lawrence Robbins, Purchase Association, quoted in Merrill Folsom, "New Zoning Voted for Pepsico Site," *New York Times,* May 23, 1967.

without requiring new schools or other public service improvements. In the past, opposition from Purchase residents had excluded International Business Machines, a racetrack, and a shopping center from their manicured acres. But the campaign against Pepsico—which included an abortive attempt to secede from Harrison—failed as the town's broader interests prevailed over those of its wealthiest residents. Three months after Pepsico revealed its plans, the Harrison town board approved a zoning change to permit commercial buildings in areas previously restricted to private estates, provided the facilities were surrounded by at least 100 landscaped acres.

Squibb's goal was 213 acres of hilly, wooded land in Lawrence Township, a bedroom suburb of 18,000 located between Princeton and Trenton in Mercer County. On this site—zoned for 1.5-acre residences and surrounded by expensive homes—Squibb hoped to build a $9 million research and administrative center to house 875 employees. Although Lawrence's master plan zoned 700 acres for light industry and research facilities elsewhere in the township, Squibb wanted "a quiet contemplative, campus-like atmosphere which our creative people would find pleasant and stimulating. We do not wish our employees to be bothered with noise, smoke, odors, traffic jams or any other disturbing elements."[51] To the residents of the affected portion of northern Lawrence, Squibb was the disturbing element. Supported by Citizens for Good Planning, the adjacent Educational Testing Service, the Lawrenceville School, and neighboring Princeton Township, the North Lawrence Citizens Association protested the rezoning of the area, arguing that "the master plan and zoning is in jeopardy in the whole township."[52] After reversing itself once in the wake of an acrimonious five-hour public meeting, attended by hundreds of angry residents, the township committee, supported by the Lawrence Committee to Reduce Taxes through Economic Growth, finally rezoned the land in favor of Squibb and its $300,000-a-year contribution to the local exchequer. As the committeeman who cast the deciding vote to create the 200-acre minimum lot commercial and industrial zone explained: "I think it is an attractive ratable; the majority of the people in Lawrence wanted Squibb."[53]

In the case of Western Electric, local opposition prevailed, and the corporation's request for rezoning to permit the development in Bedminster of a $10 million office complex employing 1,500 people on 300 acres was denied by the local government. A public hearing on the Western Electric proposal was attended by more than 400 of the Somerset County community's 2,700 residents; and the vast majority were committed to maintaining the status quo in the affluent and sparsely settled township that had no industry, no apartment houses, and five-acre minimum lot sizes. Also distressing to local residents was the presence at the hearings of critics of Western Electric who contended that the projected move to an exclusionary suburb would discriminate against minority groups, who would be denied access to jobs because of

51. "The Squibb Message," circular distributed by E. R. Squibb & Company in Lawrence Township, June 1967.
52. William G. LaTourette, president, North Lawrence Citizens Association, quoted in Leonard Sloane, "Squibb Planning to Move to New Jersey," *New York Times*, June 24, 1967.
53. Committeeman Edward T. Converse, quoted in "Squibb Move Approved, Residents Plan Appeal," *Town Topics* (Princeton, N.J.), August 3, 1967.

the unavailability of moderate-income housing in or near Bedminster.[54] After its rebuff in Bedminster, Western Electric acquired 440 acres further west in rural Readington Township in Hunterdon County, whose less affluent residents found the attractions of a large industrial property to outweigh its liabilities.

## The Results of the Maximizing Strategy

The fact that most suburbs seek to maximize internal benefits does not mean that all are successful. As the preceding discussion illustrates, political and planning skills, timing, homogeneity, areal scope, amount of vacant land, nature of previous development, location, and topography all affect the ability of a particular jurisdiction to influence development within its boundaries. In the New York region, many suburbs have had relatively little influence on market forces, whose net effect is to undermine the municipal political economy. In much of the area settled during the first decade after World War II, land-use controls were adopted in the wake of rather than in advance of intensive suburbanization. Maximizing the profits of individual landowners rather than net internal community benefits often was the guiding principle in these areas. Also, in some developing areas—especially where location, topography, and other factors have not been favorable to low-density, high-cost development—economic pressures and the lure of profits have broken down the barriers erected by land-use controls, or prevented them from being erected. Because the stakes for landowners, speculators, and developers are high, the pressures on local officials often are intense and the temptations substantial. For example, in the past twenty years, land values in Wayne have risen from $700 to well over $100,000 an acre, and charges concerning the "profitable relationship between politics, land speculation and zoning" in the Passaic County suburb have filled the air.[55] Conflicts of interest on the part of suburban officials in a position to profit from land-use changes are common, and bribery has been a factor in the turbulent land-use politics of a number of suburbs.

Although some suburbs are successful in their efforts to maximize internal benefits, it might be argued that in suburbia the public sector as a whole has little impact on the pattern of development. The successful suburbs might be too few in number to influence the overall trend. Or their success might be counterbalanced by the failures of other jurisdictions, leaving the overall thrust of the marketplace unaffected. This is the position of Wood in *1400 Governments*:

> Not one of these strategies . . . has important implications for the private sector of the Region taken as an entity. An industry barred from one locality can in all probability find a hospitable reception in another with

54. One of those who testified was Kenneth Patton, New York City's Economic Development Administrator; another was Frank Allen, chairman of the Plainfield chapter of the NAACP. See also the discussion below in the section, "Excluding the Less Affluent."

55. See Richard Reeves, "Land Is Prize in Battle for Control of Suburbs," *New York Times*, August 17, 1971.

equivalent economic advantages. High-income families take refuge in Westchester, southern Putnam, and Fairfield, while mass developers make breakthroughs in Nassau or Monmouth or Rockland to provide middle-class housing. With so many different constituencies, many options are open for firms and households alike, and though the process of industrial and population diffusion may occasionally be skewed, the forces are not, in general, thwarted, turned aside, or guided.[56]

Wood argues that the cumulative impact of suburban governments is negligible, in contrast to the private market forces he sees as determining the shape of urban growth. The logical corollary of this position seems to be that the overall pattern of suburban development would be about the same if there were no suburban governments seeking to maximize internal benefits. If the policies of suburban governments rarely "thwarted, turned aside, or guided" the forces of the marketplace, it would be reasonable to expect commercial enterprises with the greatest stakes in the marketplace for, say, suburban housing, to be relatively satisfied with the existing pattern of public policy. But this is not the case. Home builders, landowners, real estate brokers, financing institutions, and prospective home buyers are highly critical of suburban development policies that decrease the opportunities for home building, reduce the prospects of profits based on more intensive land use, and help to prevent a growing majority of the region's families from obtaining new housing in the suburbs. Thus, a New Jersey builder attacks large-lot zoning as "devastating" and speaks of the need for suburban development policies geared to meet the needs of all groups in our population, while a Long Island banker urges suburban governments to shun "localism and pettiness" in order to meet housing problems in the suburbs.[57]

The private sector is critical of the public sector in suburbia because suburban governments, in fact, do often "thwart, turn aside, or guide" the forces of the marketplace. The primary concern of developers and large landowners in the suburban housing market is the maximization of profit. In general, profits to landowners and developers correlate directly with intensity of development. Because of the region's income structure, family-size patterns, and the nature of the existing housing stock, the potential suburban market for moderately priced housing on small lots and for multibedroom apartments is larger than the market for expensive homes on large lots and for one-bedroom apartments.[58] But private actions to meet this demand are not in the interest of local governments, whose revenues and expenditures are extremely sensitive to the nature and intensity of land use. And in the process of thwarting moder-

56. Wood, *1400 Governments*, p. 112.

57. Nazario Paragano, president of the Home Builders Association of Metropolitan New Jersey, quoted in "Large Lot Zoning Declared Handicap," *Newark News*, February 28, 1964; and Arthur T. Roth, chairman of the board of directors, Franklin National Bank, quoted in Ronalo Maiorana, "Changes Urged in L.I. Land Tax," *New York Times*, February 16, 1964.

58. A Regional Plan Association study of housing needs in the New York State portion of the region concluded that 83 percent of the households in the region whose head was in the "prime" home-buying age bracket (30 to 34 years old) could not afford the average single-family house on the market in Putnam, Rockland, and Orange Counties, 89 percent could not afford housing in Nassau and the two western towns of Suffolk, and 92 percent were priced out of the market in Westchester County; see "Housing Opportunities," *Regional Plan News* (September 1969), p. 7.

ately priced residential development and encouraging more expensive housing, suburban governments have influenced the pattern of development in the
New York region in a number of significant ways. Their cumulative actions
tend to accelerate the outward growth of the region, to discourage innovation,
and to restrict the housing opportunities (and thus the employment opportunities) of a substantial proportion of the region's residents.

## Accelerating Spread

Much of the confusion over the influence of suburban governments on
development arises from the rapid outward growth of metropolitan areas. The
coexistence of strong market forces pushing development outward and suburban policies that foster decentralization has led many observers to conclude
that suburbia's public sector primarily responds to the private sector. But the
fact that two components of the urban system have similar effects does not
necessarily mean that one is wholly dependent on the other. Instead, as
pointed out in Chapter One, both may be responding to the same set of
pressures, and in so doing they may reinforce one another. This appears to be
what happened in most of the suburbs of the New York region during the
initial postwar decade. The private and the public sectors both responded to
the demand for a vast increase in suburban housing generated by the growing
number of families with the resources to satisfy their desire for space, privacy,
and mobility. The marketplace supplied land, federal and state governments
provided mortgage subsidies and major transportation facilities, the private
sector constructed housing, and the public sector (especially local governments) provided a variety of services for the new residents. By and large,
these were complementary activities, each influencing the other, and all reinforcing the basic outward trend.

Since the mid-1950s, however, land development policies have increasingly modified rather than reinforced the thrust of the marketplace. As the
interests of residents, rather than entrepreneurs, have come to dominate more
and more suburban governments, and as planning techniques and resources
have become more widely available, the newer suburban strategies have promoted a more rapid rate of decentralization than would have occurred if
market forces, coupled with the governmental service-providing roles noted
just above, determined the pace of outward movement in the region.[59] A
similar conclusion emerges from the Regional Plan Association's study entitled *Spread City:*

> the effect of the mosaic of the Region's local zoning ordinances is to
> spread the population far from the present and projected jobs which are
> likely to be relatively concentrated toward the center. First, because
> vacant land is zoned for such large lots that the cumulative effect of
> developing these lots would be to consume vast areas, hence to push
> residences great distances outward. Second, because small lots zoned

59. While these trends have become increasingly important in the 1960s and 1970s, they
were present and gathering force during the previous decade, the period examined by Wood and
analysed in *1400 Governments*. Therefore, our differences with Wood with respect to the impact of
suburban land-use policies on the overall pattern of regional development do not result simply from
the fact that we examined a longer period of time than did Wood.

*What the Regional Plan Association has termed "spread city" is illustrated in this view of suburban development in lower Middlesex County in 1970. Large amounts of open land separate scattered single-family housing developments, garden apartments, a factory, and a shopping center.*      Credit: Louis B. Schlivek, Regional Plan Association

for the outer fringes of the Region are likely to attract people who cannot afford or do not like large lots.[60]

In short, the land-use policies of suburban governments produce lower residential densities than would result if the market were unconstrained. Suburbs adjacent to employment centers and to major transportation arteries have not been settled as intensively as they would have been, while those at the fringe of the region have been developed more rapidly than would have been the case if suburban governments permitted housing development to be determined solely by market forces. Scatteration is also enhanced by the irregular pattern of local regulation. Multiple dwellings may be built in one community, but not in another. One-acre lots prevail on one jurisdiction, while a neighboring municipality permits half-acre lots but requires a minimum house size of 1,200 square feet. As a result, developers move out to the far corners of the region in search of local governments that are agreeable to their plans, bypassing attractive sites in communities whose zoning ordinances are unsuitable.

While suburban residential zoning policies have played a primary role in accelerating spread, the industrial strategies of local governments also have

60. Regional Plan Association, *Spread City*, p. 13.

influenced the diffused pattern of development. The widespread suburban quest for attractive taxable property has opened areas to industrial development that probably would not have been available under a different revenue system. Were it not for their heavy dependence on local property taxes, many residential suburbs would no doubt use their land-use controls to exclude industry rather than to attract it. Instead, the imperatives of their reliance on the property tax force many suburbs to compete for industry despite locational disadvantages and the opposition of residents. The result is more industrial scatteration in the newly developing areas than would be likely to occur in the absence of the pervasive suburban competition for industry.

By accelerating decentralization, these residential and industrial policies affect a wide range of other development issues at both local and higher levels. In fostering the outward movement and scatteration of residences and jobs, suburban governments contribute to the tremendous rise in demand for highway facilities, as well as to the incidence of conflict over the location of new roads in settled areas. Their actions also play a part in diluting the concentrations of riders essential for the economical operation of public transportation systems. On the local front, the sprawling pattern of development entails higher infrastructure costs than more intensive modes of suburban settlement. Longer water and sewer lines, more land for local schools and other public facilities to accommodate the automobile, and extensive street systems to serve low-density communities mean higher per capita costs. These in turn require higher property taxes, which of course stimulate renewed local efforts to exclude more intensive, less "profitable" forms of development.

### Discouraging Innovation

Local government policies also have a strong conservative impact on development practices in the suburbs. Zoning ordinances and building codes are essentially negative instruments—they prevent developers from doing things. Moreover, since a basic objective of these regulations increasingly is to prevent the construction of moderately priced housing, they tend to discourage innovations that might cut costs significantly. The residential developer who seeks to depart from the conventional grid pattern of building lots, or to substitute major prefabricated components for traditional on-site construction methods, invites endless negotiations with local officials, organized protests from residents, lengthy and expensive litigation, and failure a good deal more often than success. The multiplicity of jurisdictions, each with its own regulations and modes of applying them, also works against the emergence of suburban development firms large enough to achieve economies of scale and to introduce industrial methods into home building. Consequently, the private sector, whatever its inclinations, is forced to adapt to the prescribed public patterns of land use and home construction.

It is possible, of course, that the conservative bias of suburban development policies merely reflects the orientation of the market that the local governments seek to regulate. Certainly many developers are content to work within the context of single-family checkerboard lots and to employ traditional construction methods and materials, even though they chafe at the bit of zoning restrictions that limit their market. But some builders have not been satisfied with the status quo. In suburban locations throughout the region, efforts have been made to introduce cluster or planned-unit developments that depart significantly from the traditional manner of subdividing suburban land for residential purposes. Under the cluster concept, detached houses or townhouses are grouped together on a tract, with the unused land reserved for common residential usage or for green space. Even when densities are no higher than would have been the case with traditional lots, clustering cuts costs by reducing site preparation expenses, shortening utility lines, and requiring fewer streets. At Twin Rivers, a cluster development of 3,000 homes located on 700 acres in Mercer County, the developer had to put in "only 25 acres of roads, or three per cent of the total land use, compared to close to ten per cent in the standard subdivision." In addition, "at least 60 per cent of the quantity of collector mains—sewer, water, storm drainage—[was saved] because of the concentration of the housing."[61] Clustering also is more likely than conventional techniques to spare trees, preserve interesting topographical features, and produce a distinctive community setting.

Despite its attractions, cluster development won little acceptance in the suburbs of the New York region during the period of rapid growth between 1950 and 1970. Unless changed, local zoning ordinances and subdivision regulations pose an insuperable obstacle to clustering since they almost universally prescribe minimum sizes for individual lots rather than maximum densities for tracts of land. Efforts to secure an amendment or variance to local land-use regulations to permit cluster design are often resisted by local officials and residents who equate clustering with more people and higher taxes. Projects calling for townhouses are particularly vulnerable because the average suburbanite sees little difference between a townhouse and a four-bedroom garden apartment. Resistance to change in many communities has also been prompted by the fact that some developers have sought zoning changes—under the guise of cluster design or planned-unit development—that would in fact greatly increase overall residential densities.

As a result, few builders were able to break through the nearly solid wall of local resistance to clustering prior to 1970. Even the region's largest developer, Levitt & Sons, was forced by local opposition to substitute conventional single-family housing for cluster design in Manalapan Township in Monmouth County. During the 1970s, however, suburban communities became more receptive to cluster development. By 1977, about a third of New Jersey's suburbs were permitting cluster housing. In part, this change reflected greater public concern with environmental protection and the preservation of open space. It also resulted from suburban awareness that clustering need not entail higher densities or lower-cost housing.[62] Thus innovation which ad-

61. Herbert J. Kendall, quoted in Alan S. Oser, "Planned Community Is Rising," *New York Times*, February 22, 1970. Twin Rivers is located in East Windsor, a rapidly growing suburb adjacent to an exit of the New Jersey Turnpike. The project was begun in 1969, following enactment of a special planned-unit development ordinance by the local government. For an examination of the political history of the Twin Rivers development, see Lucy Hackney, "A Political Analysis of the Development Process in East Windsor Township," Senior Thesis (Princeton University, 1975).

62. See the comments of Stuart Bressler, New Jersey Division of State and Regional Planning, quoted in Carter E. Horsley, "In Suburbs, Quest for Space Pits 'Have-Nots' Vs. 'Haves,' " *New York Times*, February 6, 1977.

vances traditional suburban interests has become acceptable, although the suburbs continue to resist innovative techniques that might bring more people or higher local tax burdens.

### Excluding the Less Affluent

Almost by definition, suburban efforts to maximize internal benefits influence the distribution of moderate and low-income families in the region. Families who cannot "pay their way" are the primary target of suburban development controls that foster higher housing costs. During the past twenty years suburban land-use policies have combined with the general rise in construction and mortgage costs to price the vast majority of the region's families out of the new suburban housing market. An analysis of housing opportunities in the region's northern and eastern suburbs by the Regional Plan Association in 1969 concluded that 80 percent of the region's population was priced out of this housing market.[63] During the 1970s, housing prices rose faster than income in the region, thus further reducing the proportion of families able to afford new housing. By 1977, the minimum cost of a new single-family home built within 50 miles of Manhattan was $55,000. The rapid rise in housing costs has led many suburban owners to defer the purchase of new homes, thus slowing the "trickle down" process that traditionally has been the major source of improved housing for less affluent families in metropolitan areas.

Suburban land-use policies affect housing costs in a variety of ways. Larger lots are more expensive than smaller ones. Moreover, by reducing the supply of land available for more intensive settlement, large-lot zoning generates greater demand for the limited land available for smaller lots, thus contributing to higher prices for such lots. Higher costs also result from building codes that prohibit mass production and discourage the use of new materials and techniques. Minimum building-size requirements have an even more direct effect on housing costs since in practice they become a minimum *cost* requirement. Assuming construction costs of $35 per square foot and a conservative $15,000 for land and improvements, a 1,200 square foot minimum mandates a $57,000 house.[64] And because of the higher investments required for utility connections and other infrastructure, low-density settlement itself increases housing costs.

Of course, suburban land-use policies are not the only major factor in the rapid rise of housing costs. It is extremely difficult to measure with precision the relative weight of increased building costs, tighter money, rising land prices, and local land-use controls on suburban housing costs.[65] But certainly

63. "Housing Opportunities," *Regional Plan News* (September 1969), p. 1. Racial discrimination is also an important factor in structuring housing opportunity in the region; see "Segregation and Opportunity in the Region's Housing," *Regional Plan News* (July 1979).

64. Long Island builders estimated that required improvements for streets, sidewalks, curbs, and drainage cost $5,000 per lot in 1977; see William Tucker, "Why Production in Region Lags," *New York Times*, May 29, 1977.

65. The problem has two main facets: first, the problem of separating the impact of zoning and building codes from the other factors causing rises in the costs of construction and land; and second, the question of what would have been built on a particular parcel if the land's use had not been constrained by local regulations.

zoning and building codes contribute significantly, particularly since they raise the base cost of housing, which in turn is escalated further by the rising cost of land, labor, materials, and money. Housing built on Staten Island, where local land-use controls were essentially nonexistent during the 1960s, cost 10 to 20 percent less than similar new construction on Long Island. Moreover, almost every suburb in the region bans mobile homes, the one kind of housing priced within reach of families with modest incomes. In short, it seems safe to conclude that if suburban governments did not seek to maximize internal benefits, there would be more moderate and lower-income families in the suburbs, as well as more elderly people and young couples, and, of course, more blacks and Puerto Ricans.

One of the most important consequences of the absence of inexpensive housing in the suburbs is the growing separation of the residences of lower-income families in the core from expanding job opportunities in the suburbs. The Tri-State Regional Planning Commission estimated in 1971 that the gap in the suburbs between middle- and low-income jobs and housing within the price range of the holders of these jobs was almost 700,000 dwellings.[66] As the Regional Plan Association noted in its 1971 plan for Westchester County, "Westchester is adding to the Statue of Liberty message: 'Give me . . . your poor: but only during the day to man the factories, clean the houses and maintain the hospitals.' "[67]

The mismatch between housing and jobs in the suburbs reduces employment opportunities for lower-income families, particularly for blacks and other minorities most concentrated in the core. Because of the inadequacy of public transportation in linking inner-city residences with suburban industry, those without automobiles are isolated from more and more blue-collar and service jobs. For those with access to automobiles, journeys-to-work of an hour or longer are common in a region as large as New York. And the growing travel between suburban jobs and lower-income residential areas augments the demand for additional highway facilities in the region.

Moreover, as a result of the lack of moderately priced housing in the suburbs, many suburban employers encounter labor shortages, particularly in recruiting for lower-paid jobs. In Somerset County, for example, over half the major employers were unable to meet their labor needs in 1970 because of residential restrictions. And almost 60 percent of the companies believed that inadequate housing would restrict their plans for expansion within the county. Despite these concerns, business interests have not been willing to bring pressure on suburban governments to lower housing barriers. Typical of the attitude of most corporations was the response of Western Electric to suggestions that the company had an obligation to insure that housing was available for its employees if it were to move to Bedminster: "Western Electric is not against low- or middle-income housing for anyone. But we do think that this is a matter that local zoning officials have to decide for themselves. . . . [We] don't think this is something we as a company can properly go to a community and say we want changed." In fact, in its effort to persuade Bed-

66. See Tri-State Regional Planning Commission, "Jobs and Housing in the Tri-State Region," Interim Technical Report 4240-2223 (New York: June, 1971), pp. 5–7.

67. Regional Plan Association, *Westchester County Supplement to the Second Regional Plan* (New York: 1971), p. 64.

minster to alter the local zoning code to permit the construction of a corporate facility, Western Electric emphasized not the need for more moderately priced housing, but the argument that its impact on the area would be very modest—since only about 25 of the 1,500 new employees would become residents of Bedminster or Far Hills, a nearby exclusive suburb.[68]

Fear that industrial or commercial development might open the way to a modest flood of lower-income residents has fueled opposition to nonresidential development in some suburbs, such as that mounted by the Citizens Continuing Committee for Conservation against the construction of executive offices by the RCA Corporation in New Canaan in the Connecticut portion of the region. In some instances, opponents of industry (and of moderately priced housing) have argued that business development and lower-cost housing are part of the same package. State Assemblyman John H. Ewing, a Bedminster resident, opposed the Western Electric proposal because: "If we accept the ratables, we have the responsibility of providing adequate housing. If people want the offices, they have to take the housing problem with it."[69] As it turned out, Bedminster wanted neither housing nor industry, and rejected the corporation's plea.

But most suburbs cannot afford to reject an attractive addition to the tax base such as Western Electric. Moreover, given the logic of maximizing internal benefits—as well as class and racial prejudices—most communities refuse to make any connection between the acquisition of industry and the easing of residential restrictions. The arrival of more than forty new industries between 1965 and 1971 brought no significant reduction in the zoning barriers of Nassau County's Oyster Bay. Similarly, despite the presence of a large Ford Motor Company assembly plant and lower taxes than neighboring communities, Mahwah in Bergen County rebuffed requests for zoning changes necessary to permit the United Auto Workers Housing Corporation to build federally assisted housing within the price range of Ford's 5,200 workers—40 percent of whom were black. In neighboring Franklin Lakes, which welcomed a large IBM installation but not garden apartments, the local beneficiaries of the taxes generated by nonresidential development are equally unwilling to provide housing for workers: "There is lots of empty land and cheap housing further out—there's no reason why people should feel that they have to live in Franklin Lakes just because they work here."[70]

Because there is very little moderately priced housing in the suburban areas settled during the past quarter-century, most of the lower-income families who live outside the New York region's core are concentrated in a few older suburbs and smaller cities of the inner ring. Largely settled at relatively high densities before the advent of the automobile, these suburban jurisdictions contain most of the older housing stock in suburbia. And during the past twenty-five years these communities—such as Yonkers and Mt. Vernon in Westchester, Plainfield and East Orange in New Jersey—have attracted almost

68. See David K. Shipler, "Western Electric Rebuts City on Relocation to Jersey Town," *New York Times*, November 11, 1970.

69. Quoted in John L. Davnar, "Bedminister Committee Will Decide on Office Project," *Newark Sunday News*, November 15, 1970.

70. See National Committee Against Discrimination in Housing, *Jobs and Housing* (New York: March 1970), p. 116.

all of suburbia's low-income migrants, an overwhelming majority of whom were black. Affluent white families, on the other hand, have been deserting these older suburbs for the newer or more expensive areas where the market and public policy combine to exclude the less fortunate. Thus, in addition to keeping the less affluent out of the suburbs in general, the individual suburb's quest to maximize internal benefits tends to concentrate lower-income groups in a relatively small number of jurisdictions that have to bear the primary burden of servicing the needs of an important component of the suburban population.

The exclusion and concentration of lower-income groups also means that most suburban jurisdictions lack a significant lower-income constituency. Few residents in the typical suburb question policies based on the desire to avoid the costs that come with lower-income residents. Almost everywhere in suburbia, constituency pressures for programs designed to improve housing conditions for the poor are weak. Moreover, proposals for low-income projects meet overwhelming opposition from residents who fear reduced property values, higher taxes, and neighborhood changes in the wake of an influx of poor black families into their suburb. All of the lower-income housing proposals developed in the early 1970s by the Suburban Action Institute—a public advocacy group located in Westchester County—were rejected by suburban governments.[71] Because of the intense local opposition, few suburbs in the New York region have sought to participate in federal or state housing programs aimed at low- and moderate-income families. An exception in some jurisdictions has been subsidized housing for the elderly, which serves a local need and does not threaten a community with "outsiders"—by which suburbanites usually mean low-income blacks.

As a result, very little subsidized housing for low-income families has been built in the suburbs. Suffolk County, for example, had 48 family units and 100 elderly units in 1977, a far cry from the 27,000 low-income units the county estimated it needed. Moreover, almost all of the little low-income housing built in the suburbs since 1950 has been located in areas that already had concentrations of lower-income and black families. Even in these communities, the lower-income suburbanites rarely have a major influence on local development policies. In very few suburban communities are the concentrations of poor or black residents sufficiently large to produce an authoritative role for their spokesmen in the local political system. Moreover, as in the larger cities, ethnic and racial conflicts undermine the prospects for concerted action by the less affluent. And like their brothers in the inner-city ghettos, until recently suburban blacks have been unable to mobilize their political resources for an effective challenge of local development policies. As a result of the political weaknesses of these groups and the desire of their more affluent and influential neighbors to maximize internal benefits, older suburbs have been more interested in getting rid of low-income families and preventing more from coming than in improving conditions for (and thereby probably attracting even more) residents who are widely perceived as community liabilities.

71. Suburban Action Institute proposed large-scale housing developments in Brookhaven, N.Y., Mahwah, N.J., New Fairfield, Conn., Readington, N.J., and Ridgefield, Conn. For a discussion of Suburban Action's program and the reaction of suburbanites, see Danielson, *The Politics of Exclusion*, pp. 118–123.

Like many of the region's cities, the older suburbs relied heavily on the federal urban renewal program in their efforts to maximize internal benefits at the expense of their low-income residents. The typical suburban redevelopment plan has sought to replace deteriorated commercial or industrial structures and adjacent low-income residences with attractive tax sources. In Morris County, for example, Morristown proposed an urban renewal program to replace a low-income residential neighborhood with two department stores, a shopping mall, movie theatre, motel, office tower, 100-unit apartment complex, and a 2,300-car parking deck. Englewood initially sought federal renewal assistance to clear for industrial reuse a tract of sixty houses occupied by poor blacks in the Bergen County community. Rarely is sufficient housing provided in the older suburbs for the low-income families displaced by commercial and industrial redevelopment schemes. In Westchester, the urban renewal programs of thirteen municipalities in 1967 called for the demolition of 1,200 housing units and the construction of only 700 low-rent dwellings.[72]

As in the cities, low-income blacks pay the heaviest costs and receive the fewest benefits from urban renewal plans implemented in the suburbs. Blacks are most likely to have their homes bulldozed. For example, 50 percent of the dwelling units scheduled for clearance in Port Chester were occupied by blacks, as were 70 percent of those demolished in Huntington Station, and all of those in the target area in Englewood. Blacks also have the bleakest prospects when it comes to relocation, both because of the scarcity of low-rent housing in the suburbs, and because racial discrimination drastically reduces the suburban housing opportunities of blacks at all income levels. Consequently, urban renewal has been a major cause of racial tension in the older suburbs. Local black leaders and civil rights groups have denounced suburban redevelopment programs as "Negro removal," demanded more low-income housing, and insisted that such housing be dispersed throughout the community.

Few older suburbs, however, want urban renewal if the price includes dispersing low-income housing into areas currently white. Throughout suburbia, redevelopment schemes have been delayed or halted whenever implementation has been conditioned on the construction of public housing in white neighborhoods. In Port Chester, 2,400 signatures were collected in 1967 opposing "subsidized" housing for those displaced by redevelopment. During the same year, residents of one section of the sprawling Westchester town of Greenburgh sought to incorporate as a village in order to foreclose the construction of low-income housing for blacks.

In each instance, the arguments against low-income developments are the same as those heard in the white neighborhoods of Queens or Staten Island when City Hall proposes to scatter public housing. A resident of a $50,000 home near a proposed low-income site in Yonkers assured reporters that "it is not that I don't believe in racial or social integration, [but] really those people . . . would feel so out of place here," while the local councilman for the area never mentioned race in terming the proposal "outrageous" because it would increase crime, decrease land values, and "aggravate school

72. Urban League of Westchester County, Housing Council, "Urban Renewal in Westchester County: Its Effect on the General Housing Supply and on the Housing Occupied by Negroes," (White Plains, N.Y.: November 1967), p. 3.

problems for the neighborhood."[73] But as White Plains' Mayor Richard Hendy pointed out in discussing his city's urban renewal problems in 1965, "the crux of our . . . trouble is that residents just don't want colored people moving into their neighborhoods from the slum we have to raze."[74] The attitudes of White Plains' white residents are shared by the vast majority of public officials, realtors, home builders, and private citizens—in suburbs large and small, rich and poor, from one end of the region to the other. Racial bias and a desire to maximize internal fiscal benefits work together to ensure that suburban blacks will be concentrated in a small number of jurisdictions. While 13 percent of the residents of Essex County outside of Newark were black in 1970, 89 percent of these black suburbanites lived in three municipalities— East Orange, Orange, and Montclair—where they accounted for 42 percent of the population. In the other 18 suburban communities in Essex, only two percent of the population was black. The Suffolk County Human Relations Commission concluded in 1967 that "about 95 percent of available housing [in the county was] closed, in effect, to Negro customers."[75] In words that could be applied to almost every suburb in the region during the past two decades, a Bergen County fair housing committee found in 1965 that "discrimination is an ugly fact of life in Dumont and Bergenfield, practiced by many real estate agents, apartment owners, and homeowners."[76] A decade later, these practices were still prevalent in much of Bergen County, prompting civil rights groups to file a sweeping antidiscrimination action in federal court.[77]

By and large, suburban governments have been responsive to the views shared by so many of their constituents. Local officials typically have tacitly endorsed exclusionary practices in the private sector. Few have been eager to adopt fair housing ordinances, or otherwise assure blacks equal access to housing opportunities within their boundaries. Instead, as the previous discussion illustrates, they have fostered exclusion by bulldozing black neighborhoods and ignoring the housing needs of those displaced. In addition, suburban governments have rezoned for commercial use land adjacent to black neighborhoods; school officials have frozen and manipulated school boundaries in order to foster and preserve segregated schools; and welfare agencies in some suburban counties have concentrated black welfare recipients in suburbs with large black populations, thus accelerating the flight of whites and further concentrating suburban blacks. As a result of public policies that encourage discrimination and segregation and the fact that the maximization of internal benefits has a disproportionate impact on nonwhites, the behavior of suburban governments has an even greater influence on the settlement patterns of the region's blacks than on the distribution of less affluent families in general.

73. City Councilman Nicholas Benyo, Jr., Yonkers, Westchester County, N.Y., quoted in Samuel Kaplan, "Yonkers Debates Slum Integration," *New York Times*, May 5, 1965.

74. Quoted in Merrill Folsom, "Renewal Is Near for White Plains," *New York Times*, June 7, 1965.

75. George B. Pettengill, executive director, Suffolk County Human Relations Commission, quoted in Francis X. Clines, "L.I. Housing Plan Stirs Fears of Bias," *New York Times*, April 30, 1967.

76. Fair Housing Committee of Dumont, Bergenfield and New Milford, "Discrimination in the Twin Boroughs," May 1965.

77. See Ronald Sullivan, "Sales of Homes by Race Alleged in a Bergen Suit," *New York Times*, March 8, 1976.

### Suburbanization Without Maximization:
### The Case of Staten Island

Any discussion of the impact of public actions on the process of urban development inevitably is handicapped by our uncertainty about what would have happened if government had acted differently or not at all. Unfortunately, the events of a quarter century of suburban development cannot be rewound and replayed without local controls over residential densities, apartment sizes, and land use generally. Nor, given the great similarities in suburban political systems and development goals, is it easy to find a large suburbanizing area which has been settled under a different set of rules. During the 1960s and 1970s, however, one section of the New York region—Staten Island—was rapidly suburbanized in the absence of public policies which seek to maximize internal benefits for the local community. And on Staten Island, a largely unfettered private sector has produced a different pattern of residential development than that which occurred elsewhere in the region under much more stringent public regulation.

Staten Island (the Borough of Richmond) contains 18 percent of New York City's land area but in 1960 its 222,000 residents accounted for less than three percent of the city's population. About half its fifty-seven square miles were vacant, and the borough encompassed 60 percent of New York City's undeveloped acreage. Underlying Staten Island's lack of development was its relative isolation from the remainder of the city. No direct surface links with the other boroughs were available until 1964 when the Verrazano-Narrows Bridge was opened.[78] The bridge unleashed a building boom that led to the rapid suburbanization of much of Staten Island's vacant acreage. Approximately 2,500 housing units, most of them single-family dwellings, were built annually between 1964 and 1979, adding 130,000 new residents to the borough during the 1960s and 1970s.

Compared with the region's typical suburb, Staten Island has been a paradise for the home building industry. Land use has been controlled by a distant city government with a city-wide tax base, rather than by a small-scale political system whose financial prospects were closely linked to local land use. As a result, City Hall has been far more responsive than suburbia to the pressures of the private sector and potential home owners. Minimum lot sizes on Staten Island are so small—40 by 100 feet, or less than a tenth of an acre—as to constitute virtually no regulation, since market considerations would prevent most builders from constructing "suburban" housing on plots any smaller. During most of the decade, other public constraints on development were virtually nonexistent. The city had no master plan for the borough. Subdivision regulations were not employed. And in many instances, building permits were issued for the construction of homes on unmapped land where neither street access nor water or sewer service were available. In fact, far from constraining the private sector, the city government fueled the boom by

---

78. Before 1964, residents of Staten Island could reach the rest of New York City via ferries to lower Manhattan and Brooklyn, or via the Bayonne Bridge joining Staten Island to Hudson County, and then via bridge or tunnel to Manhattan.

*New housing on Staten Island constructed in the mid-1970s demon-
strates the relatively high residential densities that result when private
builders are not restrained by restrictive local zoning codes.*

Credit: Michael N. Danielson

selling city-owned land to private developers. About one-third of the borough's vacant land came into city hands because of nonpayment of taxes after
the Staten Island land speculation bubble burst in the 1920s. Eager to raise
money from any source, the hard-pressed city government sold $50 million of
its holdings between 1960 and 1965, thus forfeiting a golden opportunity to
guide development on Staten Island.

Freed from the constraints imposed by local government's typical strategy for maximizing internal benefits, the private sector has produced housing on Staten Island that is smaller, less expensive, more crowded, and less
attractive than that built during the same period in the suburbs of the New
York region. With eight or more houses to an acre, residential densities are
far greater than in any of the suburbs developed in recent years. Small lots
also mean lower land costs and moderately sized units, which together permitted Staten Island builders in the mid-1960s to construct single-family
homes in the $15,000 to $25,000 range. At the same time, an unfettered
private sector has sought with great success to maximize profit in exploiting
Staten Island's undeveloped land. In practice, the minimum lot size became
the maximum, and the 40-by-100-foot grid has been imposed indiscrimi-
nately on Staten Island's hills and dales. New housing has been scattered
through the borough's 13,000 acres of vacant land, often with no consideration given to drainage, access, or the availability of city services. As for the
housing itself, the City Planning Commission calls much of it "ticky-tacky
housing [of the ] crackerbox variety," while the *New York Times* architec-

tural critic, Ada Louise Huxtable, writes contemptuously of the "jerry-built, rubber-stamp rowhouses."[79]

What has been called the "sack of Staten Island" outraged planners, civic leaders, conservationists, editorial writers, and some top officials in City Hall, particularly in the administration of Mayor John Lindsay (1965–1973).[80] During the Lindsay years, efforts were made without much success to enhance and coordinate city controls over the island's development, to encourage cluster and other innovative techniques, and to use urban renewal funds to build a planned community on 1,080 acres in the largely undeveloped Annadale–Hugenot section of Staten Island's south shore. None of these approaches aroused much enthusiasm among the moderate-income families who flocked to Staten Island from Brooklyn because a largely unregulated housing industry offered a reasonable facsimile of space, privacy, and "the country" at cut-rate prices. As Steven V. Roberts pointed out, "if better planning means larger lots, bigger houses, and increased costs, many people who want to find a better life on Staten Island would be priced out of the market."[81] Just as clearly, if large sectors of postwar suburbia had been developed under the conditions prevailing on Staten Island during the past two decades, rather than under a system designed to maximize internal benefits, residential densities would be higher in the inner and outer suburban rings, housing costs would be lower, and moderate-income families would be more evenly dispersed throughout the region.

### Maximization and the Passage of Time

For those who see the private sector as having the primary role in shaping suburban development, the analysis presented here may appear shortsighted. Demands from developers and potential suburban residents will continue to mount in the suburbs, they argue. As the pressures for more intensive development intensify, zoning restrictions will collapse, be subverted, or be swept away by higher levels of government more responsive to the interests of those groups who are disadvantaged by local policies. For example, in discussing the prospects for redevelopment at higher density in Nassau County, Edgar M. Hoover argues that "zoning regulation in most types of communities seem in the past to have been quite pliable in the face of really strong private incentives and fiscal and political pressures."[82] Thus,

79. New York City Planning Commission, *Staten Island Development: Policies, Programs and Priorities* (New York: 1966), p. 26; and Ada Louise Huxtable, "Staten Island's Beauty Losing to Builders," *New York Times*, August 9, 1965. In order to maximize housing supply and builder profits, some of the developments were semiattached units, with each unit on a 25-by-100-foot lot. By 1977, cost pressures had led developers on Staten Island to cut lot size further, with semiattached units now on 20 by 100 foot lots; see Alan S. Oser, "Soaring Costs Shrinking Homes," *New York Times*, February 13, 1977.

80. The quotation is from a *New York Times* editorial entitled "Staten Island Down the Drain," January 22, 1966.

81. "The Development of Staten Island: Will It Become Another Queens," *New York Times*, April 23, 1967. For a recent discussion of these issues, see Alan Richman, "A 'Forgotten' Staten Island Concentrates on Its Future," *New York Times*, March 9, 1979.

82. Edgar M. Hoover, "Introduction: Suburban Growth and Regional Analysis," in Dieter K. Zschlock, ed., *Economic Aspects of Suburban Growth* (Stony Brook, N.Y.: Economic Research Bureau, State University of New York at Stony Brook, 1969), p. 3.

Hoover echoes Wood and Vernon in implying that suburban land-use controls are ineffective, or at least have no lasting impact on the distribution of people and jobs.

The passage of time, of course, will bring changes to all jurisdictions in the region. Market forces undoubtedly will continue to play an important role in the continuous process of urban growth and change, as housing demand increases, land values mount, structures age, neighborhoods rise and fall, and jobs move. Inevitably, these changes will have an effect on local land-use controls. But many local governments will be no more susceptible to pressures in the future than they have been in the past. Nor are the hundreds of local governments that control land likely to make uniform changes in their policies, unless local control over land is drastically altered by the state legislature or the courts, which seems unlikely. Moreover, unless the higher levels of government radically revise the rules of the development game, changes in land-use policies will not occur simultaneously throughout the region. Thus, local governments can be expected to respond to the market forces as in the past, but not everywhere in the same way at the same time. This differential pattern of local response will continue to exert considerable influence on the distribution of people and jobs.

Of course, even in the unlikely event that all local controls were swept away, the fact that they existed would leave an indelible mark on the distribution of people and jobs in the New York region. For example, the moderately priced housing that private developers were prevented from constructing by local restrictions cannot be built today without substantial governmental assistance because housing costs have risen much faster than family income. As a result, a permanent gap in the supply of such housing in the region is likely to persist, regardless of future changes in land-use control policies in the coming decades.

# 4

## Minimizing Outside Intervention

No matter how skillful or timely the application of local controls on private development, few suburbs are able to maximize internal benefits in a vacuum. Federal, state, regional, and county agencies locate roads and bridges, develop parks and colleges, and undertake a variety of other development projects that can enhance or undermine local plans. Unlike private developers, these outside public agencies are not subject to direct local control. Municipal zoning codes and master plans do not apply to state transportation departments and highway authorities, the U.S. Department of Defense, and other large-scale public users of suburban land. Over the objections of local officials and residents, projects undertaken by higher levels of government may remove large amounts of property from a suburb's tax rolls, drastically increase local traffic burdens, or radically alter the character of the community.

Lacking direct controls, suburbs must try to minimize these adverse local consequences by participating in the larger political arenas of county, state, region, and nation. In these arenas, however, suburbs with their limited areal scope and meager political resources are frequently at a disadvantage, particularly when they pursue specific local objectives that are not widely shared by other local jurisdictions. In most contests with outside agencies, suburbanites must rely heavily on elected representatives, whose constituencies often encompass conflicting suburban viewpoints on major public projects. Moreover, many of the suburbs' adversaries are large and powerful agencies that are insulated from normal budgetary controls and political pressures.

While limited areal scope weakens the suburb in the larger political arenas, small size and suburban reliance on local property taxes magnify the impact of outside development activities within individual jurisdictions. Consider, for example, the case of Fairfield, an Essex County suburb of 7,200 souls, where a state agency sought 3,000 acres of Passaic River meadowland in connection with flood control and wildlife conservation projects. The land in question accounted for almost half of Fairfield's ten square miles, and produced 25 percent of the municipality's revenues. Although resigned to parting with 2,400 acres of the meadowland tract, Fairfield vigorously contested the inclusion of 600 acres of prime industrial land adjacent to Interstate 80. This parcel, local officials contended, was desperately needed for development that would generate additional local tax revenues.

Small size also means that projects of outside agencies often have differential impacts on adjacent suburbs. A highway interchange that devastates the tax base in one municipality may precipitate a boom in land prices in a neighboring community, enabling the latter to reap the benefits of improved access with little direct local cost. By the same token, a new campus of the state university can be a godsend for the suburb that hopes to attract industrial and commercial tax ratables, while for another suburb such development implies only unwanted changes in the local residential character. Such differences in impact make it difficult to build suburban coalitions against outside threats, particularly in areas of public policy such as highway building where one community's victory in a locational dispute is usually at the expense of its neighbors.

In the pages that follow, we look more closely at these interactions among suburban governments and other governmental actors, focusing on program areas and issues that have been especially important in shaping development in the New York region. We begin with road-building during the 1950s and 1960s, exploring factors that, despite vigorous resistance in the suburbs, gave the region a vast network of new highways in these two decades. The chapter then turns to airport location, where the impact of suburban interests—which successfully resisted the building of a fourth jetport over twenty years—contrasts dramatically with their very limited influence upon highway development. Finally we take another look at road-building but now in the 1970s, examining recent changes that have bolstered the capabilities of suburban opponents of new highways, and thus sharply reduced the ability of the highway coalition to determine the shape of regional development.

In Chapter Three, our attention was focused on two primary concerns: interactions between suburban governments and private economic interests, and the central theme of the Wood-Vernon studies—whether governmental organizations do indeed "leave most of the important decisions for Regional development to the marketplace." In Chapter Four, the main actors are governmental units, and the role of private economic interests fades into the background. Thus the chapter is less directly concerned with the "marketplace" issue than with the second major theme of our study: the relative influence of different governmental units in shaping the region's growth. We focus particularly on the strategies, successes and failures of suburban governments in grappling with the demands of their larger regional brethren, and on the factors—areal scope, functional scope, and the ability to concentrate resources—that underlie suburban influence vis-à-vis the pressures of regional enterprises.[1]

---

1. Although our primary concern in this chapter is the interaction among governmental units, this interaction is imbedded, of course, in a broader pattern of relationships that includes the behavior of nongovernmental actors and is shaped by underlying social values. Thus, as noted in Chapter One, the need for new arterial highways and their proposed locations are affected by increases in automobile and truck usage in the region, by land settlement patterns (as affected substantially by the land-use controls analyzed in Chapter Three), and by other factors that in part reflect choices made in the private marketplace. Similarly, the "need" for a fourth jetport arose partly from the expansion of air traffic in the region and from general patterns of growth in the region's economy. In Chapters Six and Seven, we explore further the relationships between governmental actions and these nongovernmental factors, focusing on the extent to which regional governmental units in the transportation field act "independently," as that term is defined in Chapter One.

**MAP 5**

## The Dispersion of Power: New Roads in Suburbia

In the past thirty years, road-building has been far and away the most significant activity by outside public agencies in suburbia. In terms of scope, costs, benefits, and community impact, highway construction and its impact on development have overshadowed all other public works in the suburbs. During the 1950s and 1960s, at least one new arterial highway traversed every suburban county in the New York region, as shown on Map 5. Unquestionably, the region's suburban areas have been the prime beneficiaries of the new roads, which have played an indispensable role in decentralizing residential, commercial, and industrial development. At the same time, some suburbs and their residents have borne a disproportionate share of the costs of these roads, which destroy homes, eliminate tax ratables, and reduce the amenities of suburban life. These disparities in the distribution of benefits and costs to communities are largely inherent in the nature of urban road building, and are at the root of most conflict over highway alignments. Wherever a road is built

*New roads and new housing have gone hand in hand for the past third of a century, as shown here in Bergen County in the early 1960s.*
Credit: Louis B. Schlivek, Regional Plan Association

in a metropolitan area, benefits accrue to a relatively large area, while community and individual costs are concentrated in the small corridor actually traversed by the highway. As a result of this mismatch between local costs and benefits, "everyone is for new roads—in the other fellow's town."[2]

The conflict between the general suburban demand for new roads, and the individual community's wish to avoid their adverse impact, structured much of the politics of highway alignment in the 1950s and 1960s. Suburbs with local constituencies in the path of the bulldozer were preoccupied with community costs, while benefits loomed larger than costs in the eyes of municipalities outside the bulldozer's reach, but near enough to benefit from a proposed highway in some way. Moreover, highway building in the suburbs during these decades was almost always a zero-sum game: one party's gain was another's loss. Consequently there was little community of interest among the suburbs that bore the principal costs and their neighbors whose favorable cost-benefit ratio could be wiped out by an alternative highway alignment.

### Perspective of the Highway Agencies

Conflicts over alignments generally result from the actions of the region's highway agencies, which are foremost among those who see new roads

2. "American Dilemma," editorial, *Newark Sunday News*, February 23, 1964.

as bringing general benefits to suburbia. In justifying their plans, spokesmen for the state highway departments and the toll authorities point to the way new roads relieve traffic congestion for suburban motorists, increase mobility and access for all suburbanites, and bring widespread development benefits to suburbia. Within these organizations, the need for new expressways and their preferred location normally is determined in terms of the capability of the region's highway system to meet anticipated demand. A new road's potential adverse impact on a few communities seldom figures in the calculation. Furthermore, highway engineers have relied almost exclusively on readily measurable costs and benefits in determining specific route alignments. As Robert Daland points out:

> Engineers are taught to calculate land acquisition costs (and therefore direct effects on property traversed), construction costs, and traffic service. Traffic service includes volume of through and local traffic and highway user costs. All of these elements may be measured objectively and may be translated into dollar costs and benefits. Using the dollar criterion, one "best route" may be ascertained.[3]

Highway planners have been understandably reluctant to introduce local community costs and benefits into their calculations. Factors such as the character of the local environment or the long-term impact of a particular alignment on a specific community are difficult to quantify. And since there is little agreement as to how to measure community costs and benefits, highway specialists consider such determinations as being more subjective, and thus more susceptible to "political" influence, than the "objective" factors employed in traditional highway cost-benefit analysis. Moreover, admitting the legitimacy of these less tangible factors in determining highway alignments would downgrade the significance of the highway engineer's technical competence, as well as intensify demands that highway officials share their authority over highway policy with urban planners and others who claim greater expertise in the determination of community costs and benefits. Because of these considerations, highway agencies prefer to make their basic determinations on traditional "engineering" grounds and to justify their plans on the basis of generalized benefits, while tackling community costs on an ad hoc basis by adjusting their plans on those occasions when grass roots pressures threaten to defeat a route judged most desirable by normal engineering criteria.[4]

### New Roads and County Government

At the county level, the benefits of highway improvements were perceived during these two decades as outweighing the costs imposed on particular communities. In discussing new roads, most county officials emphasized

3. Robert Daland, "The Realignment of Route 22" (Syracuse University, Syracuse, N.Y.: Interuniversity Case Program, unpublished mimeo, August 1964), p. 103.

4. For a fuller discussion of these factors with detailed analysis of their impact in the Minneapolis-St. Paul metropolitan area, see Alan A. Altshuler, *Locating the Intercity Freeway*, ICP Case Series, No. 88 (Indianapolis: Bobbs-Merrill, 1965), and Chapter 1 of Alan A. Altshuler, *The City Planning Process* (Ithaca, N.Y.: Cornell University Press, 1965), pp. 17–83.

new development opportunities, improved access, and reduced traffic congestion. For Somerset County officials, three new interstate routes represented "a real breakthrough for the future development of the county."[5] In Suffolk a county planner bemoaned the lack of highway connections across Long Island Sound, terming "transportation . . . the no. 1 deterrent to industrial expansion on eastern Long Island."[6] And in Westchester, while local governments and groups were mobilizing against the proposed Hudson River Expressway, the county's Commissioner of Parks, Recreation and Conservation was extolling the benefits of the new road:

> it will relieve traffic on the congested Albany Post Road and other old highways that pass through the centers of villages. . . . Construction of the expressway along [the Hudson River], near the mainline tracks of the New York Central, will clean up the riverfront and provide a magnificent scenic drive. It also will enable us to develop new marinas and waterfront parks.[7]

Countywide perspectives on development issues generally are articulated more effectively on the New York side of the Hudson, especially in the three most intensively settled suburban counties. In highway controversies in the 1960s, the county executives in Nassau, Suffolk, and Westchester responded to pleas for help from their constituents in phrases much like those employed by state officials. Typically, sympathy for those displaced was combined with the argument that new roads must be considered in the broader context of regional growth and spiraling automobile usage. Westchester County Executive Edwin Michaelian answered critics who scored him for failing to oppose the Hudson River Expressway and other highways by asserting that "we would have strangulation . . . if we did not build roads as we are doing."[8] And Nassau County Executive Eugene Nickerson vetoed a resolution of the County Board of Supervisors which expressed opposition to the proposed Long Island Sound Bridge, and castigated the county legislators for their narrow perspective on "one of the most acute problems facing Nassau County."[9]

Of course, as the Nassau County example indicates, county legislators, like their counterparts at the state level, often responded to their constituents' objections to new roads. This was particularly likely in New York counties, where local officials served on county governing bodies. Since the negative community impact of a particular alignment was considerably greater in a county than in a state as a whole, a county board of supervisors or freeholders was more likely than a state legislature to take some action against an unwanted alignment. On the other hand, such actions rarely were very influen-

5. John N. Shearn, county industrial coordinator, Somerset County, N.J., quoted in Paul McEntyre, "All Roads Are Leading to Industrial Somerset," *Newark Sunday News*, July 31, 1966.

6. Lee E. Koppelman, Director, Nassau-Suffolk Regional Planning Board, quoted in Francis X. Clines, "Long Island Searches for New Links to Mainland," *New York Times*, January 9, 1967.

7. Charles E. Pound, quoted in "Governor Signs River Road Bill," *New York Times*, May 30, 1965.

8. Quoted in Merrill Folsom, "Westchester Traffic Becomes Hot Political Issue," *New York Times*, August 22, 1965.

9. Quoted in Roy R. Silver, "Nassau's Attack on Bridge Vetoed," *New York Times*, April 6, 1965.

tial since county legislators, unlike state lawmakers, had no direct controls over the agencies building major arterials. Another factor limiting the influence of county legislative bodies was the zero-sum nature of suburban road building.

Normally supervisors or freeholders were limited to negative actions, usually a resolution opposing the construction of a road in a particular place. Positive action—such as recommending an alternative route within the county—would have risked alienating other constituents.

Professional planners working for the counties have also been sensitive to the adverse impact of highways on suburban communities. However, in contrast with the negative orientation of county legislators toward new roads, the approach of county planning officials throughout the 1960s generally tended to be pro-highway. Concern with community costs, even when it led to conflict with highway agencies and their engineering approach to route alignment, seldom blinded the planners to the countywide benefits promised by the new roads. County planners sought to minimize the disruption of established communities, parks, scenic areas, and other environmental amenities, but not at the cost of losing the benefits of a new highway. Instead of merely opposing routes considered undesirable, county planning agencies frequently proposed alternative alignments they deemed less disruptive to settled areas, as well as more likely to foster development in accordance with municipal and county plans. Occasionally these efforts bore fruit. For example, the route of Interstate 95 in Somerset County was altered in response to the analysis and proposals of county planners. Usually, however, planners' efforts placed them in a crossfire between highway engineers, who were reluctant to consider the less tangible costs and benefits that preoccupy planners, and local groups, whose preferences among alternative alignments rest on narrow local perspectives.

### Highway Costs and Benefits at the Grass Roots

Regardless of the criteria used to locate an urban highway, the interests of some individuals and communities are bound to be affected adversely. Costs are most intensely perceived by those whose homes or businesses are in the path of a new expressway. Most of these people see no offsetting benefits in the "outrageous" plans of "tyrannical" highway agencies, unless another location is found that will spare their homes. Typical is the Roslyn homeowner who asks:

> How would you feel if you spent a lot of money for a quiet and secluded home in a nice section and then found the [Long Island] Expressway in your backyard a few years later? It cuts through here like the Great Wall of China, dividing the town into two sections with a barrier between you and your next-door neighbor that jars your whole way of life. That's only part of the headache. We can't hear our television if we open our windows—which always have a film of oil on them—and the smell of gasoline exhaust is terrible. We want to sell our house and move away, but who'll buy it?[10]

10. Quoted in Joe McCarthy, "Problem: The Long Island Expressway; Solution: Close Down Long Island," *New York Times Magazine*, March 19, 1967, pp. 36, 38.

Suburbanites whose interests are threatened by highway construction usually turn to their local government for assistance. Whether help was forthcoming in the 1960s, as well as its extent and intensity, depended on the local government's perception of its stakes—on how municipal officials appraised the costs and benefits of the new road for the community as a whole. Only when the costs were considered high, in terms of the number of local citizens affected and their influence in the community, of tax ratables and public property lost, of possible deterioration of community image, and occasionally of the damage to local master plans, only then did the interests of local government and the adversely affected individuals merge.

A community of interest between the threatened citizen and his local government was most likely in residential suburbs of limited areal scope with little undeveloped land. The more residential a suburb, of course, the more sensitive were local political leaders to the interests of residents, and to the actions of outside agencies threatening residential character and environmental amenities. Such communities, as Daland indicates in his analysis of the controversy over Interstate 684 in Westchester, were "much more concerned about protection of existing tracts of property than about relief from traffic congestion."[11]

Small size also meant that a relatively large proportion of the suburb's residents would be affected by a new road, and that its impact on the local tax base would be proportionately greater than in a larger community. But small size also means limited influence. Thus the phalanx of local officials and groups that unsuccessfully fought the alignment of Interstate 287 through Morristown saw the municipality's 2.9 square miles as rendering it "powerless to cope with the problems posed by the highway."[12] Moreover, for highly developed communities like Morristown, there was less prospect of replacing the taxable property lost to the highway with the economic growth that new roads might stimulate. As the mayor of Union, which lost $2 million in assessed property to Interstate 78, pointed out: "Route 78 may be beneficial to other people, but not to us. We are a suburban community more concerned about one-family homes than industry."[13]

The interests of residents in the path of a new road and of the suburban community as a whole, however, are not always in accord. From the perspective of a municipality's officials, the benefits of a particular route within its boundaries frequently outweighed its costs. The proposed alignment was sometimes considered less disruptive than an alternative that would also pass through the community. Or a planned interchange might be well situated with respect to a local industrial park. Moreover, conflicts among local officials sometimes prevented them from defending those adversely affected by highway plans. Thus local officials often were neutralized when two or more alternative alignments lay within their jurisdiction. Often local government was ambivalent when some interests in the community perceived benefits from an alignment while others were preoccupied with costs. Conflict of this

11. Daland, "The Realignment of Route 22," p. 23. Interstate 684 is the realigned Route 22.

12. League of Women Voters of Morristown, quoted in the *Newark News*, November 16, 1964.

13. Mayor F. Edward Bierteumpfel, quoted in Harvey S. Ekenstierna, "Urban Officials See Highways as Destroyers of Ratables," *Newark Sunday News*, April 14, 1968.

sort, for example, between affected homeowners and businessmen who saw the new road primarily in terms of its benefits to the local economy, were common in the 1950s and 1960s. Ambiguous responses or neutrality on the part of local government tended to be more common in larger and more heterogeneous communities, as well as in less developed suburbs. In such suburbs, the failure of local officials to rally to the cause of the opponents of a new road placed the entire burden of the grass-roots antihighway campaign onto civic groups and neighborhood associations. Many of these local organizations, were created hastily in the wake of the announcement of a highway plan, and typically lacked enough political skills and other resources to constitute an effective opposition.

Finally, of course, there are suburbs that benefit from new roads, and bear little or no locally perceived cost. Among the suburbs with a positive orientation toward a highway alignment in the postwar era were those communities adjacent to the path of a new road who were spared by the highway agency's proposals, municipalities whose industrial or commercial development plans were enhanced by a route and undeveloped towns whose officials and landowners saw new roads as a harbinger of municipal growth and increased property values. Commercial and industrial property in Parsippany-Troy Hills in Morris County, located adjacent to the intersection of I-80 and I-287, rose from $14 million to $86 million between 1961 and 1971.[14] The suburbs traversed by I-287 in Middlesex and Somerset Counties rezoned 85 percent of the vacant land adjacent to the new highway for industrial uses. During the 1960s, industrial land values increased sevenfold in these communities, and their tax revenues increased 50 percent faster than in other municipalities in the two counties.

The benefits gained or the costs avoided enabled communities that won in the suburban highway lottery to articulate a more "cosmopolitan" view of a new road than those who lost. For example, after the New Jersey State Highway Department announced in 1963 that I-287 would go through fully developed Morristown rather than adjacent Morris Township, a municipality with considerable land available for industrial development, the latter's mayor applauded the decision as "best for the town, the township and the whole area" and expressed confidence that "Morristown will be happy with it, after they live with it."[15]

But Morristown, like most suburban communities in its position, had no desire to "live with" a six-lane expressway. For more than five years, municipal officials, local groups, and affected residents contested the highway department's favored "Alignment A," which would traverse the town of 18,000, claim $2 million in property and almost 4 percent of its dwelling units, as well as pass close to a public school and the Washington Headquarters National Park. The alignment was vehemently opposed when public hearings were held in 1960 on three alternatives for I-287 in the Morristown area. Issues raised in Morristown delayed a decision on the route for three years.

14. See David K. Shipler, "New Highways Shaping Future of City's Suburbs," *New York Times*, August 19, 1971.
15. Mayor John Bickford, quoted in Jim Staples, "Road to Bring Change, Controversy Rages in Morristown," *Newark News*, July 28, 1963.

After the choice of Alignment A by the highway department and the Bureau of Public Roads was announced, Morristown's Mayor J. Raymond Manahan promised to carry his fight against the unwanted highway to the doorstep of the White House. And he did.

During the next two years, county, state, and federal officials were petitioned and pressured. Consultants were hired to counter the state's case. Lawsuits to halt the highway's construction were initiated by the mayor, the Board of Aldermen, and the Board of Education. At one point in the bitter conflict, Mayor Manahan directed his police department to prevent state appraisers from examining property in the path of I–287. Later, local officials sought to block the state by refusing to issue demolition permits. In the course of the struggle, local groups and emergency committees met, petitioned, issued reports, organized demonstrations, marched on Trenton, and distributed a parody of Alfred Noyes's poem, "The Highwayman":

> The town was a place of refuge for the city escapees
> With shops and apartments and houses with lawns and
>   flowers and trees,
> The beloved hometown of thousands, rich and middle
>   and poor
> 'Til the highwayman came riding, riding, riding
> 'Til the highwayman came riding, riding, riding
>   to the door.[16]

During the 1960s, similar conflicts erupted in every part of the New York region in the wake of the announcement of highway plans. In Rye and Oyster Bay, officials and homeowners denounced a proposed bridge across Long Island Sound as a "nightmare," and pledged "a strenuous fight" to defeat the proposal.[17] During the construction of I–80, the mayor of South Hackensack ordered the arrest of any employees of the state highway department or its contractors who removed road blocks erected by the municipality at the construction site. And in Westchester, sixteen individuals, including a rabbi, two pregnant women, and the wife of a county legislator, were arrested while attempting to prevent workmen from cutting down 150-year-old beech trees in order to widen the Cross County Parkway.

### Political Weakness of the Individual Suburb

These conflicts delayed the construction of new highways, increased their costs, and prolonged uncertainty about their impacts on suburban communities and neighborhoods. But only rarely during the 1950s and 1960s did they result in suburban victories, especially after the highway agency had selected an alignment. Interstate 287 was built through Morristown along the

16. Quoted in "Pickets Chide Route 287 Auction of Houses," *Newark News*, October 21, 1964.

17. Mayor H. Clay Johnson of Rye City, quoted in Joseph C. Ingraham, "Plan for Bridge Across Sound Arouses Rye and Oyster Bay," *New York Times*, February 16, 1965; Anthony C. Posillipo, Supervisor of the town of Rye, quoted in "Rye Residents Move to Counter Bridge over Long Island Sound," *New York Times*, July 18, 1965; and Michael N. Petito, Supervisor of Oyster Bay, quoted in Ronalo Maiorama, "Governor Urges Bridge from Oyster Bay to Rye," *New York Times*, March 22, 1967.

alignment preferred by the state highway engineers. One of the most formidable suburban coalitions ever forged failed to keep I–684 off Chestnut Ridge
in upper Westchester.[18] Suburban successes—such as the decision to spare the
tranquil Millstone Valley in routing I–95 through Somerset County—almost
always came at an early stage, when several alternatives were still being
considered by the highway agencies.

Part of the reason for the persistent suburban failure to alter the alignments chosen by highway agencies lies in the nature of the conflict engendered by the construction of new roads. While highway disputes were
widespread, conflict has been sporadic and localized rather than persistent
and general. In part, the intermittent nature of conflict over suburban highway alignments results from the practice (and strategy) of most highway
agencies, who planned and constructed one segment of a road at a time.
Segmental planning means that relatively few conflicts occur at the same
time and in the same local area. Moreover, in most disputes, the parochial
preoccupations of local governments and groups have tended to narrow
rather than broaden the issues debated. Consequently, the highway agencies
usually are opposed by a handful of relatively isolated opponents, rather
than by a broad coalition of all the communities adversely affected by highway plans in the state or region.

Throughout the 1950s and 1960s, highway agencies could draw on resources far superior to those of their suburban adversaries. The state departments and regional authorities were staffed with full-time engineers, administrators, and public relations personnel, who were experienced in the politics
of highway alignment and had mastered the maze of procedures and intergovernmental relationships involved in highway decisionmaking. Most of the
highway agencies also had ample budgetary resources to finance their activities; and, especially in the case of the toll authorities, the deployment of these
resources was subject to little direct control by the region's elected officials.[19]
The average suburb, on the other hand, possessed neither highway specialists
nor the resources to acquire them. In most cases, suburbanites adversely affected by a planned road depended heavily on part-time amateurs, most of
whom were newcomers to the arcane world of highway alignments.

Moreover, the role of the highway agencies in determining where to
locate roads was legitimate and positive in tone, while that of municipal
governments and local groups was neither. The state legislatures had delegated to these functional agencies the power to commit public resources and
acquire public or private property in order to construct "needed" highways.
This role almost always gave the highway agencies the initiative. They proposed new roads, bridges, and tunnels; those adversely affected reacted. As a
result, the orientation of the highway agencies was positive: they wanted to
solve a problem, to build an expressway or bridge. Inevitably, the grass roots'
perspective was negative: they wanted to stop something. Like the chairman
of the Mount Pleasant Planning Board when faced with the prospect of the
Hudson River Expressway, most suburbanites' first choice for a new road that
would interfere with their lives was "a half-mile offshore and ten feet under

18. See Daland, "The Realignment of Route 22," pp. 46 ff.
19. See Chapter Six for a more detailed discussion of the capabilities of highway agencies.

water."[20] When the magnitude of the threat occasionally turned the suburb's initial negative reaction into positive advocacy of an alternative alignment, the new position was always suspect on the grounds of the obvious self-interest and limited expertise of its advocates, especially when contrasted with the highway agency, which argued that its decisions rested on professional rather than personal or political grounds.

Numerous tactical advantages derived from the highway agencies' authoritative role. Since there always were more roads to be built than available resources, the highway agency could juggle priorities to improve its bargaining position, or bring pressure to bear on dissidents by threatening to cancel a project that some suburbanites desired. By proceeding with construction at either end of a disputed segment, the highway agency could foreclose many alternative alignments it deemed undesirable. The highway agencies also controlled most of the information on which alignment decisions were made, frequently forcing protestors to base their efforts on rumor and fragmentary information. The alignments shown at public hearings were rarely precise enough to satisfy the affected local parties. This was the case at least in part because the agency did not wish to invest in expensive designs until the general alignment was fixed. Interchanges, sometimes of greater interest than the alignment itself to local parties concerned about traffic within a municipality or industrial development, normally were not located until the alignment had been set. One effect of incomplete information was to widen grassroots opposition in the early stages of the alignment process, since the number of suburbanites potentially affected was greater than that actually affected. Offsetting this, however, was the highway agencies' ability to use control over information to enhance their advantage in alignment disputes, both by permitting them to retain the initiative through their regulation of the flow of information, and by employing their virtual monopoly over technical data to bolster their claim to expertise and technical competence.

In most instances, the creation of coalitions offered the only means by which beleaguered suburbanites might overcome the advantages of the highway agencies. But as indicated earlier, the zero-sum nature of the suburban highway game was a formidable impediment to coalition building and the mobilization of legislative resources at the higher levels. Adjacent communities, like Morristown and Morris Township, were as likely to have conflicting as common interests. Newark's efforts to keep I–78 out of its Weequahic section were bitterly contested by neighboring Irvington, which would be stuck with the highway and lose $2 million in taxable property if Newark succeeded. Suburbs with common boundaries whose socioeconomic and political similarities often led them to cooperate on other issues rarely found common ground on the question of who gets the unwanted highway.

A good illustration of the inherent difficulties in coalition building is the effort by some Mercer County communities to build a common front supporting an alternative alignment for I–95, to the west of the route proposed by the state highway department. Princeton Township and a few other municipalities endorsed the proposal developed by a planning consultant,

20. Quoted in Homer Bigart, "Communities on the Hudson Assail Governor's Plan for Shore Expressway," *New York Times*, July 28, 1965.

because it reduced their costs and increased their benefits in comparison with the state department's alignment. But their appeals to other communities for support fell on deaf ears. Residents of Hopewell, which would be traversed by either of the routes, vehemently opposed the consultant's proposal. A coalition, they argued, could not be built around a proposal that "takes the road out of Princeton and puts it somewhere else. If you want us to help you, if you want Montgomery to help you, you'll have to take it out of Hopewell, Princeton, Montgomery, and all the other towns."[21] But if the consultant's alternative was too close to Hopewell, it was too distant from Lawrence. It would be "of little advantage to us and might result in another superhighway being run through Lawrence" in the future, the mayor noted, in arguing for the state highway department's proposed alignment.[22]

Once an alignment is selected, the suburbs in the road's path become pariahs. Far from rushing to the aid of their unfortunate brethren, most neighboring communities, after breathing a sigh of relief and counting their benefits, allied themselves with the highway agency to ensure that the protesting suburbs did not succeed in shifting the alignment into their own backyards. Thus, the endangered municipality—or neighborhood, in the case of suburbs internally divided over a new road—typically found itself without allies in a contest with the powerful highway agencies.

Occasionally a coalition could be organized along a substantial length of a proposed route, the essential condition being a high degree of consensus about costs and benefits along the route. This condition was likely to be met only in the case of an alignment traversing several developed residential areas. The most influential suburban antihighway alliance in the New York region in the 1960s was the Bedford coalition forged in opposition to the state-recommended easterly alignment for Westchester's Route 22, which later became I–684. The coalition enlisted municipal officials from Bedford, Mount Kisco, and North Castle, local businessmen, civic groups, estate owners, and numerous conservation organizations seeking to preserve wildlife sanctuaries on Chestnut Ridge in the path of the state's preferred route. Senior executives of a dozen national corporations and major banks were active members. Compared with most antihighway groups, the participants in the Bedford coalition, as Daland points out,

> had unusual leverages with which to fight their battle. Many of them were wealthy estate owners willing to place their bank accounts behind the effort. They included men of high competence, at the top of their professions nationally. As one would expect, many of them had rendered service of a high order to one of the two political parties and, therefore, had channels of access to the highest level of state political decision-makers.[23]

The alliance mustered sufficient pressure to enlist the support of the Westchester County Planning Department, and to persuade the New York

21. Quoted in "Hopewell Disagrees with I-95," *Princeton Packet*, March 16, 1966.

22. Mayor Joseph M. Mahan, Lawrence Township, quoted in Arthur Smith, "Now Lawrence is Upset Over I-95," *Sunday Times Advertiser* (Trenton), March 20, 1966.

23. Daland, "The Realignment of Route 22."

State's road-building agency, the Department of Public Works, to reverse itself. But success in one arena does not guarantee final victory in the complicated intergovernmental world of highway politics. The Federal Highway Administration finally rejected the county and state position. Interstate 684, completed in 1970, follows the easterly path preferred by federal highway engineers, cutting "between two extensive wildlife sanctuaries, and then through an area of impressive estates, with many horse stables and paths."[24]

## A Successful Coalition: The Fourth Jetport

Contrasting with the failure of local opposition to check the road builders in suburbia during the 1960s is the remarkable success of the grass-roots opponents to a fourth major airport in the New York region. The decision to build another airport was made in the late 1950s by the Port Authority, on the basis of studies concluding that by 1965 air traffic in the region would outstrip the capacity of the authority's Idlewild (now Kennedy), LaGuardia, and Newark Airports. In reaching this conclusion, Port Authority officials had reason to believe that they would encounter no insuperable difficulties in acquiring a site for the new airport. The Port Authority was a powerful and wealthy agency whose charter, sources of revenue, and clientele insulated it from many of the cross-pressures that frequently preclude an effective concentration of resources on development objectives. Moreover, the authority was staffed by highly skilled and well-paid professional administrators, technicians, and publicists, experienced in building major public works and in weathering local opposition to their projects.

### Defeat of the Great Swamp Proposal

Once the Port Authority decided that a fourth jetport was needed, it proceeded to evaluate fifteen sites on the basis of air traffic, accessibility to the region's core, topography, and availability of land. Fourteen sites were eliminated, leaving Morris County's Great Swamp in 1959 as "the only potential site in the area which . . . meets all the requirements for a new major airport to serve the New Jersey-New York area."[25] In its preoccupation with technical criteria, however, the Port Authority overlooked a requirement that turned out to be crucial: local acceptance, or at least the absence of influential local opposition. Because of suburban resistance, twenty years after the Port Authority's plans for a jetport in the Great Swamp became known, a fourth

24. See "Interstate Road Will Open in Westchester, Thursday," *New York Times*, November 15, 1970. The article quotes a Federal Highway Administration brochure extolling the esthetic advantages of the easterly path. FHA support for this alignment was based not only on the opportunity to open a "highly scenic area" to "all the people," but on cost considerations: the easterly route was seven-tenths of a mile shorter and $4.3 million cheaper than the alignment preferred by local groups and officials. See Merrill Folsom, "Conservationists Lose Road Battle," *New York Times*, April 8, 1966.

25. Port of New York Authority, *A New Major Airport for the New York-New Jersey Metropolitan Area: A Report on Preliminary Studies by the Port of New York Authority* (New York: 1960), p. 34.

airport neither was in use nor under construction, and the authority's preferred site had become a national wildlife preserve.

Local opposition developed immediately after the *Newark Evening News* revealed in early December 1959 that the Port Authority was planning a 10,000-acre jetport in the Great Swamp area, a sparsely settled marshland dotted with estates and surrounded by upper-income residential suburbs. Residents of the affected area were appalled at the thought of their serenity being disturbed by the roar of jets, and their amenity being undermined by 10,000 acres of airport facilities, new roads and traffic, and the other development that the jetport would stimulate. In the weeks immediately following the announcement, more than 2,000 of them wrote Governor Robert B. Meyner to protest the authority's plan. Local political leaders quickly came to the support of their constituents. The day after the story appeared, the proposal was denounced by Congressman Peter Frelinghuysen who lived near the proposed site, both of Morris County's assemblymen, and the mayors of Morristown, Chatham Township, and other municipalities in the vicinity of the site. Two weeks later, Frelinghuysen took the lead in bringing together officials from twenty municipalities to organize the Jetport Action Association (later called the Jersey Jetport Site Association), which during the next two years directed the successful campaign against a Morris County jetport.

Anguished protests from residents, an outcry from local politicians, and the formation of quasi-governmental organizations are routine suburban responses to the threat of adverse actions by outside agencies. But what ensued on the jetport issue was far from normal in contests between suburbs and major development agencies. Within six weeks after the Port Authority's plans became known, the Jetport Action Association had secured overwhelming approval by the state legislature of a resolution opposing a jetport in Morris County. In taking this action, the legislature in effect vetoed the authority's proposal, since the bistate agency needed legislative consent in both Trenton and Albany to extend its boundaries to encompass the Great Swamp. Caught by surprise by the magnitude of the hostile reaction and the near-unanimity of legislative opposition, authority officials backtracked, publicly declaring that the Great Swamp had only been a preliminary choice, and that a more thorough study would be made of it and other possible sites, while privately hoping that the "emotional outburst" would subside with the passage of time.[26]

Seventeen months later, in May 1961, the Port Authority was ready to test the climate of opinion in New Jersey with a second jetport proposal. The new report, after considering everything from noise suppression to the protection of bird sanctuaries, and after analyzing a long list of sites, again concluded that only the Great Swamp in Morris County adequately met all the criteria for the location of a new jetport.[27] The authority quickly learned that the "emotional outburst" had only temporarily subsided, and that the anti-jetport coalition had lost none of its influence in Trenton. By large majorities,

26. Unnamed Port of New York Authority commissioner, quoted in David D. Gladfelter, "Jets for the Great Swamp?" in Richard T. Frost, ed., *Cases in State and Local Government* (Englewood Cliffs, N.J.: Prentice-Hall, 1961), p. 317.

27. Port of New York Authority, *A Report on Airport Requirements and Sites in the Metropolitan New Jersey-New York Region* (New York: 1961).

MAP 6

both houses of the state legislature passed a bill outlawing the construction of a jetport in any of seven northern New Jersey counties, including Morris. The fact that Governor Meyner vetoed the anti-jetport bill afforded the Port Authority little comfort, as the bistate agency still needed affirmative legislative action to undertake construction in the Great Swamp since the site was outside the port district. Also offsetting Meyner's veto was the success of the Jersey Jetport Site Association in winning promises from both gubernatorial candidates during the 1961 campaign that a jetport would not be built anywhere in northern New Jersey.[28]

By the time the Port Authority had completed yet another comprehensive review in late 1966, the efforts of Congressman Frelinghuysen and his colleagues to protect the area from the intrusion of jetcraft had erected a further barrier. The Great Swamp had been designated a National Wildlife Preserve, and the U.S. Department of the Interior announced its intention of

---

28. Meyner was not a candidate for reelection because of a constitutional prohibition against three consecutive terms.

including the Great Swamp in the National Wilderness System, where it would "be forever protected in an unspoiled condition."[29]

Meanwhile, the Great Swamp continued to be well defended in Trenton. Release of the Port Authority's 1966 study, which considered 23 sites before once again concluding that only the Great Swamp met all the criteria for the construction and operation of a jetport, was quickly followed by another legislative resolution opposing the construction of a jetport in Northern New Jersey. And Governor Richard J. Hughes reiterated his "irrevocable" campaign commitments of 1961 and 1965 against the construction of a jetport in the Great Swamp.

## Opposition to Other Sites

At this point, the Port Authority finally was ready to admit that the fourth jetport would not be built in the Great Swamp. But no other sites appeared to be available that were technically and economically feasible, and also politically acceptable. Local leaders in sparsely settled Burlington County, New Jersey, and in New York's Orange County eagerly sought the jetport and its benefits. But sites in both areas had been ruled out by the Federal Aviation Agency and the Port Authority because of considerations of air traffic patterns, topography, and distance from the region's core. The following year, two more sites suggested by New Jersey—Bowling Green in northern Morris County and Bearfort Mountain in northern Passaic County—were vetoed by the Port Authority because of the excessive costs of constructing a major airport in mountainous terrain. And early in 1967, two additional efforts to develop an acceptable site were stymied by grass-roots opposition to the construction of the jetport in Hunterdon or Suffolk Counties.

Governor Hughes' choice to break the jetport impasse in 1967 was Solberg, astride the boundary between Hunterdon and Somerset Counties. Solberg was acceptable to the Port Authority; it was close enough to the core region to interest the airlines; and its location satisfied the FAA's air space criteria.[30] Early in April, the governor and his Commissioner of Transportation, David Goldberg, launched a Solberg trial balloon. When asked about his campaign promises not to build a jetport in Morris or Hunterdon Counties, the governor replied that "Goldberg tells me Solberg is mostly in Somerset County."[31] The governor and his aides quickly received lessons in geography and grass-roots politics, as Hunterdon mobilized against the jetport in a manner reminiscent of the Morris County campaigns of previous years. One week after the Solberg trial balloon went up, it came down abruptly as more than 1,000 Hunterdon demonstrators appeared in front of the State House carrying placards reading "Save Solberg from Goldberg" and "Richard Judas Hughes." After meeting with legislative leaders, who refused to support a Solberg jetport in the face of the public outcry, and after receiving thousands of anti-

29. Walter Pozen, U.S. Department of the Interior, quoted in Murray Schumach, "Udall Aide Pledges Fight on a Jetport in Jersey Swamp," *New York Times*, December 4, 1966.

30. Throughout 1967, the Port Authority avoided public disclosure of its willingness to accept the Solberg site, although it had informally indicated its acceptance of the site to New Jersey officials.

31. Quoted in John T. McGowan, "Solberg Picked?" *Newark Evening News*, April 5, 1967.

jetport petitions wrapped in funereal purple and black ribbons, Hughes bowed to the inevitable and told the demonstrators:

> No pledge . . . will be violated. We're not in the habit of violating pledges made to the people. . . . We renew our pledge to prevent the establishment of a jet airport in Great Swamp of Morris County, Hunterdon County, or in any other settled residential area of the state.[32]

Equally fruitless was Governor Nelson Rockefeller's effort to end the stalemate with a jetport site at Calverton, seventy miles east of Manhattan on Long Island, and the location of a naval airfield leased to the Grumman Aircraft Engineering Company. Originally proposed as a jetport site in 1966 by Suffolk's County Executive, Calverton had been rejected in the Port Authority's December 1966 report because of air traffic conflicts with Kennedy, and because of the site's poor accessibility to the region's core. Use of Calverton by commercial airlines also drew opposition from Grumman, Long Island's largest employer, as well as from large numbers of local officials and groups, the Suffolk County Board of Supervisors, state legislators, and Suffolk's congressman. Ignoring this opposition, Rockefeller endorsed the March 1967 report of his Metropolitan Commuter Transportation Authority (later renamed Metropolitan Transportation Authority) which recommended that MTA build the fourth jetport at Calverton. Local opposition intensified, and Suffolk legislator Perry B. Duryea, the Republican leader in the state assembly, prevented any action in Albany. By mid-summer 1967, the architect of the Calverton proposal, MTA chairman William T. Ronan, publicly acknowledged that Calverton was a dead issue.

Four years later, in April 1971, Rockefeller and Ronan proposed that the MTA's Stewart Airport—a former Air Force base near Newburgh, sixty-five miles north of Manhattan—be expanded as the answer to the riddle of the fourth jetport. In asking the legislature to appropriate $30 million in transportation bond funds for the jetport, Rockefeller emphasized the economic benefits for Newburgh and surrounding Orange County. The prospect of jobs won support for the plan from the mayor of Newburgh, an area of high unemployment with a declining economy, as well as from the local NAACP and some business and real estate interests. But, like all the other sites proposed since 1959, the Stewart plan was vociferously opposed by residents and officials in most of the directly affected communities, as well as by many local businessmen, environmentalists, and the area's congressman and state legislators. Responding to these pressures, and to the financially hard-pressed airlines' reluctance to invest in a site so far from Manhattan, Rockefeller retreated from his original timetable for the project, indicating that "the maximum development we're talking about is closer to 20 years than two."[33]

In 1973, MTA tried again, with a consultants' report that recommended

32. Quoted in "Hughes Renews Jetport Pledge," *New York Times*, April 11, 1967. Pressures to locate the jetport at Solberg arose again in the fall of 1968, when the Port Authority publicly endorsed the site. Once again, local opposition, led by the Hunterdon-Somerset Jetport Association, proved decisive and legislation supported by the authority died in the New Jersey legislature in 1969.

33. Quoted in Francis X. Clines, "Rockefeller Sees Delay for Jetport," *New York Times*, May 13, 1971.

a "$1 billion transformation" of Stewart Airport into a major international facility, combined with a new rail link (mostly on existing track) to Manhattan, sixty-five miles away. The report implicitly acknowledged the role of noise and other environmental concerns in defeating earlier plans, emphasizing that a "buffer zone" of 8,600 acres would screen jet noises from nearby offices and homes. The consultants also noted the positive economic impact of the transformation throughout the northern part of the New York region: 29,000 jobs would be created at the airport over a seventeen-year period, and 87,000 secondary jobs would be generated in a seven-county area. During this period, passenger traffic at Stewart would expand to 36 million a year, nearly twice Kennedy Airport's 1972 total of 20 million.[34]

The MTA board heeded one lesson of the Port Authority's ill-fated efforts, releasing the massive report for public consideration without endorsing it. But there were good reasons to believe that the proposal would be approved. It had the support of Governor Rockefeller, and the complications of bistate agreement that confronted the Port Authority's efforts could be avoided in this New York State project. Moreover, there was increasing local support for the Stewart proposal because of its anticipated economic impact in this depressed area.

Led by the Hudson River Valley Council, an environmental group, and by a coalition of local towns opposed to "more goods and people and cars and bricks and concrete," the opponents fought back. They were soon joined by a new set of forces that sealed the doom of airport expansion in the 1970s. By November 1973, as the MTA was assessing the consultants' reports and the likely impact of opposition lobbying in Albany, air passenger traffic in the New York region began to decline. The drop in traffic continued through 1974 and 1975. Thus, the energy crisis and a general slowing of the region's growth combined with environmental concerns to halt the MTA's expansion effort.[35]

By 1975, the Stewart jetport plan had been shelved, and in August of that year the MTA announced a new plan to expand the number of jobs at the airport and have "a most favorable economic impact" in the mid-Hudson region. Having been selected as the site for a new animal import center, Stewart could look forward to building up to a yearly "passenger traffic" of 1,800 cattle, 800 horses, 4,000 poultry, and 300 zoo animals. This new activity, commented the MTA chairman, is "one of the most important developments for the airport since the MTA assumed control in 1970."[36]

34. For summaries of developments at Stewart in 1973 and thereafter, see Richard Witkin, "$1 Billion Is Asked for Stewart Airport," New York Times, April 25, 1973; Richard Witkin, "Candidate for the 4th Jetport," New York Times, April 29, 1973; "Should Stewart Be Made Metropolitan Area's 4th Major Jetport," New York Times, May 15, 1973; Robert Lindsey, "Air Traffic Slump Raises Question of Jetport Need," New York Times, February 3, 1974; and Steven Rattner, "Area's Economic Declines Has Hurt Its Airports, Too," New York Times, December 2, 1974.

35. The decline in airplane takeoffs and landings (and in passenger traffic) at the three major airports in the region was due to several factors. Among the most important were the national energy crisis; a slowing in the economic growth of the region, which led to a reduction in the number of business-related trips to and from the region; and the devaluation of the dollar, which reduced overseas flights. Moreover, the advent of larger aircraft which handled more passengers per plane caused aircraft movements to drop off even more sharply than passenger traffic.

36. Metropolitan Transportation Authority, 1975 Annual Report (New York: 1976), p. 20. However, interest in a broader transformation has not died. With strong local resistance to permitting the supersonic Concorde planes to land at three Port Authority jetports, early in 1977 Governor

### The Basis for Successful Collective Action

Many factors account for the repeated successes of the suburban opponents in fighting the fourth jetport. The plans of the Port Authority and the
MTA adversely affected influential politicians, such as Peter Frelinghuysen
and Perry Duryea, who carried considerable weight in state and national political arenas. In Morris County especially, the target area was settled by
affluent residents, who raised $225,000 to finance the Jersey Jetport Site Asso-
ciation's activites in 1960 and 1961, and another $75,000 when the Great
Swamp was threatened again in 1966. Despite its reputation and past successes, or perhaps because of them, the Port Authority made a number of
critical miscalculations. Initially, the authority underestimated the breadth
and intensity of those who considered themselves adversely affected, while
overestimating the appeal of the airport's benefits, especially in its immediate
environs. Because of these miscalculations, the agency laid no preliminary
groundwork in Morris County or Trenton before its plans became known.
Once having lost the initiative, the Port Authority never regained it, largely
because overconfidence and political ineptitude led its officials to insist that
the Great Swamp was the only technically feasible site long after the site was
politically out of the bistate agency's reach. When the Port Authority finally
gave up on the Great Swamp, it was far too late to build local and legislative
support for its belated second choice, Hunterdon-Solberg. The anti-jetport
forces also were strengthened by the lack of enthusiasm among the airlines,
whose spokesman at times opposed a fourth jetport because, through Port
Authority fees, they would have to pay for it.

Underlying the grass-roots' triumph was the nature of the jetport, and
the costs and benefits associated with its development. In contrast to a highway, a jetport has a much greater impact on its surroundings. An airport like
that planned for the Great Swamp is a huge physical facility occupying 10,000
acres or more. Moreover, the noise and pollution produced by modern aircraft
extend its adverse effects far beyond an airport's boundaries. The impact of a
major airport on its environs is much less ambiguous than that of an expressway. While an expressway brings costs to some and benefits to other areas
along its route, an airport is perceived by most suburbanites almost totally in
terms of costs. Only in rural areas like the Pine Barrens in Burlington County,
or economically depressed areas such as Newburgh, was there any significant
local support for airport construction. Airport user benefits also are far less
directly related to a particular location than highway user benefits. Moreover,
fewer people use airports than highways. And in the case of Morris County,
air travelers already had ready access to nearby Newark Airport, which imposed almost all of its environmental costs on the residents of Elizabeth and
Newark.

The jetport's widespread and almost universally negative impact made
it possible for those most adversely affected to forge coalitions of considerable

---

Hugh Carey of New York asked the MTA to explore the possibility of extending Stewart's runways
to accommodate the huge aircraft. As one local spokesman who favored expanding the airport noted,
the economic impact of such a step in the area would have to be weighed "against a little bit of noise
pollution"; see Edward Hanson, "Newburgh Divided over the Possibility of Flights by SST," *New
York Times*, April 3, 1977.

areal scope. Because of their breadth, these coalitions exercised far more in-fluence in the larger political arenas than the typical localized suburban oppo-sition to a highway alignment. Frelinghuysen heralded a major theme of the Morris County forces when he initially condemned the Great Swamp proposal as undesirable to "hundreds of thousands of North Jersey residents."[37] The jetport's far-reaching impact created a community of interest among local groups and legislators, which produced the repeated resolutions against a jetport anywhere in northern New Jersey, as well as the early demise in Albany of the Calverton proposal. The geographic breadth of the opposition in northern New Jersey even led Governor Hughes and other political leaders who wanted the jetport and its benefits for the Garden State to pledge that a jetport would not be built where it was not wanted, something no regional leader ever promised the suburbs with respect to a highway program.[38]

Coalition-building also was enhanced because the nature of the jetport made it possible for those who opposed the facility to make common cause with those who sought the airport. Only one jetport was to be constructed. If located where local opposition was intense, the jetport could not be built in an area where it was desired. Conversely, construction of the airport where it would be welcomed would remove the threat to communities near other pos-sible sites. Thus, unlike the normal situation in road-building, the interests of those who sought the facility and its benefits were consonant with the inter-ests of those who perceived only costs. These considerations led the Jersey Jetport Site Association to join forces in January 1960 with South Jersey groups that wanted the jetport in the undeveloped Pine Barrens. From this alliance came statewide backing in the legislature for resolutions opposing a jetport in northern New Jersey and supporting one in the south. The north-south alliance of jetport opponents and promoters also aided both sides in their quest for endorsements from candidates running for statewide office during the 1960s.

## Environmentalism and Suburban Victories

"We are witnessing a truly historic moment, something that never could have happened . . . five years ago," declared Assemblyman Albert W. Merck on a March day in 1972, as the New Jersey Assembly overwhelmingly rejected the Turnpike Authority's proposal to build a $322 million, thirty-eight mile extension through Middlesex, Monmouth, and Ocean counties. To Merck and

37. Quoted in Gladfelter, "Jets for the Great Swamp?" p. 305.

38. The Hughes position was also adopted by Robert B. Meyner, campaigning in 1969 for the governorship. Meyner's opponent, Congressman William T. Cahill, went even further, indicating that he was opposed to the construction of a jetport anywhere in the state. Two days after his election in November of 1969, Cahill joined the other members of the New Jersey congressional delegation in a successful move on the floor of the House to delete a provision from the Aviation Facilities Expansion Act of 1969 that would have empowered the U.S. Secretary of Transportation to select a site for the fourth jetport if state officials in New York and New Jersey were unable to agree upon a site within three years. While that provision was opposed by the New Jersey congressional delegation, it was favored by Brooklyn and Queens congressmen, who preferred a fourth jetport to further expansion of facilities at Kennedy Airport, which would bring further discomfort to resi-dents of their areas.

the coalition of environmentalists and suburban spokesmen, whose towns would have been carved apart by "the most carefully planned road ever conceived in the United States," this successful fight signaled the "end of the American love affair with the automobile."[39]

Two decades of massive road-building came to a close in the early 1970s. Due to several interrelated developments, the willingness and the ability of suburban areas to resist the highway agencies grew incrementally until, by the mid-1970s, it was almost as difficult to construct a major arterial highway in the New York region as to build a fourth jetport.

A major underlying reason was increased concern with environmental issues among articulate segments of the general public. In the New York area, the battle of the Great Swamp jetport had heightened the sensitivity of newspaper editors and other suburban spokesmen to the negative ecological and other environmental impacts of large-scale public construction. Nationally, widespread concern with air and water pollution had led to the creation of the federal Council on Environmental Quality in 1969 and the Environmental Protection Agency in 1970.

Even before environmental issues generated broad public interest, the highway agencies had been under attack because of their alleged narrow approach to transportation problems, and because of their tendencies to operate in isolation from the public. Since the 1950s, the highway coalition had been criticized intermittently if ineffectually for its failure to coordinate road-building programs with broader transportation and land-use planning.[40] In addition, highway officials had made little effort to involve local residents in the evaluation of specific routes; public hearings on general alignments were often held years before construction commenced, long before affected communities learned of detailed route plans, and could consider their concrete impact on specific towns and the countryside.

By the mid-1960s, these concerns began to affect the structure and regulations of highway agencies, even if not their operating behavior. Several states, including New Jersey, created departments of transportation that combined mass transport with highway programs. Federal regulations required highway plans to be developed in the context of "comprehensive planning" guidelines for particular regions.[41] In 1967, the federal Department of Transportation was created, with the federal highway agencies shifted from the Department of Commerce to the new department. Under the DOT statute, the Secretary of Transportation was given broad formal authority over federal

---

39. Quoted in Ronald Sullivan, "Jersey Assembly Rejects Major Extension of Pike," *New York Times*, March 17, 1972. The view that this was "the most carefully planned road ever conceived . . ." was that of the Turnpike Authority's executive director, William J. Flanagan, quoted in the same article. The extension project was not finally killed until 1975, after further legislative and court battles.

40. See, for example, Michael N. Danielson, *Federal-Metropolitan Politics and the Commuter Crisis* (New York: Columbia University Press, 1965) and Jameson W. Doig, *Metropolitan Transportation Politics and the New York Region* (New York: Columbia University Press, 1966).

41. Federal "comprehensive planning" requirements date from the enactment of the Federal-Aid Highway Act of 1962, which conditioned federal highway grants in metropolitan areas on the existence of "a continuing comprehensive transportation planning process carried on cooperatively by state and local communities." New Jersey combined its highway department with mass transportation and air transport functions in a new Department of Transportation in 1967.

highway planning, and was charged with assessing highway programs in the context of broader transportation and community concerns.

Federal highway officials now required highway plans to include assessments of the "environmental impact" of each major arterial proposal, and the department adopted a "two-hearing" rule, which ended the traditional reliance on a single early public hearing, and required a second round of public testimony when detailed plans had been developed. By changing the rules to make highway determinations more accessible to local interests, the federal government has increased suburban influence over highway locations at the expense of the power exercised by state highway officials.

By the early 1970s, therefore, those who perceived proposed highways as direct threats to their towns and open areas had greater access to highway planners—especially through the second hearing—and a wider base for effective challenges. They could ask whether the highway plan had been developed in coordination with other transport and land-use concerns, or whether there had been a careful assessment of environmental impact. Moreover, the opponents no longer faced the technical skills of highway engineers, armed only with generalized fears for the destruction of community life. Now they could draw upon sympathetic technicians: the environmental experts at EPA and in state agencies, whose evaluations of pollution and ecological damage were scientifically sophisticated and dealt with matters of legitimate concern to increasingly wide segments of the public, particularly well-educated upper-income suburbanites. In addition, the highway opponents had, through long experience, developed greater political skills: greater abilities to organize community residents, to use newspaper publicity and public hearings to good effect, and to utilize technicians in challenging the highway coalition's traditional control over expertise.

Finally, the historical tendency of towns not directly in the path to favor a new highway—as a stimulus to economic growth in their own areas—was undercut by heightened sensitivity toward air pollution, as well as the first suburban glimmerings of another, basic question: was growth of population, industry, and the economy generally always to be applauded and encouraged?

These factors joined to produce yet another effect. No longer was road-building a zero-sum game, as in the previous two decades, with suburban communities wary of aiding neighboring towns threatened with new arterials, for fear that the route might be shifted to their own communities. Instead, it now seemed possible to stop an arterial route altogether. As a consequence, it became possible to build suburban coalitions linking many municipalities that had once shunned cooperation.

All of these factors combined to make grass roots interests more influential in highway controversies, and to make regional political leaders more responsive to adverse constituency reaction. "The people have spoken," conceded one of the region's most enthusiastic proponents of new roads, New York's Governor Nelson A. Rockefeller, in pronouncing "the proposed Hudson River Expressway and the five alternative routes . . . a dead issue."[42] Rockefeller's 1971 announcement ended six years of conflict between state

42. Quoted in David Bird, "Hudson Expressway Plan Is 'Dead,' Rockefeller Says," *New York Times*, November 21, 1971.

and local officials, environmentalists, and other interests in a slice of West-chester County bordering the Hudson River.

As the legitimacy of highway-building as a goal in itself declined, and as opponents acquired new tools and broader areal scope, the highway agencies found their own resources dwindling. In part the problem was inevitable: the major arterials constructed first were those that were cheaper and easier to build in terms of engineering difficulties, people displaced, communities disrupted. The early highways, such as the New Jersey Turnpike, and the Narrows Bridge, joining Staten Island and Long Island, were also the most essential in terms of traffic patterns. By the early 1970s, the remaining potential arterial routes were more costly per mile, more difficult to design, more likely to displace population, and less essential to the region's basic traffic flows. In addition, under pressure from the environmentalists and other opponents, the highway agencies' budgets did not increase proportionately with rising costs, so that the ample resources of the 1960s became the limited budgets of the 1970s.[43]

During the past few years, these factors were joined by two others that also affected airport development in the 1970s: the energy crisis, and the gradual slowing of economic growth and population increase in the tristate area. Both developments reinforced the arguments of those who urged sharp curtailment or termination of major arterial construction in the New York region.[44]

So the era of the highway-builders—vigorous, resourceful, and single-minded entrepreneurs whose projects both responded to consumer demands and also powerfully shaped those demands—came to a close. Their activities left an indelible imprint on the region's pattern of residential and commercial development. In the next two chapters, we look more closely at their resources, their strategies, and the impact of their efforts. For the present we note their decline, and with the two following examples illustrate the crucial role of suburban actors in curtailing these once-powerful regional enterprises.

### The Long Island Sound Bridge and I-287

A number of examples might be used to illustrate these pronounced changes in the road-building arena. The most important project to be halted in the 1970s, measured in dollar cost and dramatic appeal, was a new bridge across the Long Island Sound. As one observer noted, it led to "one of the region's longest and hardest fought controversies over public works."[45] The

43. In New Jersey, for example, all three transportation bond issues put forward by the state department in the years 1972–76 were rejected by the voters. In May, 1977, it was reported that the federal highway trust fund contained $514 million designated for New Jersey projects; the funds could not be spent for lack of matching state money. See Mark Brown, "Jersey Has $514 Million Claim on Unused U.S. Highway Funds," *Trenton Times*, May 4, 1977.

44. The 1974 annual report of the New Jersey Turnpike Authority captures some of these themes in its opening paragraphs, referring to "a year dominated by the energy crisis and adverse economic conditions," in which traffic "fell short" of earlier levels. By 1975, all the major road-building agencies in the New York region were devoting most of their energies to modest improvements in parking facilities, landscaping, and repair of existing roadways and structures.

45. John Darnton, "Many Groups Engaged in Battle over Bridge," *New York Times*, June 21, 1973.

***Artist's rendition of the Long Island Sound Bridge proposed by Robert
Moses.*** Credit: Triborough Bridge and Tunnel Authority

effort to complete Interstate 287 was more typical, involving extension of an
arterial route that generated more effective opposition than earlier sections
had in the 1960s, leading to doubts as to whether the highway would ever be
completed. The evolution of each of these two controversies is outlined
below.[46]

A bridge across Long Island Sound was proposed in the mid-1960s by the
region's premier builder, Robert Moses.[47] The span would extend 6.5 miles
from Oyster Bay on Nassau County's north shore, to Rye, a Westchester community just below the Connecticut border. When completed, it would provide a
shorter connection between central and western Long Island and the mainland,
thus decreasing traffic congestion on existing vehicular routes. Moreover,

46. Other controversies in the 1970s that illustrate the changing environment of highway-
building politics include the continuing battle over the proposed Hudson River Expressway noted in
the text, the New Jersey Turnpike extension project (also discussed in the text) and the conflicts over
the completion of Interstate 95 in central New Jersey, the proposed widening of the Garden State
Parkway through Union County, and the construction of a new freeway along the path of Route 7 in
Connecticut, among others. The status of the region's highway projects is reported regularly by the
Tri-State Regional Planning Commission; see for example its report, *Maintaining Mobility* (New
York: 1976).

47. Moses outlined the project in a brochure released to the press in February 1965, and in a
revised plan made public in July 1965. See Joseph C. Ingraham, "Moses Is Seeking Bridge from Long
Island to Port Chester," *New York Times*, Febrary 15, 1965; Roy R. Silver, "Bridge Authority Split on
Long Island Plan," *New York Times*, March 11. 1965; Stanley H. Schamberg, "Moses Retreats on
Long Island Bridge Bill," *New York Times*, March 19. 1965; Phillip Benjamin, "Triborough Commis-
sion Ends Differences," *New York Times*, March 23. 1965; and Joseph C. Ingraham, "Moses Revises
Plan on Long Island Sound Bridge," *New York Times*, July 17, 1965. For a detailed discussion of the
controversy over the Long Island Sound crossing, see Marilyn Weigold, "Bridging Long Island
Sound," *New York Affairs* 2(1974), pp. 52–65. Proposals for bridges spanning Long Island Sound
had been made by Moses and others intermittently in earlier decades.

argued those who favored the new span, by reducing the isolation of Long Island communities, the new bridge would enhance their opportunities for attracting new commercial and industrial development.[48]

Although the proposal generated early opposition in Rye and Oyster Bay, it was endorsed by the county executives of Nassau and Suffolk, the Long Island Association of Commerce and Industry, the Builders Institute of Westchester and Putnam counties, and representatives of organized labor. "It is generally acknowledged," wrote *New York Times* analyst Joseph C. Ingraham, that a bridge across the Sound was "needed."[49] For the *Times*'s editors, "the growing population and economy of Long Island" made it imperative in 1967 that "the Oyster Bay crossing . . . should be started without delay."[50] Governor Rockefeller also gave the plan vigorous support, and in 1967 the state senate and assembly passed legislation authorizing the state's Metropolitan Transportation Authority (MTA) to build the bridge. Local officials then turned to the judiciary, but in 1969 the courts rejected a suit, and it seemed likely that construction would soon begin.[51]

The opponents did not give up. Employing a strategy used earlier by the anti-jetport coalition in the Great Swamp controversy, Oyster Bay generously donated 3,000 acres of shorefront in the bridge-approach area to the federal government as a wildlife preserve. "Citizens for Sound Planning" and other local groups raised money, hired a public relations firm, and argued in nearby towns and legislative halls that the bridge would seriously damage the ecology and recreational value of the sound, as well as generate more traffic that would burden surrounding roads and communities. In 1971 and again in 1972, opponents succeeded in obtaining favorable votes in the state senate and assembly for bills to prohibit the MTA from carrying out the project, only to have Governor Rockefeller vigorously defend the bridge proposal and veto the legislation. In October 1972, the Nassau citizen groups persuaded the county's planning board to alter its position, and the board denounced the bridge as "detrimental to Nassau County residents," because of its impact on traffic conditions, air pollution, and other environmental concerns.[52]

48. For some proponents, a bridge over the Sound was viewed as "the key to the economic well-being of the eastern half of Long Island"; see Frank J. Prial, "Long Island Bridge Dispute," *New York Times*, May 9, 1973. See also Hoover and Vernon, *Anatomy of a Metropolis*, p. 253, and the comments on the bridge's positive impact quoted earlier in this chapter in the text associated with notes 6, 8, and 9.

49. Joseph C. Ingraham, "Moses Is Pressing for Long Island-Westchester Bridge," *New York Times*, February 23, 1965.

50. "To Ease the Traffic Flow," editorial, *New York Times*, March 24, 1967.

51. Developments during the 1960s in the battle of the bridge are summarized in Joseph C. Ingraham, "Moses Is Seeking Bridge from Long Island to Port Chester," *New York Times*, February 15, 1965; Joseph C. Ingraham, "Plan for Bridge Across Sound Arouses Rye and Oyster Bay," *New York Times*, February 16, 1965; "Rye Residents Move to Counter Plan for Bridge over Long Island Sound," *New York Times*, July 18, 1965; Ronalo Maiorana, "Governor Urges Bridge from Oyster Bay to Rye," *New York Times*, March 23, 1967; "Nassau Asks State Not to Build Long Island Bridge," *New York Times*, March 28, 1967; Ronalo Maiorana, "Transit Program Sent to Governor; Long Island Bridge Voted," *New York Times*, April 1, 1967; and John Sibley, "State Court Backs Rye-Oyster Bay Bridge," *New York Times*, April 25, 1969.

52. See Harvey Aronson, "The Fury Over the Sound," *New York Magazine* 2 (October 19, 1970), pp. 32–34; Francis X. Clines, "Assembly Says No to Long Island Sound Span," *New York Times*, April 21, 1971; Frank Lynn, "Rockefeller Expected to Veto Bill Barring Bridge Over Long Island Sound," *New York Times*, April 27, 1971; David A. Andelman, "Long Island Opponents of

The suburban opponents were dealt a severe blow a month later, in November 1972, when the Federal Highway Administration approved the 318-page environmental impact report prepared by the MTA and New York State's highway department, which concluded that the bridge would have a "minimal" impact on plant and animal life along the waterfront. But before the MTA could hold the public hearings that were then required, the opponents produced their own experts, challenged the impact statement in court, and obtained a court ruling in January 1973 finding the impact statement inadequate and requiring it to be set aside. By now the *New York Times* had added its voice to the growing chorus of opponents of the bridge. Condemning the project in an editorial entitled "Un-Sound Bridge," the *Times* emphasized environmental and community concerns rather than the traffic considerations it had focused on earlier. The once imperative link in the regional highway network was now seen as a "mammoth threat to the water, air, wetlands, housing and tranquility of Oyster Bay and Rye" that would "require an ever-growing network of supporting roads, constantly to be widened at the expense of the retreating green. . . ."[53]

Meanwhile, the anti-bridge forces took their case to Washington, winning two crucial victories in March and April 1973. The Department of Interior, responding to the environmental concerns of area residents, ruled that the bridge could not pass "over, under, through or on" the new National Wildlife Refuge that Oyster Bay had donated. An active campaign also brought several area congressmen, as well as Connecticut's Senator Abraham Ribicoff and Governor Thomas Meskill—who were concerned about additional traffic from the bridge in lower Fairfield County—into the opposition camp. These efforts finally resulted in votes on Capitol Hill to prohibit the use of federal funds to pay for access roads to the bridge. The House bill went further than the Senate version, prohibiting any connection between the new span and the interstate highway system.[54]

Finally, in June 1973, Governor Rockefeller, the bridge's most vigorous advocate, yielded. While noting with approval that the project offered economic and traffic-related advantages, the Governor concluded that citizens "have gradually come to adopt new values in relation to our environment," and to "forego certain economic advantages to achieve these values." It was now, Rockefeller explained, a matter of public debate whether "all growth is automatically good." The Governor directed that there be a halt to all work on the Long Island Sound Bridge, which he termed "a lightning rod in this period of evolution."[55]

Bridge Assail Report," *New York Times*, January 31, 1972; and "Nassau Planners to Oppose Bridge," *New York Times*, October 22, 1972.

53. "Un-Sound Bridge," editorial, *New York Times*, February 1, 1973.

54. See Frank J. Prial, "Proposed Bridge on Sound Passes Environmental Test," *New York Times*, November 29, 1972; "Suit Filed Against Long Island Sound Bridge," *New York Times*, February 8, 1973; Steven R. Weisman, "U.S. Blocks All State Plans on Rye-Oyster Bridge," *New York Times*, March 17, 1973; Richard L. Madden, "Governor Says U.S Opposition Won't Stop Long Island Sound Bridge," *New York Times*, April 6, 1973; "House Votes to Tie Up Long Island Bridge Aid," *New York Times*, April 20, 1973; "The House Delivers a Sharp Blow," *New York Times*, April 22, 1973; and Frank J. Prial, "Rye-Oyster Bridge Dispute," *New York Times*, May 9, 1973.

55. John Darnton, "Many Groups Engaged in Long Battle at the Bridge," *New York Times*, June 21, 1973.

In New Jersey, the road builders faced a simpler task—completion of the northernmost section of Interstate 287, a sixty-three-mile, $226 million artery that traversed part of Central New Jersey and then turned northward, through Hunterdon, Somerset, Morris, Passaic, and Bergen counties. As I–287 had pushed northward during the 1960s, the state transportation department had employed the usual strategy, developing detailed route alignments incrementally, as construction moved north. Construction of the segment through Morristown, referred to earlier in the chapter, represented another chapter in the successful battle to divide and overcome suburban resistance.

In the early 1970s, however, the battle of I–287 was renewed ten miles north of Morristown by the "I–287 River Route Committee." Rather than simply objecting to the destruction of homes along the route preferred by the state, the committee set forth an alternative route, and used skilled advisers to argue that the state's preferred route would cause extensive drainage and sewage problems along the remaining twenty-mile route to the New York State border. Confronting widespread and sophisticated opposition, the state Department of Transportation finally yielded in 1976, adopting the alternative route along the river, which promptly generated fierce opposition from the newly affected towns. The following years, local opponents used a new round of hearings on environmental and pollution problems to ensure additional delay in the project's completion, raising doubts in the view of the state commissioner of transportation whether this last section of Interstate 287 would ever be completed.[56] In fact, as the New Jersey transportation department noted, the northern section of I–287 was but one of several "vital sections" of the region's arterial system with a "questionable future." Unless current environmental, financial and other difficulties were resolved, the department concluded in 1973, the completion of these suburban highways "may be abandoned."[57] Eight years later, no further work had been undertaken on the disputed highway, although New Jersey's transportation chief insisted that the missing section of I–287 in Morris and Passaic counties was "the last vital link in what is otherwise a completed system."[58] And as the 1970s drew to a close on Long Island, unsuccessful attempts were made to revive the moribund scheme to bridge the Sound. For supporters of the Long Island Sound crossing, the span was "as inevitable as death and taxes"; while for local residents, environmentalists, and their representatives, Moses's dream remained "a bridge too far."[59]

56. See Martin Gansberg, "A New Highway Irks Morristown," *New York Times*, April 19, 1973; Michael Monroe, "Route I–287: Change Unlikely," *New York Times*, May 17, 1973; Martin Gansberg, "Local Opposition Again Blocking Highway Work," *New York Times*, December 27, 1976; and Robert Hanley, "Bergen Protests I–287 Extension, Asserting Road Would Skirt a Park," *New York Times*, September 9, 1977.

57. New Jersey Department of Transportation, *1973 Report of Operations* (Trenton: 1974), p. 16.

58. Louis J. Gambaccini, Commissioner of Transportation, quoted in Alfonso A. Narvaez, "State to Winnow Highway Program," *New York Times*, September 2, 1979.

59. State Senator John Caemmerer, Williston Park, Nassau County, N.Y., chairman of the New York State Senate's Standing Committee on Transportation, quoted in John T. McQuiston, "Long Island Sound Span Remains a Bridge Too Far," *New York Times*, November 4, 1979.

# 5

# Political Actors of Regional Scope

Of all the governmental institutions in the New York region, those with very broad areal scope have the greatest potential to influence development, a potential that some have been able to realize through the effective concentration of resources. For example, while the Port Authority was prevented from building a fourth jetport, its extensive territorial jurisdiction and skill at focusing resources have enabled it to shape development in the New York region through a number of major projects.[1] Construction of the George Washington Bridge opened the northwestern sector of the region to intensive suburban development. Port Authority investments at Kennedy International Airport created an employment center so large that, measured by number of jobs, it ranks second to the Manhattan CBD in the entire region. Construction of the World Trade Center strongly influenced employment and travel patterns in lower Manhattan. And the highway agencies have, of course, powerfully influenced jobs and residential location throughout the region. With few exceptions, whatever broad-scale development policies have evolved in the New York region are due to the efforts of the Port Authority, state highway agencies, and other regional bodies.

In discussing regional agencies that affect development, we include those state and federal organizations whose jurisdictions encompass all or significant portions of the region: the state governments and their component agencies; public authorities and other public agencies such as the Tri-State Regional Planning Commission created by one or more of the states; and the federal government. What is striking about this group of public institutions is how few of them are oriented toward the region as a whole. Only the Tri-State Regional Planning Commission has a jurisdiction approaching that of the New York metropolitan area.[2] All of the other "regional" agencies are either smaller than the region, in most cases because their jurisdiction is limited to a single state, or far larger—in the case of federal agencies whose activities in this region are part of national programs.

None of these regional agencies is a *general-purpose* political institution

---

1. The Port Authority's jurisdiction, the bistate port district, extends approximately twenty-five miles in a radius from the Statue of Liberty and encompasses 1,500 square miles in New York and New Jersey.

2. Tri-State's twenty-four-county planning area is somewhat smaller than the 31-county region defined by the Regional Plan Association. Excluded from Tri-State's jurisdiction are the seven outlying counties of Ocean, Mercer, Hunterdon, Warren, and Sussex in New Jersey, and Sullivan and Ulster in New York.

that encompasses essentially all of the region, and whose principal concern is the New York region. There is no counterpart in the New York area to the metropolitan governments in London and Toronto which are examined in previous volumes in this series.[3] Nor has the region emulated other American metropolitan areas such as Indianapolis, Jacksonville, Miami, and Nashville, which have created areawide governmental units with broad responsibilities and considerable impact on urban development.[4] Moreover, the obstacles to regional integration in the tristate area have precluded evolution of either a strong metropolitan planning agency or a powerful regional council, such as those organized in Dayton and Minneapolis-St. Paul which are able to influence key development decisions.[5]

In this chapter, we first examine the underlying reasons for the New York region's failure to create areawide political institutions with broad functional scope and the ability to concentrate resources effectively on development goals. Then we turn to the existing regional institutions. These agencies have been shaped by the same legal, demographic, attitudinal, and other factors which have precluded the development of strong, broadly based metropolitan institutions. In general, the interplay of these factors has produced a regional governmental system in which specialized regional agencies with relatively narrow functional scope are able to concentrate resources more effectively than regional institutions with broad functional scope such as the governors' offices. The result is a political system in which the net effect of the activities of state agencies, regional public authorities, and national officials is to reinforce fragmentation. Most of these regional organizations have been created in response to the demands of particular constituencies seeking better highways, cheaper housing, more effective sewage treatment, improved mass transportation, or revitalization of marine terminals. Consequently, their development programs commonly reflect the narrow concerns that are embodied in their statutes, reinforced by organized private groups, and accepted and often applauded by much of the region's populace—which neither perceives the need for broadly based regional government, nor wants to bear the costs involved in creating such a public instrumentality.

## Impediments to Regional Integration

Size poses a substantial obstacle to the creation of strong areawide public agencies with broad functional scope. With 19.2 million inhabitants, the

3. See Donald L. Foley, *Governing the London Region: Reorganization and Planning in the 1960's* (Berkeley, Calif.: University of California Press, 1972), and Albert Rose, *Governing Metropolitan Toronto: A Social and Political Analysis, 1953–1971* (Berkeley, Calif.: University of California Press, 1972).

4. For brief discussions of metropolitan government in these four areas, see U.S. Advisory Commission on Intergovernmental Relations, *Regional Governance: Promise and Performance*, vol. ii—Case Studies (Washington: U.S. Government Printing Office, 1973), pp. 2–73.

5. For a brief discussion of the Miami Valley Regional Planning Commission (the planning and development review agency for the Dayton metropolitan area), see Michael N. Danielson, *The Politics of Exclusion* (New York: Columbia University Press, 1976), pp. 250–258. The Metropolitan Council of the Twin Cities, the most influential regional council in the United States, is discussed in John J. Harrigan and William C. Johnson, *Governing the Twin Cities Region* (Minneapolis: University of Minnesota Press, 1978).

New York region has a larger population than any state but California. The region's 12,750 square miles make it larger than nine states.[6] Of particular significance, the region is far larger than any American metropolitan area that has created a general-purpose areawide government. The biggest of those units, Metropolitan Dade County in the Miami area, encompasses a population of 1.6 million, only one-twelfth that of the tristate region. In fact, the New York region is so large that, as indicated in Table 15, a number of its individual counties outside New York City are bigger than many entire areas with metropolitan governments. The region's enormous size, in turn, increases political complexity, reduces awareness of regional interdependence, and enhances fear of areawide "super" government, which is bound to be large and distant from most of the region's citizens.

Table 15—*Selected Regions with Metropolitan Governments and the Largest New York Area Counties: A Comparison*

| County | 1980 Population |
| --- | --- |
| Miami-Dade* | 1,626,000 |
| Nassau | 1,322,000 |
| Suffolk | 1,284,000 |
| Westchester | 867,000 |
| Essex | 850,000 |
| Bergen | 845,000 |
| Indianapolis-Marion* | 765,000 |
| Jacksonville-Duval* | 571,000 |
| Nashville-Davidson* | 477,811 |

*Note:* Regions with metropolitian governments indicated by asterisk. Counties of New York City excluded.

### The Obstacles of Political Complexity

The fundamental political fact of life in the New York region is the division of its turf among three state governments. Any formal regional arrangement must be approved by three state legislatures, rather than by the single legislative action required for all of the metropolitan governments created in the United States. The need for consent from three states poses formidable hurdles to regionalism. As pointed out in Chapter Three, each state has different traditions and forms of local government. Counties, for example, are particularly important in New York, while in Connecticut they no longer exist as functioning units of government. All three of the legislatures, as well as the governors and their aides, are responsive to local concerns about regional arrangements that threaten home rule, may enlarge local fiscal burdens, or bring entanglements with older cities. But these concerns are not identical in each of the states. Connecticut includes only a relatively

6. Connecticut, Delaware, Hawaii, Maryland, Massachusetts, New Hampshire, New Jersey, Rhode Island, and Vermont are all smaller in area than the thirty-one-county region.

small portion of the region, so areawide considerations usually carry little weight in Hartford. New York City's problems are an understandable preoccupation of state officials in New York, but count for little in Connecticut or New Jersey. In those two states, New York City is viewed with deep suspicion by almost all political leaders and interests, both city and suburban. Major subregional interests, particularly county governments, have considerable influence in Albany, where they provide a political counterweight to the localism of small suburban jurisdictions. In the other two state capitals, however, municipalities are the unchallenged spokesmen for a typically parochial perspective on the region, its development, and its problems.

Division of the region among three states combines with the political complexity of local government to involve the states heavily in any regional arrangements that are developed for the New York area. In less complex areas, local interests often are able to organize regional instrumentalities directly, under authorizations provided by general state enabling legislation. In the New York area, leadership for regional approaches is more likely to come from the states, as seen in the creation and evolution of the Tri-State Regional Planning Commission and the Metropolitan Transportation Authority in the past two decades.

The states also tend to be more heavily represented on regional agencies in New York than in other metropolitan areas. For example, all 12 of the commissioners of the Port Authority are appointed by the governors of New York and New Jersey.[7] All but four of the 15 voting members of the Tri-State Regional Planning Commission are state officials, who have dominated the agency since its formation in 1961.[8] And New York State's Metropolitan Transportation Authority has an 11-member board, all appointed by the governor, with three of the 11 nominated by the mayor of New York City.

The large number of county governments also inhibits areawide integration.[9] In sharp contrast with New York, all of the areas that have created metropolitan governments are single-county regions. Areawide government was achieved in these regions either by merging the city and county governments—as in Davidson County (Nashville), Duval County (Jacksonville), and Marion County (Indianapolis)—or by using the county as the basis for a federated metropolitan government, as in Dade County (Miami). The New York region also has many more counties than those multicounty metropolitan areas which have developed strong areawide planning agencies or regional councils. The jurisdiction of the Miami Valley Regional Planning Commission in the Dayton area, for example, encompasses five counties, while the Metropolitan Council of the Twin Cities includes seven counties.[10]

Beyond numbers alone, the county structure of the New York region

7. Each governor appoints six residents of his state to the Port Authority board of commissioners.

8. Five federal officials and a representative of the Port Authority also are nonvoting members of the Tri-State Regional Planning Commission.

9. The thirty-one-county New York region has twenty-three general-purpose county governments, since five counties are part of the New York City government, and three are in Connecticut where counties no longer exercise general governmental functions.

10. According to the federal definition of the Minneapolis-St. Paul Standard Metropolitan Statistical Area, three additional counties are included in the area.

imposes other significant impediments to regional integration. As already noted, many of the region's counties are large, and some have substantial governmental responsibilities. Both in New York where county governments are powerful, and in New Jersey where they have been seeking to expand their responsibilities, counties are not eager to share their growing powers with regional government. In fact, because of their large populations and relatively broad areal scope, many of the region's counties see themselves as "regional" institutions. They would prefer to tackle urban development questions on their own, or in cooperation with neighboring county governments, without interference from a powerful regional agency.

In Passaic County, for example, the local business and civic leaders who founded the Paterson Regional Development Corporation see "regionalism" as a cooperative effort by blighted Paterson and the surrounding suburbs to tackle common problems.[11] On Long Island, regional cooperation is represented by Nassau and Suffolk counties' creation of a joint planning agency to articulate a general development strategy for an area with over 2.6 million residents. The size of the two counties—Nassau-Suffolk is the nation's ninth largest SMSA, even though it encompasses less than 14 percent of the tristate region's population—has prompted repeated efforts by Long Island's political leaders to secede from the New York region.[12] In 1969, the two counties and their representatives in Congress were successful in securing the designation of Nassau-Suffolk as a separate Standard Metropolitan Statistical Area, distinct from the New York SMSA.[13] A decade later, the bicounty agency—the Nassau-Suffolk Planning Board—was able partially to detach the counties from the jurisdiction of the Tri-State Regional Planning Commission, after arguing that the region was so large that Tri-State was unable to understand local conditions and needs.

Thus, the area's counties inhibit regional integration by their very numbers, which prevent any one or two of them from acting for anything but a relatively small portion of the metropolis; by their size, which makes a number of them substantially larger than the average metropolitan government; and by their aspirations to influence development without sharing powers with broader regional institutions. These aspirations are often backed up by substantial political strength.

A final aspect of political complexity that severely handicaps regionalism in the New York area is the sheer number of municipal governments. Even if the states were willing to yield control over such agencies as the Tri-State Commission, there is no practical way to devise representational arrangements directly involving more than a handful of the region's 775 municipalities. Indeed, the membership of Tri-State in 1976 included only four local officials—one representative from New York City, the mayor of Bridgeport, a Union County freeholder, and one suburban mayor. Lack of representation on Tri-State from Long Island was one of the complaints that spurred

11. See Alfonso A. Narvaez, "Leaders Weigh Regional Plan Centered on Paterson," *New York Times*, October 16, 1976.

12. In 1975, only the SMSAs for New York, Chicago, Los Angeles, Philadelphia, Detroit, San Francisco-Oakland, Washington, and Boston were larger than Nassau-Suffolk.

13. Nassau-Suffolk was the first SMSA designated by the federal government which lacked a central city of 50,000 or more.

Nassau and Suffolk toward secession from the regional planning commission's jurisdiction.

### Lack of Regional Awareness

The region's size and complexity make the concept of a metropolitan community extremely tenuous for most of its inhabitants. Residents of various sectors of the region are separated by substantial distances. From Mercer County to Litchfield County, or from Ocean to Ulster, or from Warren to Suffolk, involves a journey of 150 miles or more. Also reducing the sense of a single region are the area's multiple centers. Many citizens see themselves as living in the New Haven region, or in the Paterson area, or in Greater Trenton, not in the New York region. And some relate to no center at all— they live and work in Nassau or Westchester or Morris County, and rarely have reason to go to any of the region's older cities. Regional identification is further dimmed by the steady movement of jobs out of the core. By the mid-1970s, less than one-eighth of the region's workers who lived outside New York City were commuting to the Manhattan business district. Thus in spite of the area's substantial economic, social, and political interconnections, many of its citizens are oriented mainly to their own small sectors of the metropolitan region.

Another factor contributing to the lack of regional awareness is the absence of institutions that focus attention on the tristate area. As already noted, most governmental jurisdictions are either smaller or larger than the region. As a result, public attention is almost always directed toward other arenas—municipalities, counties, states, or the federal government—even when the issues involve the region as a whole. Nor do political actors with broad areal scope make much effort to raise the level of regional consciousness. Regionalism is the subject of an occasional speech rather than a constant concern of the three governors, the mayor of New York, and other political leaders in the area. And each of the region's functional agencies tends to operate within the framework of its own specialized concerns, rather than in a broad regional context. Thus, their focus is the highway network or airport needs, with the region viewed as a source of particular demands for public goods.[14]

Even less visible are those agencies whose raison d'être is a concern for regional development and cooperation. The Tri-State Regional Planning Commission has deliberately maintained a very low profile, seeking to avoid controversy by devoting most of its efforts to technical analyses of growth patterns, transportation demands, energy needs, and related subjects. Unlike some metropolitan planning agencies, Tri-State has not given priority to articulating and dramatizing the common interests and problems of the region. In 1975, for example, only seventeen stories on Tri-State appeared in the *New York Times*. Also receiving minimal public attention was the Metropolitan Regional Council, a voluntary association of local elected officials that at-

---

14. In their planning efforts, however, the Port Authority (in particular) and a few other functional agencies have paid some attention to the region's general development trends.

tempted to promote regional cooperation for twenty years until it died quietly in 1979.[15] In contrast with Tri-State, the Metropolitan Regional Council some times sought visibility, but its activities aroused relatively little public or press interest. During the whole of 1975, for example, there were no articles on the MRC in the *New York Times*, compared with 137 on the Port Authority and 39 on the city of Newark.[16]

Size and complexity have also fostered a multiplicity of organs of communication in the New York area, most of them with a local or subregional focus. No one or two newspapers blanket the region as they do in smaller metropolitan areas like Boston, Cleveland, Phoenix, or Seattle. Instead, as shown in Table 16, seven daily papers with circulations of more than 100,000 each are published in the region. Most concentrate on urban issues in local or subregional terms. For some, like the *Bergen Record* or *Newsday* on Long Island, this frame of reference may be quite extensive, but on essentially all issues it remains subregional rather than areawide.

**Table 16 – *Daily Newspapers in the New York Region with Weekday Circulations of More Than 100,000: 1980***

| Newspaper | Circulation |
| --- | --- |
| *New Haven Register* | 102,000 |
| *Bergen Record* | 155,000 |
| *Newark Star Ledger* | 408,000 |
| *Newsday* (Long Island) | 498,000 |
| *Daily News* (New York) | 1,607,000 |
| *New York Post* | 631,000 |
| *New York Times* | 842,000 |

**Source:** The Ayer Directory of Publications (Philadelphia: Ayer Press, 1980).

Of all the newspapers in the region, only the *New York Times* consistently presents its readers with a regional perspective.[17] The *Times* provides substantial coverage of regional development, areawide issues, and related news. Over the years, its editorials have preached regional interdependence, the evils of parochialism, and the need for areawide approaches to common problems. Thus, in supporting a fourth jetport in New Jersey, the *Times* urged Governor Hughes to "put the total interests of the metropolitan area first and

15. The Metropolitan Regional Council and its difficulties are discussed in detail later in Chapter Five.

16. The Port Authority articles included 27 on its rail subsidiary, the Port Authority Trans-Hudson Corporation (PATH), and 110 on other authority activities.

17. Regional issues received relatively little attention in New York City's other two major dailies, the *New York Daily News* and the *New York Post*, which tend to focus almost entirely on the city's affairs.

abandon his opposition."[18] For the *Times*, "the fate of this great metropolitan region comprising more than nineteen million people . . . is indivisible. The future of city dwellers and suburbanites alike depends on the early development of more comprehensive and effective machinery for mutual cooperation."[19]

The *Times'* regionalism, however, is heavily oriented toward the primacy of New York City and the Manhattan business district. As the city goes, so goes the region: "If self-interest threatens to block . . . a turn to regionalism, the ultimate impact of an enfeebled city on its surroundings will be to accelerate the decline of the entire area."[20] From the *Times'* Manhattan vantage point, regionalism often means that the parasitic suburbs must come to the aid of the life-giving city. "New York gets little in return," is a common refrain on the *Times* editorial page, "although the vast and still growing commuter radius derives from the city much of its economic and cultural strength."[21] Viewing the region in these terms may raise the regional consciousness of the *Times'* readers, who tend to be the most cosmopolitan inhabitants of the area. But the *Times* also reinforces the fears of those outside New York City who see area-wide approaches as a Trojan Horse that will carry the city's problems into suburbia, and view the *Times'* perspective as a counsel for suburban disaster.

Among the other communications media, television has the greatest potential for raising regional awareness.[22] The seven VHF channels in New York City—three network stations, three independents, and one public broad-casting outlet—are received almost everywhere in the region.[23] At best, however, television provides sporadic coverage of the region, its development, and its problems. Local news broadcasts devote most of their time to New York City, where the largest single bloc of the region's viewers live. And this coverage—which tends to feature crime, drugs, racial conflict, commercial sex, corruption, official incompetence, and fiscal plight—serves to reinforce suburban fears of the city, rather than bolster feelings of regional togetherness. Outside New York City, disasters, crime, and other sensational events are more likely to get attention on the local television news than problems such as regional transportation or water supply. Areawide developments receive more coverage on occasional public-service broadcasts. And a number of the channels did broadcast a series of programs on the area developed by the Regional Plan Association in 1973. All in all, however, television's impact on regional awareness has been marginal; the only consistent regional image

18. "Start the Fourth Jetport," editorial, *New York Times*, May 1, 1969.

19. "Metropolitan Imperative," editorial, *New York Times*, May 18, 1975.

20. "The State of the City," editorial, *New York Times*, May 11, 1975.

21. Ibid.; see also "State of the City: Linking the Region," editorial, *New York Times*, May 24, 1975, which emphasizes that "while commuters do pay sales taxes and generate business, the total return scarcely pays for the city's constant service to a transient population."

22. Most of the radio stations in the region have a local focus, or devote little of their programming to news and public affairs. The major exceptions are WCBS-AM and WINS in New York City, with all-news formats. Of the two, WCBS pays more attention to news throughout the region, although the focus of most of this coverage is local news, rather than regional issues and problems.

23. A number of other stations are available to viewers in parts of the region, including the VHF stations in Philadelphia in the southwestern portion, VHF channels in New Haven and Hartford, the UHF network operated by the New Jersey Public Broadcasting Authority, and a variety of other local television stations.

projected by the major stations is the nightly weather report, which invariably features a map of the tristate area.

Economic interests provide another potential source of support for viewing public issues in a regional perspective. In some metropolitan areas, major firms play an important role in defining problems in areawide terms. The New York region, however, is so large that no individual employer or small group of firms has anything approaching the regional interests or influence that corporations like Kodak and Xerox have in the Rochester area. Moreover, state boundaries restrict the sphere of such regulated industries as major banks and public utilities, which are regional in scope in most metropolitan areas. As a result, Chase Manhattan Bank and Consolidated Edison focus on New York rather than the region as a whole, while the First National State Bank of New Jersey and Public Service Electric & Gas restrict their operations to the west side of the Hudson. Organized labor is similarly divided by state lines, and most other economic interests in the area are organized along jurisdictional or functional lines rather than regionally.

An exception to this general pattern is the Regional Plan Association of New York, whose primary aim since its founding in the 1920s has been to promote coordinated development in the area.[24] The Association was involved in the preparation of general plans for the region in 1929 and again in 1967.[25] The RPA has also conducted or sponsored numerous studies of the region, prepared plans for sections of the tristate area, and evaluated plans and proposals of other agencies.[26] In the process, the planning association has frequently attracted the attention of the area's leaders and press to the regional implications of various developments and problems. Some of RPA's efforts also have had a significant effect on the region's development, most notably the first regional plan which provided the blueprint for a number of key development decisions made during the 1930s and 1940s. The RPA also played an important role in raising questions about the Port Authority's analysis of the need for a fourth jetport.[27]

Despite its past successes and continuing efforts, the Regional Plan Association speaks to a small audience, most of whom already have a relatively high level of regional awareness. In recent years, the RPA has had scant success in its main endeavor, checking the sprawl that results in what the Association calls "spread city."[28] Like the *New York Times*, the RPA is sus-

---

24. For an examination of the origins and activities of the Regional Plan Association through the early 1960s, see Forbes B. Hays, *Community Leadership: The Regional Plan Association of New York* (New York: Columbia University Press, 1965).

25. See Staff of the Regional Plan, *The Graphic Regional Plan*, Vol. I of *Regional Plan of New York and Its Environs* (New York: Committee on the Regional Plan, 1929); Regional Plan Association, *The Region's Growth: A Report of the Second Regional Plan* (New York, 1967), and Regional Plan Association, *Regional Plan Bulletin, 110—The Second Regional Plan: A Draft for Discussion* (New York, 1968).

26. The most ambitious of RPA's efforts was the New York Metropolitan Region Study launched in 1955 under the direction of Professor Raymond Vernon of Harvard University, which led to the publication of nine volumes, including the Hoover, Vernon, and Wood studies discussed earlier.

27. On the influence of the first regional plan, see Hays, *Community Leadership*, Chapter 3. For RPA's critiques of the jetport, see "The Region's Airports," *RPA News* 89 (July 1969), and "The Region's Airports Revisited," *RPA News* 93 (December 1973).

28. See Regional Plan Association, *Spread City* (New York, 1962).

pect outside New York City because of its strong orientation toward Manhattan and its office economy. Most of RPA's support comes from New York business interests, which have historically dominated its board of directors.[29] The RPA continually stresses the importance of the Manhattan business district, arguing that "most corporate headquarters should remain in Manhattan."[30] To be sure, it also promotes the clustering of employment outside Manhattan in Stamford, White Plains, Hackensack, New Brunswick, and other subcenters readily accessible by public transportation. For suburbanites, however, concentrating jobs in Manhattan or in the region's smaller cities poses a direct threat to local freedom of action, which is the basic source of resistance to regionalism in most of the tristate area.

### The Pervasive Fear of Regionalism

In the view of the Regional Plan Association, the "region's economic strengths are regional. Its economic weakness has been caused by excessive localism."[31] This perspective is not widely shared at the grass roots. For most inhabitants of the region, "localism" is a virtue rather than the problem. As seen in Chapter Three, local autonomy provides suburbanites with the major means of influencing development. Autonomy also is considered a necessary concomitant to municipal dependence on the property tax for most local revenues. Regionalism, on the other hand, is a widely feared evil. Areawide approaches pose serious threats to local autonomy. They also raise the specter of unequal costs and benefits, of tax burdens levied without compensating benefits for local residents.

Illustrative of resistance to regional approaches that threaten local costs far in excess of perceived benefits was the experience of the Metropolitan Rapid Transit Commission, a study group established in the 1950s by New Jersey and New York to ponder the problem of trans-Hudson rail commutation.[32] The MRTC recommended creation of a locally financed fourteen-county district which would construct and subsidize a bistate transit loop, and also underwrite the losses of the New Jersey commuter railroads connected to the loop. The Manhattan business-district orientation of the plan and the MRTC's reliance on local subsidies were a fatal combination in the eyes of most of New Jersey's political and business leaders. Hudson County's *Jersey Journal* captured the "regional" sentiments that produced vociferous opposition on the west side of the Hudson: "North Jersey businessmen ask why they should pay taxes to subsidize taking customers from their doors. Municipalities ask why they should levy heavy taxes to solve New York City's transit problems."[33] The widespread lack of a perceived common interest in the Manhattan business district and its rail commuters was epitomized in an

29. Beginning in the late 1960s, the proportion of business leaders on RPA's board began to decline as women, blacks, and Hispanics became directors.
30. John P. Keith, "To Survive in Adversity, Region Must Pull Together," *New York Times*, April 4, 1976. Keith was the president of RPA when he wrote this article.
31. Ibid.
32. For an extensive analysis of the origins and political tribulations of the Metropolitan Rapid Transit Commission, see Jameson W. Doig, *Metropolitan Transportation Politics and the New York Region* (New York: Columbia University Press, 1966).
33. *Jersey Journal*, July 17, 1957.

editorial in the *Perth Amboy Evening News:* "There is no more logic in expecting Middlesex [to help pay for the loop] than to ask this county to make a contribution to improve the transit system of Pittsburgh."[34] These attitudes prevailed in New Jersey, where the MRTC's recommendations died in the legislature in the winter of 1958–1959.

As indicated by the New Jersey reaction to the MRTC, regionalism also arouses fear of New York City. In the New York area as in metropolitan areas across the nation, most advocates of regional cooperation are found in the core. The *New York Times,* the Regional Plan Association, and New York City's political leaders emphasize the common interests of the city and the suburbs, stressing the economic dependence of suburbs on the city, and the need for cooperation rather than competition within the metropolitan community. Similar arguments are heard from mayors, civic leaders, downtown businessmen, and editors in the region's secondary cities, although their frame of reference is almost invariably subregional rather than areawide. As the social, economic, and fiscal problems of the region's older cities have intensified with the steady loss of jobs and white residents, and their replacement by poor blacks and Hispanics, the cry from the cities for closer bonds with their suburbs has become louder and more insistent.

Few suburbanites, however, are moved by either the cities' arguments or their plight. Instead, they fear being swallowed up by the cities and their problems, and especially by New York City. Even the most innocuous proposal for cooperation with an older city is denounced as the forerunner of the loss of local autonomy, racial integration, or unlimited local costs with few benefits to the particular community. Worsening conditions in the older cities prompt suburbanites to lengthen rather than shorten the political distance between themselves and the cities and their residents. In Essex County, for example, Newark's problems have stimulated separatist rather than cooperative sentiments among suburbs unhappy over being forced to pay county taxes which underwrite a substantial portion of Newark's large welfare costs. The nine affluent suburbs beyond First Mountain have proposed secession and the formation of a new county. One of these communities, Livingston, also petitioned the state legislature to transfer the municipality from Essex to Morris County, because "nearly 25 per cent of our property tax income goes to the county for welfare costs [which] are problems of the larger cities, not of our suburban communities."[35]

As indicated earlier, suburbs also are very wary of the brand of regionalism typically marketed by the older cities and their supporters. For the *New York Times,* the RPA, and New York's City Hall, regionalism tends to be what benefits New York City. Regional planning, in the view of city officials, is needed to ensure that businesses are located in concentrated areas and that suburbs are prevented from grabbing "the tax ratables and not the problems— provision for low-income housing, welfare, etc."[36] Constructing a stadium in the marshes of Queens is good regionalism, but building one in the Hacken-

34. *Perth Amboy Evening News,* December 24, 1957.
35. William H. Clark, quoted in the *Newark Evening News,* March 16, 1965.
36. See Michael T. Kaufman, "Nabisco Leaving City for Jersey," *New York Times,* January 4, 1973; and Maurice Carroll, "City Seeks to Mold Suburban Change to Regional Needs," *New York Times,* December 6, 1970.

*Giants Stadium in the Hackensack Meadows, located only fifteen minutes from mid-Manhattan, was opposed by those who define the region largely in terms of New York City.*
Credit: Hackensack Meadowlands Development Commission

sack marshes in New Jersey is regional treason, condemned by the *New York Times* for hastening "the decaying process" of the region and injuring "all those enterprises and people dependent on . . . municipal luster."[37] These sentiments often are echoed in the region's secondary centers. The *Trenton Times*, for example, condemns a proposed shopping mall in suburban Lawrence Township because it "would not make an essential contribution to metropolitan development," while urging the concentration of business in downtown Trenton "in a metropolitan center" which would benefit "the whole area—city and suburbs."[38]

That suburbanites reject a conception of regionalism which sees the area through city lenses is understandable. There are few incentives for suburbs to support the creation of regional instrumentalities designed to skew development away from suburbia and toward the older cities. Reinforcing suburban suspicion that regionalism is a one-way street is the selectivity of city perceptions as to what problems should be dealt with on an areawide basis. A good

37. "The Mets and Jets on Barren Turf," editorial, *New York Times*, February 17, 1977. In 1963, Shea Stadium was built by New York City in Flushing Meadows, Queens, as part of the arrangements that led to the establishment of the New York Mets baseball team. In 1971, the New York Giants football team agreed to move to a new stadium, to be built in the Hackensack Meadowlands by the newly created New Jersey Sports and Exposition Authority, and that agreement generated widespread criticism in New York City. After the new stadium opened in 1976, the New York Jets football team, which shared Shea Stadium with the Mets under somewhat unfavorable conditions, sought to follow the Giants across the Hudson, prompting the editorial cited above.
38. "Spread City," editorial, *Trenton Times*, November 25, 1968.

example of such selective perception is provided by New York City's reaction to a state proposal in 1974 that the city share its water supply with eight suburban counties in a regional system. For New York's Mayor Abraham Beame, a regional approach in a functional area where the city held the upper hand was an "unconscionable assault on the tradition of home rule."[39] Which, of course, is just the way suburbs feel about suggestions that they forego local controls over development in order to promote regionalism by focusing growth in the cities.

Suburbs are also skeptical of the proposition frequently advanced in New York City that regional prosperity requires a healthy city at the core. "If the city goes," New Yorkers insist, "so does the rest of the region."[40] But fewer and fewer suburbanites have a direct economic connection with New York City. Among suburbanites surveyed by the *New York Times* in 1978, only 20 percent of the principal wage earners worked in New York City, and less than 10 percent of the secondary wage earners were employed in the city.[41] Rather than seeing themselves in the same boat with the city, suburbia fears being forced into the city's boat and thus being pulled under by New York's enormous economic, social, and financial problems. The region's secondary centers also share these qualms. In the view of many of their leaders, proximity to New York City has tended to stunt rather than stimulate development of their cities. Nor are state leaders in Connecticut or New Jersey eager to embrace a regional perspective that heavily emphasizes the interdependence of their portions of the area with New York City. Like their local subdivisions, the states want taxable property, jobs, and other prizes that result from successful competition with New York City for desirable development. So do a host of state-oriented interests, since banks, utilities, developers, labor unions, and others in the Garden State and in Connecticut benefit far more directly from development in Bergen County or Stamford than from anything that happens in Manhattan.

These diverse interests make regional competition far more common than areawide cooperation. Instead of joining forces with New York City, the rest of the region commonly tries to take advantage of opportunities presented by the city's problems. A good example is the threatened move of the New York Stock Exchange when the city proposed an increase in stock transfer taxes in 1966. For most of the region, the stock exchange's threat to abandon lower Manhattan was a local opportunity, rather than the regional crisis portrayed in New York's City Hall and on the editorial page of the *New York Times*. Union City in Hudson County offered the Exchange a six-block plot above the Lincoln Tunnel approaches. Dover in Morris County was ready to give the Exchange a 50-acre site. Woodbridge, in Middlesex County, sent 2,500 brochures to stockbrokers throughout the nation promoting its plan to transform the local clay pits into a new business center. Newark, Jersey City, Hoboken, and Weehawken in New Jersey, along with Stamford, Greenwich, and Darien in Connecticut, and North Hempstead on Long Island, entered the

39. Quoted in "Regional Water," editorial, *New York Times*, March 20, 1974. The *Times* criticized Beame for engaging in "just the kind of self-serving parochialism that city leaders have been trying for many years to persuade their suburban colleagues to set aside in the interest of mutual survival."

40. Felix Rohatyn, chairman, Municipal Assistance Corporation, quoted in Michael Sterne, "Economically, Suburbs and City Can't Escape Each Other," *New York Times*, June 13, 1976.

41. *New York Times*, "1978 Suburban Poll" (1978), p. 18.

spirited competition for the valuable prize. The governors of Connecticut and New Jersey sought to bolster their localities' comparative advantage, as each proposed a constitutional amendment to prohibit stock transfer taxes within his state. And the *New York Times* responded with a typical monocular view of the metropolis: "New York offers unique advantages as a market. If the Stock Exchange did move to Hoboken or to the wheatfields of Kansas, it would run the risk of becoming just another regional market."[42]

Although the stock exchange remained in Manhattan after persuading the city to moderate its tax proposals, nearby cities were able to attract some brokerage activities to New Jersey during the next decade. By 1976, 11 firms had located some functions in Jersey City, including one whose move from Manhattan was facilitated by a $2.1 million loan arranged by state officials.

Interstate competition in the region is also illustrated by New Jersey's Economic Development Authority. Created in 1974 to aid industrial and commercial development, the Authority avoids financing projects that would "cause a substantial removal of jobs from one part of the state to another." No such restriction hinders its attempts to lure firms across the Hudson, however, and the agency points with pride to its successful efforts in using tax-exempt financing to attract corporations from the New York sector of the region to the Garden State.[43]

### The Metropolitan Regional Council

Perhaps the best illustration of the barriers to regional integration posed by the size, diversity, and political structure of the New York area is provided by the tribulations of the Metropolitan Regional Council.[44] Initiative for the creation of the organization came from New York's Mayor Robert F. Wagner, who invited more than fifty county and municipal officials to City Hall in 1956 to discuss the possibility of creating a mechanism to facilitate cooperation among local governments in dealing with common problems. Most of Wagner's guests concurred with his conclusion that the existing institutional arrangements in the region were inadequate and that a new metropolitan organization was needed, and they agreed to the formation of a council of local elected officials.[45]

Nine counties in New Jersey and six in New York initially joined the MRC, as did twenty municipalities in addition to New York City.[46] Support

---

42. "Stock Exchange on Rollers," editorial, *New York Times*, March 5, 1966. On the Stock Exchange negotiations, see in particular the *New York Times*, March 4, 1966, February 2 and August 3, 1967, and June 23, 1968.

43. See New Jersey, Economic Development Authority, *Guidelines for Financial Assistance* (Trenton: 1977), p. 4, and *1976 Annual Report* (Trenton: 1977), especially pp. 1–9.

44. The development and political problems encountered by MRC are examined in detail in Joan B. Aron, *The Quest for Regional Cooperation: A Study of the New York Metropolitan Regional Council* (Berkeley, Calif.: University of California Press, 1969).

45. The MRC originally was called the Metropolitan Regional Conference.

46. The New Jersey counties were Bergen, Essex, Hudson, Middlesex, Monmouth, Morris, Passaic, Somerset, and Union; New York's were Nassau, Orange, Putnam, Rockland, Suffolk, and Westchester; and the municipalities other than New York City were Darien, Greenwich, New Canaan, Norwalk, Stamford, and Westport in Connecticut; Elizabeth, Hackensack, Hoboken, Jersey City, Linden, Morristown, Newark, Passaic, Paterson, Plainfield, and Rahway in New Jersey; and New Rochelle, White Plains, and Yonkers in New York.

for the new organization's modest annual budget of $50,000 came entirely from New York City, primarily in the form of city employees who served part-time as the council's staff. Most of the council's members participated in committees that worked on a variety of problems and projects, including park and recreational needs, traffic communications, the rail commuter issue, preparation of a regional housing census, development of a master map of water pollution for the region, and organization of an air pollution alert system.

Despite this encouraging start, many of MRC's leading figures were dissatisfied with its voluntary and unofficial format. The MRC had no legal standing; it was not eligible for federal or state assistance; and it could not tax its members in order to hire a staff and reduce its financial dependence on New York City. Concern with these shortcomings led the MRC to ask the three states for formal recognition as a federation of municipal and county governments. The organization would have no formal operating powers, but it would be authorized to undertake research and promote cooperation among its members. It would also have a full-time staff and be empowered to levy a modest per-capita tax on its member governments.

Few people at the grass roots had been troubled by the initial activities of the MRC or the participation of legal officials in a voluntary organization with no powers. Once the council sought legal status, however, fears of supergovernment and loss of home rule were aroused across the region. Almost all of the suburban speakers at hearings held on the MRC proposal viewed the creation of an official regional council as a potential threat to local autonomy. Typical was the statement of a representative of Greenwich, who indicated that his town did "not want its independent action restricted at any time without [its] full consent."[47] Only at the hearing in New York City was substantial support voiced for a change in MRC's status. Among the regionally oriented interests which dominated this session, the basic issue was whether MRC should be limited to an advisory role or be given the authority to implement its plans and make policy for other public agencies in the region. Talk of the MRC guiding development and acquiring power to implement its plans, however, served only to stimulate further suburban hostility to regional institutions and city-led encroachments on local prerogatives.

Within the MRC, a 1960 canvass of members found support for legal recognition among many of the cities and towns and in several counties. But some of the largest units were wary: Bergen County opposed legal status, financial support, or a full-time MRC staff; Essex County objected to legal recognition; and Nassau and Suffolk counties abstained.[48] Suburban fears of supergovernment and suspicions of New York City hardly were allayed when Mayor Wagner, MRC's chairman and leading spokesman, wrote in 1962 that he foresaw New York in the future as a "supercity" and suggested the need for a "supergovernment to which all local government in the area—along with the three state governments of New York, New Jersey, and Connecticut—will have to yield some of their present authority."[49] By this time, opposition to the MRC throughout the suburbs also was being fanned by right-wing groups

47. Donald H. Mackenzie, quoted in the *New York Times*, November 19, 1958.
48. See Aron, *The Quest for Regional Cooperation*, pp. 28 ff.
49. "Forecast of New York in 2012 A.D.," *New York Times Magazine*, October 7, 1962, p. 7.

which saw the council as the forerunner of a metropolitan government that would force racial integration on the suburbs while communizing local government. Conservative elements in northern New Jersey organized the Tri-State Conference on Community Problems, which campaigned against local ratification of the MRC agreement in Bergen, Union, Morris, and Essex counties.

Ultimately, none of the region's four largest suburban counties—Bergen, Nassau, Suffolk, or Westchester—ratified the agreement. In Suffolk, only three proponents appeared at a public hearing in Riverhead, while thirty-five speakers denounced the MRC. Among the opponents were the Long Island Federation of Women's Clubs, the Committee to Protect Suffolk County from Metropolitan Regional Government, the Citizens Planning Council of Huntington, Young Americans for Freedom, two influential state legislators, Robert Moses (wearing his hat as Long Island State Park Commissioner), and the county's Republican chairman, who saw MRC as "the first step toward total centralization of all government under a huge bureaucracy directed by political appointees" and the means by which New York City "would like to take over control of Suffolk County . . . and make the Eastern seaboard one unit of government with appointed bosses responsible to no one."[50]

Following defeat of its efforts to obtain official status, the MRC almost expired. Meetings were no longer held, committee activity came to a halt, and in 1965 the MRC ceased publishing its bulletin. The following year, the council was revived under the leadership of Mayor John Lindsay of New York. The MRC was to remain a voluntary organization, with legal status secured through incorporation, a move that was not controversial. Having legal status, the MRC became eligible for federal grants from the Department of Housing and Urban Development. Using federal funds and local contributions, MRC carved out a modest role as a voluntary association of local officials. Among its main activities were training programs and a regional communications network.

Despite the usefulness of these activities, the MRC remained a marginal participant in the politics of development in the region. It had no official role, nor any capability to influence public agencies whose decisions affect development. The overall task of regional planning and coordination which MRC's founders sought for the council were assigned to the Tri-State Regional Planning Commission, an agency organized and controlled by the three states. By the late 1970s, MRC membership—never greater than 38 of the region's 700-odd local governments—had dwindled to 15 municipalities, and its few activities were largely funded through grants from Tri-State. Even its main champion, New York City, withdrew as a dues-paying member, and when Tri-State finally ended its financial support in 1979 the Metropolitan Regional Council quietly passed over the River Styx, its death hardly noticed. So it was that in the New York area—in contrast with regions across the nation—immense scale, political complexity, and pervasive fear of regional integration foreclosed an effective local role in the areawide planning process that had emerged in the 1960s.[51]

50. Quoted in Aron, *The Quest for Regional Cooperation*, p. 52.
51. See *Metropolitan Regional Council, 1956–1979* (New York: August 1979), and the exchange of letters between Evan Liblit of the MRC staff and Frank T. Johnson, Tri-State executive director, in the *New York Times*, July 21 and August 4, 1979.

## Agencies of Broad Areal Scope

The remainder of this chapter will analyze the capabilities for shaping development of existing official agencies whose activities encompass substantial portions of the region. As noted at the outset, included in this category are state governments and their components, authorities and other agencies created by the states, and federal agencies. After this general appraisal, the next two chapters turn to a more detailed analysis of the regional agencies that have shaped the area's transportation network.

For this discussion, we divide regional institutions into two general groups. Most of the organizations, whether independent public authorities or line agencies of the state and federal governments, have their attention focused on particular functional problems. A few, however, such as the governors' offices and the Tri-State Regional Planning Commission, are concerned with a broad range of functional areas, and with the combined impact on urban development of various public policies. In dividing regional public agencies into two groups—functional and coordinating institutions—we make a somewhat arbitrary distinction. In practice, government organizations range along a continuum from those with fairly narrow functional responsibilities (for housing, highways, parks, or sewerage) through those with increasingly wide obligations. Consequently, some organizations labeled as functional, such as the state transportation departments and the Port Authority, also provide some coordination across functional lines. And the Tri-State Regional Planning Commission, whose primary role is coordination, began as a transportation agency and has retained a heavy emphasis on transport planning and development.

### *Functional Agencies and the Advantages of a Focused Mission*

Great diversity characterizes the region's major functional institutions. They vary widely in programmatic and areal scope, and in their ability to concentrate resources effectively on development goals. In terms of functional scope, some are highly limited—being concerned, for example, only with a particular toll road, or with parkland in a few counties. Others combine responsibilities in closely related areas, such as rail and highway transportation, or housing and commercial development. The Metropolitan Transportation Authority operates commuter railroads in New York state, as well as New York City subways and buses, the strategic river crossings built by the Triborough Bridge and Tunnel Authority, and airport facilities.[52] New York's Urban Development Corporation is authorized to engage in housing, commercial, industrial, recreational, and civic development. Even broader is the Port Authority's functional scope, encompassing road, rail, airport, harbor, terminal, office, industrial development, and trade responsibilities.

52. The Triborough Bridge and Tunnel Authority was an independent public authority operating within New York City from its founding in 1933 (as the Triborough Bridge Authority) to its merger in 1967 into the Metropolitan Transportation Authority. The MTA now includes the following constituent units in addition to the TBTA: the Long Island Rail Road Company, the New York City Transit Authority, Stewart Airport Land Authority, Staten Island Rapid Transit Operating Authority, and two bus units, the Manhattan and Bronx Surface Transit Operating Authority, and the Metropolitan Suburban Bus Authority.

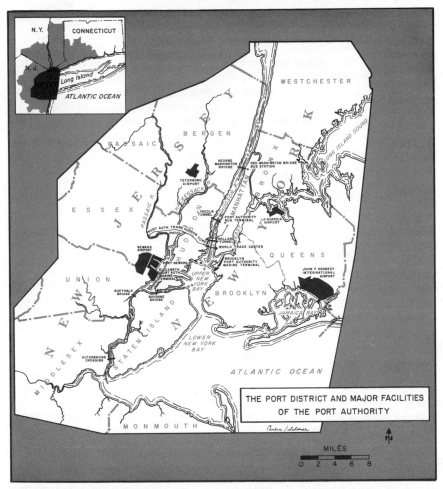

THE PORT DISTRICT AND MAJOR FACILITIES
OF THE PORT AUTHORITY

**MAP 7**

As to areal scope, most functional agencies in the region are limited to a single state or an area within a state. The state transportation departments and housing finance agencies operate throughout each state. Among functional agencies with more limited territorial jurisdictions are the Metropolitan Transportation Authority, the state toll road authorities, the Urban Development Corporation, the Connecticut Public Transportation Authority, and the Hackensack Meadowlands Development Commission, the latter agency being restricted to 19,600 acres of strategically located marshland in Hudson and Bergen counties. The bistate Port Authority has broader areal scope, operating facilities in a port district that extends in a radius of approximately twenty-five miles from the Statue of Liberty (as shown in Map 7), and the Tri-State Regional Planning Commission extends still further, with a planning area that includes 24 of the region's 31 counties. Even broader, of course, is the territorial scope of the federal functional agencies—the Federal Highway Administration, the Urban Mass Transportation Administration, the Federal Aviation

Administration, the Corps of Engineers, and the specialized programs administered by the Department of Housing and Urban Development.

With reference to the third development variable—the ability to concentrate resources to achieve specific developmental goals—the variations are particularly complex. As outlined in Chapter One, seven factors are especially important in assessing developmental influence. Differences in the first two factors—formal independence of other governments in policy-making and in obtaining and allocating funds, and the variety and intensity of constituency demands upon an agency—are especially important in understanding the impact of functional agencies on urban development.

In the case of formal independence, one could distinguish between the semi-independent public authority and the typical line agency of a state or the federal government. The following four-way division, however, is more useful. First, some functional organizations are highly autonomous. Their governing boards are composed mainly of "independent citizens" rather than persons holding other governmental positions and serving ex officio. Also, their funds are largely derived from their own facilities, through tolls and rents, rather than being allocated from tax revenues by legislatures and political executives. In the New York region, the New Jersey Turnpike Authority and the Port Authority illustrate this category of relatively independent functional agencies.

Other agencies are moderately independent. Their funds are largely self-generated, but their governing boards are composed at least partly of persons holding other full-time government posts. The New Jersey Housing Finance Agency is an example. The agency's chairman is the commissioner of the Department of Community Affairs, and two of the other four members also head major state departments. In this situation, the organization will probably be responsive to the policy concerns represented through overlapping membership on the governing board.

A third group of organizations reverses these constraints. While their governing boards are largely independent, they rely substantially on external funding, which requires them to compete with other demands on the resources of general units of governments. The Metropolitan Transportation Authority illustrates this situation in its operation of the deficit-ridden Long Island Rail Road and New York City subway system. New York's Urban Development Corporation also has been unable to generate sufficient revenue from its projects to provide an independent financial base. As a result, the corporation had to depend heavily on state funds and federal housing subsidies. This dependence crippled the UDC when federal housing funds were severely restricted during the last years of the Nixon Administration. Declining federal support combined with inadequate project revenues and other fiscal problems to prevent the UDC from selling bonds needed to finance its program, leading to the agency's financial collapse in 1975, and a severe contraction of its programs before a firmer financial footing was achieved in 1977.[53]

53. The UDC's financial problems are examined in *Restoring Credit and Confidence: A Reform Program for New York State and Its Public Authorities*, A Report to the Governor by the New York State Moreland Act Commission on the Urban Development Corporation and Other State Financing Agencies (New York: March 1976).

Finally, some functional agencies are formally dependent. As operating subdivisions of the state or national government, they are under direct authority of an elected official and his appointed agency head, and also must compete for funds in the general budgetary and appropriations processes. An example is the New Jersey Department of Transportation. Somewhat more independent financially, at least with respect to road building, are the transportation departments in the other two states, since Connecticut and New York dedicate gasoline taxes to highway construction. The Federal Highway Administration and its predecessor, the Bureau of Public Roads, also have enjoyed greater financial independence than most federal functional agencies, because gasoline and other taxes dedicated to road building supply a significant share of its funds.

Functional agencies rarely confront constituency demands that are as varied and intense as those which form the standard fare for mayors, governors, and legislators. Even so, the behavior and roles in urban development of these organizations are affected by differing patterns of public pressure. For some agencies, external pressure is focused on a narrow set of issues, and is of low intensity. For example, some turnpike authorities deal mostly with demands for good traffic conditions (and at times for expansion in the number of lanes) over routes determined long ago, as well as intermittent conflict over proposed toll increases. Other agencies, with more varied functions, must be more sensitive to competing interests in setting policy and investing resources. For example, the Port Authority has constituencies that seek additional investment in harbor terminals or rail service, from funds that might otherwise be used to expand the World Trade Center or add to airport facilities. Still other functional agencies, such as the highway departments, must balance directly conflicting demands—for new highways, and for avoiding local disruption where those highways would be constructed—while at the same time competing for funds in the legislative arena with other public agencies.

When constituency demands are intense and involve conflicting goals, the development activities of even the most powerful functional agencies can be checked. This is especially true when pressures are brought to bear on general governments having authority over the functional organization. An example is the Port Authority's inability to build a fourth airport, in the face of a broad coalition of grass-roots interests supported by key state and federal officials. Also, as seen in Chapter Four, the ability of the region's highway agencies to implement their plans has been sharply reduced as environmental restraints have enchanced the influence of those who oppose particular highway facilities and alignments.

Even when a functional agency has a high degree of formal independence, it will sometimes find that the few remaining strings of broader public control can be tightened abruptly. In the case of the fourth jetport, for example, the need for legislative action to expand the port district provided a crucial route for constituency action to prevent the Port Authority from constructing its airport in the Great Swamp. Similarly, the need for formal approval by the state legislature before the New Jersey Turnpike could be extended into Monmouth and Ocean Counties allowed opponents to contest the proposed road in the state's general political arenas, rather than within the unpromising decision-making confines of the New Jersey Turnpike Authority.

Constituency pressures may also become so intense that the functional agency suffers a significant loss of formal independence. A case in point is the authority of the Urban Development Corporation to override local zoning and building codes in order to develop its projects. When the UDC tried to use these powers to build low- and moderate-income housing in the affluent suburbs of northern Westchester County, intense pressures were brought to bear on state legislators to strip the public corporation of its override power. The UDC was particularly vulnerable at the time (1973) because of its deepening financial problems, and legislative authorization for $500 million in bonds was desperately needed. To get the money UDC had to relinquish its power over local land-use controls in suburbs, and in the process its ability to have any significant impact on suburban housing patterns.[54]

Despite these great variations in scope, formal independence, and constituency demands, the region's functional agencies share several characteristics that greatly enhance their ability to significantly affect urban development. Most important is the narrow functional perspective these agencies bring to bear on every problem. This perspective, shaped by statute and reinforced by the background and experience of the agency's officials, tends to ensure that the organization will be insensitive to many of the values that are affected by its actions. There is nothing like a wide perspective and concern with the multiplicity of human problems in a metropolis to render a participant immobile. In contrast, there are few characteristics more valuable in "getting the job done" than a vigorous, single-minded concentration on, for example, placing a highway where land costs are lowest.[55]

This limited focus is strengthened by the pattern of organizational relationships which has evolved in important areas that affect urban development. Commonly, the most active constituencies of functional agencies are the trucking and automobile associations, real estate entrepreneurs, and other private interests that expect to benefit from agency activities. Moreover, alliances have been created among federal, state, and local agencies in various functional areas, and through these alliances, substantial amounts of funds—especially from the federal government—have been made available to finance particular functional programs. Access to these funds reduces a functional agency's dependence on funds controlled by state and local elected officials, and thus decreases the responsiveness of these organizations to broader policy concerns felt in the offices of the governors and mayors. Insulation from such concerns also occurs, of course, when agency funds are largely derived from its own revenue-producing projects.

As a result of these circumstances, policy decisions in important program areas often do not evolve from public discussion of alternatives and their implications. Instead, they frequently are determined by informal, low-

54. The state legislature permitted the UDC to retain its power to override local codes in older cities. For a general discussion of the UDC, local zoning, and the state legislature, see Danielson, *The Politics of Exclusion*, pp. 306–322.

55. These observations, are not, of course, intended as an endorsement of a narrow approach to urban development. Some of the "accomplishments" that result from the tunnel vision of functional agencies are projects that should never have been undertaken at all, or that would have been more useful (at least by some criteria) if they had been modified with regard to a broader perspective on the urban development process.

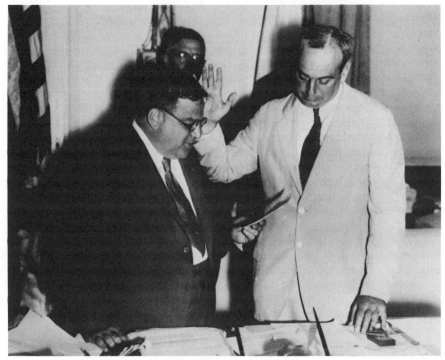

*Mayor Fiorello LaGuardia swears in Robert Moses as a member of the Triborough Bridge Authority in 1935.*
Credit: Triborough Bridge and Tunnel Authority

visibility negotiations among government agencies in a particular functional area, joined or supported by prospective beneficiaries in the private sector. These constituency relationships stand in sharp contrast to the variety of conflicting public demands that confront, for example, the mayors of the region's older cities.

Another key advantage of many functional agencies is their ability to attract skillful leadership. The organizational and financial autonomy of these enterprises provides opportunities for their leaders to exercise significant influence. Consequently, individuals who like to wield power—especially when visible and dramatic achievements can result—and who are skilled in the use of power are attracted to these organizations. Robert Moses was the archetype of the political leader whose influence derived from personal chemistry joined with the organizational and financial independence available to leaders of the public authority. With great energy, vision, and ruthlessness, Moses welded the Triborough Bridge and Tunnel Authority, the Long Island Park Commission, and other functional agencies into a formidable power base, and in the process exercised substantial influence on the region's development.[56] Other major public corporations in the region have also at-

56. Moses's career is examined in exhaustive detail in Robert A. Caro, *The Power Broker: Robert Moses and the Fall of New York* (New York: Alfred A. Knopf, 1974). For a different version of his accomplishments, see Robert Moses, *Public Works: A Dangerous Trade* (New York: McGraw-Hill, 1970).

tracted highly skilled leaders, such as Austin Tobin at the Port Authority, William Ronan of the Metropolitan Transportation Authority, and Edward Logue of the Urban Development Corporation.

In addition to strong leadership, these agencies can draw on large and able staffs, and on a host of specialized consultants. Public authorities are in a better position than line functional agencies (e.g., state highway departments) with respect to staff and consultant resources, since the authorities are generally less constrained by civil service regulations and formalized bidding procedures. Formally autonomous agencies also are less vulnerable to outside political pressures to hire particular individuals or consulting firms. Of all the region's functional agencies, the most impressive staff resources have been developed by the Port Authority, which is run by a corps of well-paid officials, many of whom have spent much of their careers with the authority and are strongly committed to the agency's relatively narrow organizational and developmental goals. Over the years, this group usually has provided the Port Authority with skillful financial management, effective long-range and project planning, efficient project development and management, and imaginative public relations.

Finally, functional agencies frequently demonstrate strong planning capabilities, compared with other organizations in the metropolis. As defined in Chapter One, planning is the "application of foresight to achieve certain preestablished goals in the growth and development of urban areas." For general urban planning agencies, and for many program agencies, this activity is fraught with difficulties. Long-range goals are frequently unclear, and the extent to which particular programs aid in achieving broader goals (when such goals can be specified) is very difficult to measure. These problems are more tractable in functional agencies concerned with highways, bridges, urban development projects, and other programs where direct output can be assessed in quantitative terms, such as miles of highways built, or traffic flow improved, or land cleared. Consequently, these organizations often develop skilled and aggressive planning staffs, whose members are of great value to the agency's leaders in providing guidance regarding specific strategies that will maximize the organization's ability to achieve its long-run goals.[57]

---

57. See, for example, Harold Kaplan, *Urban Renewal Politics: Slum Clearance in Newark* (New York: Columbia University Press, 1963). This discussion touches on a broader set of issues regarding an organization's "goals." Analytically, three distinct kinds of goals are pursued by officials of functional agencies (and all other organizations as well). First, there are external goals, those purposes the organization was created to accomplish. In the case of urban development, these include goals like improved transportation, better housing, or a more prosperous economy. Such goals provide the public rationale for government action in various policy areas, and they are usually stated in the statutes that establish the agency.

Second, there is the goal of organizational maintenance. At the most basic level, this refers to keeping the organization in existence. More broadly, it involves protecting the ability of the organization's officials to exercise discretion in making decisions and allocating resources, so that the organization can grow in size and influence.

The third goal is personal maintenance. Individuals often join an organization because they support its external goals. And they may, especially after long service, come to identify with the agency's survival and growth. But most organization members will sacrifice or disregard external goals and organizational-maintenance goals if pursuit of those goals is likely to conflict with personal self-interest. Such conflicts occur if agency policies intended to achieve those broader goals

These characteristics of functional agencies do not operate in isolation from one another. As the discussion above suggests, they reinforce and strengthen each other. The narrow path set by statute justifies functionally limited planning and action, and discourages political opponents—who might challenge narrowly focused policy were it not already legitimized by statute and rule. Insulated revenue sources, combined with this legitimacy, encourage leaders to act vigorously and decisively, and attract those who seek public influence unencumbered by the need for wide consultation and compromise.

We are not arguing, however, that these organizations operate without constraints. Compared with general governmental units such as the governor's office, their scope is restricted functionally, although such program areas as highways and housing tend to have a wide collateral influence in shaping development. Some are highly restricted in areal scope as well, being limited to particular sectors of the region. This limitation is mitigated, however, through vertical and horizontal alliances in such areas as road building, which tend to ensure similar policies and results across much of the metropolis. The operation of such an alliance in the case of highway construction is examined in the next chapter. In addition, these agencies often find their lack of control over land to be an important obstacle to action. Examples of the delays and failures that result from this limitation are recorded in Chapter Four, where the highway agencies' struggles to complete major routes and the unsuccessful effort of the Port Authority to locate a site for a fourth jetport are described.

Moreover, like all institutions, functional agencies are faced with the continual necessity to adapt to change. The inability of Robert Moses to adjust to changing development values and political realities, as well as the decline of his personal skills with advancing age, eventually cost the Triborough Bridge and Tunnel Authority its independence. The failure of road building agencies in the region and the nation to secure additional sources of revenue for new projects greatly constrained their developmental capabilities in recent years. And the sharpened public interest in official misconduct in the post-Watergate era—as well as heightened interest on the part of journalists and their editors in corruption and improper official behavior—made the revelations of expense-account padding on the part of some Port Authority officials far more damaging to the agency's image and credibility in 1977 than it would have been a decade earlier.[58]

---

are viewed as likely to affect adversely a member's personal well-being (e.g., leading to his being fired, demoted, fined, or merely inconvenienced in his regular activities within the organization).

Generally, an organization's policies cannot be understood by reference to only one of these kinds of goals. Decisions that enhance the prestige of agency leaders, for example, often increase the prospects for the agency's continuance and expansion as well. And not infrequently, such decisions do advance at least some of the organization's external goals. But a pattern of action that seems to undermine some of the agency's external goals, while strengthening its survival aims and perhaps some personal-interest values, is common enough to justify making this distinction among different aspects of an organization's goals.

58. A 1960 investigation of the Port Authority by Representative Emanuel Celler of Brooklyn, a longtime critic of the agency, produced some evidence of improper activity on the part of the Port Authority, but these disclosures had little impact at the time on the PNYA's reputation for probity and businesslike efficiency; see Doig, *Metropolitan Transportation and the New York Region*, pp. 263–264, 299–300; and U.S. House of Representatives, Committee on the Judiciary, *Port of New York Authority*, Hearings before Subcommittee No. 5, 86th Congress, second session (Washington: U.S. Government Printing Office, 1960). The 1977 investigations are discussed in Chapter Seven.

In summary, the activities of functional agencies tend to be characterized by narrowly focused rationality rather than responsiveness to a broad
range of constituency interests. While the general political leadership of the
older city, a state, or the nation must be sensitive to a wide variety of demands, the program agency enjoys a substantial degree of isolation from these
pressures. Statutory and financial insulation are joined with skilled leadership and specific yardsticks of success to permit the functional organization
to calculate its future goals and current strategies more clearly, and with
greater likelihood of success, than is true for hard-pressed mayors, governors,
or members of Congress. The cumulative result is a set of organizations that
operate from narrow perspectives and yet can have a broad impact on urban
development in the region.[59]

### The Coordinating Agencies: Modest Resources and Multiple Constraints

We now turn to those institutions which have the broadest range of
public concerns with urban development: the three states, the federal government, and their coordinating agency in the New York area—the Tri-State
Regional Planning Commission. Our concern, however, is not with the states
and the federal government as a whole. As pointed out above, most state and
federal agencies whose actions have an impact on urban development are
limited to narrow functional concerns. Our interest in this section is those
regional actors who are responsible for the interrelationship of programs
across a wide range of development areas. At the state level, these include the
governor's office, the legislature, and the agencies responsible for regional
planning and development; at the federal level, the President and his staff,
Congress, and the Department of Housing and Urban Development; and
within the region, the Tri-State Regional Planning Commission. For some of
these actors, such as the gubernatorial office in a state, the coordinating role is
an inevitable part of a general responsibility for policy-making and resource
allocation. For other coordinating agencies, such as the New Jersey Department of Community Affairs, functional scope is more restricted but still em-
braces a wide range of state and local policies that affect urban development.

Although the explicit coordinating responsibilities of these organizations imply that they have a major role in shaping urban development, in fact
their influence as coordinators is greatly restricted, for a number of reasons.
First, the most powerful of these organizations—the executive and legislative
units at the state and federal levels—devote much of their time and resources
to issues that do not have a primary influence on the pattern of urban development. The White House and Congress are preoccupied with foreign affairs,
defense, national economic policy, and general social programs. At the state
level, urban development competes for executive and legislative attention
with a variety of other matters, such as education, health, welfare, and criminal justice. Moreover, many federal or state issues with important implications for urban development—such as energy policy, interest rates, environ-

59. The perspectives and behavior of public authorities are analyzed in Annmarie Hauck
Walsh, *The Public's Business: The Politics and Practices of Government Corporations* (Cambridge,
Mass.: MIT Press, 1978). On the nature of authority leadership, see especially Chapters 7–8.

mental constraints, or school-aid distribution formulas— rarely are considered in Washington or the state capitals primarily in terms of their impact on the distribution of residences, jobs, and transportation facilities.

A second limitation is the existence of significant state and federal constituencies that lie beyond the New York region. In 1975, 33 percent of New York State's population lived outside the region, as did 21 percent of New Jersey's inhabitants and 45 percent of the residents of Connecticut. Approximately the same proportion of each state's legislators represent districts wholly or largely outside the metropolis. Moreover, because of the region's size and complexity, most of the state legislators whose districts were within the tri-state area did not perceive the region as a whole as a relevant frame of reference either for themselves or their constituents. City-suburban conflict divides the New York area's representatives in all three state legislatures, and is particularly sharp in New York State—where suburban legislators are far more likely to make common cause with upstaters against New York City than to join forces with the city's representatives in Albany. For their part, governors and their staffs tend to think in statewide rather than regional terms on most issues.

Similar considerations are at work in Washington. Less than 10 percent of the nation's population lives in the region, and the proportion steadily declines as people move south and west. Only thirty-eight members of Congress had districts primarily in the region in the 1970s. And the diversity of their constituencies combines with individual differences within the area's congressional delegation to foreclose cohesive action on most federal issues affecting the New York region. At the White House and in federal coordinating agencies, the primary concern is with general national policies rather than with the problems of individual regions. As a result, urban development programs emanating from Washington often fail to take account of the special problems raised by the nation's largest and most complex metropolitan area.

Another restraint on these coordinating agencies is the absence of a political culture of constituency demands that are favorable to broad-gauged planning and coordination. Most of the demands from the region that are pressed upon governors or Congress come from specific functional or territorial interests. Underlying this structure of demand is a political heritage in the United States that favors public policy outcomes resulting from bargaining among organized interests, and which gives rise to suspicion when "comprehensive planning" by central units of government is advocated.[60]

In confronting this antagonism to planning, central organizations bring varying strengths and limitations. The potential influence of elective institutions—the President and Congress, the governors and state legislatures—is substantial when measured in terms of their high degree of formal independence and financial capacity. The states also possess potential control over land use in every city and town. Yet the ability of these political institutions to shape urban development is heavily constrained, both by the diversity of

60. See, for example, Alan Altshuler, *The City Planning Process* (Ithaca, N.Y.: Cornell University Press, 1965), and Edward Banfield, *Political Influence* (New York: Free Press of Glencoe, 1961).

constituencies and an "antiplanning" tradition, and by several characteristics that flow out of and reinforce these conditions. Actual control over the use of land has been ceded by the states to municipalities. A variety of public authorities have been given a wide measure of formal autonomy and fiscal independence from central control. Moreover, elected officials rarely have urban planning units attached to their own offices.

In sum, the institutions with the greatest potential influence would face considerable obstacles should they attempt to establish goals for urban areas and shape public policy to achieve these objectives. Moreover, elected officials often share in their personal attitudes the widespread belief in the advantages of local and functional autonomy. And, regardless of personal preferences, they commonly seek to avoid involvement in such conflict-laden issues as coordinated planning, where proponents are likely to be denounced for "undermining home rule" or for "playing politics" with independent agencies.

All of these constraints are illustrated by the failure of various efforts to have state governments exercise greater control over land use in the region's suburbs. Legally, the three state governments have complete power over their subdivisions. They can restrict local zoning authority so as to eliminate large-lot zoning or prevent certain types of commercial activity. Or the states could take back the powers to regulate land use which have been delegated to local government, either performing the function themselves or assigning it to the counties or regional agencies. The legal potential of the states is largely neutralized, however, by political realities. All local governments—in older cities, rural areas, and suburbs—perceive a common interest in maximizing local control over local turf. These interests are well-represented in the legislatures of Connecticut, New Jersey, and New York. In addition, all three states have strong home-rule traditions that provide a rationale for those who defend the municipal status quo in zoning.

As a consequence, measures that threaten local control over land in the name of more rational and coordinated development rarely attract much support in the state capitals. In 1967, suburban opposition foreclosed action on a Connecticut bill setting one acre as the maximum lot size in the state. The fight against the bill was led by officials from Darien, New Canaan, and other affluent suburbs in Fairfield County where lots of two to four acres were common. Proponents of the bill argued that zoning laws designed "to keep the peasants out are putting out the flame under America's melting pot." Suburban opponents answered that "the issue is simply whether or not communities can continue to determine their own destinies"; and countered with a proposal that the state constitution be amended to guarantee municipal control over land-use regulation.[61]

Two years later, a furor developed in New Jersey when the administration of Governor Richard J. Hughes sought to take away some of the authority delegated to local governments in the Municipal Zoning Enabling Act of 1928.

---

61. Representative Norris L. O'Neill, Democrat of Hartford, and Representative Lowell P. Weicker, Jr., Republican of Greenwich, quoted in William Borders, "Suburban Zoning is Again Attacked," *New York Times*, March 26, 1967. Weicker at the time was also first selectman (i.e., mayor) of Greenwich.

The proposed law required local zoning ordinances to consider the housing needs of all economic groups, as well as regional transportation and open space requirements, and state, county, and regional plans. It prohibited the use of zoning to exclude anyone for racial, religious, or ethnic reasons, and shifted the burden of proof in such matters from the challenger to the municipality. Also proposed was a state role in land-use regulation in flood plains and in areas adjacent to airports, highways, and parks. Less than two weeks after the proposals were made public, adverse reaction had become so vehement that Commissioner Paul N. Ylvisaker, whose Department of Community Affairs had developed the new legislation, found it necessary to begin a discussion of the issue by emphasizing what was *not* in the bill: "There is no state zoning. There is no reduction in local zoning power," Ylvisaker insisted. "There is nothing here that can force a municipality to provide low-income housing. . . . No state planning czar or super-agency is created to oversee local zoning."[62] But Ylvisaker failed to put local fears to rest. Municipal opposition was overwhelming, and legislators responded to their constituencies by killing the bill in committee.

In New York, state legislators gave short shrift in 1971 to proposals to prohibit discriminatory zoning, establish state standards for acreage and floor space in new housing, and require that towns which zoned for industry also zone some areas for housing within the financial means of industrial workers. At the same time, another effort was underway in New Jersey to modify suburban land-use controls in order to ease what Governor William T. Cahill called the state's "crisis in housing."[63] Although Cahill's actual proposals were modest, his tough talk about "statewide zoning" and the need for "harsher measures if nothing else works" alarmed local officials and legislators.[64] Reaction was so vehement that Cahill was abandoned by most fellow Republicans in the legislature, and his program perished in committee. Suburban dissatisfaction with what opponents of the zoning proposals called a "Cahill power grab" also played a part in the governor's defeat in his bid for renomination in the 1973 Republican primary, at the hands of a vigorous defender of local autonomy.[65]

Cahill's successor, Democrat Brendan Byrne, was equally unsuccessful

62. Quoted in Arthur G. Kent, "The Zoning Issue: A Study of Politics and Public Policy in New Jersey" (Senior Thesis, Princeton University, 1972), p. 44. Kent provides a useful account of the local and legislative reaction to Ylvisaker's proposal.

63. *A Blueprint for Housing in New Jersey*, A Special Message to the Legislature by William T. Cahill, Governor of New Jersey (December 7, 1970). Cahill, a Republican, succeeded Governor Richard J. Hughes in January, 1970, following his successful 1969 campaign against former Governor Robert B. Meyner.

64. Quoted in Earl Josephson, "Cahill Wants Zoning Solutions," *Trenton Times*, August 13, 1970; and Ronald Sullivan, "U.A.W. Maintains a Jersey Suburb Keeps Out Poor," *New York Times*, January 28, 1971. Cahill's housing and land-use program called for state-determined quotas for low-income housing with voluntary compliance by municipalities, creation of a Community Development Corporation whose proposed projects would be subject to local veto, a uniform statewide building code, and simplification of the laws governing local zoning. The proposal for state-determined housing quotas was the most controversial element of the package.

65. John Chappell, president, United Citizens for Home Rule, quoted in Dan Weissman, "Home Rule: Local Forces Line Up Against Statewide Planning Bills," *Newark Sunday Star-Ledger*, April 24, 1973. Cahill was defeated in the primary by Representative Charles W. Sandman, Jr., who then was beaten in the general election by Brendan T. Byrne.

in persuading the legislature to alter local control over zoning. On the most controversial aspect of the zoning issue—the provision of low-income housing in the suburbs—Byrne sought to bypass the legislature by directing the Department of Community Affairs to prepare a "fair share" plan which would provide low-income housing guidelines for each community in the state. Localities that failed to comply with the plan could face the loss of state aid for education, sewers, and other programs. Suburban legislators attacked Byrne, challenging in state court his authority to alter local control over land by means of an executive order, and proposing an amendment to the state constitution that would safeguard local zoning.[66] In the face of suburban hostility, Byrne soft-pedaled his support for dispersing low-income housing and emphasized the need for rehabilitation in the older cities rather than new subsidized construction in the suburbs.[67]

Appointed officials concerned with urban development and regional planning tend to be more oriented than most elected officials toward the advantages of broader coordination. Career officials of state planning agencies usually have been involved in developing the housing and land-use proposals which legislators have resisted. Despite their location in state agencies with access to the governor, however, state planners and other appointive officials with broad perspectives typically play modest roles. State plans do not govern the actions of local governments or other state agencies. As a result, state planners offer advice and serve as public advocates for a broad-gauge approach to urban development, while—as described in Chapter Three—local governments regulate actual land use using very different criteria. And functional state agencies undertake the highway, sewer, water, and other public projects which strongly influence the pattern of development in the region.

Federal efforts to coordinate urban development are thwarted by similar forces and pressures. Most federal resources reach the metropolitan area through functional programs—for roads, sewers, water supply, mass transportation, mortgage insurance, and a variety of other housing, transport, and community development programs. Functional agencies and their clienteles have strongly resisted efforts that threaten to dilute the specific goals of narrowly focused programs. For example, the attempt by the Department of Housing and Urban Development in 1969 to use water and sewer grants as a lever to force suburbs to accept lower-income housing was successfully resisted by beneficiaries of the grant program and their supporters in Congress. Bergen County's Republican congressman, William B. Widnall, led the attack against HUD's efforts, arguing that local needs for water and sewers rather than regional housing considerations "should be primary" in distributing federal funds under the program.[68]

66. See Ronald Sullivan, "Housing Goals: List Stirs Debate," *New York Times*, September 19, 1976; and Martin Waldron, "What Limit Executive Power?" *New York Times*, July 17, 1977.

67. See State of New Jersey, Division of State and Regional Planning, *A Statewide Housing Allocation Plan for New Jersey*, Preliminary Draft for Public Discussion (Trenton: November 1976); Ramona Smith, "Governor Waffles on Poverty Housing," *Trenton Times*, December 9, 1976; and Joseph F. Sullivan, "A Softening of Some Issues," *New York Times*, December 10, 1976.

68. Quoted in Barbara Gill, "Readington May Seek U.S. Aid Again," *Trenton Sunday Times Advertiser*, August 8, 1971. Widnall was one of the original sponsors of the water and sewer legislation, as well as the ranking minority member of the Banking and Currency Committee which handled the water and sewer program and other HUD activities.

Efforts by HUD to coordinate and guide urban development are also weakened by its own functional activities. Water and sewer officials in HUD were much more interested in advancing their program than in spreading low-income housing—especially since the housing objectives aroused suburban and congressional hostility, and thus threatened the water and sewer program. Similarly, the broad goals of the Housing and Community Development Act of 1974, which sought to increase housing opportunities in the suburbs, have been subordinated to HUD's desire to maximize suburban participation in the community development grant program. In the program's initial years, HUD made little effort to ensure that participating suburbs were preparing housing plans that complied with the statutory federal requirements.

Because of these constraints, federal officials concerned with urban development have attempted to encourage coordination through institutional development at the metropolitan level. A principal federal goal has been the creation of areawide institutions capable of planning comprehensively and of coordinating the development activities of local, regional, state, and national agencies. Federal grants have been available for comprehensive planning since the late 1950s. Beginning with the Federal-Aid Highway Act of 1962, an expanding list of federal functional grants in metropolitan areas has been conditioned on the existence of a comprehensive planning process carried on by state and local governments. Since 1966, Congress has required that all applications for federal grants in a number of key urban programs be reviewed by a regional agency to ensure that the project was "consistent with comprehensive planning developed or in the process of development for the metropolitan area."[69]

In response to these federal requirements, regional agencies sprang up in every metropolitan area in the nation, and they soon were grinding out all sorts of comprehensive plans. Few of these agencies, however, have evolved into influential participants in the development process. Most were organized in order to ensure the continued flow of federal aid, not because of strong commitment to regionalism on the part of local or state officials. A number have been dominated by highway interests because the earliest federal requirements for comprehensive planning dealt with roads and mass transit. Consequently, most of the plans produced by these agencies reflect the particularized interests of existing governments in the area and of major functional groupings. Controversial issues typically are avoided, particularly those arising from social, economic, tax, and service differences in the metropolis. With few exceptions, regional agencies have not obtained control over land use, important operating responsibilities, an independent financial base, or other means of ensuring the implemention of their plans.[70]

Reinforcing the weakness of the regional coordinating agencies has been the ambiguity of the federal government's commitment to its metropolitan offspring. Little real power has been provided to these agencies by Washing-

---

69. Section 204, Demonstration Cities and Metropolitan Development Act of 1966, 80 *U.S. Statutes at Large* (1966), p. 1262. Under this law, programs subject to review were airports, highways, other transportation facilities, sewers, water supply, open space, conservation, hospitals, law enforcement, and libraries. Over the next decade, scores of other federal grants were added to the list, which totalled over 140 grant programs in the mid-1970s.

70. See, for example, Melvin B. Mogulof, *Governing Metropolitan Areas: A Critical Review of Council of Governments and the Federal Role* (Washington: Urban Institute, 1971).

ton, largely because of resistance by functional agencies and grass-roots interests to any authoritative role for general-purpose regional bodies. Thus regional agencies evaluate federal grant requests in terms of their compatibility with metropolitan plans, but federal agencies that administer the various aid programs are free to disregard their recommendations. And when general revenue sharing and block grants for community development were initiated in the early 1970s, neither program made any provision for distributing funds to metropolitan agencies. Instead, all federal assistance was allocated to local governments, thus reinforcing their development capabilities and reducing further the relatively weak role of regional planning units in the development process.

In the New York area, federal ambiguity has combined with the region's size and complexity to produce a coordinating agency with almost no independent influence on urban development. The Tri-State Regional Planning Commission was created by the three states to ensure federal funding of highway and transit projects in the metropolis. Organized as the Tri-State Transportation Committee in 1961, the agency initially served as a planning and coordinating body for the major transportation agencies in the region. Its functional scope expanded in 1971, not in response to pressures from within the region for a broad-gauged planning body, but because Washington steadily increased the list of grant programs covered by comprehensive planning and review requirements.[71]

Despite its functional expansion, Tri-State remained heavily skewed in the direction of its original transportation mission. Throughout the 1970s, five of the nine state officials on the commission were from transportation agencies, as were three of the five federal members.[72] The Port Authority has been closely involved with Tri-State from its beginnings. A top Port Authority official was "loaned" to Tri-State at the outset to organize the new agency as its first executive director, and the Port Authority has always been represented on the commission by a nonvoting member. Tri-State's top staff also reflects its transportation origins. Its executive director from its founding to 1978 was a transportation planner, as were many of his deputies. Inevitably, Tri-State's general orientation has reflected its initial tasks, the interests of its dominant commissioners, and the perspectives of its staff. As a result, Tri-State has naturally tended to look at the region through the prism of transportation needs and facilities.

Tri-State's perspective also is strongly influenced by the dominant role of state officials on the agency. The commission was created by the states, and from the beginning it has primarily served state interests—and particularly those of their transportation agencies. Nine of the 15 commissioners are state

71. The agency was renamed the Tri-State Transportation Commission in 1965 following the passage of enabling legislation in the three states. Six years later its name was changed to the Tri-State Regional Planning Commission to reflect its broadened functional scope over water and sewer grants.

72. The five state transportation officials included the heads of the three Departments of Transportation, the chairman of the Connecticut Public Transportation Authority, and the chairman of the Metropolitan Transportation Authority. The three federal transport officials were the regional directors of the Federal Aviation Administration, the Federal Highway Administration, and the Urban Mass Transportation Administration.

officials, and all but one of the local members is a gubernatorial appointee.[73] Tri-State's agenda is set largely by the states, the chairman of the commission has always been a state official, and state representatives dominate the agency's executive committee. Discussions within Tri-State typically are framed in terms of state interests, priorities, and objectives. From the beginning, state officials on Tri-State have functioned almost exclusively as representatives of their agencies and their states. Given the structure of the commission—five members from each state, with voting arrangements requiring that a majority of each state delegation agrees with a proposal—all of the commissioners tend to think of themselves primarily as members of state delegations, whether they are state officials or not. Because of this structure the commission functions essentially as a logrolling body, with almost all decisions made on the basis of an implicit agreement that "you back my plan and I'll back yours."[74] As a result, Tri-State has reinforced the major political divisions of the region rather than mute them with an areawide perspective.

Within this framework, Tri-State's staff has primarily served the states rather than the abstraction called the "region." The commission's work is almost entirely derivative, reflecting the development goals and particularly the transportation-oriented priorities of its dominant members. The staff maintains a low profile, emphasizing its technical role and seeking to avoid controversy and publicity. Staff work is long on data, and short on analysis and recommendations. As the Regional Plan Association notes, "the Tri-State staff performs like a consulting firm, primarily providing data and responding to study requests of state and federal agencies. They seldom take the initiative to raise hard issues for Commission consideration, and little of their research reaches the public."[75] Tri-State's basic regional development guide has been characterized as "a vague mixture of what will happen and what should happen [which] masks rather than illuminates the critical issues."[76] Until the late 1970s, public attention rarely was directed to Tri-State's plans or reports; hearings were not held on its proposals; few reporters or group representatives attended meetings; and many major regional issues—such as the fourth jetport controversy—never came before the commission.

Tri-State also is constrained by the pervasive fear of regionalism discussed earlier in the chapter. An effort by the commission to play the independent planning and development role advocated by the *New York Times* and the Regional Plan Association would be opposed by suburban officials, local private interests, and their political representatives in Albany, Hartford, and Trenton. A case in point is suburban reaction to Tri-State's cautious efforts in the 1970s to comply with federal requirements that each metropoli-

73. The exception is the chairman of the New York City Planning Commission, who is an ex-officio member. This official also is the only local representative among New York's five commissioners.

74. Michael Sterne, "For Planning Purposes, L.I. Wants to Be a Breakaway Province," *New York Times*, April 9, 1978.

75. Regional Plan Association, *Implementing Regional Planning in the Tri-State New York Region*, A Report to the Federal Regional Council and the Tri-State Regional Planning Commission (New York: 1975), p. 4. See also Regional Plan Association, "Report to the Three Governors and Legislatures on Official Regional Planning in the Tri-State Region" (New York: December 7, 1977).

76. Ibid., p. 24; see also Tri-State Regional Planning Commission, *Regional Development Guide* (New York: 1968), *passim*.

tan area develop a comprehensive housing plan that addressed the needs of low-income families. Tri-State's effort was typical of its activities—low key, research oriented, and developed with little publicity.[77] But the suburbs reacted adversely, expressing fear that low-income families would be dispersed from the older cities under some kind of regional housing plan. On Long Island, these fears fueled the demand for separation of Nassau and Suffolk counties from Tri-State, a demand which found a sympathetic audience among the two counties' state legislators and with New York's Governor Hugh Carey, who was eager to please voters in the state's two largest suburban counties. In 1979, Tri-State's critics won a partial victory. The Long Island Regional Planning Board was designated in place of Tri-State to review most federal grant applications for Nassau and Suffolk counties, with only those Long Island projects deemed by the state as having broader regional impact to be reviewed by Tri-State. And in 1980, a strong movement developed in Connecticut to withdraw from Tri-State.

The limited role of the Tri-State Regional Planning Commission in the 1970s underscores the comparative advantage of functional over coordinating agencies in terms of influencing development. Lacking resources, autonomy, and a clearly defined mission, Tri-State has been reduced to monitoring trends and processing paper—once decisions are made by functional agencies in the region—so that federal planning and review requirements can be met.

Tri-State's weaknesses also underscore the importance of the ability to concentrate resources. Tri-State has broad areal and functional scope, yet it cannot bring much influence to bear on development. Important limitations are found in its lack of formal independence, its dependence on federal and state grants, and its complete absence of control over land use. Skillful leadership might have overcome some of these shortcomings by dramatizing the agency's role and proposals. But Tri-State's leadership has been provided by its dominant state commissioners—who have sought to restrict rather than expand the agency's independent role, and who have utilized Tri-State in part to serve the commissioners' own state-agency needs. Consequently, Tri-State is left only with planning skills to go with its broad but shallow functional and areal scope, a combination which generates a great deal of paper but very little independent impact on the pattern of development in the New York region.

77. The housing plan attracted more public attention than most Tri-State programs, in part because of the sensitivity of the question of dispersing low-income housing, and in part because the Coalition for an Equitable Region (a group of civil rights and fair housing organizations led by Suburban Action Institute) publicly urged Tri-State to play an active role in securing compliance in the region with the Housing and Community Development Act of 1974 and other federal laws.

# 6

# Concentrating Resources on Highway Development

Of the many public and private activities that shape the metropolis, transportation developments are perhaps the most significant. The rail lines that spread across the countryside from the largest American cities in the latter nineteenth century, together with streetcars, elevated trains, and subway systems, were powerful forces in determining the patterns of residence, employment, and recreation in urban areas. Similarly, during the past sixty years urban America has been reshaped by the automobile, the bus and the truck, and by the vast highway network that serves their needs as it encourages their proliferation. New highways, thrusting into unsettled areas, attract developers who convert farmland into suburbs and inspire the movement of businesses as well as erstwhile city residents into the outer reaches of expanding metropolitan regions. Changes in urban transportation also modify recreation opportunities and other aspects of the urban environment. New rail lines and highways have prompted the creation of parks and resorts; expansion of the road system has threatened wildlife refuges; increasing numbers of automobiles and buses generate air pollution problems throughout urban areas.[1]

No one seriously contests the view that transportation developments have had an important impact on metropolitan America. Nor could it be argued that government is a mere spectator in the evolution of transportation facilities. State highway departments and regional turnpike authorities across the nation have financed and constructed bridges, tunnels and highway networks, and the federal government has been heavily involved in funding these facilities. State and federal agencies regulate rates, routes, and conditions of service for railroads, trucks and buses. City governments were owners and underwriters of early streetcar and other municipal transportation enterprises. More recently, direct public subsidies have helped maintain commuter railroad service as well as subway and bus service in the Boston and New York areas. New York State has taken over complete ownership and operation of the Long Island Rail Road, and government agencies have underwritten the

---

1. For detailed consideration of urban transportation developments in the United States and their impact, see Sam Bass Warner, Jr., *Streetcar Suburbs* (Cambridge, Mass.: Harvard University Press and MIT Press, 1962); Wilfred Owen, *The Metropolitan Transportation Problem* (New York: Doubleday, 1966); Edgar M. Hoover and Raymond Vernon, *Anatomy of a Metropolis* (Cambridge, Mass.: Harvard University Press, 1959), especially pp. 215 ff.; and Alan Altshuler et al., *The Urban Transportation System: Politics and Policy Innovation* (Cambridge, Mass.: MIT Press, 1979).

construction of new subway routes in the nation's capital and in other urban regions.

What has been asserted—in fact, what has been a widely held scholarly view—is the argument that government organizations involved in transportation are unimportant with respect to shaping urban development because their actions are not independent. These agencies, particularly those involved in highway transport, are viewed as inconsequential because "they leave most of the important decisions for Regional development to the private marketplace."[2] Our general position, that this oversimplifies a complex pattern of relationships, has been set forth in Chapter One. In this and the following chapter we examine these relationships in urban transportation more closely.

It is true, of course, that major transportation developments are not simply the result of governmental action, and that activities in the private marketplace are among the most important influences in shaping urban transport networks. While the same conclusion applies to a wide range of urban development projects, the transportation system illustrates the interconnection of factors particularly well. But if the activity of governmental organizations provides only one of many factors, is there any way to sort out the causal linkages? Can we identify evidence that bears on the question of whether government's role is merely to facilitate the achievement of goals determined elsewhere (especially in the private marketplace)? Or, alternatively, do government agencies in the transportation field have a significant role in shaping development?

The discussion in Chapter One suggests two modes of analysis that may be useful. One would explore cases where governmental agencies preferred different outcomes from those desired by other actors, in order to determine how often and under what circumstances government organizations "win"— that is, how often their actions significantly modify private-marketplace behavior. That approach was especially useful in Chapter Three, where zoning and other land-use regulations were found to conflict with unhindered (preferred) buyer-seller relationships regarding the sale and use of land for residential and commercial uses, with such regulations affecting locational patterns in important ways.

But that approach is not very useful in analyzing government's role in highway development during the past fifty years. In the road building era, the goals of the main consumer groups (users of automobiles, trucks, and buses) and private-sector producers (motor vehicle manufacturers) generally paralleled the goals of the major governmental agencies—the highway departments and road-building authorities. For all of these groups, the primary goal was more and better highways, tunnels, and bridges for motor vehicles. This similarity of goals lends plausibility to the view that governmental actions simply "abet the economic forces already at work," so that public programs are "of little consequence" in regional development.[3]

In this arena of governmental action, we can, however, make use of the

2. Robert C. Wood, *1400 Governments*, (Cambridge, Mass.: Harvard University Press, 1961), p. 173.

3. Ibid., p. 175. Quite different urban transportation goals were put forward by other groups, such as rail transportation organizations (public and private) and rail commuter associations. See discussion in Chapter Seven.

second mode of analysis described in Chapter One. That is, we can explore the perceptions and motivations of the main governmental actors in order to determine whether they are simply facilitating the interests of private transport users and producers, or whether their actions are shaped (partly or largely) by other concerns. Insofar as other concerns are important motivators, a governmental agency can be said to be an independent force in shaping urban development. Moreover, when government decisions—whatever their motivation—have an important role in the *location* and *timing* of crucial transportation developments, it is doubtful that such public programs should be characterized as being of little consequence.

This chapter explores the capacity of highway agencies in the New York region—based on areal scope, functional specificity, and the ability to concentrate resources—to determine the location and timing of major highway projects, and their motivations in using these sources of influence. The discussion includes more detailed scrutiny of several especially significant transportation projects of the past fifty years—the construction of the Holland Tunnel, George Washington Bridge, and Port Authority Bus Terminal; and the studies in the 1950s of highway arteries throughout the region, resulting in the building of the Verrazano-Narrows Bridge and other important additions to the highway network.

To many observers of urban development, the highway agencies have seemed too dependent—too responsive to the pressures from automobile associations and other highway user groups, too ready to build still more highways and bridges when traffic volumes increased or roads were criticized as outmoded. At the same time, the road and turnpike agencies have been too independent—far too reluctant to coordinate their plans with those of regional planning and rail organizations, and too resistant to cooperation in financing arrangements that would ensure the vitality of the regional transport system as a whole.[4] The campaign to harness the Triborough and Port Authority, the state highway department, and their brethren to a chariot labelled "coordinated metropolitan transportation," and to tap their healthy treasuries to assist the ailing mass transit system, began before World War Two and still continues. There have been a few victories, some symbolic, some real. As a result, the region's rail and bus services have been partially stabilized, or have declined more slowly since the 1950s than they would have in the absence of new government initiatives; and these actions have had some influence on the distribution of residences in the region, and on the concentration of employment in Manhattan and other urban centers. The next chapter reviews these continuing efforts to maintain a viable mass transportation system in the New York region.

## Contenders for Influence

The actions of a public agency to build a turnpike, subsidize a railroad, or carry out any transportation program are imbedded in a complex pattern of

4. See Owen, *The Metropolitan Transportation Problem*, especially Chapters 3–6, and Wood, *1400 Governments*, pp. 123 ff., 173–175, 192.

human activities and preferences, some proximate and others more distant in time and place. Other forces also are at work. As noted in Chapter Two, technological change and topography strongly shape the transportation system. The impact of technology is illustrated by the invention of the internal combustion engine, which made possible the creation of an efficient motor vehicle, and by the development of manufacturing methods that require more horizontal space, impelling businessmen to seek suburban locations where such space is available more readily and at lower cost. In the New York area, the role of topography is seen most prominently in the major waterways that divide the metropolis. The Hudson River, the East River, and New York Bay long retarded the construction of rail and highway facilities to join various parts of the region. Their existence also helped to induce public officials to create new agencies that could concentrate resources in order to overcome these obstacles to commerce and general mobility in the region.

Another key factor is public demand—the demand for highways and other transportation facilities needed to achieve desired travel objectives, especially the minimizing of congestion and travel time. As noted in Chapter One, the pattern of transportation demand in recent decades has been shaped by widespread interest in greater privacy and open space. When combined with increases in per capita income and automobile ownership, these preferences have generated greater effective demand for housing and recreation in the suburbs, thus adding to pressures for more transport facilities, particularly to serve automobiles. These pressures have been exacerbated by substantial population growth in the suburbs, and by the dispersion of manufacturing plants and other employment centers in the decades following World War II.[5]

In general, then, public demand has been a significant causal factor in the expansion of highway, bridge, and tunnel facilities. In the New York area, residents have also shown declining interest in using rail and subway services, especially during off-peak hours. Yet there are exceptions that demonstrate the interconnections among factors shaping transportation patterns. For example, Long Island's shape and the barrier of the East River have restricted transportation corridors from Nassau and Suffolk into New York City, so that the major rail system serving the area, the Long Island Rail Road, has attracted a high and fairly stable volume of passengers throughout the past two decades.[6]

In addition to technology, topography, and consumer demand, transportation development is affected by the activities of a wide variety of governmental agencies and organized private groups. While some of these organizations are not primarily interested in modifying the transport system, their

5. See, for example, Raymond Vernon, *Metropolis 1985* (Cambridge, Mass.: Harvard University Press, 1960), especially Chapter 9, and Benjamin Chinitz, ed., *City and Suburb* (Englewood Cliffs, N.J.: Prentice-Hall, 1964).

6. The annual passenger volume on the Long Island Rail Road declined from 75 million in 1956 to 69 million in 1961, rose into the 70 millions in the 1960s, fell to 69 million in 1971, was 66 million in 1974, and increased slightly in 1976 to 67 million. The past four years have seen greater increases in ridership, and the 1980 total was 81 million.

actions may have a crucial impact. Among the most important in this category are residential developers, business firms, and municipal governments, whose zoning and other land-use decisions influence the location and density of residences and the distribution of employment centers, and as a consequence affect transportation demand. Other political actors are directly concerned with shaping the transport network in the context of a broader set of social-development goals. In this category are such organizations, discussed in Chapter Five, as the Tri-State Regional Planning Commission, the Regional Plan Association, and the governor's office in each state.

The final category of contenders for influence are governmental and private organizations primarily concerned with construction, operation, and regulation of transportation facilities. Our main interest in this chapter and Chapter Seven is with public agencies in this category, whose activities range from minimal, stop-gap actions in response to immediate pressures from other sources, to a significant role in determining the pattern of transportation (and therefore the pattern of urban development) in the region. The more modest role is illustrated by the actions of state and federal regulatory agencies, confronted with demands from private railroads or bus companies to increase fares or reduce service because of declining patronage, and with opposition from commuters using the service. In this situation, the regulators have generally been limited by statute and tradition to a rather passive role. They receive requests from the private companies, weigh the proposal's impact on the users (as well as the prospects for political retribution from the users), and usually grant some portion of the change requested.

Far more significant are the actions of government agencies to grant substantial subsidies to private rail and bus corporations, or to purchase and operate rail and bus lines so that service can be maintained and perhaps expanded. New York City's decisions during the Depression to buy the several subway and elevated lines, and the purchase of the bankrupt LIRR by a state agency in 1966, illustrate an important governmental role—assuring continua tion of rail service in major sectors of the region.

In highway transportation, the government role has also varied widely—from the important but highly constrained function of deciding which route will be used in meeting increased traffic demand in a particular corridor, to developing major new projects with widespread effects on transportation patterns and land development, such as the George Washington Bridge in the 1930s and the Narrows Bridge in the 1960s.

To demonstrate that governmental agencies have in fact had an important role in determining the pace and direction of highway development, we can—as suggested in the opening pages of this chapter—direct our attention to questions of motivation and of location and timing. As to motivation, available evidence demonstrates that the policy decisions and programs of the major highway officials in the New York region were not simply responses to the demands of automobile drivers, trucking firms, and others interested in expanded vehicular facilities. Their actions have also been shaped by desires for institutional growth and personal prestige. To be sure, enhancing their own power required sensitivity to consumer demand and to social values held by the region's publics; it also required manipulating valued symbols to modify public pressure in ways that would permit and encourage the growth of their own organizations. Formal structure, leadership skills, and tax and revenue dollars were ably bent to this task.[7]

Even if public officials intended simply to let consumer demand determine their actions, in the complex arena of regional highway politics their responses would inevitably not be "simple." The timing and location of highway developments are not mandated authoritatively in the marketplace, and determining a project's feasibility depends on governmental calculations and cooperation that inevitably must shape the direction and pace of settlement in any large urban region. Thus the Narrows Bridge was completed in the 1960s, rather than in the 1920s or 1980s; and the 125th Street bridge across the Hudson was not built at all. The decision to go forward with the first was consistent with consumer demand for more arterial facilities; the decision against allocating funds for the second was not. Both actions were based on calculations of benefit and cost made within staff offices of two transportation authorities, using a set of rather narrow assumptions that were barely understood by other interested parties, public and private. The negative decision on the trans-Hudson bridge was reported by the Port Authority and Triborough Bridge and Tunnel Authority in 1955, but was never considered in detail outside the constellation of transport agencies—perhaps inevitably so, given the complexities of financing priorities and traffic flows that typically shape program decisions.[8]

In general, the more complex and expensive a project is, the less likely that simple consumer demand will be the determining factor. This can be illustrated with an example from the field of sewerage. If a homeowner in a rural area decides to replace his outhouse with a septic tank, he solicits bids and decides which tank best meets his standards of quality and price. The private market has responded to his consumer demand. But when a developer seeks approval for a new sewer trunk to serve a 50-acre site for residential housing, he is likely to become enmeshed in a complex pattern of organizational rules and personal interactions—even if there is widespread support for the proposed development. With public works projects of even greater areal scope and technical difficulty, as in the regional highway programs of the 1960s, the complexities and discretion necessary increase exponentially. Feasibility, timing, and location will depend on the planning and negotiating skills of officials operating within large bureaucracies and complex intergovernmental networks, and on their motivation and ability to allocate time and other resources needed to develop and carry out complex projects.

7. In his discussion of regional agencies, Wood agrees that their behavior should be seen as the result of "conscious design" by agency officials, but their motivation is seen as primarily a matter of survival in a world controlled by the private marketplace: "Considerations of institutional survival often tend toward programs which accelerate trends already underway," and thus the system of regional agencies, like the local governments, "arrive at . . . positions of negative influence." (*1400 Governments*, pp. 173–74.)

8. The definitive public reports on the Narrows and 125th Street bridges are found in Port of New York Authority and Triborough Bridge and Tunnel Authority, *Joint Study of Arterial Facilities* (New York: January 1955).

## The Highway Coalition

In the earlier years that concern us—from the late 1920s through the late 1940s—the agencies involved in rubber-based transportation could hardly be called a coalition. Like nations trying to carve out spheres of influence in a new-found land of riches, the highway agencies sometimes cooperated and sometimes went to war in their efforts to attract motorists and truck drivers. In those more competitive years the motives of leaders and organizations are seen more starkly, and the role of consumer demand must be placed in the context of a quest for power. The battle between the Holland Tunnel commissions and the Port Authority, recounted below, illustrates this phase, as does the often-bitter conflict between Robert Moses and the Port Authority during the 1930s and 1940s.[9]

As areas of influence stabilized in the early 1950s, and the flow of funds from tolls and federal coffers increased, cooperation became the norm, and the dozen major agencies concerned with the highway system evolved into a coalition dedicated to increasing the length and breadth of road facilities, and to resisting efforts of mayors, urban planners, and other "interlopers" to re-shape their priorities and plans based on allegedly broader development goals.[10] Conflict among members of the highway alliance was not entirely ended, but disagreements were usually resolved by staff discussion and compromise, without public display of differences.[11]

Underlying the ability of the highway coalition and its members to affect the timing and location of major projects, and to shape arterial programs partly in terms of their own motives, were a number of interrelated factors, which reinforced one another: wide areal scope, skilled leadership, complex and sophisticated bureaucracies, relatively abundant resources, enthusiastic support from narrowly focused constituencies, and—especially for the public

9. See particularly Herbert Kaufman, "Gotham in the Air Age," in Harold Stein, ed., *Public Administration and Policy Development: A Case Book* (New York: Harcourt, Brace, 1952), pp. 143 ff. Erwin Bard, the leading student of Port Authority activities in this period, characterized the PA and TBTA as "bitter enemies" during these years. (Telephone conversation, July 28, 1977.)

10. See J. W. Doig, *Metropolitan Transportation Politics and the New York Region*, Chapters 2 and 10. For purposes of this discussion, the highway coalition includes the following government organizations as they operate in the New York region: the state highway agencies (in New York, the State Department of Public Works, and in New Jersey and Connecticut, the state highway departments—all three being retitled departments of transportation in the late 1960s); the Triborough Bridge and Tunnel Authority, which operates in New York City, the Jones Beach State Parkway Authority on Long Island, and other authorities on Long Island chaired by Robert Moses; the Port Authority, whose highway-related enterprises include three Hudson River crossings (the Holland Tunnel, Lincoln Tunnel, and George Washington Bridge), three bridges between Staten Island and New Jersey, two bus terminals in Manhattan, and truck terminals in New York City and Newark; the four turnpike authorities listed at the end of note 12; and the federal government's major highway agencies—the Bureau of Public Roads until 1966 and the Federal Highway Administration thereafter.

11. There were, however, occasional breaks in the public display of cooperation. For example, when the New Jersey Turnpike Authority announced a plan in 1964 to widen a section of the turnpike from six to 12 lanes, the Port Authority calculated that such an expansion would cause congestion on its trans-Hudson crossings (the Holland Tunnel, Lincoln Tunnel) and thus negatively affect its public image and perhaps its financial position; it then opposed the expansion, appealing through the press and directly to New Jersey's governor. The Turnpike Authority's staff and board continued to favor the project, however, and its independent legal and financial position, as well as strong backing from contractors and construction unions in New Jersey, enabled the program to go forward.

authorities that were coalition members—a relatively high degree of independence in formal structure and in the allocation of financial resources.

From the 1920s onward, central roles in highway construction in the New
York region were held by the quasi-independent public authorities—the Port
Authority, Robert Moses' Triborough Bridge and Tunnel Authority and his several parkway authorities operating on Long Island, as well as four separate state
turnpike authorities.[12] For these agencies, insulation from partisan politics—
and from broader policy direction—was provided when they were created.
Under state laws, boards of private citizens, serving part-time, appointed the
executive director and other senior staff officials, and were given formal governing power. Moreover, these agencies were required to finance their projects
mainly with tolls and rents from their own facilities. Thus two important
sources of public control—appointment of top-level administrators by elected
executives, and the review and approval of annual budgets by governors, mayors, and legislators—were essentially excluded.[13] In terms of the fourfold division outlined in Chapter Five, the public authorities in the highway field fall in
the first category of "highly autonomous" government organizations.

Formal autonomy does not, of course, ensure actual autonomy. Without a
large flow of paying customers, a public authority must appeal for tax-generated
funds to survive, thus opening a wedge for close supervision of its activities by
suspicious state auditors and legislative committees. This issue was well understood by the early Port Authority leaders, and their strategy, discussed below, set
a pattern for authorities across the United States. Fortunately for the highway
authorities, public demand and agency activities were joined harmoniously in
the postwar era, producing balance sheets with large surpluses. For example, the
Port Authority's net revenues (after debt service) rose from $15 million in 1950 to
$37 million in 1960, and $73 million in 1970, while the New Jersey Turnpike
Authority's net revenues reached nearly $40 million in 1970. With these funds
available, autonomy in name became discretion in fact, permitting authority
officials to weigh choices among widening highways, improving interchanges,
building new bridges or major arterials—or even allocating funds to a new arts
center, to airport expansion, or to a world trade complex.

---

12. The Port Authority was created in 1921; its activities in the highway field began in the
late 1920s. The Triborough Bridge Authority dates from 1933, when it was formed to build a single
bridge connecting Queens, Manhattan, and the Bronx; the creation and merger of several additional
authorities in New York City led in 1946 to the establishment of a unified agency, the Triborough
Bridge and Tunnel Authority, headed by Robert Moses. The Long Island authorities were created in
this same period. During the first decade following the end of World War II, the states created
authorities to construct new major toll roads—the New Jersey Turnpike Authority, the New Jersey
Highway Authority (which built and operates the Garden State Parkway), the Connecticut Turnpike
Authority, and the New York Thruway Authority.

13. In contrast to most public authorities, Port Authority actions were subject to gubernatorial veto. That formal power was almost never used, however, until the mass transit conflicts of the
1970s discussed in Chapter Seven.

For thoughtful studies of public control of authorities in the New York region, see Wallace S.
Sayre and Herbert Kaufman, *Governing New York City* (New York: Russell Sage Foundation, 1960),
Chapter 9; and Annmarie Hauck Walsh, *The Public's Business: The Politics and Practices of Govern-
ment Corporations* (Cambridge, Mass.: MIT Press, 1978), especially Chapters 4, 7, and 8. The Port
Authority is considered from this perspective in Jameson W. Doig, "Regional Politics and 'Business-
like Efficiency,' " in Michael N. Danielson, ed., *Metropolitan Politics*, second edition (Boston: Little,
Brown, 1971), pp. 111–125.

Choices of these kinds, and the implementation of complex programs, cannot effectively be controlled by boards of part-time officials. It was inevitable, therefore, that actual power would devolve largely on senior staff officials. Moreover, since challenging opportunities were combined with ample resources, the authorities were able to attract men and women interested in developing and carrying out programs that would enhance their organizations' prestige and power, while adding luster to their own personal reputations.[14] So the partial leadership void created by part-time commissioners was quickly filled by able and aggressive staff. And with the development of the large-scale federal highway program in the 1950s, the federal and state highway departments also were able to attract to top positions individuals with an interest in and talent for the effective use of power.[15]

Even if these highway agencies had been led by officials with cramped imaginations and an aversion to the use of power, it would still have been difficult for the coalition simply to abet the goals of consumers in the marketplace. In any large bureaucracy, rivalry and negotiation among departments, staff units, and individuals deflect and modify signals and demands from the marketplace, or other outside sources.[16] And the highway agencies were large and complex bureaucracies, particularly in the road-building era. New Jersey's turnpike authority, for example, had more than 1,400 staff members in 1971. The Port Authority, embracing a much wider range of functions, had already expanded to 3,600 staff members in 1952, allocating these among 15 major departments with 43 divisions. Twenty years later, in 1972, there were 19 departments and 72 divisions, employing a total of more than 8,000 individuals. The other authorities and line departments enjoyed similar growth in the 1950s and 1960s.

But size and complexity were not the most significant characteristics of these agency staffs. In terms of potential for influencing regional development, their ability to attract high-quality planning and public-relations staff members was far more important. Able planning staffs could analyze the dynamics of regional growth and changing travel patterns, harnessing economic and technical data to the agencies' own goals, and providing solid if narrowly focused interpretations of current transportation problems and possible solutions. Moreover, their reports, carefully honed and replete with charts and statistics, could overwhelm the reservations of potential opponents, and gain the applause of editorial writers and governors who admired

14. For many authority staff members, there was an added dimension: the decision to join a government agency rather than a private corporation was attractive because they preferred to work in the "public service"—in organizations whose resources and goals were presumably harnessed to serve the needs of the region and its people.

15. In terms of Anthony Downs's typology of officials, these authorities and line agencies attracted *climbers* (those interested in power, income, and prestige) and *advocates* (whose motives also include promoting the goals and enhancing the power of their own organizations) rather than attracting *conservers* (those primarily concerned with individual security and convenience). See Downs, *Inside Bureaucracy* (Boston: Little, Brown, 1967), pp. 88 ff. Because of his unique personality and style, Robert Moses was an exception to the generalization that part-time officials largely yield power to full-time staff members. Moses was always the dominant force in "his" public authorities.

16. See Melville Dalton, *Men Who Manage* (New York: Wiley, 1959) and Downs, *Inside Bureaucracy*.

an aggressive and authoritative style, even when they did not always understand substance. Moreover, when dissenters attempted to gather planning staffs with different values, whose studies might challenge highway expansion and coalition independence, the highway alliance successfully rushed funds and staff expertise into the fray.[17]

Meanwhile, spokesmen for the road coalition maintained a steady drumfire of press releases and reports during the 1950s and 1960s, urging additional construction and announcing progress toward meeting ever-expanding goals. A third tube at the Lincoln Tunnel was "badly needed," the Port Authority asserted in 1952, and the agency "announced its readiness to make this great contribution" toward meeting traffic demands. "The building of roads must catch up and keep pace with the output of cars," Robert Moses proclaimed in 1964. "We are behind and shall keep losing ground unless we act fast." For New Jersey's Turnpike Authority, millions of pounds of "steel, asphalt and concrete" formed the basis for "another highly productive construction season" in 1965, but its northern section would need to be expanded to 12 lanes to alleviate traffic congestion.[18]

Throughout the nation, the highway coalition's public-relations approach, aimed at ensuring public support for its efforts (and public willingness to pay the toll fares and taxes needed to expand the highway network), was supplemented by more focused communication with organized groups in the private sector. The preferences of consumers in general were represented (and sometimes distorted) by the views of organized associations of truckers, automobile users, automobile and truck manufacturers, and others whose profits and advancement were closely linked to expansion of the arterial system. Representatives of these groups were kept informed of the coalition's assessment of road-building needs, and spokesmen for the private groups joined their government brethren in negotiations with legislators and others to ensure continued access to funds and land needed for highways and interchanges.[19]

17. Thus a major effort in the 1950s to develop a comprehensive study of transportation in the New York region was undercut by the Port Authority in an adroit series of maneuvers, which is described in the next chapter. Ultimately, the authority provided most of the funds for the study, in return for a treaty assuring that the study commission would *not* attempt to develop a coordinated plan for rail and road facilities. The significance of this restriction was lost on the region's major newspapers, who greeted the announcement of the authority grant with praise for a "highly constructive turn in Port Authority thinking," and for a "courageous decision" to finance a study "that starts without preconceptions or prejudices." (Doig, "Regional Politics and 'Businesslike Efficiency,' " pp. 120–121. The quotations above are from editorials in the *New York Times,* January 14, 1955 and the *Bergen Evening Record,* January 15, 1955.)

18. The quotations are from Port of New York Authority, *Thirty-Second Annual Report: 1952* (New York: 1953), p. 6; Robert Moses, remarks to the National Highway Users Conference at their meeting in the Indonesian Pavilion at the World's Fair, New York, May 8, 1964; New Jersey Turnpike Authority, *1965 Annual Report* (New Brunswick, N.J.: January 14, 1966), p. 18.

19. See, for example, the discussion of interest groups in Robert S. Friedman, "State Politics and Highways," in Herbert Jacob and Kenneth N. Vines, eds., *Politics in the American States,* second edition (Boston: Little, Brown, 1971), pp. 477–519. One of the major national successes of the coalition and its private-sector allies was their campaign to require that gasoline taxes and all other funds from highway-related sources be used solely for highway projects. By the early 1960s more than half of the states had passed laws forbidding diversion of highway revenues to other uses, and the coalition and its allies won a signal victory at the national level in 1956, when the Highway Trust Fund was created and all federal highway-related taxes were reserved to that fund, to be used to aid state road-building efforts.

Bondholders were particularly important for the public authorities. They formed a distinct interest group that constrained authority officials, while at the same time enhancing their discretion. In general, the authorities did not have access to tax revenues so most of the funds to construct their bridges and turnpikes were raised by selling tax-exempt revenue bonds to individual and institutional investors, with the bonds secured by revenues from each authority's tolls and rents.[20] Thus the bondholders and their representatives were constantly watchful, to ensure against actions that might undermine the agencies' ability to repay the interest and principal on outstanding bonds. At times, the bondholders' views clashed with those of the average motorist and the organized highway lobby. For example, bondholders opposed the recurring demand that turnpike tolls be reduced or eliminated, seeing this as a hazard to authority solvency. And they were wary of proposals for authority construction of new bridges, tunnels, and turnpike extensions if there were any uncertainties as to the profitability of a new project.

Although the private highway lobby and the financial community were uneasy allies, the authorities found the bondholders quite comfortable bedfellows. To the leaders of the highway, thruway, turnpike, and port authorities, the bondholder perspective provided an essential component of their agencies' strength and their own power. Revenue bond financing provided the justification for toll roads, and without the constitutional obligation to protect bondholder interests, public pressures undoubtedly would have led to reduced toll rates. Lower tolls would soon convert the authorities from vigorous agencies seeking new projects to custodial agencies, engaged in the sweeping and painting of aging facilities. Thus the financial strength of the public authorities—and their ability to attract skilled and aggressive leadership— were crucially aided by the bond-market constraint.[21]

Moreover, revenue-bond financing was a central element in the authorities' ability to maintain an image of competence and independence. Because these agencies had to meet their expenses without recourse to the taxing power, they could be viewed as similar to private firms, requiring "businesslike efficiency" and insulation from control by elected officials to survive. This image was readily grasped by the region's press. "All too frequently," a leading New York newspaper observed, "men elected to office are not qualified to tangle with complicated modern municipal management. . . . Time after time when the politicians have gotten in a jam they have had to create an

---

20. The Port Authority's use of revenue-bond financing dates from the 1920s. Its success in using this approach played a crucial role in popularizing revenue-bond funding for public projects in the United States. See Erwin W. Bard, *The Port of New York Authority* (New York: Columbia University Press, 1942), Chapter 8.

21. Debt service on bonds issued by a public authority is paid from the revenues produced by its facilities. Efforts to reduce tolls and rents substantially would jeopardize the ability of the authority to meet its financial obligations to bondholders, thus raising the prospect of a legal challenge under the contract clause of the U.S. Constitution (Article I, 10:1, prohibiting any state law " . . . impairing the Obligation of Contracts . . ."). Such reductions would also make it very difficult for the authority to sell bonds in the future, unless its bonds were secured by tax revenues as well as toll receipts. See the discussion in the U.S. Supreme Court opinion in *United States Trust Company v. State of New Jersey*, 431 U.S. 1 (April 27, 1977).

authority and call on successful businessmen to bail them out."[22] Public officials also heaped praise on these agencies, with special compliments directed toward the Port Authority. "Through its great public works," exclaimed New York Governor Thomas E. Dewey in the 1950s, the Port Authority "has set an example for the administration of public business on a sound and efficient basis."[23]

These encomiums to the Port Authority and to public authorities generally were not simply "natural events." They were cultivated by the authorities' leaders to stimulate public support for their efforts to meet transportation needs, and to enhance their ability to determine the pace and location of major arterial projects. In speeches, press releases, and reports—on every possible occasion—spokesmen for Triborough, the Port Authority, and their brethren emphasized that their efforts, "financed by prudent investors," were essential to the region's expansion. These are "immensely productive, independent ad hoc agencies," argued Triborough chairman Moses, which "represent government in business and accomplish what theorists promise and do not perform."[24] They place revenue-producing facilities "on their own feet and on their own responsibility," commented another authority spokesman, and "free them from political interference, bureaucracy and red tape. . . ."[25] That these themes were reflected in the assessments by governors and legislators, and in the "1400 favorable editorials in the New York and New Jersey press," should not be surprising, for the authorities and their associates in the highway coalition were engaged in an immensely successful campaign of public education.[26]

The authorities' themes of independence and prudent financing were emphasized and then extended to include "cooperative planning" among all highway agencies, and the "urgent necessity" to build more roads in order to

22. "Government by Authority," editorial, *New York World Telegram and Sun*, March 12, 1952. Similarly, the *Newark Evening News* commented editorially that the Port Authority "continues to confound those who deny that government can engage in economic activity with imagination, boldness, efficiency and profit" ("Success Story," editorial, April 20, 1959). Ironically, the search for profit eluded both of these newspapers, and they succumbed to bankruptcy some years ago.

23. Dewey's statement is reprinted in Port of New York Authority, *Thirty-Second Annual Report: 1952* (New York: 1953), frontispiece; cf. the highly favorable comments by New Jersey's Governor Alfred E. Driscoll in the same report, and by later Governor Richard J. Hughes of New Jersey, quoted in Clive Lawrence, "Port of New York Authority: A Towering National Presence," *Christian Science Monitor*, June 9, 1971. See also New Jersey Senate, Special Senate Investigating Committee (under Senate Res. No. 7 of 1961), *Report* (Trenton: June 28, 1963), which describes the Port Authority as a "vital organization" through which the two states have "procured vast public improvements without charge to the general taxpayers" and notes that this agency, "like many other public authorities . . . is expected to operate on business principles." Substantial portions of the Senate committee report are reprinted in Port of New York Authority, *Annual Report 1963* (New York: 1964), pp. 64–75; the quotations above are on pp. 64, 69.

24. Robert Moses, remarks to the National Highway Users Conference at their meeting in the Indonesian Pavilion at the World's Fair, New York, May 8, 1964. For a compilation of his other public statements, see his *Public Works: A Dangerous Trade* (New York: McGraw-Hill, 1970).

25. Austin J. Tobin, executive director of the Port Authority, in "The Work and Program of the Port of New York Authority," February 10, 1953. Cf. other addresses by Tobin: "The Authority Method of Handling Large Projects," May 19, 1955; "Address of Acceptance of the Annual Award of the Henry Laurence Gantt Medal," September 25, 1962. Tobin joined the Port Authority staff in 1927, and served as its chief full-time official from 1942 until December 1971.

26. The quotation is from Austin J. Tobin, "Public Relations and Financial Reporting in a Municipal Corporation," May 23, 1951. The tally of 1,400 covered the period 1945–1951.

"catch up and keep pace with the output of cars."[27] Contrary themes—the possible need for coordination of rail and road planning, or a concern for community disruption as new highways cut through villages and cities—were heard only sporadically through the 1960s. Instead, the highway builders responded to one important set of public concerns, and strongly influenced the way transportation problems were defined by elected leaders and in the press, thereby shaping the kinds of solutions that seemed desirable in the public mind. It was surely a performance worthy of the Silver Anvil award of the American Public Relations Association.[28]

The highway coalition was not, of course, all powerful. While some observers, such as Robert Caro, have characterized Moses and his coalition colleagues as the prime initiators of suburban sprawl and rail service decline in the New York region, neither Moses nor the highway alliance as a whole had that strong an influence.[29] Individually and collectively, however, they did help to shape the values and expectations of the region's opinion leaders and citizens, building on a growing interest in mobility and suburbanization, and focusing that interest on projects and programs of immense scope and—from some perspectives—immense benefit.

Even in their early years, the individual members of the alliance were able to plan and act using a canvas far larger in regional terms than that available to even the largest cities or to the counties. As a highway builder, Moses could range across New York City and far east into Long Island. The Port Authority crossed state lines, with a jurisdiction that included more than 350 municipalities in a dozen counties, in addition to New York City. While the state highway departments and turnpike authorities took a more partial view of the region, their geographic scope was, of course, wide-ranging. In the 1950s, cooperative efforts among these agencies increased substantially, enhancing their ability to influence the location and timing of projects, and to tip the scale toward public approbation of large programs.[30]

27. The quotations are drawn from the Port Authority and Triborough Authority, *Joint Study of Arterial Facilities*, 1955, pp. 6–7, and from Moses's Remarks, May 8, 1964.

28. This was one of several awards received by the Port Authority's director of public relations during the 1950s and 1960s.

29. In his monumental study of Robert Moses and New York City, Caro argues: "By building his highways, Moses flooded the city with cars. By systematically starving the subways and the commuter railroads, he swelled that flood to city-destroying dimensions. By making sure that the vast suburbs, rural and empty when he came to power, were filled on a sprawling, low-density development pattern relying primarily on roads instead of mass transportation, he insured that that flood would continue for generations if not centuries. . . ." As to the public authority, Caro observes that it "became the force through which he shaped New York and its suburbs in the image he personally conceived." Robert A. Caro, *The Power Broker: Robert Moses and the Fall of New York* (New York: Knopf, 1974), pp. 15, 19. The similarities in development patterns between the New York area and other metropolitan regions immediately cast doubt on Caro's interpretation that saw Moses individually as the cause of what happened in New York.

30. The interconnections between greater cooperation and magnified influence worked in several ways. For example, the augmented flow of toll revenues gave authority leaders an incentive to envision larger and more expensive programs for their individual agencies; but in the transport field such efforts would almost inevitably require collaboration with other agencies across city and state lines. Similarly, the Federal-Aid Highway Act of 1956 provided millions of dollars of additional federal funding for use by state highway departments, encouraging their officials to think more expansively—and more cooperatively—as well. The important role of federal officials, in the Bureau of Public Roads, in allocating these funds also encouraged cooperation across state lines. Cooperative efforts and larger influence were also aided by rotation and overlapping appointments

The independent authority structure, and the motivations of its leaders, were crucial to the timing of development in the New York region. Without these agencies, the pace of highway development and suburban expansion would undoubtedly have been slower; and perhaps some of the most significant projects, such as the Verrazano-Narrows Bridge, would not yet have been constructed. In other urban regions, the leadership of the highway coalition was centered in state highway departments and other executive agencies. But in New York, the large obstacles of waterways and state lines made the authorities a very useful and perhaps essential component in meeting regional "needs," thus adding an important ingredient to the organizational imperatives which shaped highway-coalition strategies.

Even in the heyday of road building, however, public support often could not simply be taken for granted. It was a prize for skillful effort that at times eluded even the best of the highway-planning strategists. Illustrative of the patterns of cooperation in the alliance, and the sometimes uncertain linkage to public approval, are the arterial highway studies undertaken during the 1950s. In 1954, the Port Authority and Moses, working closely with other members of the highway coalition, carried out a major study of the region's traffic patterns, and recommended a number of "needed" improvements. Included in their proposals were a lower deck on the George Washington Bridge across the Hudson River, a six-lane Throgs Neck Bridge between The Bronx and Queens, a twelve-lane bridge across Upper New York Bay between Brooklyn and Staten Island at the Narrows, a new bus terminal near the George Washington Bridge, and dozens of miles of connecting highways and expressways in New Jersey and in the five boroughs of New York City. The Port Authority and Triborough were prepared to allocate nearly $400 million to construction of the major toll crossings and immediate approaches, while about $200 million in state and federal funds would be needed to complete the toll-free connecting highways. In addition, another $150 million would be required if two cross-Manhattan expressways were to be built, as the report recommended.[31]

In terms of the potential impact on regional growth patterns, the single most important project was the Narrows Bridge, which would extend across a mile of water at a cost of $220 million, and provide the first direct connection between Staten Island and the other boroughs of New York City, as well as permitting direct automobile and truck traffic from Staten Island to Long Island.[32] Construction of that bridge had long been an important goal for Moses, but he estimated that Triborough revenues from other toll facilities would not be sufficient to underwrite construction of the Narrows span until the mid-1960s. After extensive negotiations, the two agencies announced in

---

of officials; for example, Charles H. Sells was superintendent of New York State's highway agency (titled Department of Public Works) before becoming a commissioner of the Port Authority in 1949; and S. Sloan Colt, long-time commissioner of the port agency, was a member of the President's advisory committee that recommended the expanded federal highway program enacted in 1956.

31. Port Authority and Triborough Authority, *Joint Study*, 1955, 62 pages.

32. Before the Narrows Bridge was completed, Staten Island's vehicular traffic could journey to the rest of New York City either by embarking on the Staten Island ferry, which deposited travelers at the lower end of Manhattan, by using smaller ferries which connected with Brooklyn, or by crossing by bridge to New Jersey, then traveling north and crossing the Hudson via bridge or tunnel, finally arriving in Manhattan.

January 1955 that the Port Authority would finance and construct the Narrows Bridge, thus permitting its completion a decade earlier than would otherwise be possible, and encouraging rapid population growth in this "last large undeveloped area adjacent to Manhattan." Triborough would operate and maintain the bridge and some years later, when its credit position permitted, would purchase the Narrows Bridge from its wealthier partner.[33]

In order to carry out the massive program, the highway alliance would have to obtain large amounts of state and federal funding. To win political support in New Jersey, the Port Authority agreed to tap its own bountiful reserves in order to pay for the state's share of the $60 million in federal/state funds required for the new arterial highway that would cross Northern Jersey to the George Washington Bridge.[34] But larger amounts would be needed for the expressways on the New York side, and voter approval of a transportation bond issue would be essential. Members of the state's highway department and the authorities developed a $750 million proposal that would provide funds for highway improvements throughout New York State, submitting it for voter approval in 1955. To enhance prospects for support of the bond issue, New York City's construction coordinator, the ubiquitous Robert Moses, wearing one of his many hats, agreed to open two nearly completed expressways a few days before the referendum—thus providing a dramatic opportunity to emphasize the public benefits that could flow from expanded highway-building funds.

Unhappily for highway forces, the public whose needs were being served found the price tag too high, and the bond issue went down to defeat in November 1955. The coalition then regrouped, pared the total sum down by one third, to $500 million, mounted a vigorous campaign to dramatize the necessity for an ever-expanding highway system, and won approval at a bond referendum in 1956.

## The Highway Coalition at Work

The interplay between public demand, the strategies and motivations of government officials, and other factors that shape transportation patterns—and through transportation patterns alter the distribution of population and jobs—are inevitably complex in a large and variegated metropolis. In the remainder of this chapter, we give three cases closer scrutiny to show this interplay in more detail. The first case describes the steps leading to construction of the Holland Tunnel and the George Washington Bridge. Here we see the limitations of relying on the private sector for the development of large transportation projects. Also underscored is the importance of organizational motivations and strategies in encouraging and crystallizing "public demand" for highways, and in shifting regional priorities from rail projects toward a road-building program. Moreover, in the Port Authority's successful effort to

33. Ibid., pp. 7, 21, 30. In fact, Triborough revenues built up more rapidly than expected, and the agency assumed full responsibility for constructing and financing the Narrows Bridge at the end of 1959.

34. Ibid., p. 38.

absorb a rival agency—to ensure that there would be no competition in tolls among trans-Hudson facilities, and that the "profits" would be at the disposal of the Port Authority—we see the importance of strategic skill in laying the groundwork for the authorities' later capacity to engage in regional development works.

A second case focuses on construction of the Manhattan Bus Terminal, and illustrates the importance of planning and political capabilities in carrying out a significant project in the face of opposition from the private sector and governmental rivals. In the third case, we look more closely at the motivation and results of the major project resulting from the highway coalition's studies of the 1950s, the Verrazano-Narrows Bridge.

### Under and Over the Hudson River

Demands for vehicular routes that would overcome the Hudson barrier to regional commerce and travel began long before 1900. The initial efforts failed because of differences in perspective and priorities between the states, and because of a desire to rely on private enterprise.

As early as 1868, New Jersey chartered a private company to construct a bridge across the Hudson, but concurrent authority was not obtained from New York State until 1894; the company made no progress and finally lost its charter in 1906 for nonpayment of taxes. In 1890, a second group obtained a federal charter for a private toll bridge, but could not raise money to begin construction. In 1917, the Public Service Corporation of New Jersey studied the possibility of a tunnel under the river but decided against it because of high costs.

As Erwin Bard notes, "private enterprise struggled for a long period with the problem of providing interstate crossings" for motor vehicle traffic.[35] Meanwhile, vehicular passengers and freight were compelled to use ferries and barges to cross the Hudson. Their slow journeys contrasted sharply with travel between New Jersey and New York City by rail tunnels after 1910. The completion of these tunnels under the river permitted the Pennsylvania Railroad and the Hudson and Manhattan rail company to bring their passengers from New Jersey directly into Manhattan terminals.

In the period between the two world wars, three major vehicular crossings were completed: the Holland Tunnel in 1927 and the George Washington Bridge in 1931, followed by the Lincoln Tunnel, which began operation at the end of 1937. Among the reasons for this sudden surge, with its considerable impact on the region's patterns of population growth and commerce, were the sharp rise in motor transportation during the 1920s, coupled with appeals from Bronx and Manhattan business groups, who favored the crossings as a way to reduce ferry congestion on the river and to improve business by reducing transportation time for customers west of the Hudson. Perhaps even more significant was the creation of new government organizations to overcome the interstate hiatus, together with the allocation of public funds for their construction activities, and the skillful efforts of these new agencies to enhance their power.

---

35. Bard, *The Port of New York Authority*, p. 192. The factual data in this section are drawn mainly from Bard's definitive study.

*The roads linking the New Jersey Turnpike and the Lincoln Tunnel in Hudson County were built through cooperative efforts of three major components of the highway coalition—the Port Authority, the New Jersey Turnpike Authority, and the New Jersey Highway Department.*
Credit: Port Authority of New York and New Jersey

After the early private efforts failed, the two states created commissions in 1906 to study ways of spanning the Hudson. Intermittent cooperation and several sporadic reports followed. The commissions suggested a tunnel under the river between lower Manhattan and Jersey City, but were unable to agree on how it would be financed or administered. "After years of groping and fumbling," the two states finally agreed in 1919 to establish independent state commissions to function in unison (it was hoped) and construct the proposed tunnel. The cost of the tunnel would be financed by tolls. Conflicts between the two commissions were frequent during the next several years, and cost overruns required additional state aid, but the Holland Tunnel finally opened in November 1927.[36]

Meanwhile, the Port of New York Authority had been established in 1921 as a joint agency of New York State and New Jersey. The authority was given broad responsibility for solving transportation problems in the region, but the main motivation for its creation was the widespread desire to improve the handling of rail freight. The agency's officials soon entered into complex

36. Ibid., pp. 178–183; the quoted phrase is on p. 180. The original estimated completion date had been 1923.

negotiations with the railroads aimed at devising a more efficient system of consolidated freight yards and related facilities throughout the region.

At the same time, business and civic groups urged both states to approve additional vehicular crossings for the Hudson River. Neither governor was pleased with the performance of the dual commissions, and both agreed in 1923 that future bridges and tunnels should be "constructed and financed by the Port Authority." Initially, the authority showed little interest in turning to vehicular projects, as its negotiations with the railroads "seemed on the verge of important accomplishments." But when these discussions foundered, Port Authority officials began to look actively for an alternative program. As Erwin Bard, historian of the authority's development, commented:

> Within the Port Authority the center of gravity began shifting to vehicular traffic. . . . The "do-something" policy in terms of construction was rising. It was imperative that the Port Authority's credit, hitherto entirely theoretical, be established. The bridge-building program offered a chance.[37]

The major project under consideration at this time was a bridge across the Hudson between upper Manhattan (about 178th Street) and Fort Lee, in Bergen County. A bridge in this location was favored by business and civic interests in Manhattan, and the proposal was pressed actively in the early 1920s by government officials and civic leaders in Bergen, who saw the bridge as a key factor in Bergen County's ability to attract the new wave of suburbanites. Among the leading New Jersey supporters of the project were the editors of the *Bergen Record* (whose economic strength and influence would grow with an expanding population) and state senator William B. Mackay (who hoped that leadership in meeting public concern for improved transportation facilities would advance his gubernatorial aspirations), as well as other civic leaders and government officials in the county.[38] Thus the campaign for the bridge illustrated the interrelationship between public demand, the interests of civic and business leaders, and strategic aims of public officials. Among the government units centrally involved was the Port Authority, whose leaders were actively seeking a path to success. They found it through undertaking the bridge project, and then used that effort to eliminate a rival organization and to establish a long-range financial strategy for institutional growth and power.

The Port Authority's leaders did not believe they could move publicly and decisively to harness the support which the 178th Street bridge commanded. For the proposal attracted opponents as well as enthusiasts. Some

37. Ibid., pp. 182, 185.

38. The most active civic group in the New Jersey campaign for the bridge was first named the Mackay Hudson River Bridge Association. The efforts of Mackay, the *Record*, local officials, and others are recounted in Jacob W. Binder, *All in a Lifetime* (Hackensack, N.J.: published privately, 1942; available in New Jersey libraries), pp. 181–198. Binder served as executive director of the Bridge Association. On the campaign for a bridge at 178th Street, see also "For Hudson Bridge Above 125th Street," *New York Times*, December 28, 1923; "Chamber Opposes Bridge at 57th Street," *New York Times*, January 4, 1924; "Greene Tells Plan for Hudson Bridge," *New York Times*, May 4, 1924; "Bridge Across Hudson at 178th Street is Discussed at Interstate Conference," *New York Times*, January 21, 1925; "Approves Hudson Bridge," *New York Times*, February 3, 1925; "Diners Hail Mackay as Father of Bridge," *New York Times*, April 23, 1925.

business and civic groups strongly favored a rival plan for a combined railroad-vehicular bridge, perhaps to be built by a private corporation, at 57th Street in Manhattan. Several conservation groups objected to the loss of park land that would occur if the bridge were built in the vicinity of 178th Street. Regional jealousy reared its expected head, when spokesmen for Queens criticized the project as catering to New Jersey's interests while the city's transportation needs were neglected. And some legislators in Trenton argued against expanding the Port Authority's role to include highway bridges.[39]

Amid these conflicts, the Port Authority moved cautiously. After a series of hearings in 1923, it concluded that a vehicular bridge should be built "north of 125th Street." As sentiment in favor of a span at 178th Street crystallized during the next year, the authority's chairman called such a crossing a "great necessity," and circumspectly announced in December 1924 that the authority was "ready to perform whatever tasks are designated to it" by the two states.[40] But when the authority was attacked as an advocate of the bridge proposal, its officials explained that the Port Authority had only concluded that "perhaps a bridge at some point" north of 125th Street was needed.[41]

Out of the public eye, however, Port Authority lawyers and engineers worked closely with both governors and with citizen groups who favored the bridge, as they pressed for legislative approval. Finally, in the spring of 1925, both states enacted legislation authorizing the Port Authority to construct the Hudson River bridge.[42]

Two years later, the Port Authority could speak about the project more expansively. The bridge across the Hudson, the agency declared, "means that the dream of many years and of many millions of persons will finally be realized." The "agitation" for such a bridge "took on the form of a public demand from the populations on both sides of the stream," the authority explained, "until the demand could be no longer logically be resisted."[43] Construction was begun at the 178th Street site in 1927, and the George Washington Bridge was opened to traffic in 1931, ahead of schedule and at a cost below the original estimate.

If Port Authority officials wished to satisfy their newly developed interest in motor transport, however, it seemed imperative that the revenue-

39. The opponents' views are set forth in "Sees Need for Five New Hudson Tubes," *New York Times*, December 6, 1923; "Chamber Opposes Bridge at 57th Street," *New York Times*, January 4, 1924; "Insist on 57th Street Bridge," *New York Times*, January 6, 1924; "Ferries, Bridges and Tunnels," editorial, *New York Times*, January 15, 1924; "Hudson Bridge Bill Passed," *New York Times*, February 10, 1925; "Committee Favors 57th Street Bridge," *New York Times*, February 28, 1925; "Move to Save Park at Fort Washington," *New York Times*, March 18, 1925; "Fear Effects of Bridge," *New York Times*, March 28, 1925.

40. Port of New York Authority, "Report to the Governors," December 21, 1923, reprinted in Port Authority, *Third Annual Report: 1923* (New York: February 1, 1924), pp. 43–50; Julian Gregory, chairman of the Port Authority, quoted in "Explains Bridge Plan," *New York Times*, December 30, 1924.

41. W. W. Drinker, Chief Engineer of the Port Authority, quoted in "Move to Save Park at Ft. Washington," *New York Times*, March 18, 1925.

42. *Laws of New Jersey*, 1925, c. 41; *Laws of New York*, 1925, c. 211. In 1924–26, the authority was also authorized to build three smaller vehicular bridges between Staten Island and New Jersey.

43. Port of New York Authority, *1926 Annual Report* (New York: January 20, 1927), pp. 55–56.

producing Holland Tunnel be acquired. For the Holland Tunnel, opened by the dual commissions in the fall of 1927, proved an immediate success. High traffic volumes and substantial revenues generated enthusiasm within the two commissions for more projects, and in 1928 they recommended to both states that they be authorized to construct a tunnel to midtown Manhattan immediately, and three other crossings thereafter. Meanwhile, sagging toll revenues on the Port Authority's facilities raised doubts as to the ability of the authority to meet its financial obligations.[44]

At this point, the Port Authority exhibited the tactical skill that would become a hallmark of its operations. In private discussions and public debate, it argued for the following approach to regional transport development:

**1.** Interstate rail and highway projects should not be considered separately, but instead as part of one comprehensive transportation plan. (Since the Port Authority already had rail responsibilities and the dual commissions did not, this principle would support vehicular expansion by the authority and cast doubt on the legitimacy of the commissions' efforts.)

**2.** All interstate motor vehicle crossings should be financed by revenue bonds, not by using the credit of the states. (The authority was authorized to issue revenue bonds, while the commissions used state funds to be repaid out of toll revenues.)

**3.** To ensure that revenue bonds could be sold to investors, all interstate bridges and tunnels should be under the control of one agency. Otherwise, tolls on one facility (for example, the Holland Tunnel) might be reduced below that of other facilities, and this "unfair competition" would drain off traffic and revenue from the other crossings.

**4.** As a further aid to revenue-bond financing, income from all projects should be pooled, so that "excess returns from the more profitable enterprises" could support weaker or new facilities.

The authority put forth two other arguments that would not reappear in its later reports and announcements. "It is perfectly obvious," the authority declared, that the general level of tolls "could be placed on a much lower basis" if all facilities were under one management rather than under divided authority. Also, the revenues pooled in the general fund would be devoted to paying off the debt on the interstate crossings, "with a view to making these facilities free from tolls within the least possible time."[45] In fact, the general level of tolls remained at fifty cents until 1975 when it was raised to seventy-five cents.

At a series of meetings in 1930 and 1931, officials of both states finally accepted the Port Authority's arguments, the dual commissions were abolished, and the Holland Tunnel was transferred to the authority. Moreover, the states agreed that future interstate crossings would be developed by the

44. The Port Authority opened two of its Staten Island bridges in 1928. In 1929 and 1930 revenues from these bridges were far below original estimates, and the first series of bonds seemed likely to face a default. See Bard, *The Port of New York Authority,* pp. 237–238.

45. See Port of New York Authority, *Eighth Annual Report* (New York: December 31, 1928), pp. 59–61; and Port of New York Authority, *1929 Annual Report* (New York: December 31, 1929), pp. 51–52.

authority, under the four principles summarized above. Perhaps understating the importance of the Port Authority's deft maneuvers, Bard concludes that the authority's "reputation for efficiency, its autonomous power to finance, and its established credit won in the race for survival."[46]

Through its activities and successes during these early years, the Port Authority established an approach to governmental action that would be repeated again and again in the New York area, as well as in other parts of the country. First, it set a precedent for financing highway facilities by revenue bonds, supported by tolls. This strategy obviated the need for state legislatures to appropriate moneys for such facilities out of general funds, or to approve the issuance of bonds backed by the full faith and credit of the state. Thus, the speed with which self-supporting bridges, tunnels, and turnpikes were constructed during the next four decades was greatly increased. The availability of revenue-bond financing also encouraged state officials to create additional public authorities as a way of avoiding direct responsibility for additional taxes.[47]

A second precedent, that each facility would be supported by the pooled revenues of all other authority projects, shaped the development of later public authorities in the transportation and port development fields.[48] It also had a decided impact on the evolution of the Port Authority itself. The pooling concept provided the rationale and financial base for extensive authority activity in airport, harbor and rail development. Otherwise, the agency would have been limited to those very few projects whose "self-supporting" nature was so evident from the outset that cautious investors would buy bonds without broader security. The pooling concept permitted the Port Authority to insulate individual projects from the short-run (and in some cases even the long-run) impact of market forces. Surpluses from bridges and tunnels could be used to underwrite new enterprises that might incur initial or continuing deficits, if those new projects seemed desirable in terms of overall regional development—or, at times, if they seemed beneficial in terms of the financial strength and public image of the authority and its officials.

---

46. Bard, *The Port of New York Authority*, p. 191. In 1931, the Port Authority was authorized to proceed with the midtown Lincoln Tunnel. Strictly speaking, the dual commissions were not abolished, but merged with the PNYA, which absorbed some of the commissions' staffs.

47. For example, the New Jersey Turnpike Authority was created in 1948 partly as a way to overcome the reluctance of the New Jersey legislature to provide substantial sums for highway building in the early postwar years.

Members of the dual state commissions and other critics of the authority concept argued that it would be less expensive, and therefore better, to finance new road facilities with state advances, to be repaid through toll receipts. This approach was used for the Holland Tunnel, and it probably *would* have been less costly for the later bridges, tunnels, and toll roads to have been financed in this manner, since interest rates on state-backed loans would have been lower than interest on bonds backed mainly by an authority's projected toll revenues. The political disadvantages of state appropriations, however, combined with the mixed administrative record of the dual commissions, were more persuasive at the time. See Bard, *The Port of New York Authority*, pp. 180 ff.

48. On the influence of the Port Authority's structure and early evolution on the development of other public authorities, see Council of State Governments, *Public Authorities in the States* (Chicago: 1953), p. 23; State of New York, Temporary State Commission on Coordination of State Activities, *Staff Report on Public Authorities under New York State* (Albany: 1956), p. 15; and Richard Leach and Redding S. Sugg, Jr., *The Administration of Interstate Compacts* (Baton Rouge: Louisiana State University Press, 1959), p. 8.

*The George Washington Bridge, looking east across the Hudson River
at upper Manhattan with the Port Authority's toll plazas in the fore-
ground.*                         Credit: Port Authority of New York and New Jersey

The Port Authority had spanned the Hudson River, and the new George
Washington Bridge soon proved a major revenue producer for the authority.
Along with the Holland Tunnel it provided the financial base for constructing
the midtown Lincoln Tunnel in the 1930s, and for entering a wide range of
other activities a decade later. The bridge also proved a valuable resource in
maintaining the image of the Port Authority as an efficient and important
regional enterprise. Opened with great ceremony in the fall of 1931, the

George Washington Bridge was widely praised for its design and construction—it was the longest suspension bridge in the world—and because of its impact on Bergen County. During the next two decades, the authority was frequently commended for inaugurating "a new era in bridge building" with this majestic span, and the bridge was called the "greatest single factor in Bergen County's growth."[49]

The new bridge did indeed have a significant impact on development west of the Hudson. Previously, rail lines and ferries provided only circuitous, time-consuming access to Bergen, and the sprawling county had remained a semirural enclave while nearby counties with better access to Manhattan urbanized rapidly before World War I.[50] Once the two states had approved the bridge in 1925, real estate speculators packed the county office building in anticipation of the land boom.[51] The next thirty years saw a tripling of Bergen County's largely middle-class population, many of the new residents having departed from the Bronx and other parts of the core to "reside in the pleasant environment of Bergen County."[52]

Property values also climbed rapidly. Between 1920 and 1954, assessed values increased by more than 250 percent in Bergen, compared with about 100 percent in Essex County and in the Garden State as a whole during this period. And the decision to span the Hudson at 178th Street, rather than at 125th Street or 57th Street (the latter across from Hudson County), altered the attractiveness of land and the pattern of growth within the county. Changes in property values among Bergen's towns illustrate the impact of the bridge: municipalities nearest the span saw their taxable property increase especially sharply, rising from three to ten times the 1920 values.[53]

For Port Authority strategists who recognized favorable publicity as a route to enhanced power, the George Washington Bridge and its impact gener-

49. The quotations are, respectively, from "Development of New York Port Lesson in States Co-operation," *Christian Science Monitor*, May 5, 1946, and "The Birth of a Bridge," editorial, *Bergen Evening Record*, April 30, 1946.

50. Much of Bergen County was as close to the Manhattan CBD as the Bronx and southern Westchester County, which were served by direct rail service and a growing highway network, and no more distant than Essex and Union counties in New Jersey, which had direct rail service to Manhattan. Travelers from Bergen County who did not wish to swim the Hudson reached Manhattan by journeying south via rail or road into Hudson County, where they could cross by the Weehawken ferry, or (going farther south) via the Hudson and Manhattan rail system (now PATH).

51. "The proposed bridge over the Hudson River," reported the *New York Times* in December 1925, "has so stirred up real estate activities in Bergen County that the searcher's room in the new $1 million court house at Hackensack is wholly inadequate. Today petitions were circulated asking the Freeholders to provide more room for the lawyers' clerks and searchers." ("Bridge Talk Stirs Bergen County," *New York Times*, December 4, 1925.)

52. Donald V. Lowe, "Port Authority Behind Bergen's Boom," *Bergen Evening Record*, October 30, 1953. During the period 1920–1954, while Essex County added 46 percent to its population and New Jersey as a whole gained 66 percent, Bergen's population rose by more than 200 percent. In addition to the bridge, other factors, such as a relatively large amount of undeveloped land (as of 1920), influenced Bergen County's high rate of population growth. For discussions of the interrelation of factors in suburban growth, see Chapters 1–3 above and Edgar M. Hoover and Raymond Vernon, *Anatomy of a Metropolis*, Chapter 8.

53. Bergen County taxable property as a whole increased between 1920 and 1954 from $207 million to $760 million. Among the towns nearest the bridge, Teaneck's taxable property rose most sharply, from $4 million to almost $45 million; Hackensack's increased from $16 million to almost $52 million, and Cliffside Park from $4 million to more than $15 million. See PNYA and TBTA, *Joint Studies of Arterial Facilities*, p. 34.

ated a steady flow of heart-warming journalistic comments. The span was mentioned prominently in many articles during the 1930s and 1940s reviewing the authority's "far-sighted intelligence" and "monument of vast public works."[54] And if attention lagged, the agency was able to assist friendly editors by preparing informative essays such as the 1953 *Bergen Record* article, "Port Authority Behind Bergen's Boom," written by Donald V. Lowe, then vice-chairman of the Port Authority.[55]

### Bringing Manhattan Closer to the Suburbs with Buses

Despite the Depression, the region's motor vehicle traffic continued to increase throughout the 1930s, and the Port Authority and its fellow road-builders added additional highways and river crossings. The Port Authority's main contribution was the Lincoln Tunnel, opened in 1937, taking traffic from New Jersey under the Hudson River directly into mid-Manhattan. And as the highway alliance built, still more travelers journeyed into New York City by motor vehicle, and Manhattan's CBD became choked with automobiles, trucks, and buses.[56] Expanding traffic had a more positive impact on the Port Authority than on city streets. The port agency's toll income increased, its surpluses grew, and by the early 1940s a once-struggling rail freight planner had become a wealthy and dynamic bridge and tunnel entrepreneur.[57]

Close study of vehicular patterns revealed, however, that traffic expansion on the authority's crossings was being retarded by financial difficulties in

54. "Port Authority Birthday," editorial, *New York Times*, April 30, 1946. For a selection of other comments on the bridge and the authority, see PNYA, *25th Anniversary* (New York: 1946), a booklet of articles and editorials.

55. *Bergen Evening Record*, October 30, 1953. One of Lowe's fellow Port Authority commissioners was John Borg, long-time publisher of the *Record* and an early advocate of the 178th Street bridge.

Sometimes those friendly editors relied so fully on the authority's press writers that they seemed to confuse the Port Authority's activities and their own. Thus the *Journal of Commerce*, in a full page review of the agency's "majestic" bridge and other accomplishments, waxed warmly on the authority's landmark financing efforts, which were notable because "our first issues" were much larger than any previous public revenue-bond issue. The *Journal*'s writer then commented, no doubt to the surprise of the newspaper's stockholders, that "any surplus from our operations ultimately belongs to the States of New Jersey and New York," and concluded with the sober admission that "we cannot turn to the taxpayers for reimbursement of losses." "New York Port Authority Traces 25 Years of Progress: It Has Accomplished Much in Many Fields of Endeavor," *Journal of Commerce*, May 22, 1946; emphasis added.

56. For example, trans-Hudson vehicular traffic rose from 16.9 million vehicles in 1934 to 30.6 million in 1941. Under the impact of gasoline rationing and "pleasure-driving" bans during World War II, traffic then dropped sharply, hitting a low point of 21.9 million in 1943 before rising again in 1944, reaching 27.2 million that year. See Port of New York Authority, *Fourteenth Annual Report* (New York: March 18, 1935), pp. 34, 36; *Twenty-First Annual Report: 1941* (New York: March 31, 1942), p. 15; *Twenty-Third Annual Report: 1943* (New York: April 1944), pp. 1–2, 7–8; *Twenty-Fourth Annual Report: 1944* (New York: November 15, 1945), pp. 2, 6–7.

57. Investment in facilities had risen from $38 million in 1928 to $238 million in 1944. Net annual revenues (after payment of debt service), which had been a deficit figure until acquisition of the Holland Tunnel in 1931, rose from $2,854,000 in 1934 to $6,424,000 in 1940 and $8,740,000 in 1941. Even during the war, annual net income never fell below the 1940 figure. See Port of New York Authority, *Eighth Annual Report*, p. 82; *Fourteenth Annual Report*, p. 55; *Twenty-First Annual Report: 1941*, p. 14; *Twenty-Third Annual Report: 1943*, p. 33; *Twenty-Fourth Annual Report: 1944*, p. 44.

New Jersey. The state highway department, supported by tax dollars rather than tolls, had managed to construct the Pulaski Skyway and related roads bringing traffic to the Holland Tunnel, and two major highways joining with the George Washington Bridge. But its efforts to build other highway projects had been curtailed by limited tax dollars. Conceivably the Port Authority might have allocated some of its toll profits in order to assist in financing related highway networks—thus adding, in the long run, to its own toll revenues while accelerating suburban mobility. But the authority did not embark on this course. As Bard comments, reflecting the views of the agency's officials at the time, "it is too much to expect that a bridge or tunnel, as a toll gate, should finance the construction of miles of highway." Much of the total cost "must be shouldered by the states and localities," so that in a "general program of highway expansion . . . toll collection is merely an auxiliary method of paying for the costs."[58]

This modest view of the toll agency's "auxiliary" role in regional highway development was not without advantages to the Port Authority, of course. While state and local agencies struggled, in these lean years, to attract enough tax dollars to meet growing highway needs, authority officials could turn their thoughts and surpluses to other challenges. The original Port Compact hardly envisioned a Port Authority devoted solely to subsidizing highway construction, and as available funds grew in the early 1940s authority officials sought new ways to shape the "development of the port" and to enhance the influence of the port's chief advocate.[59] This was a time for expansion.[60]

58. Bard, *The Port of New York Authority*, pp. 213–214. "The bridges and tunnels have been built and they are in operation," the Port Authority commented in 1940, but "the situation which now confronts the States, and particularly New Jersey, is that . . . a comprehensive system of arterial roads to *feed these facilities* . . . has yet to be constructed." Port of New York Authority, "Report Submitted to the New Jersey Joint Legislative Committee Appointed Pursuant to the Senate Concurrent Resolution Introduced March 11, 1940" (New York: June 1940), p. 32; emphasis added. See also pp. 30–32, 63–64; Port Authority, *Twenty-First Annual Report: 1941*, p. 11; and *Twenty-Third Annual Report: 1943*, letter of transmittal (pp. 6–7), and p. 16.

This distinction also underlay the reaction of a long-time authority official when reading a draft of this chapter. "The Port Authority should not be characterized as a highway-building agency," he protested; "in the field of vehicular transportation, it is only a bridge-and-tunnel agency."

59. In the 1921 compact, the two states agreed to "faithful co-operation in the future planning and development of the port of New York" (Article I), and created the Port Authority, "with full power and authority to purchase, construct, lease and/or operate any terminal or transportation facility" (Article VI). Thus the authority's officials could roam across this wide field, although they were limited by the need to ensure a long-term income flow that exceeded costs. (The compact is reprinted in its entirety in Bard, *The Port of New York Authority*, pp. 329–339.)

60. In their search for new tasks, the authority's leaders were motivated not only by the challenges of the postwar era they saw ahead of them, but also by a look behind—at the host of automobile users, truck drivers, and bus companies pursuing them, demanding lower tolls on Port Authority bridges and tunnels. The authority had already faced one legislative inquiry on this issue, in 1940, and successfully defended its view that the existing (50-cent) toll level must be maintained in order to provide funds for "future improvements" in the port district. But its officials realized that pressure to reduce toll rates would become irresistible if the agency did not soon commit its growing surpluses to new projects. On the 1940 inquiry, see Port Authority, "Report Submitted to the New Jersey Joint Legislative Committee . . ." (the quotation above is on p. 40), and Port Authority, *Twenty-First Annual Report: 1941*, p. 11. On the pressures confronting the Port Authority in the mid-1940s and the views of its officials at that time, see Herbert Kaufman, "Gotham in the Air Age," in Harold Stein, ed., *Public Administration and Policy Development* (New York: Harcourt, Brace, 1952), especially pp. 182–183.

So it was that by 1943 the Port Authority had cast an admiring eye upon the problems confronting the region in the field of air transport, and after a lengthy series of negotiations the agency assumed control of the region's three major airports in 1947–1948. Meanwhile, in 1944 and 1945, it took over a marine terminal facility in Brooklyn and began a study of port terminals in Newark, leading to a lease signed in 1947 providing for authority control, rehabilitation, and operation of Port Newark.[61]

In the long run, Port Authority operation of these leased facilities might prove of great benefit to the port's commerce and to the authority's own reputation.[62] But some greater initiative was needed—something the authority could create itself. As the war drew toward a close, the agency expanded its planning staff, completed a careful analysis of traffic patterns, and announced that it was prepared to construct "the world's largest bus terminal" to help relieve the "intolerable midtown Manhattan traffic congestion."[63]

The need for such a terminal seemed evident to the region's transportation planners. By the early 1940s, the influx of bus traffic from west of the Hudson—traveling on Port Authority facilities—had become an important factor in traffic congestion in the CBD. Most of the buses brought New Jersey passengers through the Lincoln Tunnel and deposited them at eight separate private bus terminals scattered between 34th and 51st Streets. By 1944, 1,500 buses each day crossed the Hudson bound for mid-Manhattan and most of them were caught regularly in heavy midtown traffic bottlenecks. It was anticipated that a union terminal near the Lincoln Tunnel would draw off most of this traffic, eliminating more than two million miles of bus travel in midtown Manhattan annually—and thus providing traffic relief equivalent to two or three additional crosstown streets.

In fact, a bus terminal of this kind had been proposed earlier by the bus companies and by New York City's own transportation planners. But the bus lines, each wary of losing the competitive advantage of its existing midtown station, could not agree on joint terminal operations. And the city administration, its staff and financial resources stretched thin by other service demands, had made no progress. New York's mayor was therefore glad to be able to turn to the authority's able planners. With his encouragement, the Port Authority developed a proposal in 1944 for a major terminal (between 40th and 41st Streets, and 8th and 9th Avenues) that would replace individual bus termi-

61. The Port Authority's growing interest in air transport is indicated in its annual reports for 1942–1945, and its negotiations and acceptance of the airport and harbor facilities are summarized in its reports in 1944–47. See Port Authority, *Twenty-Second Annual Report: 1942*, letter of transmittal (p. 4); *Twenty-Third Annual Report: 1943*, pp. 14–15; *Twenty-Fourth Annual Report: 1944*, pp. 11–13, 20–22; *Twenty-Fifth Annual Report: 1945*, (New York: July 1, 1946), pp. 8–9, 18–23; *Twenty-Sixth Annual Report: 1946*, (New York: November 1, 1947), pp. 2–19; *Twenty-Seventh Annual Report: 1947*, (New York: November 1, 1948), pp. 6–7, 24–25, 30.

On the airport negotiations, see also the perceptive study by Kaufman ("Gotham in the Air Age," 143–197), analyzing the conflicts between Robert Moses, the Port Authority, New York City's administration, and other participants. As Kaufman's analysis indicates, the ability of the Port Authority to allocate funds to rehabilitate and operate the airports was a crucial advantage as the authority negotiated to take over these facilities from the financially strapped municipalities.

62. Actually, ownership of the Brooklyn grain terminal was transferred by New York State to the PNYA; Port Newark and the three airports were turned over to the authority on long-term leases.

63. Port Authority, *Twenty-Fourth Annual Report: 1944*, p. 17.

nals. The authority would not only plan and design, but also finance, construct, and operate the massive new terminal.[64]

The proposal attracted warm support from most of the bus companies, business leaders, the news media and some government officials. But Robert Moses was not so pleased. Wary of the Port Authority's expansionism within New York City, as its bus terminal and airport excursions brought the bistate agency further into his territorial domain, Moses thrust back. Allying himself with the Greyhound bus company (which did not want to be included in the union terminal), Moses donned his hat as a member of the City Planning Commission, persuaded a majority of fellow commissioners to join him in opposing a crucial element of the Port Authority plan, and for two years blocked the terminal. It was, as Herbert Kaufman noted, a "grim and bitter battle."[65]

As midtown bus traffic expanded to more than 2,500 interstate vehicles per day, and complaints of traffic congestion grew, the port agency pressed for approval of "this great public improvement" to relieve an "intolerable" traffic problem costing Manhattan business "an estimated million dollars a day." Finally, in 1947, the city's Board of Estimate endorsed the Port Authority plan, handing Moses one of his few defeats. Revenue bonds to finance the Port Authority Bus Terminal were sold in 1948, and the terminal was opened in December 1950.[66]

The impact of the bus terminal project was manifold. The new terminal reduced travel time for bus passengers by between six and thirty minutes. Bus travel from Bergen, Essex, and other northern New Jersey counties became more attractive, and interstate bus routes were extended more deeply into

64. See Ibid., pp. 17–19, and Port Authority, *Twenty-Fifth Annual Report: 1945*, pp. 9–14. According to one Port Authority official involved in the negotiations, New York City's ability to undertake the project itself was weakened by the fact that its staff included "planners but not builders," while the authority, having both, could draw upon its own personnel, propose a feasible plan, and carry it out as soon as the proposal was approved.

During the mid-1940s, the authority also began constructing two union truck terminals authorized before the war.

65. Kaufman, "Gotham in the Air Age," p. 177.

66. A complex situation permitted Moses to block the PNYA proposal. The authority had concluded that the new bus terminal would not be successful in consolidating terminal traffic—and thus in reducing traffic congestion and in making the terminal self-supporting in the long run—if any of the bus companies were permitted to build or enlarge existing individual terminals east of Eighth Avenue, an area more centrally located for access to offices and shopping. Therefore, the authority sought approval by the Planning Commission and the Board of Estimate of resolutions to prohibit any bus companies from future bus terminal development in the more central area. Without such action, the authority argued, it could not sell revenue bonds for the terminal; and so construction was deferred pending action by the City. But the Greyhound bus company already had a terminal in the "forbidden area" that it wanted to expand. Therefore Moses supported the Greyhound application to be exempted from the proposed resolution, using that as his vehicle to persuade the Planning Commission to oppose the blanket prohibition demanded by the Port Authority. For details on the bus terminal case, see the authority's annual reports for 1944 (pp. 17–19), 1945 (pp. 9–14), 1946 (pp. 19–24), 1949 (pp. 76–80), and 1950 (pp. 99–102). The quotations in the text are found on pp. 19–20 of the 1946 report. Commissioner Moses's views are stated in part in his letter of October 16, 1945 to Chairman Howard Cullman of the Port Authority. In that letter, he concluded that the treatment of Greyhound was "grossly unfair" because its officials were "merely proposing to extend a non-conforming use authorized by the courts," and because the bus company had also agreed to spending $300,000 on traffic improvements related to its proposed terminal expansion. (Letter made available to the authors by Mr. Moses.)

*The Port Authority Bus Terminal in mid-Manhattan is the terminus of commuter bus lines serving residents of all the counties in the region west of the Hudson River. The terminal is directly connected to the Port Authority's Lincoln Tunnel, as can be seen in the upper left-hand corner of the photo.*    Credit: Port Authority of New York and New Jersey

suburban areas. By 1952, about 5,000 buses were using the terminal each day, carrying 130,000 passengers to and from mid-Manhattan, and the number continued to rise during the next decade. Meanwhile, although the new bus terminal was hardly decisive, the reduced travel time it provided was one more factor tipping the scales against the railroads, as passenger traffic cross-ing the Hudson by rail declined steadily in the 1950s.[67]

For the Port Authority as for bus travelers, the bus terminal venture was highly successful. The agency was widely praised for providing this "greatly needed" facility, thus aiding travelers and business in the region.[68] The com-mitment of $24 million to construct the terminal helped absorb the agency's growing reserves. As financial allocations to airports, marine facilities, and truck terminals were added in the late 1940s, the demand for toll reductions faded as an active rallying cry. Yet the authority remained alert to the need to emphasize that its reserves would always be hard-pressed to meet the region's growing demands for self-supporting facilities. "The task of keeping pace," the agency proclaimed in 1950, "is a continuing one." Projects already under-way and those still on the drawing board demanded that the authority main-tain a "sound financial position," the agency warned in 1953, for "growing requirements . . . may call for an expenditure of some $550,000,000 of capital funds in the next ten years."[69]

In the language of the *Hudson Dispatch*, the Port Authority had become a "giant operator,"[70] and the efforts of the 1940s would, its officials hoped, be only a prelude to more vigorous activities in the decades ahead.

From the perspective of our more general interests, these activities illus-trate a number of important themes: leaders of large and "profitable" public enterprises have substantial discretion in choosing programs and timing their projects; these leaders' views of the proper goals of their agencies are crucial in determining how they respond to "market demand" and how they shape it; public authorities have great advantages, in comparison with local general-purpose governments, in their ability to concentrate resources on specific developmental projects; conflicts in priorities and territorial influence among public officials combine with public demand in shaping government action; new public projects, in this case the Lincoln Tunnel and then the bus termi-nal, have impacts that extend outward, affecting transportation and residen-tial patterns, and then molding the need and opportunity for future develop-ment projects.

67. Port of New York Authority, *Thirty-Second Annual Report: 1952* (New York: 1953), p. 36; Port of New York Authority, *Metropolitan Transportation: 1980* (New York: 1963), Chapter 20.

68. The quotation is from "Port Authority Report," editorial, *New York Times*, August 13, 1946; cf. the laudatory comments on the bus terminal and its benefits in "The Port Authority at 30," editorial, *New York Times*, April 30, 1951, and "New York Port Authority's 30 Years of Achieve-ment," editorial, *Courier-Post* (Camden, N.J.), May 1, 1951. A decade after the terminal opened, increased traffic led the authority to undertake a $30 million expansion of the terminal, which it said would save five minutes or more in commuting time. The new plan generated another round of media applause. The article in the *Sunday News* placed particular emphasis on the nexus between improve-ments in transport terminals and suburban growth. "Over the next six months, more than 91,000 commuters from Bergen and Passaic, Hudson, Essex, Union Counties and points west will be 'moved closer' to New York," the article announced. "Real estate men, advertising suburban dream houses as '30 minutes from New York,' will be able to claim 25 minutes, or 20." Douglas Sefton, "Eureka! N.J. Commuters Nearing a Utopian State," *Sunday News*, March 25, 1962.

69. Port Authority, *Twenty-Ninth Annual Report: 1949*, p. 116; *Thirty-Second Annual Re-port: 1952*, p. 67.

70. "Port Authority in 25 Years Becomes Giant Operator," editorial, *Hudson Dispatch*, April 30, 1946.

### Regional Arteries That "Fire the Mind"

Relations among the highway-oriented agencies have not always been free from conflict, as the bus terminal case indicates. By the mid-1950s, however, all major elements of the highway coalition were deeply involved in a cooperative program that would demand close contact for the next decade, and would significantly alter the region's transportation system. Initiated with a study by Moses's Triborough Authority and the Port Authority in 1954, the program also required major financing and planning contributions by federal and state highway agencies and by other public authorities in the region. Ten years later, the coalition could look on the results with satisfaction: the Verrazano-Narrows Bridge joining Staten Island and Long Island; the Throgs Neck Bridge between the Bronx and Queens; a second deck on the George Washington Bridge; new expressways in Bergen County, Staten Island, and New York City; and extensions of the New Jersey Turnpike and the New Jersey Highway Authority's Garden State Parkway.

During the first half-dozen years after the end of World War II, vehicular traffic on the region's major highway arteries nearly doubled, with especially large increases recorded on Triborough's bridges and tunnels to Manhattan and on the Port Authority's trans-Hudson crossings. The usual response of the highway organizations was to expand facilities incrementally to meet demand—witness the Port Authority's 1951 decision to add a third tube to the Lincoln Tunnel, to facilitate traffic pouring into Manhattan. Coordination among the region's agencies tended to be limited to those involved with particular segments of the road network, and relationships between the Port Authority and Moses were often strained.[71]

The early initiative in developing a more comprehensive and cooperative approach to highway planning was taken by the Port Authority. In a series of studies of traffic patterns in the early 1950s, the authority noted that an increasing proportion of trans-Hudson automobile trips did not begin or end in Manhattan. It concluded that detailed studies were needed of highway arteries that would bypass the Manhattan central business district, and asked the Triborough Authority to join in such studies. Moses agreed in late 1953, and after a year's study the two agencies released a report in January 1955 proposing several major additions to the highway network.

In terms of their expected impact on the region, the most important of these was the Narrows Bridge, connecting Staten Island—New York City's borough of Richmond—to Brooklyn and the rest of Long Island. The report anticipated that as a result of this bridge Staten Island, "the last large undeveloped area adjacent to Manhattan, would enjoy a significant economic improvement." Population would be "at least tripled" by 1975, and the development of the borough "would be integrated with the expanding economy of

71. Moses was immersed in a great variety of enterprises, many dating from the 1920s and 1930s, which necessarily brought him into conflict with other agencies and officials. The "necessity" was caused in part by differences in organizational goals and perspectives, and in part by Moses's acerbic style of public discussion. Conflicts with the PNYA included the bus terminal case (where Moses was acting in part in his role as member of the City Planning Commission), and the question in the late 1940s whether the PNYA or a separate airport authority should develop regional airports east of the Hudson (Moses preferring the latter). On the airport conflict, see Kaufman, "Gotham in the Air Age," pp. 143–197.

New Jersey and Long Island." Moreover, more than seven million vehicles would be diverted from the streets of Manhattan.

Other projects to be undertaken by the two authorities were the lower deck of the George Washington Bridge (by the Port Authority) and Throgs Neck Bridge (by Triborough). In addition, negotiations with other agencies led to simultaneous announcements of several related projects: the Garden State Parkway and the New Jersey Turnpike authorities would provide $85 million to extend their roads north to help provide bypass routes around Manhattan; and New Jersey's state highway department would collaborate with the Port Authority in financing and constructing a new expressway across Bergen County to the George Washington Bridge. Federal and state funds, the report suggested, might also provide an expressway across Staten Island and two express highways through Manhattan. The Port Authority and Triborough anticipated spending nearly $400 million of their own funds on the projects; the other agencies would contribute another $200 million or more. The report noted that if necessary approvals were granted "without delay," the three bridge projects could be opened to traffic in five years—by January 1, 1960.[72]

Once an affluent public authority announced that it would build a major highway facility, one might predict—in the heyday of road building—that the task would certainly, and promptly, be accomplished. The agency's financial independence, and the fact that its proposed actions appeared consistent with public needs for better arterial highways, gave assurance of success. Moreover, a successful outcome could be anticipated with greater confidence when the sponsors were two prominent authorities who had joined forces, and when their plans have attracted support from regional spokesmen. Indeed, initial reactions to the announced program, particularly among the news media, made it clear that the two agencies had scored an early public relations success. The program was acclaimed as "awe-inspiring" and "monumental," as a "spectacular" plan that would open "new vistas for the planning and development of the New York metropolitan area." "Fortunately," one major newspaper editorialized, "we have men . . . who can understand problems of such magnitude . . . and work them out while the rest of us gasp with awe."[73]

In a complex political environment, however, even spectacular projects with well-heeled sponsors can be derailed. The evolution of the Narrows Bridge project underscores the important role of leadership skills in major regional efforts. The Narrows Bridge program also shows how personal and organizational motives, as well as financial independence, are important factors distinct from "public demand" for new facilities.

72. PNYA and TBTA, *Joint Study of Arterial Facilities* (New York: January 1955). The quotations in the text are on pp. 7, 21 and 25.

73. The quoted comments are, respectively, from "Welding the Metropolitan Region," editorial, *New York Herald Tribune*, January 17, 1955; "Staggering Plans," editorial, *Paterson News*, January 18, 1955; "New Bridge-Building Plans," editorial, *New York Times*, January 17, 1955; untitled editorial, *Bergen Evening Record*, January 17, 1955; these and other editorials on the announced program are reprinted in Port Authority, *Annual Report: 1954*, pp. 14–15. New Jersey's Governor Robert Meyner and other political and business leaders also provided early endorsements. Before the authorities' public announcement, their officials had briefed the press, business groups, and public officials at extensive meetings in New York City, Bergen County, and Trenton.

The main points regarding the Narrows project can be made briefly:

1. A bridge or tunnel across the Narrows had been under consideration since the early 1900s, and New York City's governing body had approved a toll tunnel in 1929, voting an initial appropriation for design work. Yet no crossing was built for another twenty-five years, the major obstacles being technical and political complexity, as well as money. The channel was more than 7,000 feet, requiring a bridge center span longer than any yet constructed. Also, a bridge would have to be high enough for large ocean vessels to pass underneath. And there were thousands of residents in the path of bridge approaches in Brooklyn. The costs and technical problems involved in a tunnel under the deep channel were even greater.

2. The challenge of building a bridge across the Narrows was, however, an attractive prospect to Moses, for it would be a crowning jewel for the many prominent projects with which he had been associated. This would be "the longest suspension bridge in the world, and the tallest," Moses exclaimed; "it will be the biggest bridge, the highest bridge, and the bridge with greatest clearance." Struck with the personal, organizational, and regional benefits which could flow from "the most important single piece of arterial construction in the world," Moses had obtained necessary approval from the federal government in 1949 to build it as a Triborough Authority project. The estimated cost was far beyond Triborough's immediate financial capacity, however, and as of 1954, it seemed doubtful that the authority could undertake the project for at least another ten years.[74]

3. At this juncture, collaboration with the Port Authority seemed particularly attractive to Moses and his aides, as the bistate agency had the funds needed to begin construction at once. An agreement was worked out by the end of 1954, whereby the Port Authority would construct and finance the bridge, Triborough would operate it, and—when its financial resources from other bridges and tunnels permitted—Triborough would buy the Narrows bridge from the Port Authority.

The advantages of this joint arrangement were hardly one-sided, however. While enhancing Moses's prestige, stimulating development on Staten Island, and reducing travel time between Long Island and New Jersey, immediate action on a Narrows Bridge also promised several specific benefits for the Port Authority. The bridge would divert motor vehicles from the Holland Tunnel, thus allaying criticism of the authority for failure to provide more trans-Hudson facilities. The new crossing also would reduce traffic congestion in Manhattan, which promised to generate support for the Authority from the media and civic groups in Manhattan. Moreover, the project would improve the financial condition of the Port Authority's three Staten Island bridges,

---

74. Quoted in William Randolph Hearst, Jr., "To Speed Traffic Through City: Main Points in Moses Program," *New York Journal American*, December 10, 1954. In the early 1950s, the Triborough Authority's income flow and uncommitted borrowing capacity were not as large as the Port Authority's; adding both the Narrows Bridge and the Throgs Neck Bridge in 1955 would have overtaxed its borrowing capability. Later, as Triborough's toll revenues steadily rose, Moses's agency took full financial responsibility for the giant span.

Caro's discussion provides more detail on some aspects of the joint study negotiations; see Caro, *The Power Broker*, pp. 921–930. Our review of the evidence, however, suggests that Caro assigns too much credit to Moses, and too little to the Port Authority's staff, in his discussion of who took the initiative in proposing a joint study, and how the detailed plans were developed.

which had operated in the red for most of the past twenty-five years. The bridge would also absorb funds that otherwise might lie idle, opening the agency to criticism for maintaining high automobile tolls and failing to use its "excess" funds to solve the growing rail transit problem.

4. The decision of the two authorities in early 1955 to allocate funds for the Narrows span did not ensure that a bridge would actually be built. The most difficult problem was to convince the New York City Board of Estimate to authorize construction of the approaches through residential sections of Brooklyn. Vehement opposition from local residents and their elected representatives led to continuing delays in 1955, 1956, and 1957. Construction was postponed, Moses later recalled, as "opponents sought by distortion of facts, appeals to prejudice, . . . and almost incredible personal vituperation to maim or kill the project. These opponents never rested. They appeared at every forum and in every tribunal." At one Board of Estimate hearing, the critics, "with jeers, cat-calls, and billingsgate, were allowed to go on until two o'clock the next morning. . . . No rule of debate was observed. We were treated as if we were speculators asking for a franchise to build a private toll bridge."[75]

Moses led the counterattack, arguing that unless the city gave prompt approval, Triborough would drop the arterial projects. Moreover, Moses doubted that he could then be of any use to New York City as its general coordinator of highway construction (a separate post he had held since 1946), since he would not "be able to speak with any authority or any expectation of support" from the city administration. Moses found it "hard to believe that New York City under its present Mayor will go on notice as not having the imagination and guts to take advantage of funds largely from other sources."[76]

Final approval was at last obtained from the Board of Estimate at the end of 1958, ground was broken in 1959, and in November 1964 the Verrazano-Narrows Bridge was opened to traffic—by Triborough, which had now become affluent enough to assume complete responsibility for the span. During the next six years, the population of Staten Island increased by more than 30 percent, to nearly 300,000. Stimulated by improved access to the rest of New York City and Long Island, land values on Staten Island rose from $1,500 per undeveloped acre in 1960 to $20,000 in 1964 and $80,000 in 1971.[77] Moreover, by making Staten Island more accessible, and thus facilitating construction of the relatively inexpensive new housing discussed in Chapter Three, the Narrows Bridge hastened the flow of white middle- and working-class families out of the city's older sections.

As to the bridge itself, the Triborough Authority's gross income from the crossing was $9.5 million for the first twelve months of operation, and revenues increased steadily thereafter. The last word on its esthetic contribution

75. Robert Moses, *Public Works: A Dangerous Trade* (New York: McGraw-Hill, 1970), p. 226.

76. That is, from the two authorities and from federal and state highway programs. The quotations are from Moses's letters to Mayor Robert F. Wagner, Jr., in 1955, reprinted in Moses, *Public Works*, p. 229.

77. See Port Authority, *Staten Island: A Study of Its Resources and Their Development* (New York: Staten Island Chamber of Commerce, January 1971); and Robert D. McFadden, "Verrazano-Narrows Bridge: 'A Two-Faced Woman,' " *New York Times*, December 6, 1970.

*The magnificent Verrazano-Narrows Bridge connecting Brooklyn and Staten Island provided an essential link in the highway system forged by the Triborough Bridge and Tunnel Authority, the Port Authority, and other highway agencies.*    Credit: Triborough Bridge and Tunnel Authority

to the region goes to Robert Moses, who retired soon after completion of this final monument to his ambition and his genius:

> It is a structure of superlatives, a creation of imagination, art, architecture and engineering. Its scale, magnitude and beauty will fire the mind of every stranger and bring a tear to every returning native eye.[78]

78. Robert Moses, remarks at the cable-spinning ceremony at the Verrazano-Narrows Bridge, March 7, 1963. The bridge design was the work of the great Swiss bridge designer, Othmar Ammann, who was also responsible for the George Washington Bridge three decades earlier.

# 7

---

# Mass Transportation and the
# Limited Capabilities of Government

---

Even a cursory glance at the evolution of transportation patterns in the New York region during the past half-century reveals stark contrasts between the highway system on the one hand, and the facilities available for mass transportation—travel along fixed routes by rail or bus—on the other.[1] The road system, as well as highway trips by automobile and truck, have expanded geometrically, and the impact of these changes in reshaping the urban region has been extensive and dramatic. With respect to the principal concerns of this volume, the highway-building coalition obviously deserves close attention in order to determine the role of governmental actors in the patterns and timing of highway expansion, and to identify the sources and motivations of governmental action.

In contrast, the public transportation system—especially its extensive rail component—has declined in quality and ridership during the past several decades. Every major private rail carrier in the region has gone into bankruptcy, publicly owned rail services generate large deficits, almost no new rail lines have been built for forty years, and the financial conditions of most bus operations serving cities and suburbs are distinctly unhealthy. Nonetheless, the major railroad, subway and bus lines found in the region twenty and thirty years ago still exist; commuters and mid-day travelers (if they wait patiently) still do travel on the Long Island Rail Road, Conrail, suburban bus lines, and New York city's vast network of subway and surface lines.[2] It is not a public transport system in rapid decline; instead it is a largely static system, at least when viewed in the context of the

---

1. In this study, mass transportation, mass transit, transit, public transport, and public transit will be used interchangeably to refer to transportation systems, operating on rail and road, which use fixed routes and are available to the general public. The term "rail transit" refers only to railroads, trolleys, subways, and other rail systems. The term "rapid transit" refers to subways and other rail systems that have exclusive rights of way and frequent designated passenger stops.

2. Conrail (Consolidated Rail Corporation) was created by the federal government in 1974, in order to acquire the assets of the major railroad corporations operating in the northeastern United States. Commuter passenger services and freight services provided by Conrail in the New York region include those previously operated by the Penn Central, New Haven, Erie Lackawanna, Central Railroad of New Jersey, and Lehigh Valley rail companies. The government corporation began operation in 1976 after court challenges were resolved, and after further congressional action (the Railroad Revitalization and Regulatory Reform Act of 1976). Conrail also operates intercity passenger services on behalf of the National Rail Passenger Corporation (Amtrak), another federal government enterprise.

regional dynamics described in previous chapters. For more than half a century, the region has expanded and changed through the vigorous interactions of highway builders, private businesses and homebuyers seeking new locations, aggressive developers, and cautious or unwary local officials with zoning powers. But mass transit officials—governmental and private—seem condemned to be onlookers rather than shapers of urban development. By and large they serve a declining, residual fragment of the region's residents: those so unfortunate or so wise that they do not rely on automobiles for the journey to work and all other activities but bathroom and bed.

When contrasted with the highway-building system, then, it may seem relatively unimportant to sort out the role of governmental action in shaping the evolution of mass transit in the region. For the mass transit system has hardly evolved at all. Yet the critic or reformer can justify some attention to mass transportation, if only to examine the potential, or paradise, lost: Why did government not act more vigorously—using funds and other public powers to revitalize the rail system, and in this way effectively hinder the evolution toward diffuse suburban growth in the past three decades? Moreover, through such an examination it should be possible to assess better the impact on the region's future development of government mass transit programs—programs that have become more desirable to many as a consequence of rising energy costs.

## Mass Transportation and the Region's Development

Movement outward from the central urban areas began long before the automobile was an important means of travel. As noted in Chapter Two, trolleys and railroad lines fostered and shaped suburbanization in the nineteenth century and the first two decades of the present century. The expectation of private profit was an important stimulus to these mass transit developments; but public funds and other forms of governmental collaboration were also significant factors in establishing rail lines, horse-drawn streetcars, and electrified trolleys in New York and other urban regions.[3]

The networks of transit lines created through these public and private efforts had far-reaching effects on patterns of housing and job location—effects that were to some extent foreseen by their initiators. The new transit lines allowed workers to seek housing farther removed from their job locations, since they could now travel quickly from homes in Queens and Westchester to factories and offices in Brooklyn and Manhattan. In New Jersey, suburban growth was encouraged by railroad lines extending out from Jersey City, Newark, and Paterson; and after 1910 two new rail lines under the Hudson River provided additional incentives for Manhattan workers to seek apartments and houses in the western suburbs.[4] At the same time, these

3. See Seymour J. Mandelbaum, *Boss Tweed's New York* (New York: Wiley, 1965), pp. 123–126; Wallace S. Sayre and Herbert Kaufman, *Governing New York City* (New York: Russell Sage,1960), p. 323, and sources cited on pp. 346–347; Sam B. Warner, Jr., *Streetcar Suburbs* (Cambridge, Mass.: Harvard University Press and MIT Press, 1962), especially Chapters 2, 4, and 7; Louis Hartz, *Economic Policy and Democratic Thought: Pennsylvania, 1776–1860* (Cambridge, Mass.: Harvard University Press, 1948), Chapters 3 and 7.

transportation lines made it possible for employers to tap the large and growing pool of workers—as long as their offices and plants were located at the
hubs of the expanding rail networks.

In the several decades before World War I, then, extensive rail construction activities permitted greater concentration of employment centers in the
New York region, and especially in the Manhattan business district, than
would otherwise have been possible. The rail system also encouraged residential suburbanization, and helped to determine the structure of suburban
growth—which tended to cluster along rail lines, and especially near railroad
stations and rapid transit stops, so that travel time to job and shopping locations could be minimized. Thus the developing transit system had both a decentralizing impact—encouraging residential locations in the suburbs—and a
centralizing influence—attracting business firms to Manhattan, Jersey City, and
other downtown areas of the expanding metropolis, and holding them there.[5]

After the 1920s there were few significant additions to the rail network
of the New York area. In this region as in others, however, bus transportation
expanded sharply (largely through the initiative of private companies), reaching its highest passenger levels in the 1940s and early 1950s.[6] Although government has come to play an increasingly important role in keeping the region's mass transportation system operating over the past quarter century, no
significant additions have been brought about by governmental initiative and
funds during this period. In terms of impact on population and employment
patterns in the region, there are no mass transportation counterparts to the

---

4. To recount briefly the creation of the New York region's rail system: First came the
Camden and Amboy, later part of the Pennsylvania system, which opened a line across New Jersey
in 1831. During the next 40 years, five other rail corporations—the Erie, Lackawanna, Central of
New Jersey, Lehigh Valley, and Susquehanna—laid rail lines through New Jersey cities and suburbs,
all terminating in Jersey City or other towns on the western bank of the Hudson River. At that point,
passengers and freight bound for Manhattan and other eastern points had to rely on the slow
trans-Hudson ferry system. Then, in 1908–1909, the Hudson and Manhattan Railroad (now PATH)
completed two tunnels under the Hudson River, joining Newark, Jersey City, and Hoboken with
Manhattan. A year later, the Pennsylvania completed its tunnel under the river to Penn Station in
midtown Manhattan.

East of the Hudson River, rail lines were constructed through Westchester and into Connecticut, and by 1850, the New York Central and New Haven railroads brought passengers directly into
Manhattan. Long Island's rail system was laid during the same period, although Manhattan-bound
travelers crossed the East River by ferry until 1910, when a tunnel was completed, bringing Long
Island passengers directly into Penn Station. In the latter part of the nineteenth century, elevated rail
lines were built in Brooklyn and Manhattan, and in the first years of this century the New York City
government and a private firm carried out major programs of subway construction. See John T.
Cunningham, *Railroading in New Jersey* (Newark: Associated Railroads of New Jersey, 1951), pp. 6–
16, 35–55, and *passim*; Jean Gottmann, *Megalopolis* (New York: Twentieth Century Fund, 1961),
Chapter 3; New York State, Public Service Commission for the First District, *Report . . . for the Year
Ending December 31, 1913*, Vol. V: *Documentary History of Railroad Companies* (New York: 1914),
pp. 605–620, 768–772, 881–894, 978; and the reports of the New York City Board of Transportation
listed in Sayre and Kaufman, *Governing New York City*, pp. 346–347.

5. This widely accepted view, that rail transit lines and other developments encouraged
diffusion long before the automobile arrived, is discussed in the sources cited in note 3 above, and
in Edgar M. Hoover and Raymond Vernon, *Anatomy of a Metropolis* (Cambridge, Mass.: Harvard
University Press, 1959), pp. 2, 134, 187, 190, 215–216.

6. On bus transportation, see Wilfred Owen, *The Metropolitan Transportation Problem*,
revised ed. (Garden City, N.Y.: Doubleday Anchor, 1966), pp. 243–244 and *passim*; and Port of New
York Authority, *Metropolitan Transportation—1980* (New York: 1963), Chapters 16 and 20.

interstate highway system or the Narrows Bridge.[7] Instead, public action has been directed toward more modest objectives: slowing the general decline of existing rail and bus service, stabilizing mass transit service during commuting hours, and replacing wornout equipment.

It is understandable that this kind of governmental effort may not be viewed as significant, when compared with the dramatic road-building efforts of the postwar era, or the massive projects of the earlier railroad and subway construction decades. But that perspective may be too myopic. Suppose that the railroad commuting system of the New York region had collapsed, following the bankruptcy of the major rail carriers in the 1960s and early 1970s.[8] That collapse, which was averted by government action, would have had a traumatic impact. In the short run, more than 150,000 daily commuters would have been added to the already-clogged highways, bridges and tunnels leading to Manhattan, Newark and other employment centers. Similarly, failure to provide public funds would have brought the subway system to a halt, requiring more than 1.4 million passengers to find alternative ways to get to work. And in some parts of the region—such as Bergen and Rockland counties— government inaction in the face of mounting bus company deficits would have forced several thousand additional commuters into automobiles and onto crowded highways.

In the long run, the loss of public transit services to any sector of the region—or even a sharp decline in services—could be expected to have a major impact on the distribution of residences and jobs within the region, and also to redistribute jobs toward other, competing metropolitan regions. For example, the demise of the Long Island Rail Road would render Nassau and Suffolk counties less attractive to people employed in New York City. Some firms would respond in time by relocating to parts of the region whose labor pools could more readily be tapped by public transportation and which are more accessible by automobile. Finding their ability to relocate constrained by zoning laws, perhaps by deteriorating mass transit services in other parts of the region, and by highway patterns and congestion, firms would also tend to shift services and locations to other parts of the nation. Many offices would, for example, find relocation to Chicago, Denver or Houston attractive.

The impact of railroads and rapid transit lines in the early decentralization of the New York region is widely acknowledged by students of the urban economy, including Raymond Vernon.[9] So too, there is general acceptance of

7. Perhaps the Port Authority's midtown Manhattan bus terminal, discussed in Chapter 6, and the George Washington Bridge bus station, completed in the early 1960s, qualify as the most significant additions to the New York region's mass transportation network. In contrast, in San Francisco-Oakland, Washington, D.C., and a few other regions that had not experienced the early wave of rail construction seen in the New York area, new rail systems have been built during the past two decades.

8. The highlights of this period of decay include the bankruptcy of the Central of New Jersey in March 1967; the merger of the Pennsylvania and New York Central railroads to form the Penn Central in February 1968, which added the New Haven Railroad 10 months later and then succumbed to bankruptcy in June 1970; and the collapse of the Lehigh Valley, the Reading, and the Erie Lackawanna, all of which declared that they were bankrupt during 1970–1972. For a more detailed summary see Consolidated Rail Corporation, *Annual Report 1976* (Philadelphia: 1977), pp. 4–5.

9. See Vernon, *Metropolis 1985*, pp. 21, 23. Cf. Hoover and Vernon, *Anatomy of a Metropolis*, pages cited in note 5 above.

the importance of rail facilities in the recent and future ability of Manhattan and Newark to maintain large office centers.[10]

In assessing the importance of government's role in mass transport, our differences with Vernon and Wood largely turn upon a matter of definition. Assume that government officials devise and carry out multimillion-dollar programs that resist the "economic forces at work", and the mass transportation system's basic services are thereby stabilized. We would cite such efforts as evidence that government has had a major continuing role in determining the public transportation network for the region and, through those efforts, in influencing the distribution of jobs and residences in the New York area. Wood and Vernon interpret the evidence differently: they conclude that in mass transit as in other areas, government has had little or no influence on development. Our conflicting views are not primarily caused by looking at different time periods or different facts; instead, the disagreement stems from using different standards in evaluating the role of government.

Wood and Vernon apply a severe standard in testing the impact of government mass transit policies on the pattern of regional development. To be influential, government policies must involve sustained, dependable access to public funds for mass transportation, which would lead to improved service that might attract more riders.[11] But even that would not be enough. Some increases in public funds could be expected in the coming years, but if they were to have a significant impact, they would have to be linked to a "great initiative on the part of government," a "really sharp break with the past," and "massive changes in passenger transport policy."[12] For Wood, the standard for significant influence would be government action that halted and perhaps reversed the diffusion of jobs and residences across the metropolitan hinterland. This would entail "a massive flow of public funds to support mass transit," as well as a regional organization with the power to make authoritative decisions about development throughout the New York area, and to provide funds for highway as well as rail programs only when those programs were consistent with a general plan.[13]

Since these were the criteria for success used by Vernon and Wood, it is hardly surprising that they found all government transit programs then existing or in the offing in the early 1960s to be of little importance. Continuing public financial support had been provided for the Long Island Rail Road, and funds for new equipment were available to other commuter lines, but these were but "palliative" actions. The Port Authority had agreed to spend more than $80 million on a rail project, but this did not "embrace the comprehensive coordination of modes of travel" or entail a "basic sacrifice" by the highway agencies. Therefore, such efforts were "only marginal."[14] Looking to

10. See Hoover and Vernon, *Anatomy of a Metropolis*, pp. 97, 112, 218, 245; and Owen, *The Metropolitan Transportation Problem*, Chapter 4.

11. Wood, *1400 Governments*, p. 143.

12. Vernon, *Metropolis 1985*, pp. 182, 183.

13. Wood, *1400 Governments*, pp. 170, 192. On page 192, Wood characterizes such goals as those of the " 'view with alarm' school of metropolitan affairs"; but in fact they are also the standards that he and Vernon apply in exploring the powers and policies of "a government sufficient to redirect the pattern of economic development in the Region . . ." (p. 193).

14. Vernon, *Metropolis 1985*, p. 186; Wood, *1400 Governments*, pp. 142–143, 170.

the future, Wood accurately foresaw increased public subsidies for public transport services, and he conjectured that transit services might in fact be expanded somewhat. But in the absence of a powerful regional planning agency and a "massive flow" of government funds to mass transit, the diffusion of jobs and residences would not be halted. In the field of mass transportation as in other program areas, therefore, "public policies are of little consequence."[15]

In our view, the Wood-Vernon test of significant government influence entails too extreme a standard. If government efforts fall short of the extraordinary requirements specified by these authors, the need for further analysis seems to be at an end. That is, one need not consider the relative usefulness of various public programs in stabilizing or modestly improving the region's transit system, or the impact that such programs may have on the region's development. Moreover, the Wood-Vernon conclusions on mass transportation again illustrate the weakness of viewing government policies as a set of activities that can be treated as separate from private market forces, with both categories being isolated from underlying consumer/voter demands. As we argued in Chapter One, in a relatively responsive democratic system, government programs will be closely intertwined with behavior in the private economy, and with underlying consumer/voter preferences. To stipulate that government's public transit programs can be considered significant only if they effectively undercut consumer preferences for suburban "diffusion," and only if they overcome the widespread public suspicion of powerful regional agencies, is to decide the question of governmental influence on urban development almost by definition.[16]

## Obstacles to Governmental Action

We prefer a lower threshold of significance, and therefore a wide variety of concerns deserve close attention—the goals of public officials and private groups concerned with mass transportation, the obstacles they have faced, the extent of their successes (however modest), and the conditions that have determined patterns of success and failure.

In the first decade after World War II, the environment for public action was inhospitable and disappointing—at least to those who sought a great initiative by government to meet mass transportation problems. Problems were certainly plentiful—some left over from the public agenda of the prewar era, others newly developing or reemerging. Since the 1920s, New Jersey commuter groups had urged that new rail lines be constructed across the

15. Wood, *1400 Governments*, pp. 144, 170, 175.

16. It should be noted that in *Metropolis 1985* Vernon occasionally offers comments that take a different position from the dominant Wood-Vernon argument outlined in the text. On page 182, Vernon notes that a "total breakdown in some critical service," such as mass transit, could result in "distorting the Region's development"; and on page 223, he argues that rail as well as highway services will be crucial in shaping the future of the Manhattan CBD. The implication, though not given much emphasis, is that government actions might have an important role even if they do not involve "massive changes" in policy and "comprehensive coordination of modes of travel."

Hudson, in order to reduce travel time and increase convenience for travelers from Bergen, Morris, and other New Jersey counties bound for Manhattan.[17] Then, in the early postwar years, New York City's subway system generated large deficits; and the financial condition of the commuter railroads serving the region, already weakened in the Depression, began to show signs of severe distress by the late 1940s and early 1950s.[18] Meanwhile, increasing automobile and truck congestion on the highways, caused in part by the absence of good rail and bus alternatives, led some observers to conclude that expanded mass transit service was essential for continued regional mobility and economic growth.[19]

In the arena of highway policy—described in Chapter Six—when congestion and financial constraints were identified as "highway problems" in the early 1950s, the general direction for a solution seemed clear, and within a few years a detailed strategy had been devised and a massive response was underway. It seemed evident that more highways, bridges, and tunnels were needed; responsibility for action lay in the hands of government; and new taxes and a special trust fund were created to finance the extensive federal-aid highway program begun in 1956.

In the mass transit field, in contrast, no consensus emerged from the early discussions regarding the general approach to be followed or where responsibility for action lay, and prompt action did not follow. There were several difficulties in this policy arena. First, while road building was historically a government function, rail and bus service traditionally had been the responsibility of private entrepreneurs.[20] Except for New York City's subway system, mass transit services were still provided in the early postwar years by private "profit-making" corporations. The governmental role was essentially passive, with state and federal regulatory commissions reviewing (and accept-

17. As mentioned in note 4 above, several of the New Jersey rail lines terminated at the Hudson River, and passengers had to cross to Manhattan by ferry, bus, or the H&M transit service. The efforts of commuter associations and other groups, during the period 1922–1952, are summarized in New York Metropolitan Rapid Transit Commission and New Jersey Metropolitan Rapid Transit Commission, *Joint Report* (New York: March 3, 1954), pp. 54–62. (Hereafter, this document will be cited as NYMRTC and NJMRTC, *Joint Report*.)

18. After the end of World War II, passengers deserted the rail lines and took to the highways, especially during noncommuting hours, and the trucking industry increasingly siphoned off the more lucrative freight traffic. By 1952, both the Long Island Rail Road and the H&M Railroad were in bankruptcy, while sharp passenger declines had led to reductions in rail service and to shaky financial conditions on several of the New Jersey railroads. See Owen, *Metropolitan Transportation Problem*, Chapter 3; Robert W. Purcell, "Special Report to the Governor on Problems of the Railroads and Bus Lines in New York State" (New York: March 12, 1959); NYMRTC and NJMRTC, *Joint Report*, pp. 12–13, 34–43, 63–68.

19. See, for example, NYMRTC and NJMRTC, *Joint Report*, pp. 2–10, and the testimony of public officials, citizen groups, and others at the commissions' hearings in 1953, summarized in *Joint Report*, pp. 73–102.

20. This tradition had plenty of exceptions, however. During the nineteenth century, in addition to providing land and other assistance to private railroad corporations, government units were at times actively involved in the development of rail service through "mixed corporations," which included both public and private funds as well as joint policy control. In New York City, the local government constructed the Interborough Rapid Transit (IRT) subway system beginning in 1904, and then leased it for operation to a private firm, and in 1925 construction was begun on a second city-owned system, the Independent (IND). See Hartz, *Economic Policy and Democratic Thought*, Chapter 3, and the sources cited in note 4 above.

ing or rejecting) proposals by rail and bus corporations to alter fares and service. There was no set of public officials with a mandate to act more directly in defining and proposing solutions to the growing mass transit problem, no recent history of public action that would lead the general public to expect government to take the initiative in this field, and no readily available source of public funds to underwrite mass transportation.

Closely related to the tradition of government non-responsibility was the fragmentation of government authority in the New York region. Rail and bus routes crossed municipal, county and state lines, and the fractionalization of formal and informal governmental power was even greater than in the highway field. Rail transport had no counterpart to the integrating efforts of Robert Moses with his many hats, or the Port Authority with its bistate jurisdiction. Moreover, because federal and state government efforts in the rail and bus field were essentially regulatory and passive, there was even less incentive for—and little tradition of—cooperative effort among relevant state and national public agencies.

In fact, the governmental and private groups in the New York region concerned with mass transportation were a remarkably motley crew, with limited political resources and an unpromising future. User interests were represented by the commuter organizations of North Jersey, Long Island, and Westchester, whose efforts to improve mass transportation and to involve the Port Authority in rail enterprises extended back to the 1920s. Yet by the early 1950s, these associations—the Inter-Municipal Group for Better Rail Service, the Transit Committee of Bergen County, the Westchester Commuters Group, and others—were devoting most of their energies to campaigns simply to save existing services. Thus they were caught up in continual rearguard action— with statements to the press and at regulatory hearings that did little more than resist efforts by the railroads to curtail service and increase fares.[21]

The suburban railroads were far more interested in reducing or abandoning service on deficit-producing passenger lines than in improving mass transit. Rail spokesmen occasionally did argue that additional rail facilities were needed, and some urged the Port Authority and other highway agencies to help meet mass transportation needs. But their understandable concern with corporate solvency led railroad officials to adopt an essentially negative stance—cutting services and increasing fares, rather than devising imaginative programs of transportation improvement.[22]

Then there were the business and civic interests that were anxious to maintain mass transportation services to New York City, Newark, and other downtown locations. Most of those active in this group were Manhattan-based associations which saw rail service stability as essential to the economic strength and dominance of the Manhattan CBD. A few viewed improved rail and bus service as part of a complex strategy for improving economic health and living patterns in the region as a whole. In the conflict between the railroads and commuter organizations, some of the civic-group spokesmen were sympathetic to the economic plight of rail corporations and their desire

21. See NYMRTC and NJMRTC, *Joint Report*, pp. 54–60, 92, 101–102, and Jameson W. Doig, *Metropolitan Transportation Politics and the New York Region* (New York: Columbia University Press, 1966), pp. 22–24.

22. Ibid., pp. 21–22, and NYMRTC and NJMRTC, *Joint Report*, pp. 91–100.

to reduce deficit-producing services. Others agreed with suburban commuters that existing services should be maintained, while the search continued for other sources of funds to save public transportation.[23]

In contrast to the highway coalition, then, the private interests concerned with mass transit policies differed greatly among themselves as to short-run priorities and long-run goals. They did not produce a coherent set of constituency demands that legislative committees and other government agencies would be compelled to weigh carefully as representing an agreed-upon program of action. Consequently the efforts of the rail interests to obtain effective government action were severely handicapped. The underlying problem—the limited ability of governmental actors to shape urban development when confronted by diverse constituency pressures—is one we have seen before, in the Chapter Four discussion of environmentalism and highways in the 1970s. We will see it again in the analysis of the older cities in the next two chapters.

Moreover, in contrast to the widespread and growing use of automobiles, the most directly involved constituency—the users of mass transit service—comprised a small percentage of the region's population, and in the case of rail commuters a declining proportion as well. Between 1930 and 1952, automobile registration in the three states increased sharply, while railroad commuter traffic dropped by 25 to 60 percent. By 1952, trans-Hudson commuters from North Jersey who used mass transit comprised just over 3 percent of the population of the nine northeastern counties, with more than one-third of this fraction relying on bus rather than rail. The proportion was somewhat higher in the Westchester-Connecticut sector, and highest on Long Island, where LIRR commuters made up just over 5 percent of the Island's burgeoning population. When non-rush-hour rail travel was added, the Long Island total rose, but only to 8 percent.[24]

Of course the number of residents potentially affected by mass transportation was far larger than the modest number who made regular use of the region's rail and bus services. As noted earlier in this chapter, the loss of public transit services, especially in commuter hours, would lead to massive highway congestion, and probably to long-run changes in residential and commercial location patterns that would be traumatic for Long Island, Westchester, and some North Jersey areas. Yet there was no widespread sense of concern on the part of the general public, because the main rail and bus services continued, even while some of the carriers slid toward bankruptcy. Throughout the first postwar decade, the commuters and their local communities found they could rely on their state utility commissions to resist the

23. See, for example, the views of the New York Chamber of Commerce, Citizens Union, Avenue of the Americas Association, and Regional Plan Association, quoted in *Joint Report*, pp. 5–7, 85–89, 102. The views of the RPA are discussed more fully above in Chapter Five.

24. The increase in automobile registration during 1930 to 1952 was 104 percent in New Jersey, 71 percent in New York State, and 138 percent in Connecticut. During this period, railroad commuter traffic declined by 59 percent in New Jersey, 25 percent in Westchester County, and 42 percent on Long Island. These totals, and the ratio of passengers to population in 1952 cited in the text, are based on figures compiled by the Port Authority, the U.S. Census Bureau and other sources, and are summarized in NYMRTC and NJMRTC, *Joint Report*, pp. 10–13, 32–33, 44, and 52. See also Port of New York Authority, *Metropolitan Transportation 1980* (New York: 1963), Chapters 20–22.

railroads' efforts to raise fares and reduce the frequency of service.[25] Fares did creep upward and both the quality and frequency of service declined, but only slowly, incrementally, while most of the region's populace looked on, complacently.

Those who favored governmental action to aid mass transportation faced not only public indifference, but active opposition as well from some members of the highway coalition. In the view of Robert Moses and his colleagues, government funds for urban and intercity transport should be funneled primarily into roads, not rail; and the planning and construction of new highway systems should go forward without any attempt to coordinate road and rail facilities. Local taxes paid by the railroads might be "scaled down," and subsidies to meet crises might even be provided from general government funds. However, any attempts to redirect the flow of moneys from highways and bridges, or to tie highway development to broader transportation planning goals, were vigorously opposed.

Underlying the resistance of the highway agencies and their supporters to involvement in mass transportation was the fear that the deteriorating rail services were a "bottomless pit" whose voracious needs for additional funds would destroy the ability of the Port Authority, Triborough, and their fellow road agencies to maintain their freedom of action, bountiful resources, and political independence—and thus their ability to build new bridges, tunnels, and highways.[26]

Despite these obstacles, the first postwar decade was not a period of inactivity in the mass transit field. Indeed, some significant action did take place: a new transit authority took over operation of bus and rail services in New York City; the state intervened to support the Long Island Rail Road; and state governments in Albany and Trenton created a joint commission to draw up a long-range program for the New York region.[27] However, these efforts also illustrated the weaknesses identified above—in governmental structure and leadership, in program goals, financing, and constituency support—and left the major problems unresolved.

### Responding to a Transit Crisis in New York City

In New York City, government had been involved in construction and operation of rail transit services since the turn of the century, and by the early 1940s the city's Board of Transportation had responsibility for subways, elevated railways, and bus services throughout most of the city.[28] Although lim-

25. On the railroad's mounting financial problems, and the attitudes of state utility commissions and the Interstate Commerce Commission, see Michael N. Danielson, *Federal-Metropolitan Politics and the Commuter Crisis* (New York: Columbia University Press, 1965), pp. 12–20, 24–31.

26. On the views of the highway coalition in the first postwar decade, see, for example, the statements by Austin Tobin of the Port Authority and by Robert Moses at public hearings in 1953, reprinted in part in NYMRTC and NJMRTC, *Joint Report*, pp. 77–82.

27. Another important mass transportation project was the construction of the Port Authority bus terminal in Manhattan, discussed in Chapter Six.

28. As indicated earlier (note 20 above), in the early 1900s the city government had constructed the IRT subway line and leased it for private operation, and in 1925 the city broke ground for a second line, the IND. Meanwhile, in 1913, the private Brooklyn Rapid Transit Company (later Brooklyn-Manhattan Transit, the BMT) began a subway line. By the end of the Depression, the BMT line, as well as the elevated rail lines built by private entrepreneurs and many of the bus lines in

ited to New York City, the operation was immense: The board served several million passengers each weekday over hundreds of miles of rail and bus routes. In spite of heavy usage and large city subsidies from its general tax coffers, however, deficits mounted during the first postwar decade, and additional funds were needed to meet operating expenses and finance new construction.

The city government believed these needs should be met without raising the fare; higher fares, it was argued, would increase the diversion of riders to private automobiles, especially during non-rush hours, thus adding to traffic congestion while providing little net gain in total revenues at the fare box. Moreover, increased fares would be particularly burdensome to the city's lower-income residents—who might take out their resentment against the city fathers at the ballot box.

In weighing these factors, city officials were, of course, considering mass transit policy in the context of other policy goals. But their ability to translate this broader perspective into action was sharply constrained. Except for increased fares, the two major sources of possible funds to meet transit needs were (1) siphoning off toll revenues from the Triborough and other highway authorities, and (2) increasing general tax levels within the city. State laws creating the highway authorities had placed the first option beyond the reach of city officials, unless the state consented—an unlikely prospect, particularly in view of the adamant opposition of Moses and his colleagues. And the second option would have required the state to grant additional taxing authority to New York City.[29]

Governor Dewey and the state legislature rejected both of these alternatives, and instead in 1953 replaced the Board of Transportation with a new Transit Authority which was organized to provide a stronger financial base for mass transportation in New York City. The new authority was required to meet its operating expenses from its own revenues, and would be able to increase fares as expenses rose. Yet the Transit Authority was given no borrowing power, so final responsibility for funding capital improvement still rested with New York City. This effort to "solve" the city's transit crisis by relying on the fare box and local tax funds failed as deficits mounted in subsequent years. However, Albany's intervention provided a precedent for still deeper state involvement in the region's mass transportation quagmire.[30]

### A Railroad Is "Practically Reborn"

Meanwhile, the Long Island Rail Road (LIRR) tottered on the edge of disaster. The region's preeminent commuter rail carrier in terms of passengers

---

New York City, had abandoned their profit-seeking aspirations and sold out to the city government. The Board of Transportation also took over operation of the IRT, leaving only the Staten Island Rapid Transit line and some bus routes in the private sector. For additional details, see the sources cited in note 4 above.

29. There was, of course, a third possible source of funds for mass transit—transferring money from other city programs. In practice, use of this option was highly constrained by constituency demands for larger expenditures in every major sector of its budget, a problem explored in detail in the next two chapters. Moreover, the magnitude of transit deficits dwarfed the funds that could have been reallocated at the margin.

30. For further information on the origins and characteristics of the Transit Authority, see Sayre and Kaufman, *Governing New York City*, pp. 323–343 (*passim*), and the sources listed on pp. 346–348.

per year, the LIRR steadily lost traffic to the expanding highway network in the postwar years, entering bankruptcy in 1949. A study commission appointed in 1950 by Governor Thomas Dewey recommended that a state authority be created to purchase and operate the railroad, but that proposal was rejected in Albany as the "road to socialism." Instead, state officials sought ways to continue the floundering line under private ownership. Finally, in a much-heralded state effort that departed from traditional passive state regulation, the LIRR was restructured in 1954 as a private "railroad redevelopment corporation" and given tax concessions, unusual freedom in setting fares, and other assistance which—state officials argued—would permit the railroad to emerge by 1966 as a self-sufficient private rail carrier. In the words of its publicists, the LIRR was "practically reborn" as the result of this plan,[31] but in reality the program was so modest that only a very optimistic observer could expect it to succeed, particularly if the competing highway system on Long Island continued to expand. By the early 1960s declining passenger traffic, deteriorating service, and new deficits would force wary state officials to embrace public ownership as advocated by the Dewey Commission in 1951.

### Toward Broader Regional Action

Beyond these halting efforts to meet short-term crises, there were some attempts during the first postwar years to identify broader goals and strategies—concerned with stabilizing and improving rail and bus services across the region, and with planning that included both highway and mass transportation programs. The Regional Plan Association urged that a "balanced transportation system" be developed. Goodhue Livingston of the New York City Planning Commission publicly advocated creation of a regional transportation authority to take control of the funds and duties of Triborough, the Port Authority's bridges and tunnels, New York City's buses and subways, and the Long Island Rail Road. Other public officials and private groups took similar positions.[32]

The most important action generated by this broader concern was the creation of the Metropolitan Rapid Transit Commission (MRTC) by New Jersey and New York in 1954. The bistate agency was empowered to study the region's transit problems and to recommend action to meet existing needs. In its initial meetings, the commission interpreted its mandate broadly, to include an analysis of rail and bus problems, and the preparation of a general plan for transportation development for the region.

The obstacles to an extensive study of this kind, however, were considerable. The states had set up the commission, but their support was more rhetorical than substantive. A program of action was needed, they agreed, but the $50,000 appropriated by each state was barely enough to hire a small staff, much less begin a comprehensive study. Behind this lukewarm support lay a

31. This was the phrase used in the LIRR pamphlet, *Facts 'n' Figures about the Long Island Rail Road* (New York: no date, ca. 1966).

32. See, for example, Henry Fagin (planning director of RPA), "Toward a Balanced Regional Transportation System," *Regional Plan News* 34 (May 1952), p. 1, and the views of the RPA, Livingston, the Westchester County Planning Commission, and others included in NYMRTC and NJMRTC, *Joint Report*, pp. 2–17, 22–24, 85–102.

basic political weakness: the regional transit problem had only limited constituency appeal. East of the Hudson, New York City's leaders were concerned primarily with the subway problem, and Long Island's officials had exhausted their energies in seeking state action for the LIRR. There was greater concern in Westchester and New Jersey, but no sense of crisis impelled local residents to press for larger appropriations. Moreover, the MRTC study was not directed to meeting current emergencies but toward long-range solutions.[33]

In addition, the goal of the commission—comprehensiveness in transportation planning and financing—was viewed with mixed feelings in Trenton and Albany. Would it mean, for New Jersey, direct involvement in the massive financial problems of the New York subway system? Would state officials in Albany find their ability to meet "their own" problems handicapped by the need to negotiate with Hudson County politicians and contentious leaders of other local fiefdoms? And beyond these themes of fragmented perspective, the states—and especially the governors—wondered if they really wanted to grasp the nettle of mass transportation leadership. If the MRTC did carry out a comprehensive study and recommended long-range solutions, it seemed inevitable that the pressures for action would flow to the governor's office—whether to appropriate large amounts of state funds, or to battle Robert Moses and a phalanx of Port Authority experts and their fellow highway coalition leaders. The lessons of the recent LIRR and Transit Authority struggles, and of skirmishes over the years with Moses and his friends, were that the costs of such active leadership might well outweigh the benefits.

Finally, the commission itself—composed of five members appointed by each governor—was internally divided as to its purposes. Some commissioners were deeply devoted to the goal of comprehensiveness in study and, ultimately, in action. But other commission members had reservations. A comprehensive study would require larger funding than seemed likely. Also, a wide-ranging approach would surely lead to conflict with the highway coalition. An MRTC program that called for integrated planning and funding might result in no action at all, in view of the impressive influence of highway leaders in both states. For MRTC's more cautious members, the better part of valor would be a study focused on feasible ways of providing public support to meet growing commuter rail deficits, and on possible new rail construction—without a direct attempt to confront the "rail versus road" issue.

These weaknesses in political support, financing, and internal cohesion made the MRTC highly vulnerable to outside influence. The organization most interested in shaping the commission's efforts was the Port Authority. While fashioning its joint arterial studies with Robert Moses into a public relations success in 1954–1955, the Port Authority was dismayed by the public pronouncements of some MRTC members, who argued that highway expansion had caused rail-service deterioration, and that "grandiose" road plans should be halted until the MRTC completed its study. As a bistate agency like the MRTC, the Port Authority was the most explicit object of commission criticism. Moreover, it was directly involved in two decisions, made in 1954,

33. The discussion of the MRTC is drawn from Jameson W. Doig, *Metropolitan Transportation Politics*, Chapters 3–8.

not to provide opportunities for rail transit—by excluding rail lines on the Narrows Bridge and on the lower deck of the George Washington Bridge.[34] As a wealthy and politically skilled agency, the authority also had the resources needed to neutralize the commission. Thus the Port Authority offered the financially strapped study group a half million dollars to conduct its surveys—if the commission agreed to exclude from the studies any work on a general plan for rail and road facilities, and if the authority were given joint policy control over the surveys. With no other source of funds available, the commission accepted.[35]

Thus the widely heralded comprehensive study became instead a detailed analysis of possible ways to improve the financing and quality of rail service. The commission's final report in January 1958 proposed the creation of a bistate Transit District, supported by local tax revenues. The district's taxpayers would absorb the deficits of the region's passenger railroads, and meet the costs of a proposed bistate rail loop and other improvements. The proposal was endorsed by Manhattan business and civic groups, New York City newspapers, and some commuter groups in New York, where the philosophy of local tax support for rail was already well-accepted due to the local financial assistance long provided to the city's rapid transit system.

The district bill was forwarded to Albany and quickly passed, in March 1958. In New Jersey, however, as noted in Chapter Five, these proposals were received with less than wild enthusiasm, as widespread aversion to local tax support for rail facilities was combined with suspicion that the proposed improvements would mainly benefit Manhattan. The subject of acrimonious hearings in the state assembly in November 1958, the district bill succumbed a few weeks later. So the attempt to devise a comprehensive regional program, begun rather promisingly in the early 1950s, died finally in early 1959, a casualty of the three-way conflict among the advocates of regional planning and mass transit improvement, the road coalition, and local spokesmen who were wary of the costs and loss of autonomy that might result from a regional effort.[36]

34. Rail facilities across these two bridges had long been advocated by transit proponents in order to improve rail transit between New Jersey and Manhattan (across the George Washington Bridge), and between Staten Island, the other boroughs of New York City, and Long Island (across the Narrows). The decision to exclude rail lines was made during the 1954 Port Authority-Triborough arterial highway studies, and was based, according to the two agencies, on traffic, engineering, and cost considerations. However, the Port Authority's plans for the lower deck did include structural reinforcement so that rapid transit facilities could be added "at any future time," even though "rail rapid transit across the Hudson does not appear to be an immediate prospect." PNYA and TBTA, *Joint Studies of Arterial Facilities* (New York: January 1955), pp. 8, 30, and 40.

35. The authority then joined with New Jersey's Democratic governor, Robert B. Meyner, in a series of tactical maneuvers that forced all the New Jersey commissioners to resign. Meyner's main interest was to replace the five members, all of them holdovers appointed by the previous governor, Republican Alfred E. Driscoll, with his own choices. The New Jersey members were also the most vocal critics of the Port Authority's vehicular projects, and the authority, seeing an opportunity to exclude these opponents from the MRTC, worked closely with Meyner in achieving that goal. See Doig, *Metropolitan Transportation Politics*, Chapter 5.

36. Before being defeated in the New Jersey Assembly, the district bill had squeaked through the Senate by a one vote margin, with the support of Governor Meyner and indirect but crucial assistance from the Port Authority. On the legislative battles, see Doig, Chapter 8.

## Elements of a Solution: Realistic and Otherwise

There was a certain air of unreality about the mass transit debate as it was carried on throughout the first postwar decade and extended into the late 1950s.

On the one hand, some state officials and other government leaders assured the public that tax concessions and other modest measures would enable the bankrupt LIRR to emerge as a healthy private carrier, that creation of a transit authority would provide a long-term solution for the subway system, that the commuter railroads could survive if they kept their fares low and thus attracted more traffic, and that long-range solutions to the region's transit needs could be found through reliance upon that "horn of plenty" called the Port Authority. In the absence of widespread crisis that would compel action by elected leaders, it was far easier for state officials to describe such half-measures as "solutions," to avoid direct responsibility, and to utilize their own limited time and funds on other state problems and programs.

The most articulate advocates of better mass transportation and coordinated development took a very different view, but they rarely paused to weigh feasibility or compare notes on priorities. Three major elements of a strategy for solving mass transit problems were sounded by these partisans, and then amplified by the press so that they set the framework for reformist thought during this period:

1. Any government action, if it were to be effective, must be broad in areal scope. It was argued that the problems of the LIRR and the subway system were intertwined,[37] that the New Haven and New York Central lines would soon face financial difficulties similar to those of the LIRR, and that the several New Jersey railroads, already in financial straits, might be able to retain passenger traffic if they could be extended into Manhattan with transfer stops on the subway system. But to those who held these views, such as the *New York Times* and the MRTC, the answer was not to use existing centers of government power—for example, at the state capitals—to provide leadership and funding to meet these interrelated regional problems. Instead, a new layer of government, embracing a dozen or more counties in two or three states, should be created, and through this imaginative approach would come salvation—once interstate rivalries and taxpayer suspicion had evaporated, and vigorous leadership at the new regional level had emerged.[38]

2. Planning and coordination should be "comprehensive intermodally," encompassing rail and bus, truck and automobile, and taking into account the relationship between changes in rail and highway services, on the one hand, and patterns of land use in the region, on the other. Analytically, this was a reasonable position, in view of the evidence that changes in any one of these

---

37. For example, the subway system had been extended into eastern Queens, and with its traditional use of a flat fee the average deficit per mile increased; at the same time, commuters from western Nassau County found subway service more conveniently available as the system pushed eastward, and thus commuters were siphoned off from the (more expensive) LIRR to the subway system, adding to the LIRR deficit.

38. For illustrations of this line of reasoning, see the material cited in Doig, *Metropolitan Transportation Politics*, Chapters 4–5 and 7–8.

areas strongly affected program needs in the others.[39] As the argument was applied to the New York region, however, it was often extended beyond the bounds of political feasibility and perhaps of intellectual defensibility. Thus one prominent critic advocated as the first step toward a solution the creation of a Regional Transportation Authority to control all rail and road facilities—and all existing transport authorities—in the metropolitan area. The new agency would at once place tolls on all toll-free bridges, thus diverting passenger traffic to rail lines.[40] Perhaps extremism in the service of good planning was no moral vice, but it surely left the mass transit advocates vulnerable to the barbs of skeptics and opponents. As Robert Moses commented in 1953, reviewing the arguments for region-wide and intermodal coordination through new public agencies:

> There are always those who glibly advocate an official, all-powerful regional agency to take over these problems on the curious assumption that difficulties will disappear with regional consolidation. . . . Putting all of the problems into a big new shiny basket is just a way of hastening their trip to the dump heap or the incinerator.[41]

3. The third crucial element of a program to meet the region's mass transit needs was, of course, money. Not just modest tax concessions, not simply funds to eliminate grade crossings, but a sustained inflow of millions of dollars to meet the deficits of the New York subways, the Hudson tubes, and the region's eight private rail carriers. By the mid-1950s, the total yearly deficit had reached nearly $100 million; and to this might be added additional millions to replace old commuter cars and modestly improve the quality of service on the rail lines, subways, and government-owned bus lines—thus stemming the loss of commuters and other passengers to automobiles.

That kind of money quickly catches the attention of governors and other elected officials, who as quickly move out of the line of fire, hoping that their terms of office will end before any sizable mass transit burden is laid at their political doorsteps. But even $100 million strikes no sparks in the heart of a mass transit evangelist, if such sums yield no dramatic new projects to fire the mind. For those who would put their personal stamp on the future—for rail-builders as for road-builders—larger sums, to achieve visible and enduring results on the scale of a Narrows Bridge or a World Trade Center, are needed. To the members of the MRTC, their "Narrows Bridge" was a $350 million rail tunnel and transit line, joining the New Jersey railroad systems to a new subway line under Manhattan. For others, a modern passenger rail terminal in Manhattan, with new tunnels to bring all

---

39. This was the perspective taken, for example, by Wilfred Owen in the first edition of his volume, *The Metropolitan Transportation Problem* (Washington, D.C.: Brookings Institution, 1956). Owen's analysis was widely read and discussed in the New York region and nationally.

40. This was the position taken by Goodhue Livingston, commissioner of the New York City Planning Commission; see the summary of his views in NYMRTC and NJMRTC, *Joint Report*, pp. 89–90. Another commentator, H&M Railroad president William Reid, urged that the building of vehicular facilities simply "be stopped" as an initial step in ending the "tremendous shift from rail to rubber." See his comments in the *Joint Report*, p. 91.

41. Quoted in NYMRTC and NJMRTC, *Joint Report*, pp. 78, 79.

New Jersey trains directly into the terminal, would fit the imagination if not the pocketbook.[42]

How could such sums be secured? A central element of the rail coalition's response—especially after the defeat of the Transit District bill (with its reliance on local taxes)—was "pooling." That is, funds generated by rail and road agencies would be pooled, and then used by the new metropolitan authority or other agencies to meet needs which, under a general plan, had highest priority. In reality, this would mean (in their view) that excess revenues from the Port Authority, Triborough, and other highway agencies would be siphoned off to meet the deficits of rail and bus operations.

Even without dramatic new construction, the potential bill for mass transit needs would be large enough to block achievement of the roadbuilders' own dreams. To protect their interests, the road agencies sought to discredit the pooling concept by emphasizing the gigantic total costs involved. Thus in 1958, confronting New Jersey legislators anxious to bring Port Authority money and skill to bear on the rail problem, Austin Tobin generously estimated the region's mass transit deficits at $150 million a year. Tobin thought it was "awfully clear that the Port Authority couldn't assume one little part of this . . . without assuming it all."

Behind the Tobin smokescreen was an element of real concern. Admittedly, neither the Port Authority, nor Triborough, nor the New Jersey Turnpike Authority could absorb the entire transit deficit, but it would be financially feasible for any one of these agencies to absorb part of the total. When combined with other state and federal moneys, such contributions might provide enough funds to achieve modest goals if not grand plans for mass transit. But the platform of the mass transit advocates—large amounts of money, intermodal planning, and regionwide scope—did not direct the attention of elected officials toward smaller, more manageable increments. Tobin and his colleagues eagerly accepted this monumental frame of reference, insisting that any attempt to force the authorities to meet large deficits and carry out grandiose plans would simply put an end to these paragons of "nonpolitical corporate management" which had served the region's development needs so well.[43] The result, as the decade of the 1950s drew to a close, was continuing division and debate, deteriorating mass transit service, and no feasible plan of action.


## Steps Toward Stability

What was needed, hindsight suggests, was a crisis severe enough to alter the major variables that prevented effective action by officials in the tristate region. By 1958, such a crisis was conveniently at hand in the form of massive

---

42. See Metropolitan Rapid Transit Commission, *Report: Rapid Transit for the New York-New Jersey Metropolitan Area* (New York: January, 1958), pp. 5, 32–36, and the views of other advocates of major construction projects, summarized in NYMRTC and NJMRTC, *Joint Report*, pp. 73–75, 86–89, 91, 95–97, and 100–101.

43. Tobin's comments are taken from his statement before the Committee on Federal and Interstate Relations of the New Jersey Assembly, November 24, 1958, as quoted in Doig, *Metropolitan Transportation Politics*, p. 186.

railroad deficits and heightened concern in Washington about the weakened financial situation of the nation's railroads.[44]

During the first dozen postwar years (1946–1957), rail freight traffic declined nationally, while passenger deficits increased to five times their 1946 level. It seemed evident to railroad officials, and to the U.S. Interstate Commerce Commission, that most of the rail systems serving the New York area would soon go bankrupt unless they could move quickly to curtail passenger service, especially on lightly used lines. However, efforts to reduce service often required the approval of state utility commissions, and these agencies—whose officials were sensitive to opposition from suburban commuters and town officials—commonly delayed and sometimes rejected railroad appeals. By the spring of 1958 there was widespread sentiment in Congress to alter existing federal statutes so that rail corporations could more quickly discontinue interstate service—with ICC approval required, but without necessarily holding a hearing—and so that intrastate trains could be eliminated with ICC approval, even if state regulatory commissions were opposed. A bill embodying these provisions, titled the Transportation Act of 1958, was enacted in July and signed by President Dwight D. Eisenhower. As soon as the law was signed, the New York Central and the Erie railroads initiated action to end their trans-Hudson commuter services, and soon the other commuter railroads threatened to cut service sharply and even eliminate all passenger services.

Although state and regional leaders had taken little interest in the federal bill, the 1958 act significantly altered the political channels through which mass transportation policy was shaped. The railroads' perennial threats to discontinue rail service now became real. As a result, the number of constituents demanding action to preserve rail service expanded and the intensity of their pressure greatly increased. Because of the collapse of the MRTC effort, and the weakness of the Metropolitan Regional Council and regional leadership generally (described in Chapter Five), the demands for action focused on the states and especially on the three governors. The response in Albany, Trenton, and Hartford varied in enthusiasm and in program details. None met the high standards for influence on urban development required by the Wood-Vernon approach. Nevertheless, all three states devised programs that moved appreciably toward the major goals of the mass transit planners and which, while modest, had the merit of being feasible.

First, the obstacle of areal fragmentation in the region was substantially overcome by state leadership. State transportation offices were created to prepare commuter programs extending across all counties within each state's sector of the New York region. These programs were not, however, predicated on the need for agreement on common plans between two or all three states. The initiative was taken by Nelson Rockefeller, shortly after his 1958 election as governor of New York. In breaking free from the search for interstate agreements, Rockefeller asserted that rail problems should be solved by "each state taking action itself," while cooperating across state lines where possible. His pronouncement dismayed some regional spokesmen, for it seemed in conflict

44. The discussion in this section is based primarily on Doig, *Metropolitan Transportation Politics*, Chapter 9, and Danielson, *Federal-Metropolitan Politics*, Chapters 2–3.

with the search for a truly areawide solution advocated by the RPA, the *New York Times*, and MRC leaders. However, Rockefeller's approach was congruent with the areal pattern of effective political power. Regional bodies could only debate and urge action; state officials could define new policies, allocate resources, and implement programs.

Aided by increased constituency demand, and utilizing a modicum of political skill, Rockefeller channeled new funds to mass transit. The railroads were given significant amounts of tax relief, in a package that also offered assistance to bus lines throughout the state—thus attracting support from upstate legislators not notably sympathetic to New York City and the suburban counties.[45] In addition, the governor and his aides breached the Port Authority wall, finally persuading that reluctant dragon to help meet the state's rail needs.

In the fall of 1958, the Port Authority had told the New Jersey legislature that the authority had "nothing more to contribute" to solving the transit problem. Less than six months later, the Port Authority announced that it was "quite pleased" to help by purchasing rail commuter cars and leasing them to the state's passenger carriers. Between these two statements, the authority's leaders had reluctantly accepted Rockefeller's demand that the bistate agency reverse its traditional position against taking any direct responsibility in the rail passenger field. The authority's contribution would be modest; it would administer the program, but the leases on the new railroad cars would be backed by state guarantees. Even so, the program was a first step in developing direct ties between the highway coalition and the region's rail systems.[46]

New Jersey's Governor Meyner was less inclined to exert leadership, but through the energy and skill of his chief advisers the Garden State also began to respond to the commuter crisis. An initial plan, devised in the spring of 1959, would have tapped the surplus of the New Jersey Turnpike Authority to meet rail and bus deficits. But this attack on the "integrity" of highway coalition funds, and on the image of an independent authority, proved too early and too direct. Automobile and highway interests counterattacked, and the Turnpike-surplus plan went down to resounding defeat in a statewide referendum in November of 1959.[47] The plan did, however, produce two cracks in the common front of the highway coalition, as the state's highway commissioner, Dwight Palmer, devised the proposal, and the Port Authority—seeing that the program would divert pressure from its own door—broke ranks and informally supported the Turnpike plan.

The following year, as continued railroad threats to end passenger service produced increasing concern in the commuting suburbs, state officials in Trenton developed two programs that provided a basis for long-term stability of essential mass transit services. The first was a plan to give state funds directly to private carriers, in return for contracts in which the railroads

45. The first Rockefeller program, in 1959, provided a $15 million reduction in railroad taxes, and additional tax relief to the beleaguered lines was provided by the state in 1961.
46. The commuter car program is described in more detail in Danielson, *Federal-Metropolitan Politics*, pp. 79–83.
47. Under the state constitution, a referendum was required before the state could acquire the surpluses by assuming liability for the Turnpike bonds, which otherwise were undergirded only by the Turnpike's own revenues and surplus.

would agree to maintain specified schedules of trains and fares. The legislature endorsed the plan in the spring of 1960 and provided $6 million to cover costs for the first year. During the fall, service contracts were negotiated with all major New Jersey rail carriers.

The second proposal forced the Port Authority to confront a future it had hoped to avoid—as a railroad owner and operator. After the Turnpike plan collapsed, commissioner Palmer pressed the port agency to use its own funds to provide new cars for the Hudson and Manhattan Railroad—a heavily used passenger line that ran between Newark, Hudson County, and Manhattan. The Port Authority might have fought the proposal vigorously, but in 1960 its officials viewed their position as unusually vulnerable. The failure of the Transit District proposal and the Turnpike plan had brought the authority under renewed attack for its "crass indifference" to the railroad crisis. Moreover, the Port Authority's plan to build a jetport in suburban Morris County (described in Chapter Four) had sparked vigorous opposition to the agency in North Jersey.

So the Port Authority reluctantly negotiated with Palmer, and by 1961 a plan had been hammered out which enmeshed the authority more deeply in the rail problem, but also protected the bistate agency from additional responsibilities for mass transit. The centerpiece of the plan was purchase of the H&M Railroad by the authority, which would modernize and operate the line. In return, the two states agreed that the Port Authority could undertake other rail activities only if the total annual deficit from all its rail operations would not exceed 10 percent of the Authority's general reserve fund. Since the H&M deficit seemed likely to rise close to that level, the agreement meant that the authority would be protected from future attempts to force it to operate other rail passenger services. Officials of both states argued that this absolute limitation was needed so the authority would be able to sell bonds for this and other future projects. "It gets down to how badly we need the H&M," Palmer declared. "Do we want it on the investors' terms or not at all?" The states wanted the H&M, and after a further round of negotiations, which included state approval for authority construction of the World Trade Center, the plan was approved in Trenton and Albany in the spring of 1962—and the H&M became the Port Authority Trans-Hudson rail system (PATH).[48]

In the early 1960s a few steps were taken that were consistent with the mass transit coalition's goals of regionwide planning, intermodal coordination, and greater financial resources. First, bringing Connecticut at last into the fold, state officials created the Tri-State Transportation Committee to review and coordinate highway and transit funding in the New York region.[49] The original impetus for such an agency had come from the RPA and the MRC, which sought a planning body to include representatives of local gov-

48. For further information on the H&M plan and the related World Trade Center negotiations, see Doig, *Metropolitan Transportation Politics*, pp. 215–220. On the Port Authority's role in rail transit, and its use of bond covenants in achieving its policy goals, see also Chapter 6 and Annmarie Hauck Walsh, *The Public's Business: The Politics and Practices of Government Corporations* (Cambridge, Mass.: MIT Press, 1978), pp. 94–103 and *passim*.

49. Connecticut's earlier efforts in response to the 1958–1959 railroad crisis had been directed toward maintaining service on its only rail carrier, the New Haven Railroad. These activities had been halting and unsuccessful, and the New Haven entered bankruptcy in July 1961.

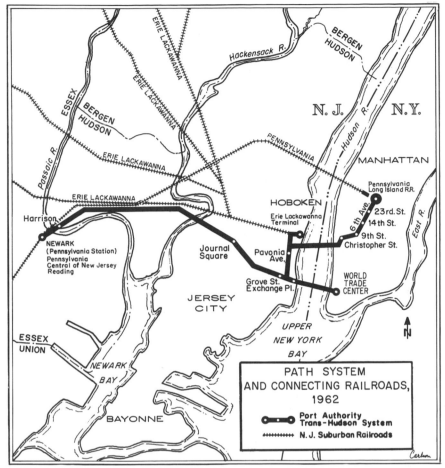

MAP 8

ernments throughout the region and of the three states. When Tri-State was formed by the three governors in 1961, however, its membership underscored the state-dominant pattern of leadership: of the original thirteen committee members, twelve were state appointees, with one allocated to New York City. On paper, at least, the new agency therefore seemed to provide a useful channel to shape state action to broader regional needs. As indicated in Chapter Five, Tri-State's role has largely been "on paper"—limited to producing reports that monitor development trends in the region, rather than shaping those patterns.

The rail crisis also prompted halting steps toward financial aid and a regional perspective for mass transit, in the place where the crisis had been set in motion—the halls of Congress. After the first months of turmoil that followed passage of the 1958 Transportation Act, a small group of northeastern congressmen—led by Senator Harrison Williams of New Jersey—counterattacked. In 1960, Williams introduced a bill to provide $100 million in federal loans for mass transit facilities, gathered support from central city mayors across the country, from railroad presidents, and from such civic groups as the Regional Plan Association, and within a year obtained passage of the first federal aid ever provided for urban transit services. Enacted as part of the Housing Act of 1961, the new law authorized $75 million in federal loans for transit improvements in urban areas, and additional planning funds to be allotted in connection with "comprehensive" approaches toward solving problems of traffic congestion and other transportation problems on a regional basis. Although the funds were modest, the perspective was broad, prompting the RPA to commend it as "pioneering legislation." While the new legislation did not directly challenge the autonomy of the highway coalition, it echoed the basic ideology of the RPA and the MRTC commissioners of the early 1950s, and augured greater federal intervention in a not-too-distant future.[50]

By the early 1960s, therefore, state and federal officials had moved the mass transit problem to a higher position in the catalog of demands for vigorous governmental action. However, the new policies still did not meet the standards of those who championed regional transportation planning and development. The Regional Plan Association viewed the state efforts as no more than "stop-gap programs" which were "keeping commuter service alive [but] do little to promote a future system" that could provide better service and be less costly to maintain. And the *New York Times* termed the programs "piecemeal," while urging in their place a "unified multi-state attack."[51]

If the views of advocates of comprehensive regional schemes seemed unalloyed by political realism, some political leaders were expressing hopes that seemed equally devoid of economic realism. Even after the New Haven had slid into bankruptcy, and as deficits rose on the LIRR and other rail lines, state officials looked wistfully to a future in which government action might be less crucial to the survival of the region's mass transit system. In 1964, William Ronan, Rockefeller's chief transportation policy adviser, attacked a report that urged public ownership as the best solution to providing commuter service east of the Hudson. Ronan argued that the new public programs had helped the railroads to "improve commuter service and lower costs," and that the economics of commuter service would "continue to improve," permitting private ownership of such major commuter lines as the New Haven and the New York Central to endure.[52]

## Dramatic Changes and an Elusive Goal

Ronan's optimism was short-lived. He soon found himself deeply involved in a new Rockefeller initiative to save the New Haven, New York-

50. The activities leading to the 1961 mass transportation legislation are discussed in Danielson, *Federal-Metropolitan Politics*, Chapters 3–9. Rockefeller, Meyner, and other state officials were absorbed in working out their own responses to the rail problem, and were not actively involved in the campaign for federal transit-subsidy legislation.

51. Regional Plan Association, *Commuter Transportation*, Report Prepared for the Committee on Interstate and Foreign Commerce, U.S. Senate, 87th Congress, first session (Washington, D.C.: 1961), and editorial, *New York Times*, March 27, 1961.

52. John Sibley, "Report Rejects Rail Agency Plan," *New York Times*, January 16, 1964.

Central and Long Island railroads—this time through *public* ownership and operation. In New York State, and in New Jersey as well, government's role in preventing collapse, in stabilizing, and in improving rail and bus service in the region has steadily deepened and widened since the early 1960s. New policies hammered out in Washington have been joined with state programs to alter, sometimes quite strikingly, the organization of transport programs and the criteria for action. Yet the broadest planning and financing goals enunciated by the Regional Plan Association and its fellow regional travelers remain unfulfilled, providing a time-honored banner to be unfurled in the editorial pages of the *Times* and in RPA bulletins, as the region's mass transit system lurches fitfully into a modest future.

In the following sections we explore the search during the 1960s and 1970s for solutions to the mass transportation problem, concentrating on changes in areal and functional scope of public institutions, and on the ways that leadership skills, funds, and other resources have been concentrated so that public officials could maintain transit services in the New York area. Our main focus is on the Metropolitan Transportation Authority, a 12-county agency established by New York State in 1968. More briefly, we examine efforts to enlarge the Port Authority's role in maintaining trans-Hudson commuter facilities. Intertwined with these activities are the efforts of the federal government, which has played an increasingly important role in financing and shaping public efforts to meet the region's mass transit problems.

### Creating a Regional Transit Agency

Despite William Ronan's professed optimism in 1964, it seemed clear that significant new initiatives would be required if the region's commuter rail services were to be kept alive. In the world of the ideal planner, the rational approach might involve combining all major rail and road facilities under one institution, embracing those portions of the region in all three states. In the world of political reality, however, even the innovator with a grand design moves slowly, incrementally, using short-term crises as opportunities to extend his power, then pausing to negotiate with potential opponents who might resist a broader role—until, drawing their fangs or lulling them to unwary sleep, he pounces.

Or, to alter the metaphor: For the political innovator, the adroit use of the "camel's nose" strategy is often the *sine qua non* of skilled leadership. The "camel's nose" is the first step in a large new government program; being small, it may seem acceptable to legislators and the public, while if the true long-term costs—the entire camel—were seen at the outset, opposition would widen and the first step might never be taken.[53]

The evolution of New York State's role in mass transit between 1964 and 1968 illustrates these political strategies fairly well. The first step was to save the Long Island Rail Road, which had been operating since 1954 under a special program of state aid. For several years public officials lived under the

53. Planners sometimes oppose the camel's-nose strategy as offensive to their principles (that programs should be based on a rational calculation of long-term costs and benefits), while fiscal conservatives object for different reasons—because the strategy makes it more difficult for them to build a successful alliance against the proposed innovation.

**MAP 9**

hope—or perhaps it was always an illusion—that the LIRR would emerge in 1966 at the end of the twelve-year program as a healthy private rail carrier. Even with tax relief and other concessions, however, the LIRR operated at a deficit or barely broke even in the early 1960s, and the modernization efforts proceeded very slowly.

By 1964, Governor Rockefeller was forced to recognize that more drastic action would be required, and he appointed Ronan, his chief transportation adviser, to head a study committee. Reporting to the governor early in 1965, the Ronan committee recommended that the state purchase the LIRR and create a new public authority (the Metropolitan Commuter Transportation Authority) to operate the rail line and carry out a wide-ranging modernization program. In order to spread the costs, and thus make the plan more palatable to the state legislature, the railroad would be purchased with state funds (but for far less than the "$2 billion in new highways that would be required . . . if the LIRR should cease to exist"), the costs of station maintenance would be met by the counties served by the railroad, and it was hoped that "much if not all" of the

$200 million improvement program would be financed under the federal mass transit program. The camel's nose was not small, but at least there seemed to be several tents. And to avoid objections from the still-influential highway coalition, no mention was made of tapping toll revenues of the Triborough Authority, whose bridges and tunnels directly competed with the LIRR for passengers bound for Manhattan.[54]

Rockefeller had been actively involved in shaping the plan, and he immediately endorsed the report. A bill to create the MCTA was introduced and quickly approved by the state legislature.[55] While the main emphasis of the Rockefeller-Ronan plan was the need to meet the immediate crisis on the LIRR, the bill empowered the new authority to develop plans ensuring the continuation of other commuter rail services in the New York region. The legislation also reflected Rockefeller's interest in exerting strong state leadership in this field. Despite local demands for a role in setting MCTA policy, all five members of the new authority's board were to be appointed by the governor. And the first chairman would be William Ronan.

During the next two years, the state bought the LIRR for $65 million and began negotiations with officials of the New Haven and New York Central, where mounting deficits again threatened the termination of passenger services.

Meanwhile, the financial and the physical condition of the city's subway system continued to deteriorate, demonstrating the limited effectiveness of the 1953 Transit Authority scheme. As Republican candidate for mayor of New York City in the fall of 1965, John Lindsay made the local transportation problem one of his major targets, criticizing past city and state actions, and promising that he would press for coordinated planning and financing of rail and highway developments in the city. Soon after his election, Lindsay had legislation introduced in Albany to extend the Rockefeller-Ronan initiatives dramatically by merging the Transit Authority and Triborough. Lindsay's bill would also give the mayor power to appoint a majority of the new governing board's members.

The Lindsay plan, which promised policy coordination for mass transit and highways, as well as a flow of funds from Triborough to the subway system, was enthusiastically endorsed by the *New York Times*.[56] It was also

54. The 1965 proposals are set forth in New York State, Special Committee on the LIRR, *A New Long Island Rail Road* (New York: February 1965); for a summary of the plan, see Charles Grutzner, "Rockefeller Urges State Buy L.I.R.R. and Modernize It," *New York Times*, February 26, 1965.

55. The Ronan committee presented its report to Rockefeller on February 25, 1965 and he released and endorsed it the same day. The MCTA bill was passed by the state assembly on May 20, and by the state senate on May 26; Rockefeller signed the bill on June 1. This and subsequent Rockefeller-Ronan initiatives in mass transportation are discussed briefly in Robert H. Connery and Gerald Benjamin, *Rockefeller of New York: Executive Power in the Statehouse* (Ithaca, N.Y.: Cornell University Press, 1979), pp. 274–280. On Rockefeller's leadership style, see especially Chapters 3, 7, and 11. On his relationship with Ronan and his use of public authorities, see also Walsh, *The Public's Business*, especially Chapter 10.

56. The enthusiasm of the *New York Times* is conveyed in its series of editorials: "Mr. Lindsay's Transit Proposal," February 18, 1966; "Transit Debate," March 12, 1966; "Unifying Transport Policy," May 5, 1966; "Time for Transit Action", May 16, 1966; "Who Speaks for Straphangers?," May 24, 1966. This "sound program," this "carefully thought-out program for bringing order" out of chaos and aiding the city's "mobility and prosperity," the *Times* argued in its May 16 and 24 essays, "must not be allowed to die because of special interests and political deals." In a perhaps unintended pun, its May 16 editorial found the Lindsay plan in "grave danger."

condemned, with even greater energy and effectiveness, by Robert Moses, the investment banking community, the automobile associations, leaders of the construction unions (whose regard for Moses and concern for a continuing flow of highway construction jobs were legendary), the existing members of the Transit Authority (whose jobs would be abolished by the Lindsay bill), and Democratic legislative leaders in the state capital.[57]

Against this phalanx, Lindsay's proposal met a quick and bloody death in the state legislature. However, Lindsay's actions exposed and underscored important weaknesses in Rockefeller's leadership. During his first gubernatorial campaign in 1958, and extending through his LIRR purchase plan of 1964–1965, Rockefeller had built a reputation for initiative and vigorous action in meeting mass transportation needs. But behind the rhetoric of leadership, the creation of the MCTA, and its efforts to stabilize commuter service, the reality was troubling. All the commuter railroads in the region and the city's vast subway system were in deep financial difficulties; and federal funds needed to help modernize these rail lines might not be forthcoming in large amounts. Upstate legislators would be wary of pouring more state money into the New York region's transit morass. And now Lindsay's vigorous campaign threatened to displace the ambitious governor as the acknowledged leader—in the Empire State and nationally—in dealing with urban transportation problems.

Meanwhile, Moses sat atop Triborough's surplus: millions of dollars a year that could be used to stabilize and improve rail services—and to bolster Rockefeller's reputation as an innovative problem solver. Moses himself was a contender for leadership; his pronouncements on urban transport always received wide publicity, and even now, in 1966, his engineers were preparing a report on highway and mass transit needs for the New York region.[58] Moreover, the history of relationships between Rockefeller and Moses suggested that Triborough's leader would always maintain a certain unruly independence.[59]

Could these problems be converted into opportunities, enabling Rockefeller to reassert his central leadership role? The governor thought so, and by the first days of 1967 he was ready to set in motion a three-pronged attack. First, he announced plans to combine state highway activities (then under the Department of Public Works) with mass transport in a new Department of Transportation, symbolizing the need for a coordinated approach. The new agency would then formulate a statewide plan for a "truly balanced" transpor-

57. The opponents' views are set forth in Samuel Kaplan, "Moses Calls Transit Unity 'Hogwash,' " *New York Times*, January 8, 1966, Emanuel Perlmutter, "Moses Calls Transit Unity an Illegal, 'Fantastic' Plan," *New York Times*, February 14, 1966; Emanuel Perlmutter, "City Transit Plan Scored by Travia," *New York Times*, February 20, 1966; Richard Witkin, "Lindsay and 'the Moses Problem,' " *New York Times*, March 20, 1966; Charles G. Bennett, "Lindsay Charges Transit Trickery," *New York Times*, May 14, 1966; Charles G. Bennett, "Lindsay Angers Council With Blunt Transit Talk," *New York Times*, May 24, 1966; and Moses, *Public Works*, pp. 899–904. For a detailed analysis of the Lindsay plan and its fate, see Caro, *The Power Broker*, Chapter 48.

58. That report, prepared by the Madigan-Hyland engineering company, was released to the press by Moses in March 1967. See Peter Kihss, "Gains in Transit Held Vital Here," *New York Times*, March 20, 1967.

59. Ronan also had had his problems with Moses. On the Rockefeller-Ronan-Moses connections, see Caro, *The Power Broker*, pp. 1070 ff.

tation system. Second, he proposed a $2.5 billion bond issue for "major capital investments in mass transportation systems" and highway arteries. Sensitive to upstate interests, his message to the legislature emphasized that these billions would meet "urgent needs . . . in the rural areas, the towns, the villages, the suburban and city areas of our state." Buses as well as rail lines would be aided by the state's program. And to meet the concerns of influential northern legislators, a Niagara transportation authority would be created to organize transport improvements in the northwestern portion of the state.[60]

The third part of Rockefeller's program incorporated the Lindsay proposal to combine Triborough and the Transit Authority and added the MCTA to create a new Metropolitan Transportation Authority (MTA). In urging that the MCTA be broadened to include both of the city agencies, the governor emphasized that this would assure "unified regional policy direction."

A central element of Rockefeller's plan, as it had been of Lindsay's, was the capture of Triborough's surpluses to subsidize mass transportation. The challenge was to overcome the legal and political obstacles that stopped the Lindsay scheme in 1966, and that had sharply limited access to Port Authority surpluses in the 1962 covenant. Rockefeller's advisers thought they could see a route to legislative approval—if a way to protect the bondholders could be devised, and if Moses could be persuaded to approve the new plan, thus muting opposition from the banking community, and from Moses's allies in the construction unions and the automobile associations.[61]

Moses was no longer a young man. In December 1966 he had celebrated his seventy-eighth birthday. He had resigned, or in a few cases been removed from, most of his many city and state positions; Triborough was his final remaining official position of real influence.[62] If he viewed the merger as ending his public career, he could be expected to attack, vigorously and adroitly, and it might then not be possible to obtain agreement to the plan from legislators and bondholders.[63] So Rockefeller and Ronan moved cautiously and shrewdly: They pointed out to Moses and his associates that a future record of achievement lay not simply with Triborough, whose successes were in the past, but in exerting leadership in creating a magnificent new structure—a Long Island Sound bridge. But Moses could not take on that

60. See Richard L. Madden, "Governor Offers $2-Billion Plan in Highways and Unified Transit," and "Text of Governor's Proposals for Action in His Ninth Message to the Legislature," *New York Times*, January 5, 1967; Ronalo Maiorana, "Governor Asks 2.5-Billion for Transport Programs," and "Text of Rockefeller Message on a Huge Bond Issue for Transportation," *New York Times*, January 29, 1967.

61. For evidence on the views and strategy of Rockefeller's advisers, see Melvin Masuda, "The Formation of the Metropolitan Transportation Authority of New York State," senior studies paper, Yale Law School, April 1968, pp. 35 ff.

62. In the spring of 1965, Mayor Lindsay had removed him as City Construction Coordinator, which had been a central position in negotiations for state and federal highway funds. On his departure from other positions, see Caro, *The Power Broker*, Chapters 46–49.

63. Caro indicates that Moses had calculated the interest payments state taxpayers would have to underwrite for the $2.5 billion issue (they totalled $1 billion); and he had analyzed the possibility that, as Ronan argued, the Triborough surplus would completely offset the subway and LIRR deficits—and concluded that the surpluses wouldn't even come close. Moses was ready to make these figures public, and the governor realized they could be devastating, especially to upstate voters. See Caro, *The Power Broker*, pp. 1134–1137.

challenge unless Rockefeller pressed for legislative approval and appointed Moses to head the project. Meanwhile, Moses was led to believe that he would be appointed to an important post with the MTA—as a member of the new authority's board, or perhaps as president of Triborough, which would retain its organizational identity though not policy control.[64]

Moses accepted these assurances. After a meeting with the governor in March 1967, he publicly supported the merger bill, and he endorsed and campaigned for the $2.5 billion bond issue.[65] The construction unions followed his lead. Meanwhile, Rockefeller had won Mayor Lindsay's support by offering some minor concessions to meet the mayor's reluctance to accept a new state-controlled authority with great influence in local affairs.[66] Having no significant opposition, the bond issue and merger bills were overwhelmingly approved by the state legislature by the end of March. And, with a slight majority upstate and an overwhelming favorable vote in New York City, the voters endorsed the highway-transit bond issue in November.[67]

The only obstacle remaining in the way of the Rockefeller-Ronan scheme was approval by the bondholders. Rockefeller had already persuaded Moses not to oppose a negotiated settlement. In a series of discussions with representatives of the bondholders during the winter of 1967–1968, it was agreed that the bondholders would accept the merger and the control of Triborough surpluses by the MTA board, in return for a modest increase in the bondholders' interest payments.[68]

On March 1, 1968, the new Metropolitan Transportation Authority came into being, with William Ronan as chairman and chief executive officer, and with eight other members. Robert Moses was not among them. Instead, Robert Moses was designated as "consultant" to Triborough. As he recalled later, "I was told by Dr. Ronan and by Governor Rockefeller several times that the building of the Long Island Sound crossing . . . would be my primary responsibility when that project was in the clear." Meanwhile, he was left with "rather undefined duties," and his former assistants now reported directly to

64. See Moses, *Public Works*, pp. 256–258, and Caro, *The Power Broker*, pp. 1138–1139.

65. Previously, Moses had attacked the merger plan as "absurd" and "grotesque"; see John P. Callahan, "Moses Denounces a Transit Merger," *New York Times*, January 22, 1967. Even after campaigning for legislative approval of the plan, Moses could not resist expressing his hostile views toward integrated transport financing and his skepticism that a merger would provide any real assistance in meeting the new agency's rail deficits. In a report released during the summer of 1967, he and his fellow Triborough commissioners proclaimed: "There is no surplus available now or in the foreseeable future for any extraneous municipal purpose such as the rapid transit operating deficiency." Triborough Bridge and Tunnel Authority, *Financial and Construction Program, 1967–1971* (New York: July 1967), p. 1.

66. The main concession was that three of the gubernatorial appointments to the nine-person MTA board would be individuals recommended by the mayor of New York City. See Masuda, "The Formation of the Metropolitan Transportation Authority," pp. 46–53, for a review of the Lindsay negotiations.

67. The favorable vote was 69 percent in New York City, 52.5 percent in the nearby counties (Nassau, Suffolk, and Westchester), and 51 percent in the rest of the state. See Masuda, "The Formation of the Metropolitan Transportation Authority," p. 58.

68. Payments were increased by one-quarter of one percent. It was perhaps helpful to the governor's cause that the central position in negotiating for the bondholders was held by the Chase Manhattan bank, whose president was Nelson Rockefeller's brother, David. On the negotiations, see Masuda, pp. 59–60, and Caro, *The Power Broker*, pp. 1140–1141.

Ronan's office.[69] And as the possibility of building the Long Island Sound bridge faded and died in the 1970s,[70] so did Moses's dream of constructing a final spectacular contribution to the road-building era that now seemed no more.

So the camel advanced by increments into the tent, and the old tiger was squeezed into a corner, and finally sent out into the dark.[71]

### Larger Resources and a "Grand Design"

What painstaking negotiations, shrewd maneuvering, and broader vision had created in the spring of 1968 was a public enterprise with many of the attributes long sought by advocates of coordinated transport and regional planning. The MTA spanned a large part of the region—New York City plus seven nearby counties, a total of 4,000 square miles in which lived twelve million citizens.[72] It was responsible for subways, buses, commuter rail services, and vehicular bridges and tunnels, and the new agency had a statutory mandate to implement a "unified" mass transportation policy for the region. Moreover, its leaders had a tilt toward rail facilities. Ronan criticized previous public policies that had "permitted our rail links to atrophy," and promised to seek a "balanced approach" in order to "save, then nurture and restore the great vitality of our troubled cities."[73] The MTA's scope and perspective made this a "tremendous forward step," commented the *New York Times* editorially. The *Times* view that this was "the greatest advance in the metropolitan transportation system in at least half a century" was no doubt received warmly at the governor's mansion in these early months of a presidential election year. The newspaper was compelled to note, however, that with New Jersey not yet included, the "truly regional agency that has been the goal of planners for decades" was yet to "evolve."[74]

The new agency not only had wide regional and transportation scope; MTA also had money—millions of new dollars that could be used to revitalize rail and bus services, and thus stabilize traffic or even reverse the trend toward the automobile. The largest chunk of new money came from the bond issue approved in the fall of 1967; together with local matching funds, this would provide more than one billion dollars during the next five years for

69. The quotations are from Moses, *Public Works*, pp. 257–258. Ronan later commented expansively to associates that he had never intended to give Moses any power at the MTA.

70. See Chapter Four in this volume.

71. Yet he remained not without hope, however slim. In December 1975, more than two years after Rockefeller had withdrawn his support for the crossing, Triborough staff updated their calculations of the cost and debt service required for the bridge; and when one of the authors visited Mr. Moses in the fall of 1978, shortly before his ninetieth birthday, he set forth with moderate passion the need for the project, and they viewed a slide show noting the decline in economic growth on Long Island and describing the anticipated benefits of the new bridge—more than 50,000 new jobs generated by improved access from Long Island to the mainland, and lower levels of traffic congestion and therefore of air pollution in the northeast quadrant of the region.

72. The seven counties outside New York City are Nassau, Suffolk, Westchester, Rockland, Dutchess, Orange, and Putnam.

73. Ronan, "Regional Transportation," an address to the Canadian Transit Association, June 25, 1968.

74. "As the M.T.A. Takes Over," editorial, *New York Times*, February 16, 1968.

transportation improvements planned and carried out by the MTA.[75] In addition, Ronan could draw upon the surpluses of Moses's Triborough empire, which were expected to be more than $25 million in the first year, with larger sums to follow.[76]

Equally important, the MTA had leadership skills and political savvy that seemed likely to rival those found earlier in the Moses regime and at the Port Authority. William Ronan had already proven to be an intelligent, forceful, and crafty adviser and executive—in his many years as a top aide to Governor Rockefeller, in his negotiations leading to the creation of the MCTA, the purchase of the LIRR, and the deposing of Moses, and in his nearly three years as chief of MCTA. And behind Ronan stood Rockefeller, whose interest in a vigorous and successful MTA was quickened by his awareness that the agency's early efforts could enhance his political power as governor, and perhaps improve his prospects for a successful presidential bid.[77] He had already fought long and hard for creation of the MCTA and the MTA, and had campaigned across the state for the 1967 bond issue. In contrast with the approach in the 1950s of Governor Dewey and New Jersey's Governor Meyner—who fought mainly to keep the mass transit problem at arm's length—Rockefeller wanted to be involved, and he wanted success.

These advantages were, however, offset by obstacles that might interfere with MTA's effort to achieve specific development goals. First, Ronan confronted a wide range of constituency demands, and some of those constituencies were in conflict with one another. There was the potential conflict between the advocates of better rail and bus facilities, and those who might demand better highway facilities or lower tolls. Even those who favored better bus and rail transit could not be counted on to support the MTA's efforts. Some of its proposals would probably aid certain parts of the region more than others, and the "others" could be expected to protest.

Moreover, among hundreds of thousands of MTA clients were many—and generally the most outspoken—whose basic orientation to the services the authority would provide was hostile and aggressive. In addition, MTA's insulation from local policy control—only New York City was represented on the authority's board—meant that elected officials from Nassau County and other local areas would adopt commuters' concerns as their own, attacking the

75. Ronan estimated that $600 million from the $2.5 billion could be allocated to MTA transit improvements; to that he added $200 million from New York City (required as matching money on a 3:1 basis), plus $100 million per year which the city had regularly been allocating from its capital budget. See "State Bonds Due to Help City Transit," *New York Times*, November 27, 1967.

76. Moses objected to these plans to drain off large amounts from Triborough, noting initially that the available surplus would be no more than $5 million a year, and later agreeing that larger sums could be obtained, but only by halting current authority plans. How could a third Queens Midtown tunnel and other needed improvements be carried out, Moses lamented, if the Triborough surplus, "honestly earned and prudently husbanded," was to be diverted to rail? By 1970 he found this policy "political folly" and asserted that Triborough's "program of expansion is dead. Future public needs are ignored. It has become another routine, static, bureaucratic agency. The original proud concept has been compromised. . . ." Moses, *Public Works*, pp. 259–261.

77. As Richard Witkin commented, dramatic transportation projects might add to Rockefeller's "political luster" and thus aid his "non-candidacy" for the U.S. presidential nomination. Witkin, "$2.9-Billion Transit Plan for New York Area Links Subways, Rails, Airports," *New York Times*, February 29, 1968.

agency for its neglect of local needs.[78] The prospect for such conflict was enhanced by the Albany-approved arrangement for meeting station maintenance costs on the LIRR: the state-run authority would maintain the railroad stations, but it would charge the local communities for these costs. As the experience of the MCTA under this arrangement already revealed, these mandated expenses did not endear the agency to local officials who had to levy taxes to pay the bills.[79]

And there was, really, a problem of money. Certainly, the new authority had the great advantage of the 1967 bond funds, and a pot of Triborough gold that might increase. But more would be needed simply to meet the increasing subway and commuter-railroad deficits, fueled regularly by wage settlements beyond the means of the operating agencies. And still more money would have to be found to demonstrate that the MTA was a successful invention— not merely an agency battling to stay even, but an enterprise that could produce striking plans, marshal public opinion in support of its vision of the future, experiment with new technologies, and reconstruct the region's transport systems. The MTA's leaders were not unaware of these greater financial needs, and soon after the MTA commenced operations Ronan began to urge that "full national resources be applied" to solving urban transportation problems.[80]

First, however, if the new authority wanted to dramatize its new role, convert skeptics and adversaries into admiring supporters, and demonstrate how massive funds would be used, Ronan needed a plan. MCTA's planning skills were set to the task, and in February 1968, before the MTA was formally in being, Rockefeller and Ronan announced a "sweeping $2.9 billion blueprint." Their self-styled "Grand Design" called for a new subway under Manhattan's Second Avenue, running north to connect with a new subway line in the Bronx, as well as additional subway and LIRR service in Queens, a new rail tunnel from Queens to Manhattan at 63rd Street, and a new rail terminal in Manhattan at 48th Street. There would be a rail line built to Kennedy Airport, and hundreds of new subway cars and commuter railroad coaches for the region's rail travelers. New turbo-trains would rush Long Island commuters at speeds up to 100 mph, cutting in half commuting time from major

78. As originally constituted, the MTA board included nine members, all appointed by the governor. Three of the nine were to be appointed "only on the written recommendation of the mayor of the city of New York"; there were no provisions for recommendations or other formal involvement of the seven suburban counties with MTA facilities—Nassau, Suffolk, Westchester, Putnam, Dutchess, Rockland, and Orange counties. In the 1970s, in response to suburban complaints of underrepresentation, the board was restructured several times. By 1979, it had been expanded to thirteen members, chosen as follows: (1) the governor appointed four on recommendation of the mayor of New York City; (2) the county executives of the seven suburban counties each submitted a list of three names, from which the governor selected four members—one each from Nassau, Suffolk, and Westchester, and one from the remaining four counties; and (3) the governor appointed the chairman and the four other members, two of whom must be New York City residents.

79. Upon receiving the MCTA bill for the year ending in March 1967, for example, New York City's controller, Mario Procaccino, opposed paying $3.8 million of the total of $4.4 million; the Nassau County executive declared that "under no circumstances" would his county pay its $1.8 million bill; while Suffolk's executive expressed "shock" at its $900,000 MCTA bill, and said he would turn the matter over to the county attorney. See Charles G. Bennett, "Procaccino Calls Rail Bill Too High," *New York Times,* June 20, 1967.

80. See speech by Ronan, "Regional Transportation," June 25, 1968.

suburban stations. And true to Rockefeller's promise and Moses's dream, one or even two bridges would extend across the Long Island Sound.[81]

Upon hearing Ronan describe these visions of the future, Rockefeller stepped to the front of the assembled audience of journalists and exclaimed that he thought "we have been witnessing a historic event." The *New York Times* was less enthusiastic, for while the plan seemed basically "well-conceived," it "will not remedy all the existing deficiencies." The *Times* argued that "something akin to a system of moving sidewalks" might be added to the plan, for the enjoyment of the more agile mid-Manhattan office workers. Buried in the extensive news coverage given to the media event was a cautionary note from chairman Ronan, who said that all the cost figures had been calculated at current price levels, and that any delays might increase costs "beyond our capacity to meet them."[82]

### *"Many a Slip . . ."*

During the next decade, progress toward the "Grand Design" proceeded by fits and starts, with a bit more of the former than the latter. Although the ten-year plan was endorsed by the Regional Plan Association and other civic groups, the program came under fire from Mayor Lindsay, from elected officials in Queens and Brooklyn, and from spokesmen for the New York Stock Exchange and other groups—either because it did not go far enough, or because it slighted some parts of the city while benefiting others.[83]

Meanwhile, the subway deficit continued to rise, from $49 million in 1968 to more than $70 million in 1969 and $120 million in 1970, bringing pressure on Ronan and his MTA board to increase the transit fare, which they did in 1970. Further wage increases and larger deficits led to another fare increase in 1972. On each occasion, city officials and strap-hangers attacked the MTA for the fare hikes and continuing service deficiencies.[84] Long Island

81. Ronan and his aides estimated that these projects—except perhaps for the two Sound bridges—would be completed within ten years. The second phase, beginning in 1978, would see still further rail improvements and new transportation centers throughout the suburbs. The MTA plans are described in Witkin, "$2.9-Billion Transit Plan for New York Area Links Subways, Rails, Airports," and Charles G. Bennett, "Transportation Funding Would Have 4 Sources," both *New York Times*, February 29, 1968, and in MTA, *Transportation Progress* (New York: December 1968), pp. 16–27.

82. See Witkin, "$2.9-Billion Transit Plan," and "Program for Better Transit," editorial, *New York Times*, June 5, 1968.

83. Brooklyn officials argued that the program gave "inadequate attention" to that borough, and gave too much attention to "carrying suburbanites into and out of Manhattan." City business leaders expressed "dismay" that part of the Second Avenue subway was to be deferred until stage two of the program. Queens representatives urged that more rail lines be provided in their area. In response, the Board of Estimate and Mayor Lindsay agreed to aid these projects with $500 million in additional contributions from the city—the new funds to be raised through long-term borrowing. See Charles G. Bennett, "Ronan Warns City To Act on Transit Lest Funds Shrink," *New York Times*, August 13, 1968; Seth S. King, "Ronan Willing to Expand Subway Plans, and 'Happy' City Pays," *New York Times*, September 20, 1968.

84. In 1970, for example, Mayor Lindsay denounced the MTA and appointed a "transit watchdog" committee, "fare-dodging strikes" were carried out by groups of commuters, and several Queens officials, led by the Queens district attorney, announced an inquiry to determine whether fare increases were the result of a "criminal conspiracy." Edward C. Burks, "Lindsay Rides Subway; Calls It 'Unacceptable,' " *New York Times*, January 10, 1970; "Transit Return to City is Sought," *New York Times*, February 2, 1970.

rail commuters, faced with work slowdowns and deteriorating equipment in the first years of the MTA, were equally unhappy.[85]

But Ronan and Rockefeller fought back, with substance and with public-relations ploys. In the fall of 1968 the first new LIRR cars were delivered, and the governor announced enthusiastically that "the future in metropolitan area transportation is here now."[86] Less than a year later, as heightened labor problems and service breakdowns resulted in the LIRR's "worst service in the memory of man,"[87] and as commuters revolted against showing their tickets and paying fares, Rockefeller promised that the LIRR would have "the finest railroad service in the country" within two months. Sixty days later, to a skeptical audience, he announced that this pinnacle had been achieved. It was, as one observer noted, "one of a long list of political productions" by the embattled governor.[88] Meanwhile, Nassau County and New York City continued to withhold station-maintenance payments, wages spiralled upward, and deficits on the LIRR and the subway system grew ever larger.[89]

Still the MTA inched forward with its modernization plans. By 1971, 620 new cars were in service on the LIRR; and during 1968–1971 1,100 new subway cars, most of them air conditioned, were purchased using funds from the 1967 bond issue and placed in service. Also in 1971, the Staten Island rapid transit line was purchased for a fair market price—one dollar—and the MTA began to replace its ancient rolling stock (none had been bought since 1925) and refurbish its decrepit stations. Meanwhile, Connecticut had created a Transportation Authority to work with the MTA to maintain passenger service on the bankrupt New Haven Railroad. The two state authorities assumed full responsibility for commuter service on the line in 1971 and began a $100 million modernization program—with federal funds totaling $40 million to assist the bistate effort. The following year, the MTA took over the remaining commuter lines operating out of Grand Central Station, the Hudson and Harlem routes through Westchester County formerly provided by the New York Central.[90]

Moreover, Ronan's agency—now dubbed the Wholly Ronan Empire—began to move vigorously on bus problems, a concern that had simply been left out of the original "Grand Design."[91] In 1971, 200 new buses were put into

85. See, for example, "G.O.P. Unit Assails Service on L.I.R.R.; Change Is Proposed," *New York Times*, October 9, 1968, and sources cited below in note 88.

86. Quoted in MTA, *Transportation Progress*, p. 13.

87. This was the assessment of three transportation specialists with extensive experience in the region: Joseph M. Leiper, Clarke R. Rees, and Bernard Joshua Kabak, "Mobility in the City," in Lyle C. Fitch and Annmarie Hauck Walsh, eds., *Agenda for a City* (Beverly Hills, Calif: Sage, 1970), p. 389.

88. See Craig R. Whitney, "With Day to Go, L.I. Riders Are Wary," *New York Times*, October 6, 1969; Bill Kovach, "Governor Hails L.I.R.R.," *New York Times*, October 8, 1969; Richard Witkin, "On Stage: Transport," *New York Times*, October 8, 1969.

89. See, for example, Robert D. McFadden, "L.I.R.R. Reports $16-Million Loss," *New York Times*, December 23, 1969; Lesley Oelsner, "Long Island Railroad Faces $43.3-Million Deficit," *New York Times*, January 5, 1971; Robert Lindsey, "Transit: Ink Gets Redder," *New York Times*, March 8, 1971.

90. The details are contained in the MTA's reports. See, in particular, MTA, *1971 Annual Report* (New York: March 1, 1972), pp. 19–41; MTA, *1968–1973: The Ten-Year Program at the Halfway Mark* (New York: Undated, ca. June 1973), pp. 9–12, 18–53.

91. An early use of the phrase "Wholly Ronan Empire" is found in Sydney H. Schanberg, "Ronan Lays Transit Crisis To a 30-Year Lag in City," *New York Times*, August 25, 1968. Cf. Fred C. Shapiro, "The Wholly Ronan Empire," *New York Times Magazine*, May 17, 1970, pp. 34–52.

service on the MTA's routes in New York City. When several private bus companies in Westchester began to falter financially, the authority and the county government purchased the buses and assured the continuance of commuter bus service. And the MTA responded to a similar problem in Nassau County by creating a new subsidiary, the Metropolitan Suburban Bus Authority, which took over the facilities of ten bus companies and began operating them as a unified system.[92]

While these efforts to stabilize and modernize service went forward, deficits continued to mount on all the MTA's rail systems. The rate of increase on the Long Island was particularly striking, growing from $2.5 million in 1965 (the year before state purchase) to $54.7 million in 1971. In response, the authority raised commuter rates and subway fares, squeezed increasing amounts out of Triborough, and—as inflation ate into the funds remaining from the 1967 bond issue—saw its ability to achieve the "Grand Design" fading.

If more funds were needed, Rockefeller and Ronan concluded, the voters would have to supply them through another bond issue. The governor took the lead, carrying the issue to the electorate with a $2.5 billion proposal in 1971— and he was defeated. Undaunted, Rockefeller put together a massive $3.5 billion bond issue two years later, and it too lost in the statewide vote. Both proposals had been carefully crafted to provide large amounts for mass transit and for highways, and Rockefeller offered the prospect of lower bus fares, as well as rail and bus capital improvements. Thus the bond issues might appeal both to advocates of mass transit and auto travel, and to citizens in upstate regions as well as to New York-area voters. But upstate, the proposals seemed to offer too much for New York City and its suburbs, while downstate transit advocates denounced them as "highway plans in mass transit clothing."[93]

So the MTA limped along, with little money to carry out its large construction program, searching for ways to make modest improvements in rolling stock and to meet ever-growing deficits. Triborough tolls were increased in 1972 and again in 1975 to provide funds for rail and bus operations. Although these increases led to some traffic diversion to toll-free bridges, net revenue from the Triborough facilities continued to rise. TBTA funds transferred to mass transit operations doubled to $50 million a year in 1972, rose to $74 million in 1974, and passed $100 million in 1976.[94]

92. See MTA, *1968–1973*, pp. 5, 7, 17, 47–48.

93. The quoted characterization is that of Theodore W. Kheel, who led the successful campaigns against the 1971 and 1973 bond issues. His point was that every dollar of state funds used for highway construction would generate nine dollars of federal aid, while state dollars spent for mass transit would yield much smaller amounts of federal funds. As a result, even a 60-40 state bond issue (the ratio in favor of transit in the 1973 referendum) would generate more total dollars for highway construction than for transit improvement. For the views of Kheel and others, see Francis X. Clines, "Governor Asking 3.5-Billion Bonds for Transit Plan," and Frank J. Prial, " 'New' Transit Plan Isn't," both in the *New York Times*, July 21, 1973. The campaigns for the two bond issues were covered extensively in the *Times* during the summer and fall of 1971 and 1973. For useful summaries of the issues, see Frank Lynn, "In New York: Everybody Was for the Bond Issue Except the People," *New York Times*, November 7, 1971, and Edward C. Burks, "Transit-Bond Plan Termed an Underdog in Need of Heavy City-Suburban Vote," *New York Times*, November 4, 1973. On the evolving resistance to highway construction, see Chapter Four in this volume.

94. Triborough's contributions are summarized in MTA, *1975 Annual Report* (New York: undated, ca. April 1976), pp. 18–19, and *Annual Report—1976* (New York: undated, ca. July 1977), pp. 22–23. In 1974, New York State also began to make direct contributions to meet operating

## The Interweaving of Federal and Regional Action

Faced with mounting transit deficits, Ronan and other officials in the region called upon Washington for help. In his first months at MTA, Ronan advocated tripling federal aid for mass transit projects from its 1968 level of $175 million. He also urged that federal funds for mass transit cover 90 percent of costs as they did in the interstate highway program. MTA was a prominent member of the transit coalition that pressed successfully for passage of the Urban Mass Transportation Act of 1970, authorizing several billion dollars for capital projects. By 1971, as president of the Institute for Rapid Transit, a national pressure group, Ronan was among the leaders in lobbying for federal operating subsidies for rail and bus lines, and for use of the Highway Trust Fund to finance transit operations.

In 1972–1973, the MTA was an active member of the national coalition that finally breeched the wall, as the Federal-Aid Highway Act of 1973 permitted use of trust fund dollars for mass transit projects. The 1973 act also increased federal transit grants to $6.1 billion, and improved the federal matching ratio to 80–20.[95] A year later—spurred in part by energy-conservation arguments—Congress agreed for the first time to provide money for transit operating subsidies, and approved an $11.8 billion multiyear package for mass transportation. The new measure, passed overwhelmingly with bipartisan support, was heralded by members of Congress from the New York region, who had led the fight for approval, as ushering in a "new era for mass transit."[96]

But in MTA territory the new era looked very much like the old, as rail-system deficits continued to mount, and construction for new subway lines crept along slowly. One notable difference, however, was the absence of the old leaders: In December 1973, after nearly fifteen years at the helm in Albany, Nelson Rockefeller had resigned the governorship, leaving soon after for Washington as the third in the 1970s parade of Republican vice-presidents. And in 1974, William Ronan moved from MTA headquarters to the heights of the World Trade Center, as the new chairman of the Port Authority's governing board.

---

subsidies, through a new program to assist rail and bus operations under the MTA and elsewhere throughout the state. See New York State, Department of Transportation, *Annual Transportation Report: 1975* (Albany: undated, 1976), pp. 4–5.

95. Some of Ronan's activities on behalf of the coalition seeking more federal funds, and the increasing role of federal moneys in MTA projects, are described in Edward A. Morrow, "Heavier U.S. Aid Asked for Transit," *New York Times*, September 12, 1968; MTA, *1971 Annual Report*, pp. 6, 9, 16, 33–38 passim; and MTA, *1968–1973*, pp. 16, 73–77.

96. The quoted phrase is that of Representative Joseph G. Minish (Democrat of New Jersey), who led the battle for approval in the House. Other prominent supporters of the bill were Representative Hugh L. Carey (Democrat from New York City), who had just been elected Governor of New York and vowed to use the new funds to help save the 35-cent subway fare, Representative Edward I. Koch (also Democrat from New York City), whose support for transit aid would later be helpful in his successful campaign to become mayor of New York City, and Democratic Senator Harrison Williams of New Jersey, who once again guided a transit bill successfully through the upper house. The measure also attracted Republican support, with President Gerald Ford urging passage as a "responsible step in our efforts to reduce energy consumption and control inflation." See Martin Tolchin, "House Approves $11.8-Billion Aid for Mass Transit; Measure Now Goes to Ford," *New York Times*, November 22, 1974.

Meanwhile, the search for additional funds for mass transit continued. In 1973, Mayor Lindsay sought to reduce the $100 million annual burden imposed on the city budget by the transit system by urging a regional payroll tax. Lindsay's scheme involved creation of a regional transit district encompassing the tristate area; the new district would draw funds from federal and state sources, as well as from a payroll tax, thus putting the region's transit operations on a "firm and durable financial footing." Three years later, the MTA's new chairman emphasized the authority's need for "adequate and assured financing on a long-term" basis, and also urged that a broad-based regional tax be enacted.[97]

These sentiments released a predictable flow of encouragement from the *New York Times*. One commentator on political affairs wrote optimistically that

> New York and its surrounding communities have come to realize, more and more, that the suburbs and the city are one—that if New York dies, Scarsdale and Montclair and New Canaan may be next. . . . The regional approach is, perhaps, the only approach.[98]

Eloquent statements indeed. But wary local officials and state legislators had no interest in that kind of regional cooperation, and both the Lindsay and MTA proposals died aborning.

Cooperative action did continue, however, directed toward the goal of squeezing more funds from the occasionally reluctant guardians of the federal exchequer. In 1976, urban interests in Congress obtained additional "temporary" federal funds for commuter rail transportation, in order to "assist in an orderly transition to locally supported service." No such transition had occurred by the fall of 1977, and President Carter reluctantly signed a bill extending this aid, while expressing disappointment that "the affected cities have not yet arranged to live within these original Federal emergency payments."[99] Congressmen from the New York region pressed ahead, urging an increase in the federal gasoline tax, with the added moneys used to provide a new trust fund—for mass transportation programs. And Carter's own proposals, announced in January 1978, called for $50 billion for mass transportation and highways, with matching funds for transit finally reaching the 90–10 ratio used for interstate roads, and with increased flexibility for cities to select their own preferred mix of rail and highway projects. As approved by Congress and signed by the President in November, the Surface Transportation Act of 1978 provided nearly $14 billion for mass transit during the next four years, plus additional funds, if highway projects were

97. The Lindsay proposal, reminiscent of the 1958 MRTC district plan, is described in Frank J. Prial, "Lindsay Suggests Plan for Transit to Reduce Fares," and in "Excerpts From Lindsay's Plan," *New York Times*, April 30, 1973. Ronan's successor at MTA, David L. Yunich, set forth his support for a regional tax in his letter of transmittal accompanying the authority's annual report; see MTA, *1975 Report*, p. 2.

98. Frank J. Prial, "Mass Transit: Some Help From the Neighbors?" *New York Times*, May 6, 1973.

99. The quoted phrases are from President Jimmy Carter's statement upon signing HR 8346; see "Statement by the President," November 16, 1977.

"traded in" for transit, that might yield a total transit-aid figure of more than $16 billion.[100]

### The MTA's First Decade

In announcing the "Grand Design" in 1968, MTA leaders had said that Phase I would be entirely completed in ten years—if there were no delays. But delays there were, due to conflicting priorities among MTA, New York City, and suburban officials, between mass transit and highway proponents, between upstate and downstate voters. By 1978, there were significant improvements in the quality of rail and bus service in the 12-county MTA region, but there were important offsetting minuses as well—fares that had risen sharply, and inaction on most of the new lines that had been proposed in 1968.

On the positive side, the deterioration in the region's commuter services had been halted, and significantly reversed on some rail lines. The Staten Island line now had new rolling stock in place of its forty-five-year-old cars, the subway system and the Long Island rail system had more than 600 new cars each, and the New Haven, Hudson, and Harlem lines also sported new commuter cars and other modest improvements. Bus services in the region were stabilized, and in Nassau County the MTA's efforts had reversed the long-term decline in ridership.[101]

On the other hand, in order to meet continuously rising costs, fares had increased substantially since 1968. Although such increases affected rail and bus services throughout the region, the rate of increase was particularly notable on New York City's subway and bus lines, where fares rose from twenty cents to thirty, then thirty-five, and then fifty cents, bringing agonized cries from riders and local officials.

Moreover, while electrification, air conditioned cars and other improvements had some favorable impact on service quality, they did not meet the expectations of commuters, or even of MTA and state leaders. Here the "loss leader" was the Long Island Rail Road. In the late 1960s, Ronan and his aides had distributed to LIRR commuters their plans for the coming decade—including a table showing dramatic reductions of 40 to 50 percent in running time between Long Island stations and Manhattan. But in 1978, the actual timetables were essentially the same as a decade earlier, and some trains even took longer to reach Manhattan.[102] In the summer of 1978, equipment failures

100. On these developments in Washington, see for example Edward C. Burks, "U.S. to Open Hearings on Rail-Transit Bill," *New York Times*, July 25, 1977; Ernest Holsendolph, "White House May Let Cities Decide on Transit Funds," *New York Times*, November 25, 1977; Albert R. Karr, "Mass Transit Gets Short Shrift," *Wall Street Journal*, December 30, 1977; Message of the President, January 26, 1978; Terence Smith, "Carter Calls for $50 Billion Highway Program With Increased Share for Mass Transit," *New York Times*, January 27, 1978; Edward C. Burks, "Howard, Roe Say Carter's Transit Bill Does Not Allot Enough Funds for State," *New York Times*, February 6, 1978; Edward C. Burks, "Carter Signs a Record 4-Year, $51 Billion Bill for Roads and Transit," *New York Times*, November 8, 1978.

101. See MTA, *Annual Report—1976*, pp. 6, 12–13, 17, and MTA, *Annual Report—1977* (New York: January 1979), pp. 6–19.

102. Based on a comparison between the MCTA's original table, distributed in 1966 or 1967, and LIRR timetables in use in July, 1978. A study of LIRR running times, comparing 1903 and 1976, indicated that in general rail travel between Long Island stations had been faster in 1903 than in

*One of MTA's new subway cars operating on the express line between mid-Manhattan and Kennedy Airport.*

Credit: Metropolitan Transportation Authority

and canceled trains had begun to cause political problems for Governor Carey, as they had for his predecessor. Under pressure from the governor—whose spokesman said the railroad was in "hideous shape"—and from commuter groups, the MTA abruptly fired the LIRR president in late July. By general agreement, the LIRR was "in the throes of its worst performance since 1968."[103]

As the energy crisis grew in the late 1970s, the subways, buses and railroad lines of the MTA all experienced significant gains in ridership. But these gains, which continued into the 1980's as gasoline prices remained high, brought as many problems as benefits. MTA revenues were up; but overcrowding became severe, with hundreds of rail commuters standing during long trips from distant suburbs. The added passengers contributed to the increased delays, and at times trains bound for Manhattan were so crowded that they could not pick up passengers at the final inbound stations, leaving

---

1976. See Irvine Molotsky, "Audit Disputes L.I.R.R. On-Time Records," *New York Times*, November 18, 1978.

A typical story circulating among LIRR travelers in the 1970s was the following bit of gallows humor: Seeing a man lying on the LIRR tracks, apparently bent on suicide, a rescuer rushes forward and then notices a loaf of bread in the man's hand. "Why the bread?" he asks. "I was afraid," replies the would-be suicide, "that I might starve to death before the train comes along."

103. The shape of the railroad, and Governor Carey's political concerns (his opponent was reportedly "relishing the opportunity" to use the LIRR's problems "as a weapon" in the fall campaign) are described in E.J. Dionne, Jr., "Carey Dismisses L.I.R.R. President, Naming a Grumman Aide to the Job," *New York Times*, July 29, 1978; Robert D. McFadden, "Commuter Groups Offer Advice to New L.I.R.R. Chief," *New York Times*, July 30, 1978; Irvin Molotsky, "New L.I.R.R. Head Says He Can Be Its Moving Force" *New York Times*, November 27, 1978.

*A commuter train operated by the state of New Jersey picks up pas-*
*sengers at the old Plainfield station on the former line of the Central*
*Railroad of New Jersey.*
Credit: Barbara Reilly, Staff Photographer, *New Jersey Transit*

weary commuters stranded. The new cars needed to alleviate the crush were
not expected to arrive until 1984.[104]

Finally, the program of new construction—the centerpiece of the 1968
plan—had been largely suspended since the early 1970s, a victim of rising
costs and inadequate resources. A few segments of the 63rd Street line to
Queens, and of the Southeast Queens line, were completed and a few others
were under construction a decade later, though they were far behind the
original time schedule. Only a small part of the fabled Second Avenue subway had been started, and other projects, such as the new rail line connecting
Kennedy Airport with Manhattan and the East Side transportation center in
Manhattan, had never moved off the drawing boards. Nor were there prospects for going ahead with most of these projects in the near future. In 1968,
the estimated costs for the new transit lines were $1.3 billion; by 1973, the
total had risen to more than 2.5 billion. At that point the MTA stopped
estimating the cost. In the winter of 1978–1979 the alert pedestrian could still
see signs on Fifth Avenue near 63rd Street in Manhattan, proclaiming "the
MTA's overall program of adding over 40 miles of new subways," but these

104. The commuter's fate is aptly described in David A. Andelman, "Rail Commuters Angry
but Resigned," *New York Times*, January 24, 1980.

*A new PATH train in Newark, from which the Port Authority's com-*
*muter line provides service to Jersey City, Hoboken, mid-Manhattan,*
*and the World Trade Center in lower Manhattan.*
Credit: Port Authority of New York and New Jersey

were only monuments to past hopes now beyond the authority's means or realistic intention.[105]

### The Port Authority in Disarray

On the west side of the Hudson a similar pattern of public action emerged, although the institutional development was quite different. Under the leadership of the state Department of Transportation (which succeeded the Highway Department in 1966), service was stabilized on most New Jersey rail lines, new cars were acquired for many of the routes, and a series

---

105. The 1968 plan had called for more than fifty miles of new subway lines; by 1974 this had been cut to a promise of forty miles; and in 1978 the total had been whittled down to the Queens lines, totaling less than fifteen miles, with the hope that these segments would be open for service by 1985. Yet the MTA leadership, finding its construction plans delayed, pressed forward with rhetoric. Enticed by the same optimism and edifice complex that had captured the MRTC in the 1950s and their own predecessors in the 1960s, MTA's leaders in 1977 saw a "new awareness . . . spreading throughout the land about the problems and importance of public transportation," and felt "confident that this awareness will inspire a new resurgence of public transportation ridership." The authority therefore set forth a new 10-year $5.5 billion program to expand subway and commuter rail lines, earning the MTA a vigorous attack from New York City's planning commission, which argued that air conditioning of cars and other modest improvements would be a better use of scarce dollars than a costly building program. See MTA, *Annual Report—1976*, pp. 2–3; New York City Planning Commission, *Capital Needs and Priorities for the City of New York* (New York: March 1, 1978), pp. 23–27. See also the series of four articles by Grace Lichtenstein, "The Subways," *New York Times*, May 8–11, 1978, and Ross Sandler and David Schoenbrod, "Tunnel Vision, Too," *New York Times*, April 14, 1978.

of modest improvements in the system was initiated. State operating subsidies and funds for capital improvements were extended to bus lines, thus preserving commuter services which in New Jersey carried considerably more passengers than the rail lines. The costs of these subsidies to private bus companies grew rapidly, however, leading the state in 1979 to initiate action to take over ownership and operation of major bus lines.[106] Under the Port Authority, the Hudson Tubes became the PATH rail lines (for Port Authority Trans-Hudson) and were overhauled with new equipment and terminal facilities in lower Manhattan and Jersey City. As in New York, stabilization, overhaul, and increasing labor and other costs brought higher fares and continued dissatisfaction from New Jersey commuters. The new era also produced a series of ambitious plans for major improvements which were delayed by rising costs, conflicts over priorities, and disagreements over financing and institutional arrangements.[107]

The most serious dispute in New Jersey centered on the role of the Port Authority in mass transportation. As the 1960s drew to a close, the bistate agency seemed protected from further involvement in rail transit by the 1962 bond covenant, which effectively limited the Port Authority's rail transportation role to the PATH tubes. Friends and enemies alike viewed the covenant, which seemed to foreclose deeper authority involvement in rail transit, as a premier example of the strategic skill of its officials in defending the agency's independence and power.[108] What Austin Tobin had not expected was a governor who would demand that the covenant be changed and, when faced with resistance because of alleged constitutional barriers, would again demand that the covenant be changed—and further, insist that Port Authority officials agree with his view and make plans to plunge the agency deeply into rail transit, despite personal and legal reservations. But William Cahill, who was elected New Jersey's chief executive in November 1969, was such a governor.

Acting on his campaign promises, Cahill urged the Port Authority to press ahead with rail transit commitments and brushed off the protests of Tobin and his commissioners. By 1971, Cahill was using his veto power to delay its other programs, while advocating Port Authority action on a series of rail projects.[109] When Tobin defended the authority's position as a self-

106. New Jersey's program and results are summarized in the annual reports of the state's Department of Transportation (NJDOT). On New Jersey's bus programs, see Bus Subsidy Program Study Commission, State of New Jersey, *Report to the Legislature* (Trenton: January 9, 1978).

107. For a sampling of New Jersey's hopes, plans, and disappointments, see Peter Carter, "$300 Million Rail Plan Is Proposed by Hughes," *Newark Evening News*, May 16, 1966; NJDOT, *A Master Plan for Transportation* (Trenton: March 1968); Dick Gale, "$2.5-Billion 'Master Plan' Outlined For Rails and Highways," *Trenton Evening Times*, March 12, 1968; Richard Phalon, "Mass Transit a Key Issue in Jersey Governor Race," *New York Times*, May 29, 1973; and James Manion, "N.J. May Bench Conrail, Run Rail Lines Itself," *Trenton Evening Times*, August 31, 1978. In New Jersey, as in New York State, a crucial element in the delays and lost aspirations was the defeat of several transportation bond issues at the polls during the 1970s.

108. On the negotiations leading to the creation of PATH, the World Trade Center, and the 1962 bond covenant, see note 48 above and associated text. The role of tax-exempt revenue bonds in maintaining the independence of public authorities is described in Chapter Six; see note 21 in that chapter and associated text.

109. The Cahill projects included expansion of the PATH rail system to other areas of New Jersey, Port Authority purchase of the Penn Central railroad station in Newark, and construction of a new rail tunnel from New Jersey to Manhattan near 48th Street to provide "direct rail access to

supporting body and expressed doubt that it could assume large deficits and survive, Cahill attacked the executive director publicly. He also directed that the New Jersey commissioners caucus separately before board meetings to establish a "New Jersey point of view," and he warned them to follow his lead on the mass transit issue if they wanted to be reappointed.[110]

The Cahill barrage had an impact. In December 1971, Austin Tobin abruptly announced his retirement after nearly 30 years as executive director.[111] Five months later, the authority's vice-chairman, a respected banker who shared Tobin's views on the bond covenant, also resigned.[112] In the spring of 1972, after years of working with Tobin and his staff, Governor Rockefeller attacked the old regime and urged that William Ronan be chosen to replace Tobin and change the agency "from a rubber to a rails orientation."[113] That November the two governors announced that the Port Authority had agreed to a plan which, within the constraints of the bond covenant, would permit it to apply more than $250 million of its own funds to extend the PATH rail lines into the New Jersey suburbs, provide rail service between Manhattan and Kennedy airport, and carry out other rail projects.[114]

Then, in the spring of 1973, both states passed legislation ending the bond covenant for Port Authority bonds sold in the future, and a year later

---

mid-Manhattan for all New Jersey commuters." Early in his second year in office, Cahill said he would take "a much more aggressive, determined and stubborn approach to the failure of the Port Authority," and he referred to the 1962 bond covenant as a Port Authority "device to permit it to escape additional responsibilities," which had been accepted, "incredibly," by the state legislatures. These criticisms, together with the governor's comments on new rail projects, are set forth in William T. Cahill, "Remarks at Chamber of Commerce Dinner," February 4, 1971.

110. At a legislative hearing in early 1971, for example, Tobin protested: "Don't tell us that we can operate a mass transit system with a $300 million a year deficit on a self-supporting basis, . . . we can't, and God can't." In response to this typical Tobin strategy—emphasizing the extreme in rail transit burdens—Cahill exclaimed that Tobin "will not be making the decisions on what the Authority can or cannot do." See New York State Assembly Committee on Corporations, Authorities and Commissions, and Autonomous Authorities Study Commission of the New Jersey State Legislature, *Public Hearing* (New York: March 5, 1971), pp. 92–93; Henry Lee, "Ronan to Be Named Port Authority Head," *New York Daily News*, March 15, 1972. On the separate caucus, see Alex Michelini, "PA Commish Defends the N.J. Caucus," *New York Sunday News*, April 2, 1972.

111. Tobin announced his decision on December 12 and immediately turned over his duties to his long-time deputy, Matthias E. Lukens, who was designated acting executive director.

112. The commissioner, Hoyt Ammidon, had previously defended Tobin's actions and publicly opposed proposals that might violate the 1962 covenant. Ammidon was also chairman of the board of the United States Trust Company, an investment company which would later bring suit on behalf of the Port Authority's bondholders to protect the bond covenant; see discussion below. His views are set forth in Hoyt Ammidon, "Port Authority," letter to the editor, *New York Times*, March 24, 1971.

113. "We don't want a continuation of the Tobin structure," Rockefeller opined, "which as everyone knows was a very tight, highly political structure and opposed to mass transit." Rockefeller's attack was motivated in part by his sense that leadership in the mass transit area had been usurped by his fellow Republican from New Jersey. See Frank Mazza, "Rocky Raps PA Steamroller," *New York Daily News*, April 28, 1972, and the transcript of his interview with John Hamilton, WNEW-TV, April 9, 1972.

114. The new program is described in Port Authority, *1972 Annual Report* (New York: March 1973), pp. 6–8. Also in 1972, in response to Cahill's urging that the title of the "misnamed Port of New York Authority" be altered, the agency became "The Port Authority of New York and New Jersey."

both states overturned the covenant retroactively. With that hurdle allegedly out of the way, Port Authority tolls were raised sharply in order to provide more funds to carry out additional mass transportation projects. Ultimately, the scheme failed. The repeal of the covenant predictably brought a bond-holders' suit, and in 1977 the U.S. Supreme Court rejected the states' action as a violation of the obligations of the contract clause of the Constitution.[115] The rail transit projects announced with fanfare in the early 1970s would have to be financed in some other way, not with Port Authority funds.

But the long battle to increase the authority's activities in mass transit had other results. In the complex world of the Port Authority, a sense of institutional purpose, effective central leadership, and staff morale had been crucially linked for thirty years to Austin Tobin's energy and intensive in-volvement in all major areas—and to staff expectations that funds would be available to permit them to carry out ambitious programs. As Tobin's energies became absorbed in the battle with Governor Cahill, the potentially separate empires—airports, world trade, and the other departments—began to drift apart; and when that conflict cast into doubt the ability of the Port Authority to raise and employ the sums needed to achieve large purposes, staff members worked less for the institution and more for themselves. The process was subtle: some did not know it was happening. And the change in the institu-tion was uneven: in some areas, where there were new plans afoot, a lively interest in the future remained. But in department after department, a sense of forward motion—of the possibilities for forward motion—crept out, and staff morale fell.

Had Tobin II replaced Tobin I, it might have been different. But in December 1971 Tobin's replacement was a career staff member, designated as "acting" executive director; and he in turn was succeeded in 1973 by another careerist with the same tentative hold on the office until receiving a regular appointment in the fall of 1974.[116] Perhaps neither of them had a taste for vigorous leadership; but in view of the uncertain legal situation and recurrent gubernatorial forays, it would have required a person of quite un-usual abilities to do much better. Had Rockefeller's first choice been ac-cepted in 1972, power might again have flowed into the staff director's office; but William Ronan was not acceptable to a majority of the commis-sioners, because of his advocacy of deeper rail transit involvement and their

115. Immediately after the repealer was signed in New Jersey, the United States Trust Com-pany filed a suit against the state. In 1975–1976, the trial court and the New Jersey Supreme Court found the statutory repeal to be a reasonable exercise of the state's police power, not prohibited by the state or United States constitutions. On appeal, the U.S. Supreme Court reversed the decision, concluding that the repeal, by permitting Port Authority funds to be used without restriction to fund rail transit projects (which might generate large deficits), had substantially impaired the bond-holders' security, and therefore had violated the contract clause of the U.S. Constitution. See John H. Allan, "Law Dismays Municipal-Bond Dealers," *New York Times*, May 1, 1974; Roger Harris, "P.A. At the Crossroads," *Newark Sunday Star-Ledger*, August 21, 1977; *United States Trust Company v. State of New Jersey*, 431 U.S. 1 (1977).

116. Matthias Lukens served in an acting capacity from the time of Tobin's exodus until he retired in August 1973; his successor, A. Gerdes Kuhbach, was acting staff director until August 1974, when he was named executive director. Lukens had been with the Port Authority for 24 years prior to replacing Tobin, including eleven years as Tobin's deputy. Kuhbach had been with the New Haven Railroad until 1962, when he joined the authority as director of finance, the position he held until replacing Lukens.

fear that this effort would end the vitality of the agency as a self-supporting enterprise.[117]

For a time the leadership vacuum was filled by Ronan, who had served on the board since 1967 and became chairman in May 1974. But his strong protransit stance and earlier criticisms of other Port Authority officials made it difficult for him to gain support within the agency. For example, in 1972 he criticized his fellow commissioners publicly for appearing to "assign a higher priority to the bond market than to mass transportation" and expressed doubt that the board majority was "highly motivated toward the difficult decisions necessary" to fund large transit projects.[118] By the end of 1974, Ronan himself had been publicly rebuked by Brendan Byrne, Cahill's successor as governor, for failing to make progress in mass transportation, and he was criticized inside the agency for his unwillingness to let staff members make decisions, while being largely absent from the Port Authority offices himself. As one commissioner noted openly in November 1974, "nothing is getting done." The authority was "dead in the water."[119]

So the Port Authority drifted. Bridge and tunnel tolls were increased in early 1975 to fund mass transportation projects, an expansion of the Manhattan bus terminal was begun later that year, and in the spring of 1976 the governors of both states again announced that the Port Authority would help to finance a new mass transit program. But the 1972 program had never gotten underway, the legal uncertainties remained, and the authority's financial position had weakened—mainly due to multimillion-dollar yearly deficits generated at the World Trade Center, PATH, and Newark Airport.[120]

In the spring of 1977, frustrated by the agency's inability to devise a legally acceptable transit program, Governor Byrne began vetoing board actions on all subjects, further undermining morale and a sense of direction at the authority. Byrne demanded that the agency either find a way to use the added moneys for mass transit, or rescind the 1975 toll increase. Otherwise,

117. Ronan was known to be strongly interested in the post. He had already built a strong national reputation at the MTA, and the Port Authority, with its large net income base, would offer greater opportunities. Several factors undermined Ronan's candidacy: his sometimes arrogant style lost him support; his active effort in 1971 (as MTA chairman) to oppose federal funds for a Port Authority rail project—he argued that the MTA needed the money more—counted against him; and Governor Cahill was wary of Ronan's fondness for New York State and for Rockefeller, whose influence might tilt authority policies against Cahill's already beleaguered state. The evolution of the conflict is described in the following articles: Frank J. Prial, "Port Agency Seeks Successor To Tobin Within the Authority," *New York Times*, March 16, 1972; Frank J. Prial, "Port Authority Dissent: Ronan Gives a Hint of the Bitterness and Strife Among the Commissioners," *New York Times*, April 1, 1972; and Edward C. Burks, "Ferment in Mass-Transit Agencies," *New York Times*, April 5, 1974.

118. See "Ronan Letter to Port Unit," *New York Times*, March 31, 1972. On various occasions, he had also criticized Tobin and other agency staff members for failing to meet their mass transit responsibilities.

119. The quotations in the text are taken from Frank J. Prial, "Port Authority Has Fallen on Hard Times," *New York Times*, November 10, 1974; Prial's article accurately describes the authority's malaise during the mid-1970s.

120. The Trade Center deficit reached $7.9 million in 1974 and $11.9 million in 1975; and a $400-million expansion program at Newark Airport added several million more ($8.6 million in 1975). In 1975 the PATH deficit exceeded $37 million. Between 1973 and 1977 total Port Authority personnel shrank from more than 8,000 to less than 7,700. The Port Authority deficit figures are set forth in the report of the New York State Comptroller, "Public Authority Financial Analysis Statements, No. 8–76" (New York: November 1976).

he said, "I will not let them operate. I will veto the minutes." While authority commissioners and staff searched feverishly for a way to underwrite mass transit without violating the bondholders' rights, Byrne vetoed the minutes of the board in May and again in June, thus blocking the Port Authority from approving contracts and taking policy actions in a wide variety of areas. Continuing to apply pressure during the summer, Byrne criticized the authority as "too staff-dominated" and as populated by people who take a negative view of rail transit. While denying that his widely publicized efforts were motivated by a desire for votes in his 1977 reelection campaign, the governor acknowledged that his constituents would welcome either forward action on a transit plan or a toll reduction.[121]

Then, for the first time, scandal touched the agency's top officials. Rumors of inflated and fraudulent expense vouchers, of authority cars and helicopters appropriated for family outings of senior staff and commissioners, and of contract irregularities reached the press. By the fall of 1977 three senior officials had been disciplined, one had committed suicide, and New York State's Comptroller's Office had issued several detailed reports describing "extravagancy at public expense," "widespread padding of expense accounts," and other examples of misuse of public funds and of managerial weakness.[122]

Yet even as these past abuses were generating banner headlines, the Port Authority began to recover, drawing on its financial resources, areal and functional scope, staff skills—and new leadership. The Supreme Court decision in April 1977, reaffirming the validity of the 1962 covenant, strengthened the authority's position in the bond market, and required that rail transit advocates search for alternative ways—consistent with the covenant's constraints—to involve the agency. Soon thereafter, in June 1977, Ronan, whose relationships with Governors Byrne and Carey were not close, was replaced as Port Authority chairman by Alan Sagner, one of Byrne's closest associates. At the same time, the board broke a tradition of fifty years and hired Peter C. Goldmark, Jr., as the authority's first staff director from outside its career ranks.[123] Under its new leaders, the authority took steps to tighten managerial controls over the areas

121. Byrne's 1977 veto strategy is described in "Byrne Vows Fight for Toll Trim or Transit," *Newark Star-Ledger*, April 28, 1977; Ralph Blumenthal, "Byrne Again Opposes Port Unit; Vetoes Its Plan for Bus Projects," *New York Times*, June 22, 1977; Ralph Blumenthal, "Byrne Affirms View on the Hudson Tolls," *New York Times*, August 11, 1977.

122. Among the examples of extravagance cited in the reports were lavish overseas trips (in 1975–1976, three trips by authority officials totaled $100,000), costly dinners in honor of authority commissioners (one bill ran to $2,055), and the use of chauffeured vehicles to drive commissioners and senior officers to private clubs. More than two dozen senior staff members were accused of padding their expense vouchers, and two were involved in nepotism (one hired ten of his relatives for short-term jobs). The Port Authority vigorously resisted the view that abuses were "widespread" and after investigation disciplined six staff members for committing fraud and twenty-one others for minor abuses. See the official reports of the Office of State Comptroller, State of New York, 1977–1978; and Jameson W. Doig, "Illegal Behavior in Complex Organizations," typescript, 1979. The quotations in the text are taken from the state audit report of October 20, 1977.

123. Sagner had been commissioner of the New Jersey Department of Transportation and a member of the Port Authority board since his appointment to these positions early in 1974 by Governor Byrne. Previously, he had been finance chairman of Byrne's gubernatorial campaign in 1973. At the time of his appointment as executive director, Goldmark was serving under Governor Carey as state budget director.

where there had been abuses, and pressed for a transit program that would meet legal restrictions while providing the two states with $240 million in new funding—to purchase commuter bus equipment, develop additional exclusive bus roadways, and aid other mass transit facilities. Believing that the authority's leaders were now willing and able to move ahead in the transit area, Byrne stopped vetoing authority actions.

### Conflict into the 1980s: the Case of Westway

By the close of the 1970s, the region's two great independent agencies—the Port Authority and Triborough—had been yoked to mass transit's painted wagon. Triborough was fully submerged in a still larger enterprise, and was reduced to Moses's nightmare, collecting tolls and cleaning tunnels. The Port Authority was only partially yoked to mass transit, as it was assured by the 1962 covenant of some resources for innovative efforts in industrial development, energy recovery, or other fields that might benefit the region, its citizens, and its most venerable bistate agency.[124]

The states too were harnessed to mass transportation. Both state and city leaders continued to make vigorous efforts to secure more help from Washington, whose transportation resources might be diverted from highway building to aid the cities' transit needs, thus helping New York City, Newark, and Paterson to survive, and even thrive.

The highway-building era had ended; the highway era continued. This was the irony faced by those who supported mass transportation as they rounded the corner of the 1970s and tumbled into yet another decade. Indeed, as recounted in Chapter Four, the added influence yielded to local communities, along with the energy crisis and other forces, had ended the time of dramatic highway expansion in the New York region and, with few exceptions, around the nation. But the highways and their beneficiaries had not gone away. They fought still for the funds needed to complete Interstate 287 in Bergen County and other elements of the interstate network. Even the heralded 1978 federal act, which provided more than $14 billion for mass transportation, authorized much more—$37 billion—for highway projects.

Moreover, those who monitored the quality of the road system and lived by its largess argued that even greater amounts would be required to repair highways that were "beginning to crumble." By the end of the decade, U.S. officials calculated that a sharply increased level of federal aid would be needed simply to maintain the levels of highway quality that had existed in the mid-1970s.[125]

In the New York region, the road-building coalition found new allies in the late 1970s, as it adopted a wider vision in the massive Westway project. And here, in an urban drama that pitted regional planners against environmentalists and neighborhood groups, and divided mass transit advocates into

124. The Port Authority's explorations in these new fields are discussed in Chapter Ten.

125. See Albert R. Karr, "Operation Pothole," *Wall Street Journal*, January 31, 1978; and Fred W. Frailey, "America's Highways: Going to Pot," *U.S. News & World Report*, July 24, 1978, p. 36. According to one estimate, cited by Frailey, maintaining the quality levels of 1975 on the interstates would require $22 billion per year, twice the actual rate of expenditures in recent years.

*Crumbling piers and the relic of the West Side Highway flank the site of the proposed Westway project along the Hudson River in Manhattan.*
Credit: Sheldon Pollack

opposing camps, the many obstacles to large transportation projects and to integrated transportation and land-use development were clearly displayed.

When a truck carrying ten tons of asphalt plunged through the roadbed of the elevated West Side Highway in December 1973, it seemed evident that a major renovation of this forty-year-old roadway, which ran down the western shore of Manhattan, was past due. Major portions of the expressway were pronounced unsafe, and the highway south of 46th Street was closed, dispersing its traffic onto congested Manhattan streets.

Two plans were emphasized in the ensuing debate. One plan would simply replace the highway with a new road, probably at street level. The other, which evolved in the mid-1970s, would use the collapse of West Side Highway as an opportunity for a major project in urban renovation—with a total price tag of $1.4 billion. This ambitious scheme proposed replacing the elevated roadway with a six-lane highway, extending more than four miles from 42nd Street to the Battery, at the lower tip of Manhattan. Responding to the environmental and other anti-road concerns of the 1970s, most of the highway would be built below street level, and much of it would be covered over. The covered sections would be used to provide ninety-three acres of parks along the Hudson River and over 100 acres for commercial, residential, and industrial development. By attracting traffic from congested Manhattan streets, proponents argued, the new highway might actually reduce air pollution. In addition, the project would generate 6,000 or more construction jobs per year.

What the Westway project, as it was called, would mean in terms of new permanent jobs was a matter of some debate even among the proponents. The enthusiasts, led by a coalition of business executives and labor leaders, envisioned $7 billion in new private investment flowing to the area, and a net job impact—new jobs plus jobs that may disappear from New York without Westway—of over 150,000. Other project supporters, privately noting that such estimates were "outrageously high," anticipated at least 30,000 new jobs. There was agreement, however, that "this major economic development project" was indeed "New York City's opportunity of the century"—offering a way to revitalize not only the waterfront but the entire "decaying West Side of Manhattan."[126]

Opponents argued that the new highway would attract more traffic to the area, increasing both congestion and air pollution. They insisted that the funds should be traded in for additional mass-transit aid, as was now possible under federal law, and as Boston and other cities had done. Some argued that using "Westway funds" to renovate and improve the subway system would generate as many jobs as Westway, or even more.

The possibility of exchanging the Westway project for a modest highway at grade level, plus much-needed transit funds, was the central plank in the opposition campaign, but there were other concerns as well. Some were unhappy at the prospect of losing the old buildings and piers that gave this area of Manhattan its distinctive atmosphere. Many feared that the project would cause sharp increases in land speculation, property values, and taxes, driving out residents along the project area. Opponents also pointed to the possible destruction of fish spawning grounds, and heightened water pollution, that might result from the dredging and landfill operations required by Westway. And across the Hudson, the mayor of Jersey City noted with concern that landfill operations to build up the western Manhattan shoreline would alter the flow of the Hudson River—shifting it westward and possibly flooding Jersey City and Bayonne.[127]

To the *New York Times*, Westway's advantages clearly outweighed its costs and improved on any feasible alternative. Noting that state grants would meet 10 percent of project costs and federal funds the rest, the *Times* argued that the project "would not cost the city a cent." Moreover, this "welcome $1 billion" was not "just money for a road, or for jobs." Westway was a "comprehensive land-use project," exclaimed the *Times*; "it probably represents New York's major planning opportunity of the century." In response to the argument that these highway funds should be traded in for transit, the *Times* adopted a different view of the issue than it had in the past. If these moneys were used "to finish the Queens lines," the editorial board explained, the new transit facilities would burden the city with an additional operating deficit of "at least $20 million a year, and probably much more." "So on with it," the *Times* concluded, in its vigorous endorsement of Westway.[128]

126. Citizens Housing and Planning Council, and others, *Westway: West Side Rebirth or Decay?* pamphlet, New York, December 1978.

127. The opponents' concerns and arguments favoring the project are effectively captured in Paul Goldberger, "Uncertainty Clouds Westway's Amenities," *New York Times*, January 13, 1977; Ada Louise Huxtable, "Will Westway Turn Into the Opportunity of a Century?," *New York Times*, January 23, 1977; and Phyllis Kronick, "Westway is the Best Way," *Bergen Record*, January 21, 1979.

128. "Manna for Westway," editorial, *New York Times*, January 5, 1977; "Westway, Still the Best Way," editorial, *New York Times*, November 14, 1977; "Riding the Westway Roller Coaster," *New York Times*, December 31, 1977; "The Westway-Subway Détente," *New York Times*, April 21, 1978; and again, "Westway, Still the Best Way," editorial, *New York Times*, July 28, 1981.

As he approached the 1978 reelection campaign, Governor Carey, who had once denounced the project as a "planning and ecological disaster," found that his ability to attract crucially needed labor and business support in New York City would be greatly aided by a vigorous pro-Westway stance, and became persuaded of the project's great value. The U.S. Secretary of Transportation, after weighing the complex arguments for and against, also supported the plan, in a press conference held in Governor Carey's Manhattan office in January 1977. The Westway effort was, he concluded, "vital to the strength and future of New York City"; and as he spoke, Carey later said, "I could hear the money flowing."[129]

Other sources of opposition had to be laid to rest before the money would flow, however. In his successful 1977 mayoralty campaign in New York City, Edward Koch had refused to alter his long-standing opposition to massive highway projects in Manhattan, even though that stand would cut into his labor and business support. As a Manhattan congressman, he had opposed Westway and called for trading in the funds for additional aid to mass transit. The governor then wooed the new mayor, pledging that if Mayor Koch would support Westway the state would provide $120 million from Port Authority surpluses, and $40 million in state funds, in order to generate $640 million in federal funds for mass transit in the city. Moreover, Carey would personally guarantee that the subway fare would not be increased beyond its current 50-cent level until at least the end of 1981—after the next campaign for mayor in New York City. Koch reversed his position and endorsed Westway in April 1978. In the gubernatorial campaign that year, Carey was able to use that agreement as an example of his leadership in meeting complex transportation and economic development problems, and his Westway supporters among labor and business helped him to victory in November.

Even then, in the complex world of the 1970s, Westway could not proceed unless state and federal officials certified the project as acceptable in terms of air pollution and other environmental standards. Carey's own state commissioner of Environmental Conservation appeared reluctant to approve Westway, and this became a factor in his forced resignation in December 1978. And when a federal official opposed certification because of air pollution problems and possible damage to fishlife, Carey denounced him publicly as a "lunkhead" and urged that he be overruled or fired.

As the Westway battle extended into the 1980s, it seemed to illustrate many of the themes and divisions that had characterized transportation conflicts for the past three decades and more. There were echoes of the earlier era of highway building, when political power was concentrated and proposals for a massive George Washington Bridge or Verrazano span could sweep the opposition away through force of technical expertise, leadership skill, and asserted "public need." Indeed, some realities of that epoch remained: leaders of the construction unions who saw road building as jobs for their members; business executives who viewed such projects as essential steps in reducing traffic congestion and maintaining economic vitality for the region; elected officials who valued dramatic projects and the jobs they could provide as

129. Ralph Blumenthal, "Westway Plan Wins Final U.S. Approval; Boon to City Is Seen," *New York Times*, January 5, 1977.

steps to reelection, and whose enthusiasm was heightened when the projects also promised an economic boon (a plus for highway construction) without long-term deficits (a minus for rail projects).

There were strong echoes too of the near and distant past for those who had long fought for mass transit. Campaigners who recalled the LIRR and MRTC battles of the 1950s, and the first, grudging federal transit aid programs of the 1960s, viewed Westway as a symbol of that older era and saw a trade-in for transit as an important victory over that nearly vanquished highway foe. Moreover, the banners unfurled against Westway symbolized broader concerns as well—the importance in the present era of "doing something" about the environment, about energy, about the older cities. To defeat that billion-dollar project, and to funnel those funds into mass transit—this seemed a way to "do something" in the struggle against these several dragons.

As the Regional Plan Association attempted to explain, a careful evaluation of Westway required a more complex lens. Although the four-mile roadway was central to the project, it was only part of a far broader strategy for waterfront renovation and other new development along the West Side. Moreover, although Westway might bring some additional traffic to Manhattan, it would also siphon traffic from local streets, and might in time become crucial to a future effort to create auto-free zones in central Manhattan. And while the RPA had long advocated a better mass transit system, its officials viewed the trade-in of Westway moneys for transit funds as a "false choice," since the added transit dollars would be too little to make a significant dent in the region's problems. The RPA urged instead that the federal government make a vastly increased commitment to public transportation, including $2 billion a year for rail transit in the New York area.[130]

The Regional Plan Association, the Citizens Housing and Planning Council, the *New York Times*, and other groups made these arguments. And so did Governor Carey and his highway and planning aides. Even the chairman of the MTA endorsed the Westway project, arguing that there was no conflict between Westway and improved mass transit for the region. But now the number and variety of active constituencies were larger, their access to levers of influence—particularly via the new environmental laws—was much greater, and they were mistrustful of government action, especially on such a massive scale. As the process of gaining air-quality, water-quality, and dredge-and-landfill permits inched slowly forward, the opposition surged in at each decision point, pressing state and federal environmental agencies and the Army Corps of Engineers to reject the project. Using "transit trade-in" as a rallying cry, the Clean Air Coalition and its allies determined that if the executive agencies approved Westway, they would press a series of legal suits. "We can keep this in court" for years, a leader of the anti-Westway forces argued. "Westway won't be built—ever."[131]

130. Boris S. Pushkarev (RPA vice president), Statement before the National Transportation Policy Study Commission, February 27, 1978.

131. Brian Ketcham, quoted in Phyllis Kronick, "Westway Is the Best Way," *Bergen Record*, January 21, 1979. Materials on Westway include a vast outpouring of newspaper articles and documents, especially in 1977–1978. Files of useful materials are maintained by the RPA and the New

So it was that those defenders·of urban society who might have been united in urging both Westway and revitalized mass transit as crucial elements of a larger development strategy found themselves a house divided, exhausting their energies in a continuing war for the greater glory of the nation's largest metropolis.

## The Continuing Search for Solutions

While much of the public attention during the 1960s and 1970s was directed toward the bankruptcy of major rail lines, the deposing of chairman Moses, and the conflicts surrounding the Port Authority bond covenant, the region took some significant steps toward meeting mass transportation needs. Through the exercise of political leadership and planning skills, government agencies channeled increasing amounts of state and federal funds—and authority surpluses—into rail and bus transit, with the result that major services throughout the region have survived and some public facilities, such as PATH, have even been improved. Admittedly, it would be difficult to find a mass-transit counterpart to the George Washington Bridge, or the Narrows crossing, in their impact on residential and job distribution in the region. Nevertheless, public transport services that would otherwise have been abandoned have, through governmental action, been stabilized. As a result, established patterns of transportation, jobs, and residential development have continued—altering incrementally, without abrupt dislocation of working and living patterns in the region.

By the late 1970s, federal money for mass transit had expanded to many times its early 1960s level, but this period of growth clearly ended with the inauguration of President Ronald Reagan in 1981. In cities and suburbs alike, there would be renewed competition between mass transit and highway forces to divide the shrinking transportation. pie. It seemed unlikely that enough money would be forthcoming from federal and other sources to carry out large new rail projects in New York or other regions. Moreover, escalating costs seemed destined to absorb much of the new funding allocated to subway, bus, and commuter rail lines. With these several forces at work, it appeared unlikely that the combined efforts of federal, state and regional agencies would provide the "adequate and assured" long-term funding that might permit reduced fares and other improvements urged by the MTA chairman in a wishful moment in 1976.

---

York Chamber of Commerce and Industry (which favor the project), and at the Clean Air Coalition (which opposes Westway).

In the summer of 1981, with subway service now deteriorating further and the fare at 75 cents, Mayor Koch seemed ready to abandon Westway; then, extracting further financial concessions from Governor Carey, the mayor reaffirmed his support in late July. And Ronald Reagan, the fourth President of the Westway era, offered his support and federal dollars too. By August, as this volume went to press, only the court suits and ten years of massive landfill and road-building efforts remained—plus the need for another billion dollars to meet continually escalating costs—before the Westway vision would be reality.

# 8

# Concentrating Resources
# in the Older Cities

Without exception, governments in the region's older cities are strongly committed to using public resources to influence the pattern of development. None has been willing to accept as unalterable the economic and demographic developments of the past three decades. Instead, every city government has sought to check the employment and population trends that have changed the fortunes of the older cities. The steady decline in the cities' share of regional employment has produced a variety of public efforts designed to retain existing jobs and attract new ones. In response to the middle-class exodus from the core, cities have devoted substantial resources to urban renewal, middle-income housing, and related programs. Zoning, urban redevelopment, and other public powers have been used to enhance the attractiveness of the older cities for upper-income households. Substantial efforts also have been made to improve poor neighborhoods through public housing, slum clearance, model cities, code enforcement, and other programs.

Underlying these city efforts to influence development have been strong political pressures. City dwellers expect their governments to do something about the erosion of jobs, inadequate housing, neighborhood decay, and declining public services. Candidates for public office amplify these concerns by holding incumbents responsible for the loss of business firms and middle-class families to the suburbs. And office holders steadfastly assert that *their* programs will reverse the tide, and restore the city's economic and social health. Thus, Mayor John Lindsay exuded confidence about his administration's ability to "create more jobs and a better economy in New York City," and in so doing "help the poor [and] alleviate the fiscal crisis."[1] His predecessor, Robert Wagner, was certain that city housing programs were "inducing more and more middle-class people to move back from the suburbs into the city."[2] Wagner also sought to make New York the "first city without slums."[3] The fact that neither Lindsay's economic development program nor Wagner's housing efforts had much overall impact on development trends did not dis-

---

1. Quoted in Clayton Knowles, "Mayor Defends City's Economy, Calls Criticism 'Old and Tired,' " New York Times, July 20, 1966.

2. Quoted in Steven V. Roberts, "Slums Here Held Federal Problem," New York Times, May 6, 1966.

3. Quoted in Barbara Carter, "Biggest Slumlord on the Block," Reporter 26 (January 4, 1962), p. 28.

courage Lindsay's successors, Abraham Beame and Edward Koch, from pledging to achieve similar goals, albeit with a new set of bottles for the city's old wine.[4]

In pursuing these ambitious development goals, the older cities are severely handicapped by their limited ability to concentrate resources. Nowhere are the obstacles to concentrating resources better illustrated than in the region's major cities. As a result, several components of the "concentrating" variable are highlighted in this chapter. In particular, we examine the implications for city influence on development of:

1. the shortage of land available for development in the older cities;
2. endemic conflict within diverse populations over development goals and priorities;
3. inadequate financial resources and growing fiscal crisis;
4. the cities' heavy dependence on the states for authority and resources to undertake substantial development programs; and
5. the lack of effective integration of government agencies having responsibilities for urban development.

Before considering these factors in detail, we explore the political implications of the ambitious development goals of the older cities, and examine the role of areal and functional scope in shaping the politics of development in these jurisdictions. The analysis in this chapter draws primarily on New York City illustrations. The next chapter, which examines the efforts of the older cities to concentrate resources by creating autonomous agencies to undertake urban renewal, focuses mainly on the changing role of the Newark Housing Authority.

## Goals and Resources in the Older Cities

The nature of the older cities' goals complicates the problem of concentrating resources effectively. In contrast with the development objectives of most suburbs, city goals often require substantial intervention. Suburbs rely heavily on regulating the private marketplace to achieve their main objectives—through zoning, building codes, and other local policies restricting the activities of private developers. Moreover, the overriding goal of many suburbs is negative: the exclusion of unwanted development. Cities, on the other hand, primarily pursue positive objectives. Their basic goal is the attraction of needed development, which requires more active and extensive governmental involvement than is typically the case in suburbia.

4. See, for example, Beame's "new" economic development program unveiled at the end of 1976 in *Economic Recovery: New York City's Program for 1977–1981,* NYC DCP 76-30 (New York: December 1976), and Michael Sterne, "A Plan to Revitalize New York's Economy Is Offered by Beame," *New York Times,* December 21, 1976. To be sure, all public officials in the older cities do not share this activist perspective. One recent exception is Roger Starr, Housing and Development Administrator in the Beame administration, who has argued that New York must adjust to economic and social trends and accept a diminished role in the region and nation; see Roger Starr, "Making New York Smaller," *New York Times Magazine,* November 14, 1976, pp. 32–34, 99–106. Starr, however, was neither an elected official, nor a candidate at the time he expressed these views; instead he was a professor at New York University.

*Abandoned housing in the Ocean Hill-Brownsville section of Brooklyn, a stark symbol of the spreading decay of vast areas of the region's core.*                          Credit: Michael N. Danielson

To be sure, cities rely heavily on zoning and other regulatory devices when market forces push in the same direction as city policy, most notably in the case of office buildings and luxury housing in Manhattan. With respect to office construction in the Manhattan business district, Mayor Lindsay defined his city's task as "provid[ing] office space for the corporate headquarters that already are here and want to expand and for the new companies that are interested in moving in."[5] To provide space for new office buildings, New York has been willing to adopt a limited, facilitating role, adjusting its zoning code to meet the requirements of United States Steel, New York Telephone, and other major corporations. And when zoning has been insufficient to facilitate office development, New York City has responded with other actions. In lower Manhattan, for example, the city has moved a park and closed a number of streets to provide "superblock" sites for massive new office buildings.

But most city housing programs and economic development efforts require a far more active role for government. Without substantial public involvement, private builders are unwilling to undertake low- or middle-income housing, or even luxury housing in Manhattan. By 1980, practically no apartment construction in New York City was possible without public assistance of some kind.[6] Thus, to spur the construction of housing for most of their residents, older cities must provide tax abatement, mortgage assistance, and other kinds of subsidies. In the case of industry, older cities are trying to alter rather than facilitate market forces. Zoning by itself is too passive an instrument to attract industry to the older cities. As a result, cities have developed an assortment of other policies aimed at attracting industrial development. Low-interest loans have been advanced for plant expansion and the development of new industries. City-owned land has been made available to industrial firms at bargain rates. An even more activist approach has been public acquisition and development of industrial sites, such as the Flatlands Urban Industrial Park in Brooklyn, which New York City hoped would lead to the creation of 7,000 jobs.

As development goals require more public intervention, the problems of concentrating resources intensify for older cities. Activist policies multiply the number of local agencies involved, and in the process complicate the tasks of those who seek to integrate planning, policy-making, and implementation. New programs frequently involve securing authorization from the state, and usually rely heavily on federal or state funds, all of which increases the number of involved parties and complicates the process. Intervention also typically places new demands on the city's scarce financial and land resources, and this in turn increases conflict over the city's development goals, priorities, and means of implementation.

Ability to concentrate resources also is reduced by the variety of development objectives pursued by most older cities. Multiple goals compete for scarce resources, as well as further increasing the number of participants and relationships in the development process. Nor are different goals always com-

5. Seth S. King, "Mayor Discounts Loss of Industry," *New York Times*, February 19, 1967.

6. For a useful review of the extent of governmental involvement in housing in New York City, see Michael Goodwin, "As Housing Problems Increase, Experts See Little Hope for Future," *New York Times*, January 23, 1980.

patible. For example, there is no easy way to reconcile the "crucial challenges" posed in New York City's master plan of retaining the middle class while upgrading the position of the poor.[7] If upgrading the poor involves dispersing public housing into more attractive neighborhoods, as advocated by the Lindsay administration, middle-class resistance is certain to be substantial, with residents of the affected area loudly threatening to depart for the suburbs unless City Hall spares their communities from an "invasion" of ghetto dwellers. Moreover, housing programs aimed at either the middle class or the poor are bound to compete for funds and land. And housing of any kind will contend with other development objectives for these scarce resources. Consider the impact on industrial development of the urban renewal program in New York City, whose primary objective was increasing housing opportunities for affluent families. Between 1960 and 1963 alone, urban renewal claimed land containing almost six million square feet of loft and factory space.[8]

Broad policy objectives—such as retaining the middle class—may also embody difficult internal contradictions. Most of the middle-income housing built under New York's Mitchell-Lama program has been located in the outer reaches of the city, where land is relatively inexpensive and relocation problems minimal.[9] Peripheral locations were also attractive to middle-class families who wanted to separate themselves from lower-income and minority areas. Construction of large middle-income projects along the city's outskirts, however, compromised another development objective—the creation of stable, integrated neighborhoods in the older middle-class sections. The location of the massive Co-op City project in the northeast corner of the Bronx, for example, attracted large numbers of residents from the borough's Grand Concourse area who, in the words of the project's developer, were "running from changing neighborhoods."[10]

Conflicts over these middle-class objectives precipitated a "bloody fight" among city housing officials over a Mitchell-Lama project in Brooklyn. Some officials feared that such a large development on the fringe of Brooklyn "would attract many white families from central Brooklyn who felt threatened by the gradual entrance of Negro families into their present neighborhoods," and whose departure would "leave these neighborhoods highly unstable and ripe for real estate speculators."[11] Faced with this dilemma, City Hall opted for new housing—represented by the Twin Pines Village project—over older neighborhoods, on the grounds that the older "white areas are going to change

---

7. See *Plan for New York City*, Vol. I (Cambridge, Mass.: MIT Press, 1979), p. 5.

8. See Barry Gottehrer, *New York City in Crisis* (New York: Pocket Books, 1965), p. 92.

9. The Mitchell-Lama program was established in 1955 by New York State's Limited Profits Housing Act. Under the program, housing developers who agreed to limit their profits (to 6 percent of equity originally, later to 7.5 percent) were eligible for long-term low-interest loans from the city or state government, and for local real-estate tax abatement. Mitchell-Lama underwrote the construction of 120,000 apartments in New York City through 1979, with 60,000 financed by the city and the rest by the state.

10. Harold Ostroff, executive vice president, United Housing Foundation, as quoted in Steven V. Roberts, "Co-op City Blend of Races Sought," *New York Times*, April 30, 1967. Co-op City with 15,500 units was the largest Mitchell-Lama development and one of the largest housing projects in the United States.

11. Steven V. Roberts, "Project for 6,000 Families Approved for Canarsie Site," *New York Times*, June 28, 1967.

*Ground is broken for Co-op City in the Bronx, the largest of the hous-*
*ing projects built under the Mitchell-Lama program. Among the promi-*
*nent shovelers were Robert Moses (in the hat, second from the left),*
*and Governor Nelson Rockefeller (under "Governor" in the sign).*

Credit: Triborough Bridge and Tunnel Authority

anyway. . . . [I]f we are going to keep middle-class families of all races in the
city, we have to provide them with adequate housing choices. Co-op City and
Twin Pines Village do that."[12] Within a few years, however, rapidly escalating
construction costs and insistent pressures from established middle-class areas
led to a deemphasis of new housing, and higher priorities for stabilizing and
improving existing neighborhoods.

Goal conflicts in the older cities reflect the complexity of their problems, as well as the lack of proven answers to these problems and an inability
to foresee all of the major implications of various policies. Conflicting priorities and incompatible development objectives also result from the responses
of political leaders to diverse constituency, agency, and intergovernmental
pressures. In almost every policy area, this responsiveness has led to the
proliferation of objectives, which makes it extremely difficult to concentrate
resources effectively. In public housing, for example, New York has set itself
the impossible task of housing as many as possible of those least able to afford
satisfactory shelter in the private market, providing public housing tenants
with a decent neighborhood environment, and promoting racial and economic
integration—while in the process maintaining sufficient political support to
fund the program and secure project sites.

12. Jason R. Nathan, housing and development administrator, New York City, quoted in
Roberts, "Project for 6,000 Families."

## Areal and Functional Scope

When measured against the size of the entire New York region, none of its older cities has extensive areal scope. New York City covers much more territory than the others, with an area of 300 square miles compared to 24 for Newark and only 15 for Jersey City. But even New York encompasses only 2.4 percent of the 12,700 square miles in the 31-county region. Thus, development efforts in the older cities involve relatively small areas. Moreover, most of their land is already intensively settled, leaving comparatively little for new industry or housing. In the case of open land, New York City's position is more favorable, for it has more undeveloped land than in all the region's other cities. The availability of large tracts in Queens and Staten Island for housing development in recent years permitted New York to retain a much larger share of middle-class families than was the case in Newark and Jersey City, neither of which had much land usable for low-density residential development.

### Table 17–*Population and Land Area of Major Cities in the New York Region, 1980*

| City | Population | Square Miles |
| --- | --- | --- |
| New York | 7,071,000 | 299.6 |
| Newark | 329,000 | 23.6 |
| Jersey City | 224,000 | 15.1 |
| Yonkers | 195,000 | 17.7 |
| New Haven | 126,000 | 18.4 |
| Elizabeth | 106,000 | 11.7 |

Within the limited areal scope of the older cities are relatively large and diverse populations. Compared to suburbs, cities are both more intensively settled and considerably more heterogeneous. New York City's population density in 1980 was 23,601 people per square mile, compared with 1,504 per square mile for the region as a whole, and 4,603 in the inner ring where suburban settlement is most intensive. The presence of large, diverse, and densely settled populations within heavily developed and geographically contained jurisdictions inevitably intensifies conflict over almost all development issues in the older cities, which contrasts sharply with the situation in most suburbs, where small size and relatively homogeneous populations produce low levels of conflict on development questions.

Limited areal scope has external as well as internal political consequences. As in the suburbs, limited areal scope prevents the older cities from controlling or influencing significantly many activities in the region that affect their interests. But the consequences of the limited governmental influence are more important for the cities than the suburbs because "favorable" development tends to move from the core to suburbia for a host of reasons beyond the control of local government. Unlike suburbs, which generally want nothing to do with the older cities, the cities would like to influence suburban policies, particularly in order to curtail suburban actions that encourage the outward

## Table 18–*Population Density in the New York Region, 1980*

| Cities | Population (per sq. mile) |
| --- | --- |
| New York City | 23,601 |
| Manhattan | 64,888 |
| Brooklyn | 32,192 |
| Bronx | 27,837 |
| Queens | 17,416 |
| Staten Island | 6,103 |
| Jersey City | 14,834 |
| Newark | 13,941 |
| Yonkers | 11,017 |
| Elizabeth | 9,060 |
| New Haven | 6,848 |
| *Region* | |
| 31-County | 1,504 |
| Inner Ring | 4,603 |
| Intermediate Ring | 1,311 |
| Outer Ring | 245 |

movement of jobs and middle-class residents. The ability of city officials to exercise influence is severely limited, however, both by the region's political geography and by growing suburban influence in the state capitals and in Washington. When the cities and suburbs have common interests—as in aspects of the mass transit issue described in Chapter Seven—they can affect broader regional trends. But when their interests conflict, both must take the uncertain route of seeking help in the state capitals and in Washington.[13]

With respect to functional scope, city governments typically engage in a much wider range of activities that affect development than most suburban jurisdictions. In housing, for example, older cities usually are involved in public housing, rent control, housing rehabilitation, middle-income housing, neighborhood conservation, and urban renewal, in addition to the land-use and building regulation that preoccupy suburban governments. Among the region's major cities, New York has taken on the widest range of responsibilities, encompassing almost every conceivable governmental function with an influence on urban development.

Broad functional scope tends to reduce the ability of the older cities to concentrate resources. With more functions come more specialized public agencies and greater problems of coordination for the mayor and other central policymakers. The wide range of city responsibilities also increases dependence on other levels of government and on public authorities, thus diminishing the cities' freedom of action. State approval has been required for much of the expansion of city functions, and detailed state involvement is common in middle-income housing, rent control, and other policy areas. City programs for economic development, public housing, and mass transit depend heavily

13. The impact of these efforts on state and federal policy is discussed in Chapter Ten.

on state or federal funds. Moreover, a number of city responsibilities are shared with independent agencies. New York City's government must coexist with the Metropolitan Transportation Authority, the Urban Development Corporation, and the Port Authority in various policy areas that affect development. In other cities, control over major functions is diluted by the existence of urban renewal agencies, community development corporations, and parking authorities. All of these problems are less severe for suburban governments and for specialized public agencies whose functional scope is narrower than that of the older cities.

## The Shortage of Land

Intensive settlement, as indicated above, has left the region's older cities with relatively little land that is easily available for development. Few large tracts of vacant land remain in the cities, except in the more isolated parts of Staten Island and in Newark's meadowlands. Most of the remaining undeveloped land is in small parcels that are difficult to use for large-scale development. Moreover, vacant land in the older cities has usually been bypassed for good reasons—often because of difficult terrain, which requires substantial grading, large amounts of fill, or expensive pilings. Undeveloped areas often lack sewers, streets, access to public transportation, and other improvements. As a result, much of the open land in the older cities is costly to build on, or inaccessible, or both.

The lack of usable vacant land has a number of important consequences for the politics of development in the older cities. It reduces the usefulness of zoning as a means of influencing development, since zoning tends to have its greatest impact when land is initially used. Moreover, the absence of easily developed land combines with intensive settlement patterns to drive up prices, which increases the costs of acquiring land in the older cities for public housing, industrial parks, highways, and every other public project. In addition, most city development programs involve land that is already being used, usually complicating government's role even more. In urban renewal, for example, city officials have to select areas for redevelopment, secure a private developer interested in using the site, acquire the land, relocate those using the property, resell land to the developer, and improve public facilities serving the area, all within the framework of detailed federal regulations.

Intensive development also increases the number of people affected and the degree of conflict, particularly for programs of urban renewal, highways, industrial development, and other activities that require large amounts of land. In the case of urban renewal, more people are disadvantaged by the clearance of densely populated slums than will benefit from the new dwelling units. The fact that very few residents of renewal areas can afford to live in the new buildings further exacerbates discord. Large-scale private development efforts in the older cities cause similar problems. For example, the expansion plans of Columbia University and other major institutions in the Morningside Heights section of Manhattan have been steadfastly opposed by local residents. From Columbia's perspective, "the problem was a physical one. It simply isn't possible for institutions to grow the way the institutions feel we must grow and for the residents to remain here in the same number and location they are in now. Something has to give and a considerable number of people will have to move."[14] On Morningside Heights as elsewhere in the older cities, however, local residents refused to give in without fighting for their densely settled turf, and in the process successfully enlisted to their cause political leaders who were able to limit Columbia's expansion.[15]

Conflict over scarce land means that most major development activities in the older cities are plagued by long delays. An example is New York City's experience with the Flatlands Urban Industrial Park, the city's initial venture into industrial land development. First, local residents bitterly protested Mayor Wagner's plan to condemn the 96-acre site, and work on the project was delayed while the homeowners carried an unsuccessful legal action all the way to the U.S. Supreme Court. Then a struggle developed between the city and black groups that wanted the site developed as an educational park complex to foster integration. After years of controversy, instead of being covered by two million square feet of factories as envisaged by City Hall, Flatlands was "a glacier of mouldy mattresses, unsprung sofas, and a strange gamut of debris," populated by "rats . . . as big as cats."[16] When construction finally began in the middle of 1966, Mayor Lindsay was reminded of the intensity of competition for land in the city as he was met at Flatlands by 1,000 black and Puerto Rican demonstrators from Brooklyn's ghettos, who chanted "Industrial Park, No; Educational Park, Yes."[17]

Lindsay sought to mollify the Flatlands demonstrators by insisting that "we can do a lot of things at once. We can do this and still build more and better schools."[18] In fact, however, the scarcity of land in the older cities guarantees that industrial land acquisition will produce conflict. Implementation of Newark's $11 million industrial renewal project in the black Central Ward was delayed for years by the litigation of property owners and the protests of affected residents and their allies, who valued new housing more highly than job development in the renewal area. In New York City's 38-acre Washington Street Market urban renewal area, conflict arose between public agencies pursuing different development objectives. In line with the original plans to develop the Washington Street site for commercial and industrial use, the Public Development Corporation urged the construction of a center for the city's printing industry, which would help to keep the industry's 165,000 jobs in the city. The Housing and Development Administration, on

14. Lawrence H. Chamberlain, vice-president, Columbia University, quoted in Steven V. Roberts, "Columbia's Expansion to Uproot Area Residents," *New York Times*, November 2, 1966.

15. The major victory of local interests over Columbia involved a proposed gymnasium on a two-acre site in a city park that separates Columbia from Harlem. Announced in 1961 and initially supported by most city political leaders, the gymnasium was opposed by a broad coalition of neighborhood and minority interests, leading to second thoughts on the part of city officials, and the plan's ultimate withdrawal in 1969.

16. Homer Bigart, "Industrial Park Spelled D-U-M-P," *New York Times*, March 30, 1966. Delays also were caused by difficulties in finding a suitable developer and differences over the project between the Wagner and Lindsay administrations.

17. See Douglas Robinson, "Mayor Walks Alone into Angry Crowd and Draws Cheers," *New York Times*, July 20, 1966. Flatlands finally was opened in early 1969; for a useful review of these developments, see Joseph P. Fried, "Park Opens for Industry in Brooklyn," *New York Times*, January 12, 1969.

18. Quoted in Robinson, "Mayor Walks Alone."

**The route of the Lower Manhattan Expressway as proposed by Robert Moses.**                    Credit: Triborough Bridge and Tunnel Authority

the other hand, argued for comprehensive development in the area, including public housing and educational facilities. As with other development projects, conflict caused delays, compounded in this instance because federal and state approvals were required for a change in land use for an urban renewal site.

Nowhere is the impact of scarce land on the politics of development in the older cities more striking than in the case of road building. Highway construction in densely settled sections of the core adversely affects far more people than in the suburbs. A single mile of Robert Moses's Cross-Bronx Expressway demolished 1,530 dwelling units in the East Tremont section of the Bronx.[19] The Lower Manhattan Expressway, another major highway designed by Robert Moses in his capacity as New York's City Construction Coordinator, would if built have displaced 2,000 families and 800 businesses with 10,000 employees along a 2.5-mile corridor between the Holland Tunnel and the Brooklyn Bridge.

As the implications of urban expressways for local neighborhoods were grasped by city dwellers, highway plans met increasingly fierce opposition in the region's core. A lengthening list of projects were shelved in the late 1960s

---

19. For an excellent discussion of the routing of the Cross-Bronx Expressway through East Tremont, see Robert A. Caro, *The Power Broker: Robert Moses and the Fall of New York* (New York: Knopf, 1974), Chapters 37–38.

and 1970s in the face of intense resistance from local interests and responsive public officials. Successful opposition to the new roads developed sooner in densely settled sections of the cities than in the suburbs, and depended less on the environmental factors discussed in Chapter Four, although antihighway groups in the older cities were quick to capitalize on environmental considerations when ecological concerns moved to the forefront of the debate over road-building in the early 1970s.

The first major casualty among inner-city highways was the Lower Manhattan Expressway. Despite impressive support from downtown business interests, and substantial political backing from City Hall prior to the election of John Lindsay in 1965, the Lower Manhattan Expressway could not survive prolonged and well-organized opposition from residents of the area. First the opponents prevented the construction of the highway for over a decade, then they forced the city to redesign the road as a partially depressed expressway, and finally they persuaded Mayor Lindsay to abandon the project in 1969. The years of controversy and uncertainty also delayed implementation of urban renewal, middle-income and public housing, and other public and private projects in areas adjacent to the stillborn expressway.

In Newark, the Midtown Connector aroused the same kinds of passions as the Lower Manhattan Expressway, with the added element of racial conflict intensifying feelings in the racially divided city. Designed to connect two highways that flanked the city—Interstate 78 and Interstate 280—the 2.5 miles of road were to cut through Newark's black Central Ward, in the process eliminating almost 3,000 residential units housing 10,000 low-income blacks. Initially, the expressway was strongly supported by the city's business and political leaders, who saw the road as a means of relieving congestion, fostering economic growth, and eliminating slums. In promoting the project, Mayor Hugh J. Addonizio emphasized "the benefits Newark will derive from this undertaking," as well as "the necessity" of the road "as part of a large regional transportation network."[20] Opposition began in the affected black neighborhoods, with community, antipoverty, and church groups in the forefront. Other black interests joined in the struggle, including militant organizations like the Black Panthers. By 1970, protests against the road had escalated to the point where city leaders feared a replay of Newark's 1967 revolt, which had been triggered by black anger over the proposed clearance of a large site in the Central Ward for the construction of a state medical school.[21] Facing the prospect of another devastating conflict, city officials reluctantly capitulated to community pressure. As one explained, we "want the road, but we don't want the issue . . . [W]e're not anti-highway, but we are anti-confrontation."[22]

Among other major road projects killed by the intensity of opposition in the land-scarce older cities were the Mid-Manhattan Expressway, the Bush-

20. Quoted in Moray Epstein, "Rt. 75 Line Gets Airing," *Newark News*, February 28, 1964.

21. The medical school proposal, community opposition, and the black revolt are discussed in Chapter Nine.

22. See Douglas Eldridge, "Confidential Report Ready on Rt. 75 Plan," *Newark News*, February 15, 1970.

*Trucks inch their way across Canal Street in the transportation corridor that would have been served by the Lower Manhattan Expressway. Most of the buildings in the photo would have been demolished to make way for the highway.*

Credit: Louis B. Schlivek, Regional Plan Association

wick Expressway in Brooklyn, and the Cross-Brooklyn Expressway.[23] The Cross-Brooklyn road, which was to link the Narrows Bridge with the Nassau Expressway near Kennedy Airport, was the heart of an ambitious "linear city" scheme designed by the Lindsay administration, involving a six-mile strip of new housing, schools and other public facilities, and with commercial and industrial development to be built over the road. The attempt to market the expressway as part of a comprehensive plan intensified rather than reduced opposition, however, since even more land would be taken for the entire plan than for the road alone. Responding to widespread local opposition, legislators from Brooklyn killed the project in Albany. "The people in Brooklyn are up in arms," explained one of the borough's most influential political leaders, because "the Mayor wants to run an expressway through the heart of the residential area of Brooklyn."[24]

23. The Mid-Manhattan Expressway, joining the Lincoln Tunnel and the Queens-Midtown Tunnel, was part of Moses's plan for several elevated highways across Manhattan. The Bushwick Expressway was another Moses project, and was designed to link the Williamsburg Bridge with the Nassau Expressway. Responding to local opposition to the Bushwick road, the Lindsay administration replaced it with the equally unpopular Cross-Brooklyn Expressway.

24. Assemblyman Stanley Steingut, quoted in Maurice Carroll, "Plans for Brooklyn Road

# LANDFILL: MANHATTAN
# AND ADJACENT AREAS

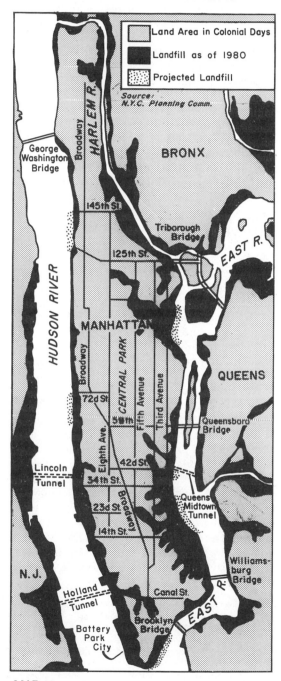

Land Area in Colonial Days

Landfill as of 1980

Projected Landfill

Source:
N.Y.C. Planning Comm.

HARLEM R.

Broadway

BRONX

George
Washington
Bridge

145th St.

Triborough
Bridge

EAST R.

125th St.

HUDSON RIVER

MANHATTAN

CENTRAL PARK

Broadway

Fifth Avenue

Third Avenue

QUEENS

72d St.

59th

Queensboro
Bridge

Eighth Ave.

42d St.

Lincoln
Tunnel

34th St.

23d St.

Broadway

Queens
Midtown
Tunnel

14th St.

N.J.

Williams-
burg
Bridge

Holland
Tunnel

Canal St.

EAST R.

Battery
Park
City

Brooklyn
Bridge

**MAP 10**

One way around some of the problems resulting from the shortage of turf in the older cities is the creation of new land. Over the decades, new land has been formed on both sides of the Hudson by fill and other means, as indicated by Map 10. About 3,650 acres have been added to Manhattan since the city's founding, and land reclaimed from the surrounding waters now accounts for about 25 percent of the island's area. Extensive reclamation has been necessary in the development of marine terminal areas in Newark and Elizabeth. With the growing scarcity of land, its high cost, the problems of relocating residents and businesses, and the intensity of pressures that confront efforts to change existing land uses, the creation of new land has become increasingly attractive to leaders in the older cities. "We're adding more land by means of platform development to lower Manhattan," explained Mayor Lindsay in connection with his ambitious plans for the eastern tip of Manhattan, "because we're not satisfied with the size of the island we bought."[25]

Creating new land, however, does not eliminate conflict. The very scarcity of land in the older cities almost always leads to disagreements over the use of newly formed acreage, as illustrated by the competing plans of New York City and New York State for 91 acres along the Hudson River created in the construction of the Port Authority's World Trade Center. City Hall saw the parcel as an integral part of its comprehensive and imaginative $2 billion plan for lower Manhattan. The state government wanted to develop the site as a $600 million free-standing project called Battery Park City, containing housing, office, commercial, and industrial development. Only after two years of disputes and hard bargaining did a compromise emerge, which retained the state's Battery Park concept, but reframed the project to comply with the city's general plan for lower Manhattan.

Particularly contentious has been the question of what kind of housing should be built on new land. In the case of Battery Park City, the state advocated a mix of housing to serve a broad range of income groups, while New York City favored heavy emphasis on luxury units, because of the high cost of reclaimed land and its desire to complement downtown office development with walk-to-work housing for executives. In the negotiations over the Battery Park project, the city's views on housing prevailed. Less than 7 percent of the project's units were to be for low-income families, and even this commitment disturbed Mayor Lindsay, who saw it as "equivalent to putting low-income housing in the middle of the East Side of Manhattan."[26] Lindsay's position was strongly criticized by black leaders and spokesmen for low-income groups, who assailed the city for using public money to house the rich in "the Riviera of the Hudson" while housing conditions for

Halted by Mayor's Order," *New York Times*, March 4, 1969. Steingut was the leader of the Democratic Party in Brooklyn, and minority leader of the New York State Assembly at the time; his successful effort to block Lindsay's scheme was supported by every member of the state legislature from the borough.

25. Quoted in David K. Shipler, "Massive Complex Planned for Platform in East River," *New York Times*, April 13, 1972.

26. Quoted in David K. Shipler, "Battery Park Plan Is Shown," *New York Times*, April 17, 1969. Because of the high costs of landfill a unit of low-income housing in Battery Park City was about 2.5 times as expensive as the average unit constructed elsewhere in the city.

*New land created from the excavation of the World Trade Center will be the site of the Battery Park City development.*
Credit: Port Authority of New York and New Jersey

the poor deteriorated.[27] A similar dispute arose over the housing mix in the city's Waterside development, involving 1,450 apartments constructed on a six-acre platform over the East River. The controversy combined with financial problems to delay the project for years, before critics were mollified by an increase in the proportion of low- and middle-income apartments.

## Conflicting Constituency Interests

As the conflicts over use of newly created land illustrate, the ability of older cities to concentrate resources on development objectives is severely limited by the diversity of their populations. Every major program must run the gauntlet of conflicting interests growing out of class, racial, ethnic, and sectional differences. Rare indeed is the development issue on which the demands of diverse groups are easily reconciled. Efforts to overcome the disadvantages of ghetto dwellers by integrating schools and neighborhoods hasten the exodus of white as well as black middle-class families. Blacks

27. Percy E. Sutton, borough president of Manhattan, quoted in Shipler, "Battery Park Plan Is Shown." Sutton was the only black member of the New York City Board of Estimate during the development of the Battery Park project. Eventually, as costs for the project rose, all the low-income housing was dropped from Battery Park City.

disagree over whether priority in housing and educational programs should be given to quality or integration. A subsidized transit fare keeps lower-middle-income families in New York City, but also increases general tax burdens, thereby weakening the city's ability to compete for jobs. Affluent whites seek more housing benefits, while poor blacks and Hispanics argue that public efforts should focus on those most in need of improved shelter. Zoning and transportation policies that foster concentration favor the business district's white-collar industries but work against the interests of manufacturers, for whom the costs of congestion offer few offsetting benefits.

In the older cities, socioeconomic differences are bolstered by the spatial separation of populations along income, racial, and ethnic lines. As a result, socioeconomic and territorial interests tend to reinforce each other, as groups and neighborhoods seek to advance their interests on development issues. Spatial differentiation is more important in the cities, because these political units are larger and more diverse than the typical suburb. As indicated in Chapter Three, most suburban jurisdictions are small and encompass relatively homogeneous populations. Thus, while spatial differentiation is important *among* suburbs, it is not a major political factor *within* the vast majority of suburban municipalities. In the cities, on the other hand, the spatial separation of socioeconomic groups plays a key role in the politics of development. Local politics is far more territorial in the older cities than in most suburbs, with city councils, party organizations, and many groups based on territorial subdivisions. Political units are particularly important in New York City, whose size, diversity, and history have resulted in its division into 5 boroughs (each with its own president and party leaders), 33 city council districts, 18 congressional districts, 91 state legislative constituencies, and nearly 60 community planning units. Of the 160 local, state, and federal officials elected from constituencies in New York City, all but three represent subsections of the city.[28] As a result, a wide variety of the city's diverse social, economic, and community interests are directly represented in the various political systems that make decisions about development.

Groups also tend to play a more important role in the politics of development in the older cities than in the suburbs. Cities encompass both wider ranges of interests and larger critical masses of individuals with shared concerns than most suburbs. Group interests that can barely fill a living room in a suburb may spawn a dozen organizations in Newark or New Haven, and generate scores of social, religious, civil rights, and community organizations in New York City. The diversity of the older cities also stimulates organization for collective action, since there is much less consensus on development issues than in more homogeneous communities. As a consequence, almost any development proposal is supported and attacked by a variety of group interests—some with broad concerns, others with a very narrow focus; some with considerable experience and resources, others organized hurriedly to block a specific unwanted project. The essential process of group formation, internal organization, and political involvement is no different in the cities

28. New York's mayor, president of the city council, and comptroller are elected citywide. The five borough presidents and two members of the city council from each borough are elected from these five large subdivisions. All other constituencies are sub-borough, with the exception of one congressional district that encompasses all of Staten Island plus lower Manhattan.

than in the suburbs, but in the older cities the range and intensity of group action on most development issues are substantially greater. Moreover, the scale of the older cities—particularly of New York—means that conflicts tend to attract other groups beyond the immediately affected area, who share interests with those directly involved. As a result, the scale of most conflicts is broadened, further compounding the problems faced by those seeking to concentrate resources on development objectives.

The communications media also play an important role in widening group involvement in the politics of development in the older cities, and especially in New York City, which, as pointed out in Chapter Five, is the primary focus of the region's largest newspapers and major television outlets. In recent years, newspapers and television have devoted increasing attention to local perspectives in highway disputes, housing controversies, and other development issues. In part because of the growing assertiveness of local groups, the press no longer covers most "improvements" from the perspective of the proposing agency, as was usually the case during the heyday of Robert Moses and the Port Authority. And particularly for television, protest activities provide inherently more interesting coverage than the unveiling of a plan. In response to growing media attention, many groups have developed considerable skill in securing coverage of their activities by reporters. The net result is more attention by the newspapers and television news programs to urban development conflicts, which tends to attract still more groups into disputes over housing projects, industrial parks, new roads, and other programs.

Group activity also is stimulated in the older cities by the high level of adversary relations in their political systems. Rival parties and factions are always ready to criticize almost any policy choice by those in power. Complex and fragmented governmental systems ensure conflict among key officials, such as New York's mayor and comptroller. Reinforcing these adversary relationships, of course, are the diverse interests of the city's heterogeneous population. As a result, unified political support rarely is achieved in the older cities for a major project or development program. Opposing groups usually can find a champion among the citywide political leadership, as well as from the elected officials who represent the particular constituency.[29]

To emphasize the role of groups is not to imply that most organizations in the older cities achieve their objectives. Nor does the wide scope of group activity mean that *all* interests are organized, or that some are not far more influential than others. On one end of the scale are powerful interests, such as the major real estate developers, banks, insurance companies, and contractors, with large stakes in a substantial range of development issues. Few groups in the city can match the financial clout or political access possessed by David Rockefeller of the Chase Manhattan Bank and his colleagues on the Downtown Lower Manhattan Association. Clearly such interests wield considerable influence on many questions, and they have been particularly effective when allied with powerful public agencies such as the Port Authority. But these influential interests do not always prevail in development contests. The strong backing of downtown and other business groups was insufficient to

---

29. See particularly Wallace S. Sayre and Herbert Kaufman, *Governing New York City* (New York: Russell Sage Foundation, 1960), Chapter 19 and *passim*.

ensure the construction of the Lower Manhattan Expressway or the location of the World Trade Center along the East River.[30]

Moreover, these influential groups often disagree among themselves on major projects. A good example of elite conflict is provided by the proposed New York City Convention Center, where the contestants have been likened to "a pair of pre-historic beasts" in the form of "two great coalitions of political, real estate, and banking power . . . locked in a tail-thrashing struggle over a new $200-million exhibition center on the banks of the Hudson River."[31] And as is usually the case, the main product of intense group conflict on the convention center was delay, with City Hall unwilling to make a decision between the rival sites that would alienate the powerful groups on the losing side. "No matter what decision he makes, he'll get criticized," explained one of Mayor Beame's aides in connection with the mayor's reluctance to break the seven-year stalemate on the project. "People will say he's choosing a particular site to please this or that political supporter."[32]

At the other end of the scale in terms of political effectiveness in the older cities have been the poor, particularly the minority poor. Large numbers of low-income city dwellers are politically inactive. Meager resources, lack of education, apathy, and alienation make the poor difficult to organize and frustrate sustained political activity.[33] Until the 1960s, those responsible for making development decisions in the older cities were able to shortchange poor blacks and other low-income groups with considerable impunity. Much of the "success" of the urban renewal program in Newark and other cities, discussed in the next chapter, resulted from the inability of slumdwellers to organize effectively to defend their interests. Increasingly in recent years, however, blacks, Hispanics, Italian-Americans, and other low-income residents of the older cities have mobilized the political influence latent in a concentration of people with shared problems. And by flexing their political muscle, the poor have made planning and policymaking more responsive to their needs, while complicating even further the task of concentrating resources in the older cities.[34]

The bitter conflicts surrounding New York City's efforts to scatter low-income housing projects into middle-class neighborhoods illustrate the inter-

30. The initial plan called for the World Trade Center to face east, toward Brooklyn, Long Island, and Europe. After extensive negotiations with New Jersey officials—whose agreement was required since the Port Authority would build the project—New York political and business leaders finally agreed that, while the gigantic structure could not cross the Hudson River to the wilds of Hudson County, it might traverse Manhattan and face west, toward Jersey City, Newark, and Trenton.

31. Nicholas Pileggi, "How Things Get Done in New York: A Case History," *New York* (February 28, 1974), p. 58. Pileggi provides a fascinating look at the interrelationships and conflicts among the major private development interests in New York City and their political allies.

32. See Steven R. Weisman, "Beame Puts Off Selection of Convention Center Site Until After Vote," *New York Times*, July 3, 1977. Beame's successor, Edward Koch, finally settled on West 34th Street rather than West 44th Street for the project, whose estimated cost at the time in April 1978 had reached $257 million; see Charles Kaiser, "Convention Site at West 34th Street Chosen by Koch," *New York Times*, April 29, 1978.

33. See Michael Lipsky, *Protest in City Politics: Rent Strikes, Housing and the Power of the Poor* (Chicago: Rand McNally, 1970), particularly Chapters 6–7.

34. See Chapter Nine; cf Clarence N. Stone, *Economic Growth and Neighborhood Discontent: System Bias in the Urban Renewal Program of Atlanta* (Chapel Hill, N.C.: University of North Carolina Press, 1976).

play of these factors. Prior to the mid-1960s, public housing in New York, as in most cities, was confined to slum locations by a combination of federal policies, cost limitations, and political considerations. By locating projects in slums, political conflict over site selection was minimized, since ghetto dwellers needed the housing and other neighborhoods strongly opposed housing projects. The political key to keeping public housing confined to the slums was the role of the borough presidents, who were able to exercise an informal veto over projects in their boroughs. After a site had been selected by the New York City Housing Authority, it was submitted to the appropriate borough president for clearance. Since the borough presidents were highly sensitive to local opposition to public housing, the housing authority tended to steer clear of unacceptable sites in white and middle-class neighborhoods.[35]

Shortly after his election in 1965, Mayor John V. Lindsay attempted to reformulate public housing policy. Lindsay was determined to end "the traditional pattern of huge, sterile public housing projects, isolated physically and socially from community life."[36] In place of ghetto projects, Lindsay sought to foster racial and economic integration by moving public housing out of the slums into middle-class areas. For Lindsay and his aides, scatter-site housing was a "moral imperative" dictated by the city's growing racial bifurcation.[37] It was also a response to black interests that had given Lindsay overwhelming support in his race for mayor. Under the new policy, vacant and underutilized sites in outlying sections were to get priority, and borough presidents were to be denied their informal veto over housing projects. "The Borough Presidents have a legitimate knowledge and concern about their boroughs and we intend to consult them regularly," explained a mayoral aide, "but they can't override our final decisions. Public housing has citywide implications and we have to have an overall plan for its development."[38] Lindsay's plan was backed by the borough presidents of Manhattan and the Bronx, who were black and Puerto Rican respectively, and strongly opposed by the other three borough presidents.

35. The borough presidents exercised an informal veto because of their membership on the Board of Estimate, the more important of New York City's two legislative bodies. Each borough president has two votes on the Board of Estimate, while the mayor, comptroller, and president of the city council have four each. The borough presidents were able to maintain solidarity on most issues before the Board of Estimate through the practice of "borough courtesy," whereby each deferred to the wishes of a colleague whose constituency was directly involved in a matter before the board, in return for similar consideration when their own borough's interests were at stake. This bloc power gave the borough presidents substantial leverage on constituency issues such as site selection. For a general discussion of the political role of the borough presidents, see Wallace S. Sayre and Herbert Kaufman, *Governing New York City*, pp. 638–639. The role of the borough presidents in site selection for public housing is examined in Jewel Bellush, "Housing: The Scattered Site Controversy," in Jewel Bellush and Stephen M. David, eds., *Race and Politics in New York City* (New York: Praeger, 1971), pp. 104–106, 110–111. On a similar veto system over public housing sites in Chicago, see Martin Meyerson and Edward C. Banfield, *Politics, Planning and the Public Interest* (New York: Free Press, 1955).

36. Quoted in Peter Kihss, "Housing Policy of City Changed," *New York Times*, July 16, 1967.

37. Donald H. Elliott, counsel to the mayor and later chairman of the City Planning Commission, quoted in Walter Goodman, "The Battle of Forest Hills—Who's Ahead?" *New York Times Magazine*, February 20, 1972.

38. Donald H. Elliott, quoted in Steven V. Roberts, "City Hall Ends Veto by Borough Presidents over Housing Sites," *New York Times*, May 11, 1966.

As the first step in the new approach to locating public housing, thirteen projects were proposed in 1966 for white middle-class areas in Brooklyn, the Bronx, Queens, and Staten Island. Reaction from the affected communities was overwhelmingly negative, with local residents angrily equating public housing with slums, crime, drugs, blacks, and neighborhood deterioration. At meeting after meeting on the scattered site projects, the message of local groups and their political representatives was always the same. "Do not change the area," pleaded a state assemblyman from Queens: "Do not give us a project. We are happy and want to stay that way."[39] At one stormy session of the City Planning Commission, several hundred opponents to scattered-site housing carried placards reading "Destroy a Community and You Destroy a City," "Low-Income Housing Breeds Slums," and "Essential Services Yes, Public Housing No."[40] Never far in the background was the threat of departure as voiced by a Bronx state senator: "This project will promote nothing but the further flight of the middle class from the city."[41]

In the face of this intense opposition, little headway was made with the scatter-site program, as the dissident borough presidents and their allies on the Board of Estimate killed most of Lindsay's proposals. In 1972, six years after the new policy was inaugurated, only one of the thirteen projects had been completed—a project for the elderly, which in New York and elsewhere has been more acceptable politically than family housing with its heavy proportion of black and Hispanic tenants. Two other projects were under construction in white, middle-class areas. And one of these—located in the largely Jewish, middle-income area of Forest Hills in Queens—was the source of an extremely bitter and wide-ranging conflict that eventually sealed the doom of Lindsay's scatter-site program.

Public housing was being built in Forest Hills in 1972 only because local groups successfully kept the project out of nearby Corona. Earlier, a deal had been struck between City Hall and the Queens borough president which switched the project to Forest Hills. Because of this agreement, the Forest Hills Residents Association and other opponents were unable to kill the project in the Board of Estimate. Local interests also failed to block the project in court, although their legal actions delayed ground-breaking until 1971. Meanwhile, the city was enlarging the size of the project from four 14-story buildings to three 24-story apartment towers with 840 units, making Forest Hills more than twice as large as the typical scatter-site development planned by the Lindsay administration.[42] By the time construction finally began, local feelings had risen to a fever pitch, and more than 500 angry demonstrators marched on the site. With the crowd shouting "Keep the ghetto out of Forest

39. Assemblyman Sidney Lebowitz, quoted in Steven V. Roberts, "Public Housing in Middle-Class Areas Assailed," New York Times, June 2, 1966.

40. See Emanuel Perlmutter, "Queens Borough President Among 200 Opposing New Low-Rent Housing," New York Times, September 12, 1967.

41. State Senator Harrison J. Goldin, quoted in Steven V. Roberts, "Public Housing in Middle-Class Areas Assailed," New York Times, June 2, 1966. Goldin was elected city comptroller in 1973.

42. The change in plans resulted primarily from the higher foundation costs incurred because of adverse subsoil conditions at the Forest Hills site. By building higher and including more apartments, these costs would be spread over more apartments, thus helping to keep the average cost per unit within federal limits.

Hills," and carrying placards declaring "Lindsay Is Trying to Destroy Queens. Now Queens Will Destroy Lindsay," rocks and flaming torches were hurled at the construction trailers.[43]

In the wake of this fiery outburst, the conflagration at Forest Hills spread rapidly, ultimately attracting a wide range of groups and elected officials. One reason for the escalation was the pervasive fear of public housing in white neighborhoods throughout the city. Another was the personal identification of an increasingly unpopular Mayor Lindsay with scatter-site housing, which was seen as another indication of the indifference of Lindsay and other "limousine liberals" to the interests of middle- and working-class whites. Most of Lindsay's numerous political enemies eagerly rallied to the defense of Forest Hills. Widespread press coverage followed in the wake of the vehement demonstrations, spreading from the local press and newscasts to network news programs and national news magazines. The conflict mobilized a wide range of Jewish groups in opposition to the Lindsay program, including the Queens Jewish Community Council, the Long Island Commission of Rabbis, the New York Board of Rabbis, the Association of Jewish Antipoverty Workers, the National Council of Young Israel, and the Rabbinical Council of America. On the other side, black groups—such as the National Association for the Advancement of Colored People, the New York Urban League, and the Architects Renewal Committee for Harlem—defended scatter-site housing, as did the New York Urban Coalition, the Queens Council for Better Housing, and one major Jewish civil rights group, the Anti-Defamation League.

As the conflict widened and groups became increasingly polarized over the issue, Lindsay bowed to the mounting pressure and accepted the necessity for compromise. In naming a mediator to explore possible alternatives in Forest Hills, Lindsay conceded that "the climate is just too destructive for our city and the future of our housing programs and community stability, so that we must try yet another way to resolve this matter in fairness to all concerned."[44] Three months later Lindsay reluctantly accepted a compromise plan that cut the size of the Forest Hills project in half, which further delayed construction as the proposal was recycled through the maze of public agencies with responsibilities for public housing in New York.[45] And the high political costs of the intense group conflict over Forest Hills effectively killed Lindsay's scattered-site program, as well as dealing the mayor a devastating political blow that contributed significantly to his decision not to seek a third term in 1973.

As more and more constituency interests are represented in the development process, political leaders in the older cities find it increasingly difficult to carry out coordinated plans to meet housing and job development needs.[46]

43. See "Rage in Forest Hills," *Newsweek* 78 (November 29, 1971), p. 82; and "Fear in Forest Hills," *Time* 98 (November 29, 1971), p. 25.

44. Quoted in Murray Schumach, "Mayor, in Compromise Move, Names a Lawyer to Study Forest Hills Plan," *New York Times*, May 18, 1972. The mediator was Mario R. Cuomo, a Queens lawyer, who later served as New York's secretary of state under Governor Carey and ran unsuccessfully for mayor in 1977.

45. For a detailed account of the development of the Forest Hills compromise, see Mario R. Cuomo, *Forest Hills Diary: The Crisis of Low-Income Housing* (New York: Vintage Books, 1975).

46. For a discussion of the impact of fragmentation in older cities, see Douglas Yates, *The Ungovernable City: The Politics of Urban Problems and Policy Making* (Cambridge, Mass.: MIT Press, 1977).

Instead of comprehensive schemes devised by housing, planning, transportation, and industrial development agencies—singly, or preferably with collaboration across agencies—city governments typically wind up with patchwork programs aimed at satisfying the competing interests of diverse constituencies. A good example of the result of these kinds of pressures is New York's Washington Market urban renewal plan, which started off as renewal for the printing industry and wound up being "parceled out . . . in the best New York tradition [with] a community college, an industrial complex, middle-income housing with some subsidized low income units, luxury housing and office buildings—each marked off by the tidy boundaries of compromise."[47]

## The Fiscal Straitjacket

Money constitutes a major constraint on the ability of all the region's older cities to concentrate resources. Large public investments are required for the cities to realize most of their ambitious development goals. Local financial resources for these purposes, however, are hard to find because the older cities have been caught in a tightening squeeze between rapidly rising costs and a stagnant tax base. Between 1957 and 1977, New York City's operating budget rose from $2 billion to $13.6 billion while the city's population was declining by 270,000, or 3 percent. During the same period, spending in Newark increased from $82.4 million to $216 million, and the population dropped 17 percent. Part of these increases in public expenditures is attributable to factors affecting all governments in the region: growing demands for public services, rising prices, and increased labor costs without corresponding increases in productivity. But an additional factor of great importance in the older cities has been the steady increase in the proportion of poor people in the core, causing welfare and other social expenditures to consume an ever-larger share of the city tax dollar.

In New York City, these expenditure trends have been amplified by the size of the local public sector, which reflects the city's huge population and intensive settlement pattern. Size increases unit costs because of the need for elaborate organizations to provide education, police protection, sanitation, and other public services. A densely settled population and the massive concentration of business activities necessitate heavy public outlays for mass transit and sophisticated fire-fighting equipment, as well as contributing to high land costs that affect all public activities. The enormous size of New York's public sector also results from the responsiveness of the local political system to human needs. New York spends far more per capita for health care, welfare, social services, and higher education than other major cities. A final factor has been the political power of the city's public employees, which enabled them to claim a steadily larger share of New York's budget from the mid-1950s through the mid-1970s.[48]

47. "The Washington Market Plan," editorial, *New York Times*, August 1, 1968.

48. These characteristics of New York City's politics are examined in Lyle C. Fitch and A.H. Walsh, eds., *Agenda for a City* (Beverly Hills, Calif.: Sage, 1970). See also Thomas Muller, "Economic Development: Dealing with Contraction," *New York Affairs*, 5(1978), pp. 23–36, and other articles in this issue.

Rising costs have steadily squeezed the older city's tax base, which has not grown nearly as fast as local outlays. Underlying the lack of substantial growth in city tax resources, of course, has been the departure of businesses and better-off families to the suburbs. Further complicating the cities' financial problems has been the concentration of the region's tax-exempt property within their boundaries. Governmental, educational, health care, religious, charitable, and other tax-exempt activities occupy much more property in cities than in all but a few suburbs, and the proportion of tax-exempt city land has been steadily increasing. In New York, 40 percent of all property was exempt from local property taxes in 1976, up from 28 percent in the mid-1950s. Newark faces an even more serious problem, since more than 62 percent of its land is tax exempt. Between 1968 and 1976, the number of tax-exempt properties in Newark rose from 2,700 to 6,900. In addition to the city governments themselves, the large public authorities are major holders of tax-exempt property in the region's older cities. The Port Authority occupies about one-fifth of Newark's land area. In the early 1970s these facilities generated $1 million annually in lease fees, compared to $64 million if the Port Authority were taxed at the same rate as other property owners in Newark.[49]

### Table 19—*Tax-Exempt Property in New York City: 1975*

| Nature of Property | Amount (billion $) | Percentage of Tax-Exempt Property |
|---|---|---|
| City Government | 11.1 | 47.4 |
| Nongovernmental | 4.1 | 17.5 |
| Public Authorities | 3.9 | 16.7 |
| Subsidized Housing | 3.1 | 13.2 |
| Federal Government | 0.6 | 2.6 |
| State Government | 0.5 | 2.2 |
| Foreign Governments | 0.1 | 0.4 |
| Total | 23.4 | 100.0 |

*Source:* New York City Finance Administration.

The further city tax bases have lagged behind expenditures, the more city governments have had to raise tax rates and find new sources of income. Increasing local taxes, however, has been highly counterproductive to the cities' development goals. Tax rates which are much higher than those in the suburbs, and in other sections of the country, substantially increase the likelihood that businesses and middle-class residents will leave the region's cities. Nowhere is this process more advanced than in Newark, whose property taxes are the highest in the nation, reaching $10 per $100 of assessed valuation in 1976. With tax rates this high, only 88 percent of Newark's potential property tax revenues are collected, and 1.5 percent of its taxable properties is aban-

49. On the financial arrangements between the Port Authority and Newark, see the testimony of Newark Mayor Kenneth A. Gibson and Port Authority Chairman James C. Kellogg III in State of New Jersey, Autonomous Authorities Study Commission of the State Legislature, *Public Hearing* (Trenton: March 12, 1971).

doned annually. Real estate taxes in New York City have not lagged far behind, increasing from $4.41 per $100 in 1964 to $8.75 in 1980.

To ease the burdens on property owners, cities have sought revenue sources less damaging to their competitive positions. Such taxes are difficult to find, as Mayor Lindsay learned in 1966 when he sought $520 million in new levies, including a city income tax applicable to nonresidents, and a substantial increase in the city's stock-transfer tax. Manhattan's business leaders reacted negatively to both proposals, arguing that raising taxes would undermine the city's ability to maintain its position as the nation's business capital. Particularly vehement in its opposition was the securities industry, whose perceived dependence on a Manhattan location had singled it out for special tax treatment over the years. Lindsay's proposed 50 percent hike in the $100 million stock-transfer tax was denounced as "misguided, short-sighted, and self-defeating" by the New York Stock Exchange, which raised the specter of departure of the security industry's 400,000 jobs and $2.5 billion payroll should the tax proposal be enacted.[50] To bolster its threat to depart, the exchange scrapped plans for a new $80 million headquarters in lower Manhattan, raised the possibility of establishing a second trading floor in New Jersey in order to avoid the New York tax on large stock transactions, and encouraged other cities and suburbs to offer alternative sites and tax advantages. In the face of these moves City Hall eventually backed down, settling for a smaller increase in the tax, and substantial tax concessions for nonresidents and for transactions involving large blocks of stocks.

These economic and political impediments to raising local taxes resulted in annual net tax increases of only 5 percent in New York City for the years after 1960, while city expenditures were increasing by 10 to 15 percent each year. Part of this gap was closed by increased assistance from Albany and Washington, the rest by borrowing and fiscal legerdemain. New York City began borrowing to meet operating expenditures in 1965 during the final year of the Wagner administration. A heavy price was paid for this new policy, since the city's credit rating was lowered immediately by Moody's Investors Service and Dun & Bradstreet. Moody's justified its action by arguing that "there is increasing evidence that over the years the city government has tended to succumb to the pressures of special interests and minority groups, thus permitting spending to get out of hand."[51] The following year Standard & Poor's followed suit, emphasizing the city's vulnerability "to loss of taxpaying businesses and middle-to-upper income families."[52] The reduced ratings combined with a tightening money market to force New York to pay 50 percent more interest for all its loans in 1966 than it had the previous year. In 1967, Newark's credit rating was downgraded as a result of its worsening financial problems, and by 1975 the city had one of the lowest bond ratings of any major public instrumentality in the nation.

Mayor Wagner's borrowing practices were roundly criticized by the two men who would follow him into City Hall. John Lindsay railed against Wagner's financing policies throughout his successful mayoralty campaign in

50. Keith Funston, president, New York Stock Exchange, quoted in Richard Phalon, "Funston Terms Tax Misguided," *New York Times*, March 4, 1966.

51. *Moody's Bond Survey*, July 18, 1965, pp. 6–7.

52. *Standard & Poor's*, July 25, 1966, p. 7.

1965. Abraham Beame, the city's comptroller, condemned bond financing of operating expenditures as an "unsound proposal which threatens the credits and financial standing of the city."[53] But both Lindsay and Beame turned increasingly to short-term borrowing as city budgets soared in the late 1960s and early 1970s. In order to "balance" its budgets and reassure lenders, the city "fudged its books to hide the extent of its borrowing."[54] By 1975, New York was spending 17 percent of its budget for debt service, and the city's deteriorating financial situation led to the suspension of its credit rating, an inability to market new bonds, a failure to meet existing fiscal obligations, and a dire fiscal crisis that further undermined the city's ability to achieve its many development objectives.

In the painful aftermath of the fiscal collapse of 1975, New York City struggled to develop policies that would be least harmful to its basic development goals. Higher taxes were inevitable, despite the certainty that increased taxes would speed the departure of jobs and more affluent residents. Initially the Beame administration sought to increase revenues through a heavy reliance on additional business taxes, including higher stock-transfer, bank, and corporation taxes. As in the past, business reaction was extremely negative, with major economic interests arguing that additional taxes were totally counterproductive for a city whose appeal for business investment was fading rapidly. More than three dozen large corporations had moved their main headquarters out of New York City in the years 1965–1975, and during the Beame regime one survey of corporate leaders in the city predicted "a tidal wave exodus of large corporations" unless city taxes were lowered rather than raised.[55] In response to these warnings and strong business pressures, Mayor Beame completely reversed his approach to business taxes. By 1977, Beame was advocating tax cuts as the major element in his economic development program, including repeal of the stock-transfer tax and credits for new enterprises locating in the city.[56] A year later, his successor, Edward Koch, worked

53. Quoted in Steven R. Weisman, "How New York Became a Fiscal Junkie," *New York Times Magazine*, August 17, 1975, p. 8.

54. "A Healthy Shock for City and Nation," editorial, *New York Times*, April 7, 1977. See also U.S. Congress, Congressional Budget Office, *New York City's Fiscal Problem: Its Origins, Potential Repercussions, and Some Alternative Policy Responses*, Background Paper No. 1 (Washington: U.S. Government Printing Office, 1975); Ken Auletta, *The Streets Were Paved with Gold* (New York: Random House, 1979); and Charles R. Morris, *The Cost of Good Intentions: New York City and the Liberal Experiment* (New York: Norton, 1980).

55. See Michael Sterne, "Corporations Fret About New York Tax," *New York Times*, March 3, 1977. The survey was conducted by the Labor Committee of the New York State Senate. Similar findings emerged from a survey of business leaders conducted by the *New York Times* in 1976; see Michael Sterne, "Lower Taxes and Better Government Called Keys for City to Hold Industry," *New York Times*, May 16, 1976. The tally of corporate departures, 1965–1975, was based on the "Fortune 500"; during this decade, the number of these corporations with their headquarters in New York City dropped from 128 to 90. See "Exodus of Corporate Headquarters from New York City: What Impact?," *Civil Engineering* 48 (November 1978), pp. 97–98.

56. See Michael Sterne, "Beame Proposes New Business Tax Cuts as Lure," *New York Times*, May 25, 1977. The stock transfer-tax was to be phased out over four years, and cuts totalling $100 million made in taxes on business property, corporation profits, commercial rents, and new equipment. New firms would be given tax credits against the city's business income tax for each job created, and real-estate taxes held constant for at least 10 years. See also Mayor Beame's program as set forth in *Economic Recovery: New York City's Program for 1977–1981* (New York: Department of City Planning, DCP 76-30, December 1976).

feverishly to persuade the state to give the American Stock Exchange an "economic development" grant, and offered other concessions in order to keep the exchange from leaving the city.[57] As the final agreement that kept Amex in the city illustrates, the subsidy approach can generate large benefits for private parties and large burdens for the public exchequer. Government funds will pay for most of the $53 million capital cost for the new Stock Exchange building, with the Amex rent fixed at less than one-half the going rate in the private market.[58]

Reducing financial burdens for some classes of taxpayers inevitably places higher costs on other groups. As a result, tax benefits of this type are extremely sensitive politically, particularly in the complex constituencies of the older cities. For example, New York's efforts to stimulate the construction of luxury apartment developments through tax abatements and other subsidies, as at Battery Park City and Waterside, have been steadfastly opposed by spokesmen for lower- and middle-income groups. As the city's fiscal problems intensified, resentment mounted against the use of scarce public funds to subsidize the affluent. Similar problems arose with middle-income housing, as mounting costs and interest rates led to a steady increase in the income limits for Mitchell-Lama developments. By 1975, a program initially designed to serve families with incomes in the $6,500 to $7,500 range was accepting those with incomes as high as $50,000 annually, to the growing consternation of representatives of lower-income groups. At the same time, escalating operating costs were squeezing lower middle-income residents of Mitchell-Lama housing, many of whom refused to pay the higher charges in an effort to force an increase in public subsidies.[59]

New York City's financial crisis also left substantially fewer resources available for development projects. Capital funds for industrial parks, sewers, and other projects were cut by a quarter in the austerity budget that resulted from the 1975 financial collapse. Similarly, in nearby Yonkers, a city of 200,000 which nearly went bankrupt the same year, "the city's capital projects—longer-range plans to revive a sagging economy" suffered most in the retrenchment of 1976–1978. The fiscal crisis not only slowed physical renewal efforts; the impact was psychological as well, as the "arrested development deprived residents of the feeling that progress was being made and that Yonkers was a city on the move."[60]

57. For a detailed study of New Jersey's efforts to entice the exchange across the Hudson, and of New York's halting responses, see James P. Sterba, "How New York Almost Lost the Amex," *New York Times*, November 27, 1978.

58. See Edward Schumacher, "State Aid for New Amex Building Criticized at Legislative Hearing," *New York Times*, October 31, 1979.

59. By the late 1970s, local tax abatement for Mitchell-Lama projects was close to 80 percent. The most militant tenants were the residents of Co-op City in the Bronx, whose refusal to pay increased monthly carrying charges eventually led state officials to agree in 1977 to relieve the project of $25 million of its debt to the state and city; see Joseph P. Fried, "Co-op City Leaders Arrive at Pact with State Aides on Project's Debt," *New York Times*, July 16, 1977. By the end of the decade, tenant resistance to higher charges had again produced acute financial problems at Co-op City, and was a major factor driving many other Mitchell-Lama projects deeply into the red. See Joyce Purnick, "Growing Deficits Peril Entire Program," *New York Times*, December 6, 1979.

60. Ronald Smothers, "Yonkers, With Spending Curbed, Takes Control From State Today," *New York Times*, November 27, 1978.

Lack of money in New York and the region's other older cities has also drastically reduced the funds available for housing development. In the wake of financial collapse, New York was forced to shelve almost all of its housing development activities, including the construction of 50,000 apartments for low- and middle-income families. As a result, the gap steadily grows larger between the rhetoric of the slum-free city and the reality of meager housing programs, which are unlikely to have a significant impact on development patterns.

Last but hardly least, financial adversity has undermined development efforts in the older cities by reducing the level and quality of public services. "Our parks are filthy," pointed out Manhattan's borough president at the end of 1976, "our highways are strewn with garbage, there are more potholes, our bridges are deteriorating, schools and day-care centers are being closed."[61] For New York City, austerity meant less police and fire protection, fewer garbage collections, and a 25 percent increase in class size in the schools. In Yonkers between 1975 and 1978, police and fire department personnel were reduced by 10 percent and park crews were cut by nearly two-thirds. Reduced services inevitably decrease the attractiveness of the cities for business and middle-class families. And the need to stretch scarce resources more thinly, in order to meet essential city services, further limits the ability of city officials to husband resources and concentrate them on development projects with long-term benefits to the economic and social well-being of these declining urban centers.

## Dependence on State Government

Cities, like suburbs, depend heavily on state governments, from which they derive all of their governmental powers and a significant share of their financial resources. Dependence on the states, however, affects the politics of development in the older cities more than in the suburbs. As already emphasized, the cities undertake a wider range of development activities than the vast majority of suburbs, and most of these city activities involve extensive governmental intervention. Consequently, the cities need more from the states, in terms of both formal authority and resources. And because of the cities' need for state action, state legislators and officials tend to become more deeply involved in city development efforts than those in the suburbs.[62]

City dependence on state government has been reinforced by fiscal crisis. New York City avoided bankruptcy in 1975 only through state assistance permitting the city to meet its most pressing financial obligations. In return for its help, Albany forced City Hall to accept the creation of an Emergency Financial Control Board dominated by state officials to oversee city finances. The board was empowered by the state legislature to approve contracts, make budget cuts, and "review the operations, management, efficiency and produc-

---

61. Percy Sutton, quoted in Steven R. Weisman, "Indications of Deterioration Abound in New York Crisis," *New York Times,* December 5, 1976.

62. For a detailed analysis of the patterns of state intervention, see Sayre and Kaufman, *Governing New York City,* Chapter 15.

tivity" of all city agencies.[63] The effect of this legislation was to increase
detailed state involvement in all phases of city government, thus reducing the
ability of city officials to concentrate resources on their preferred development goals.[64]

The superior constitutional position of the states also means that state
government can preempt city development powers and controls. In 1968, Governor Nelson Rockefeller persuaded the New York legislature to create a new
state agency to rebuild the state's older cities. The Urban Development Corporation was empowered to override local zoning and building controls if necessary, with its sweeping powers justified by Rockefeller because of the failure of
the older cities to concentrate resources effectively on improving housing and
meeting their development objectives.[65] New York City bitterly and unsuccessfully opposed the creation of the Urban Development Corporation. "Our
cities," argued Mayor Lindsay, "cannot be renewed by state-operated bulldozers which move into local communities without their consent and without
knowledge or concern about the increasing need for supportive services connected with all development."[66]

Cities, of course, are not powerless in dealing with state government.
Urban mayors—and certainly the city executives of New York City, Newark,
and Jersey City—are usually powerful political figures in their own right.
State legislators from city districts typically respond to the strongly expressed
concerns of local elected officials. Moreover, state officials are generally reluctant to assume full responsibility—and thus the possibility of bearing the
blame and receiving political flak—for city programs. Thus, the Emergency
Financial Control Board proceeded cautiously rather than boldly in fulfilling
its mandate to oversee New York's financial affairs. And the Urban Development Corporation quickly sought an accommodation with Mayor Lindsay and
other city leaders to ensure that UDC projects within older cities were coordinated with overall local programs.[67]

A good illustration of the exercise of state power and the countervailing
role of city influence is provided by the Battery Park City project referred to
earlier in this chapter. By proposing the creation of a state Battery Park City
Authority in 1966, Governor Rockefeller sought to take control of the development of the land along the Hudson River adjacent to the World Trade Center.
The new authority was to have sweeping power to develop the area, with
little provision made for local participation. City resistance both to the proposed authority's powers and to Rockefeller's plan for the area (discussed

63. See *New York State Financial Emergency Act for the City of New York*, New York State
Statutes Chapter 22 (Laws 1975, Chap. 868), effective September 9, 1975. The Emergency Financial
Control Board has seven members: the governor, state comptroller, mayor, city comptroller, and
three members appointed by the governor with the advice and consent of the state senate. The
quotation in the text is taken from Section 7 of the act.
    64. Emergency Financial Control Board supervision was also applied to Yonkers in 1975, as
one step in staving off bankruptcy.
    65. See Rockefeller's statements in Sydney H. Schanberg, "Governor Offers a $6 Billion Plan
to Rebuild Slums," *New York Times*, February 29, 1968.
    66. "Text of Statement by Mayor Lindsay on His Proposal for an Urban Bill of Rights," *New
York Times*, March 7, 1968.
    67. On the creation and evolution of the Urban Development Corporation, see Michael N.
Danielson, *The Politics of Exclusion* (New York: Columbia University Press, 1976), pp. 307–322.

above) produced a protracted conflict between Albany and City Hall. In the end, the city won substantial concessions from the state in the physical plan and the powers of the authority. But the state nonetheless secured basic responsibility for overseeing the development of a highly strategic area, thus reducing the city's ability to carry out development in accordance with city objectives and priorities.[68]

## Lack of Executive Integration

Another important set of constraints on the older cities' ability to concentrate resources are the impediments to effective political leadership posed by administrative complexity and functional autonomy. Because of the wide functional scope of their responsibilities, Newark, Jersey City and most older cities in the region have many agencies carrying out program responsibilities in interrelated areas, but often with little coordination or central control. Organizational diffusion is most pronounced in New York City, which has scores of agencies operating a bewildering variety of programs that affect urban development. In the case of housing, separate agencies have often been responsible for middle-income developments, urban renewal, rent control, public housing, rehabilitation, and code enforcement, as well as for broader programs stimulated by federal or state aid such as the model cities effort. A similar pattern has characterized the city's industrial development efforts. As it attempted to devise an effective program, New York City created a Public Development Corporation to make loans to industrial firms and develop industrial properties for lease to manufacturers, an Industrial Development Corporation to take advantage of New York state's industrial loan fund, a Commercial Development Corporation to use federal loan funds, and an Economic Development Administration to attempt to direct the overall program.

In addition to the profusion of city agencies with development responsibilities, major areas of policy are determined by agencies outside the cities' sphere of control, such as the Port Authority, the Metropolitan Transportation Authority, the Urban Development Corporation, the state transportation department, and the toll-road authorities. Although New York City's chief executive ranks as one of the nation's more powerful mayors, past incumbents have had limited influence on the policies of such agencies—even of

68. Fifteen years after Rockefeller's original proposal, meager progress had been made with Battery Park City, beyond the land fill and the laying of foundations for the first six apartment buildings in the project. In addition to conflict between the city and state, the project was delayed by rising costs and the softening of demand for offices in lower Manhattan during the 1970s. By 1980, the futuristic plans prepared under Rockefeller had been scrapped in favor of more conventional development featuring low-rise apartments. The failure of the Battery Park City Authority to advance the project, and the prospect of default on the authority's bonds because of the lack of revenues, led Governor Carey in 1979–1980 to fold the authority into the state Urban Development Corporation and seek additional state funds to keep the project afloat. In addition, the city reluctantly agreed to permit UDC to bypass normal city approval processes. See Edward Schumacher, "13 Years Later, Battery Park City's an Empty Dream," *New York Times,* October 26, 1979; Edward Schumacher, "Carey and Koch Accept New Battery Park City Plan," *New York Times,* November 9, 1979; and Paul Goldberger, "6 Builders Chosen for Housing at Battery Park City," *New York Times,* August 19, 1981.

some agencies whose operations take place entirely within city limits, such as the Triborough Bridge and Tunnel Authority and the New York City Transit Authority (both now part of the state-controlled Metropolitan Transportation Authority). This limited control was especially clear in conflicts between City Hall and Robert Moses, whose autonomous power base gave him far more influence on the development process than any of the five mayors he "served."[69] In Newark, public housing and urban renewal have been administered by the Newark Housing Authority, an independent public corporation which long held "large amounts of discretion in the policy realm," and which (next to the local board of education) was for many years "the largest spender of funds and the largest dispenser of contracts in the city government."[70]

Among this welter of city, state, and special-purpose agencies, overlapping responsibilities are common and coordination among related programs usually inadequate. As a result, in the older cities different agencies often work at cross purposes, to the detriment of advancing general development goals. As the *New York Times* noted some years ago, "the list of interdepartmental fumbles that become permanent physical mistakes in New York is endless." The *Times* provided the following examples:

> Real Estate defies Planning as the sell-off of city-owned land on Staten Island continues unchecked. . . .
> Public Works and Parks cross signals on a major sewage plant designed with no relationship to the changing objectives of the Manhattan waterfront.
> A Landmark Preservation Commission is appointed after Highways has replaced historic buildings and areas with parking lots and street widenings.
> Superauthorities impose superhighways on neighborhood patterns; roadway spaghetti disrupts attempts at a coordinated civic center; public structures are pushed willy-nilly into empty real estate lots. . . .[71]

Efforts by mayors to draw together the disparate strands of development policy tend to be undermined by the sheer complexity of the governmental system, as well as by the influence of agencies and their clienteles, the formal autonomy of many key public organizations, functional ties between city agencies and state and federal funding sources, and the reluctance of other elected officials to strengthen the mayor's hand. All of these factors were at work during a decade of political conflict over the administrative structure of New York City's government. After a campaign in 1965 stressing the need for vigorous political leadership and centralized direction of housing, renewal, and transportation programs, Mayor Lindsay sought to attack the problem of

69. As Caraley notes, however, the creation of semiautonomous agencies is at times encouraged—not opposed—by city officials, who are glad to " 'spinoff' and reduce their responsibility for programs and functions that have become especially and chronically troublesome." Demetrios Caraley, *City Governments and Urban Problems* (Englewood Cliffs, N.J.: Prentice-Hall, 1977), p. 113.

70. Harold Kaplan, *Urban Renewal Politics: Slum Clearance in Newark* (New York: Columbia University Press, 1963), pp. 11, 60. The Newark Housing Authority is examined in detail in Chapter Nine.

71. "New York Program: Planning," editorial, *New York Times*, December 26, 1965.

diffusion by creating superagencies to encompass all of the city's major administrative units. Lindsay's proposals were resisted by many city agencies and their clients, who were unhappy about the loss of both agency autonomy and of direct access to the mayor. Key independent agencies, such as the New York City Housing Authority and the Triborough Bridge and Tunnel Authority, lobbied successfully to avoid inclusion in the new superagencies.

From Lindsay's perspective, what consolidation did occur provided City Hall with a better opportunity to control policy development and implementation. But the sheer size of New York's administrative apparatus, and the multiplicity of its internal linkages and ties with outside agencies, were insurmountable obstacles to effective coordination.[72] More often than not, creation of the new superagencies merely added another participant to an already crowded field, leading to more paperwork, more official clearances and approvals, and further delays in designing and carrying out development programs. The least successful of Lindsay's superagencies was one of the most important for development policy, the Housing and Redevelopment Administration, which a City Council report accurately characterized five years after its creation as "a large, clumsy bureaucracy which served to frustrate rather than further housing goals."[73] After Abraham Beame succeeded Lindsay in 1974, the Housing and Redevelopment Administration was dismantled, as were many other Lindsay innovations.

Although his city is only one-twentieth the size of New York City in population, Mayor Kenneth A. Gibson found the complexities of Newark's administrative pattern equally frustrating. After eight years in office, Gibson was still trying to locate adequate handles of central control in order to reduce "duplication and fragmentation" of services in the city. Facing an increasingly severe fiscal crisis in the winter of 1978–1979, the mayor attacked the existing "confusion of responsibility" and called for a major reorganization of city agencies, sharply reducing the number of departments. Donning the necessary mask of optimism, Gibson looked forward to the success of this strategem in enhancing executive control, governmental efficiency, and the ability of the beleaguered city to meet its service and development goals.[74]

City planning agencies provide another means to enhance a mayor's control over the development process. In New York City, the planning agency has substantial analytical and design capabilities, and has been responsible for most of the comprehensive development proposals generated within city government. The City Planning Commission has substantial formal powers

72. For an analysis during this period of the fragmentation of power in New York City, and a lively debate on possible ways to improve coordination and executive leadership, see David B. Hertz and Adam Walinsky, "Organizing the City," and Herbert Kaufman, "Organizing the City: Commentary II," in Lyle Fitch and A.H. Walsh, *Agenda for a City*, pp. 451–501, 505–511. See also Wallace S. Sayre, "The Mayor," in Fitch and Walsh, pp. 563–601.

73. The report was prepared by the council's Committee on Charter and Government Operations in connection with allegations of "fraud and ineptitude" in the agency's management of the Municipal Loan Program, which provided funds for housing rehabilitation. See Edith Evans Asbury, "H.R.A. Disbanding Urged in Council Panel's Report," *New York Times*, March 1, 1972; City Council, "The Municipal Loan Program: Blueprint for Failure" (New York: 1972).

74. See Alvin Davis and Michael Wright, "Newark Goes on a Crash Diet," *New York Times*, December 24, 1978; Newark Public Information Office, City Hall, "Gibson Seeks Major Reorganization of Newark Agencies," December 17, 1978.

over zoning, siting of public facilities, and capital budgeting. These capabilities prompted various mayors to attempt to use the planning commission to enhance their influence, primarily by installing a close associate as chairman. While these efforts have strengthened the mayor's hand in some development areas, they have been constrained by the nature of the commission. Like most municipal planning agencies, New York's planning commission was designed as a semiautonomous body. Formal decisions are made by a multimember board appointed for eight-year terms, restricting the amount of influence exercised by an incumbent mayor. In addition, the dominant city planning tradition in New York—as in most large American cities—has emphasized an apolitical role for planners rather than service as an instrument of mayoral power. Consequently, a number of commissioners, staff members, and clientele of the agency have strongly resisted subordination of the planning agency to the mayor's office. A final, and crucial, limiting factor is the City Planning Commission's lack of formal authority over the activities of public authorities and other key public actors in the development process.[75]

Still another approach to the problem of executive integration is the creation of a specialized agency under mayoral supervision to undertake a particular development activity. Here the challenge for City Hall is to employ the mayor's time and other scarce resources in order to control the agency. Otherwise the new agency is liable to drift away and further complicate the problem of concentrating resources. Illustrative of these difficulties was the effort of the Lindsay administration to create a South Richmond Development Corporation to direct the planned development of more than 10,000 acres of largely vacant land on Staten Island. Lindsay and his aides saw their new agency as a means of concentrating city resources on a high-priority objective. Among the Island's residents, however, the mayor's proposal was almost universally denounced as a power grab "through which the Mayor gains control of Staten Island for twenty years."[76] Heightening local resistance was the widespread fear that the city's plan would include low-income housing, encouraging an influx of blacks and Hispanics to Staten Island. Responding to these constituency concerns, legislators from Staten Island forced major changes in the South Richmond bill, including a substantial dilution of the mayoral role by providing that a majority of the agency's members be residents of Staten Island.

The ability of Staten Islanders to check City Hall on South Richmond, like that of Brooklyn residents to kill Mayor Lindsay's linear city scheme and the vetoes successfully exercised by other sections, reflect another significant obstacle to executive integration in the older cities. Neighborhood and district interests typically pull in different directions from those of city hall. These concerns have always been well-represented in the political systems of the older cities, primarily through the city council and the local political parties.

75. The best analysis of the role of New York City's planning commission is found in Sayre and Kaufman, *Governing New York City*, pp. 372–380. In the region's other older cities, the planning agencies have far less expertise and typically defer to (or if they resist lose out to) urban renewal authorities and other narrowly based city departments. See for example the analysis of city planning in Newark, in Kaplan, *Urban Renewal Politics*, pp. 114–134.

76. Borough President Richard T. Connor, quoted in Edward C. Burks, "City Hall Dominance of S.I. Plan Is Fought," *New York Times*, April 27, 1971.

As already noted, these centripetal forces are particularly entrenched in New York City, with its borough presidents, district-based city council, large number of state legislative and congressional districts, and the active political party organizations in each of the five boroughs. Further enhancing the significance of territorial interests in development politics in the older cities have been the insistent demands in recent years for greater governmental concern with neighborhood interests, and for community control over key policy areas such as housing, land use, highways, and education.[77]

In New York City, the most significant response to demands for decentralized government has been the development of community planning boards. Initially created in the mid-1960s to advise city agencies on actions affecting their sections, the local planning boards have steadily enlarged their role. In 1970, the City Council required the City Planning Commission to notify local boards before making zoning, housing, and other development decisions, thus ensuring that local interests would have an opportunity to make their views known to city officials. Building on this advisory role, a number of community planning boards have become influential participants in the politics of development. One on Manhattan's East Side was able to block a large shopping mall strongly supported by the Beame administration. Another in Manhattan has been influential in blocking the construction of Westway. And others have strongly opposed scatter-site housing. A more important role will be played by these agencies in the future since charter revisions approved by New York voters in 1975 empowered the fifty-nine local boards to hold public hearings on most public and private development proposals, as well as requiring the City Planning Commission to justify the rejection of any recommendation by a local planning board. Each of the local boards now has a small staff headed by a district manager, and beginning in 1980 police, sanitation, and other local service district boundaries must conform with those of the community planning boards.

Whatever the virtues of more community influence, the growing power of neighborhood interests in the older cities seems certain to increase the formidable problems faced by mayors in attempting to concentrate resources on complex development goals. Which brings us back to the point of this chapter, which is *not* that older cities are unable to undertake development activities. Vast amounts of public investment have been made by the region's older cities, producing thousands of units of housing, large amounts of urban renewal, and a variety of other important changes. Moreover, some efforts by the older cities clearly have influenced development patterns in the region. For example, even more middle-income families would have departed from New York City had government not actively sought to retain the middle class. Land-use controls have been used successfully to protect middle-class neighborhoods from industry, the poor, and blacks. Zoning has also facilitated single-family housing development in Queens and Staten Island. Subsidization of the transit fare has exerted a strong influence on the locational decisions of the CBD's clerical workers in the lower middle-class neighborhoods

77. See J. Clarence Davies III, *Neighborhood Groups and Urban Renewal* (New York: Columbia University Press, 1966); Walter G. Farr, Jr., Lance Liebman, and Jeffrey S. Wood, *Decentralizing City Government* (New York: Praeger, 1972); and Joseph D. Sneed and Steven A. Waldhorn, eds., *Restructuring the Federal System* (New York: Crane, Russak, 1975), pp. 143 ff.

of Brooklyn, Queens, and Staten Island. Rent control has substantially reduced the cost of housing for many middle-class families, thereby lessening
the attractiveness of a move to the suburbs.

Our basic point, however, is that the size and complexity—social, economic, and political—of the older cities make the concentration of resources
on coherent development objectives extremely difficult for these governmental systems. Instead of focusing their efforts, the older cities tend to spread
their investments widely, responding both to the breadth of their problems
and the diversity of their constituencies. The fact that the cities' deepening
problems reduce the resources available further undermines the ability of
these governments to concentrate their remaining resources effectively.

# 9

# Urban Renewal: Political Skill and Constituency Pressures

One major strategy to overcome the obstacles to concentrating resources in the older cities is the use of semiautonomous functional agencies. One of the region's most influential governmental institutions—the Triborough Bridge and Tunnel Authority—was organized as an independent functional agency operating entirely within the boundaries of New York City, as was the New York City Transit Authority.[1] The use of such functional agencies within older cities has been particularly extensive for public housing and urban renewal. All of the public housing in the region's older cities has been developed by housing authorities. Functional agencies of one kind or another, usually operating with considerable financial and policy independence from city hall, also undertook urban renewal in the cities, with the same agency often responsible for both public housing and redevelopment.

In this chapter we focus on urban renewal in the older cities, and in particular on the ability of renewal agencies to concentrate resources on their development objectives. Although the federal urban renewal program largely expired in the mid-1970s, urban renewal deserves serious attention in any examination of the impact of government on the distribution of jobs and residences in metropolitan regions.[2] For a quarter of a century the renewal program was the major source of funds, plans, and programs for the revitalization of older cities. Through urban renewal and associated programs, the region's cities sought to redevelop their commercial centers, augment the supply of high-quality housing within their boundaries, stimulate economic development, and otherwise increase their share of jobs and better-off families in the region. Taken as a whole, urban renewal has had less impact on the distribution of jobs and residences than the region's transportation programs and zoning policies. Urban renewal has, however, exerted

1. As indicated in Chapter Seven, in 1968 both Triborough and the NYC Transit Authority were incorporated into the Metropolitan Transportation Authority, an agency whose jurisdiction reached far beyond the boundaries of New York City.

2. Federal grants for urban renewal were consolidated into the community development block grant program by the Housing and Community Development Act of 1974. Henceforth, funds for slum clearance and rehabilitation of cleared areas were no longer allocated by Congress and distributed by the Department of Housing and Urban Development to local urban renewal agencies on the basis of project application. Instead, renewal activities were funded by city governments out of their community development block grants, along with a wide range of other community and housing investments that can be financed by the federal block grants.

an important influence in some of the region's cities by modifying "private market" decisions regarding the location of office buildings, apartments, and other development.[3]

## The Federal Framework

Urban renewal was created by the federal government. As a result, the roles and capabilities of the participants were strongly influenced by federal laws, regulations, and policy determinations. The Housing Act of 1949 sought to halt the spread of "slums and blight" through slum clearance and redevelopment. Under Title I of the 1949 legislation, federal aid would be given to cities to encourage clearance of blighted areas, and redevelopment of the cleared areas for housing, industry, or other purposes. The financing arrangements assured that private developers as well as public agencies would be actively involved in carrying out the purposes of the new program. A local public agency would purchase and clear the land, and provide sewers and other facilities. The public agency then would sell or lease the land to a developer, who would construct housing or other mutually agreed-upon projects. And the federal government would repay the city for two-thirds of the net cost of the total project package.[4]

In effect, Title I of the Housing Act of 1949 required renewal projects to meet the perceived goals of private developers, as well as those of local governments. Federal insistence on close cooperation between developers and public agencies resulted partly from congressional reluctance to allocate large amounts of public funds directly to such a vast field—in contrast, for example, with the reliance on direct public construction in the more narrowly defined public housing program. This reluctance to engage in massive government construction was reinforced by intensive lobbying by the housing industry, whose demands were bolstered by the nation's long tradition of private action in constructing housing, industrial plants, and office buildings.[5] As a result, governmental action in urban renewal has been much more actively influenced by the preferences of specific private firms—particularly large-scale developers capable of undertaking renewal projects— than has been the case in, say, the development of the regional highway network. And the *independent* role of governmental actors in shaping re-

3. Most close observers concur with this overall assessment of the impact of the urban renewal program on the pattern of settlement. For the New York region, see Robert C. Wood, *1400 Governments* (Cambridge, Mass.: Harvard University Press, 1961), pp. 155 ff. For more general assessments, see Charles Abrams, *The City Is the Frontier* (New York: Harper & Row, 1965), Chapter 9; and the commentators whose views are collected in James Q. Wilson, ed., *Urban Renewal: The Record and the Controversy* (Cambridge, Mass.: MIT Press, 1966).

4. For a detailed discussion of the evolution of federal urban renewal legislation, see Ashley A. Foard and Hilbert Fefferman, "Federal Urban Renewal Legislation," in Wilson, *Urban Renewal*, pp. 71–125. The basic operation of the urban renewal program is explained in William L. Slayton, "The Operation and Achievements of the Urban Renewal Program," in Wilson, *Urban Renewal*, pp. 189–229; Slayton, at the time, was head of the Urban Renewal Administration in the U.S. Housing and Home Finance Agency.

5. See Scott Greer, *Urban Renewal and American Cities* (Indianapolis, Ind.: Bobbs-Merrill, 1965), pp. 17 ff.

newal programs is more difficult to sort out from other influences than is the case, certainly, with mass transportation, or suburban zoning.

Before any portions of the urban landscape could be cleared and redeveloped, the differing priorities of private developers, federal agencies (the Federal Housing Administration and the Urban Renewal Administration), and the local renewal authority would have to be reconciled. Initially, cities sought to use urban renewal programs to clear slums and replace blighted housing with moderately priced homes. Newark's experience was typical. The staff of the Newark Housing Authority (NHA) perceived slum clearance under Title I primarily as a means of providing middle-class families with new apartments. But NHA officials soon learned that unless a private firm could make a profit on middle-income housing, "no redeveloper would buy the site," and "no FHA official would agree to insure mortgages for construction there."[6] Developers invariably demanded choice sites and higher rents than those originally planned by NHA. In the face of the constraints imposed by the requirements of private involvement, NHA shifted its attention to less blighted areas and a higher-income clientele for the new apartments. Under skillful leadership that maximized the authority's autonomy from much of the local political system, NHA pursued its revised goals with considerable success. As Harold Kaplan notes, "high-priced apartments on sites immediately surrounding the central business district" rather than the original goals of "slum sites" and "moderate rents" were the principal product of Newark's first decade of urban renewal.[7]

New York City's Slum Clearance Committee also quickly discovered that the economics of urban renewal under Title I facilitated the construction of luxury apartments and other high-value projects rather than the middle-income units initially promised by the program. Under the aggressive direction of Robert Moses, New York launched a monumental Title I program which by 1960 had redeveloped more land than all other cities in the nation combined. In place of moderately priced housing in the cleared neighborhoods rose luxury apartment buildings, a $22 million exhibition hall, office buildings, hospital and university facilities, and the Lincoln Center for the Performing Arts.

Out of the framework provided by the Housing Act of 1949 came a set of relationships among three major participants. One was the federal Housing and Home Finance Agency—which in 1965 became the Department of Housing and Urban Development—whose officials would have to concur in the plans of any project before federal funds could be reserved or paid to the city. The second was the private developer, whose willingness to purchase the land for specified uses would be required if any renewal was to occur under Title I. The third was the local public agency, which under the federal law could be the city government itself or any agency designated by the city. In order to avoid local debt limitations, as well as to combine the renewal function with existing public housing responsibilities, the local agency chosen was frequently a public authority.

6. Harold Kaplan, *Urban Renewal Politics: Slum Clearance in Newark* (New York: Columbia University Press, 1963), p. 16.
7. Ibid., p. 25.

*The site of the Atlantic Terminal Urban Renewal Project in Brooklyn, one of a number of renewal schemes in the region that never progressed beyond the clearance stage.*     Credit: Michael N. Danielson

## Elements of Success and Failure

In order to make an impact on land use patterns in its city, the renewal agency had to forge effective relations with both federal officials and developers. This required the local agency to be able to concentrate resources on specific projects that would satisfy the other key participants. To achieve this goal, urban renewal agencies needed some insulation from the mayor's office and from other city elected officials and local constituencies, all of whom were likely to press in diverse directions, complicating relations with Washington and with private developers. In addition, leadership skills were required to seek out the opportunities and constraints inherent in Title I, and to deal with other elements of the city political system, both at city hall and in the affected neighborhoods.

In this section we explore the interplay of these factors in two of the region's older cities, Newark and Trenton, which had very different experiences with the urban renewal program during its first dozen years. Our comparison focuses on the period from 1949 to the early 1960s, when both cities had housing authorities serving as their urban renewal agencies. Thus two public authorities are compared, and the relative impact of their urban renewal efforts and the factors that underlie their differential impacts are examined. "Impact" on development is measured in terms of the number of urban renewal projects completed or initiated during the period, the percentage of city land directly involved in authorized projects, and federal funds expended or allocated in the two cities.[8]

In these terms, the differences between the Newark Housing Authority and the Trenton Housing Authority (THA) are dramatic. The Newark agency had completed two renewal projects by 1961, and had received federal grant approval for 10 additional projects. Trenton's housing authority had received funding for only two projects, and neither had been completed. The Newark projects encompassed nearly 1,000 acres, or close to 7 percent of the city's land area.[9] The Trenton total was 133 acres, about 3 percent of the city. Even greater were the differences in federal urban renewal funds, both expended or reserved. By 1961, the Newark Housing Authority's total was more than $60 million, placing it in the nation's top 10 renewal agencies in terms of total federal funds received. Trenton, on the other hand, had been allocated only about $2 million. Newark's population was about four times that of Trenton, so Newark's per capita federal funds were approximately seven times as large as those for Trenton.[10]

In accounting for the very different impact of urban renewal in the two cities, areal scope and functional breadth are not helpful variables. Both the Newark Housing Authority and the Trenton Housing Authority operated within the boundaries of their cities, and their functional scopes were similar, with each agency responsible for urban renewal and public housing. Nor were differences in "objective" need for renewal projects significant, since deteriorated commercial and residential structures were widespread in both cities. The two agencies also were similar in their fairly high degree of political and financial independence. Commissioners of both authorities were appointed by the mayors, but they all were private citizens rather than officials of other city agencies. The federal government was the primary source of funds, which gave the agencies potential leverage in obtaining the necessary one-third matching funds from their city governments.[11] On the other hand, neither of these renewal authorities could match the financial independence—in relation to local and state governments—of the highway

8. Similar measures of impact are used by Wood, *1400 Governments*, pp. 155 ff; Kaplan, *Urban Renewal Politics*, pp. 2 ff; and Raymond Vernon, *Metropolis 1985* (Cambridge, Mass.: Harvard University Press, 1960), pp. 142 ff. It would also be possible to include other factors in an assessment of impact—for example, the effect of the urban renewal program on economic development in the city. Because of problems of definition and difficulties in sorting out the interrelated causal factors, we do not include these measures here. We are not arguing, however, that these indices, or even broader measures of impact on economic development, are definitive ways of measuring whether an urban renewal agency is "successful," either in terms of the broad objectives stated in the Housing Act of 1949 or other social welfare goals. At this point, we are simply concerned with the following: When two agencies are created with similar overall goals, project objectives, and organizational structures, what factors account for the differences in the ability of the two agencies to achieve their purposes?

9. The proportion of Newark's city-controlled land that was involved in urban renewal was even greater, since the Port of New York Authority uses about 20 percent of Newark's land area for Newark Airport and other facilities.

10. The totals are calculated from the annual reports of the two authorities. See also U.S. Housing and Home Finance Agency, Urban Renewal Administration, *Urban Renewal Project Directory* (Washington: U.S. Government Printing Office, 1962).

11. The argument was often made in these cities as in others that to obtain two dollars in outside funding for every one dollar in local money was an "efficient" and attractive way to use local funds.

agencies, where the proportion of federal funds reached nine-to-one in the interstate highway program.

What was distinctly different between the Newark and Trenton agencies was the political skills of renewal officials in the two cities, particularly in their ability to handle constituency demands. Leadership and constituency factors were crucial to the contrasts in program results of the two authorities. These factors can usefully be compared through a brief review of the development of each of the agencies.

### Conflicting Pressures in Trenton

The Trenton Housing Authority was created in 1938 to construct public housing under the federal Housing Act of 1937. During the next 10 years, THA built three projects. In constructing its first two projects, the authority was criticized by protest groups involving black and white residents of the designated areas, was attacked for its decisions by both Trenton newspapers, found its plans temporarily halted by a vote of the city council, and finally built the housing projects only after the reluctant intervention of the federal housing administrator. Underlying these constituency problems was the initial attempt by THA to exercise its powers in a truly independent fashion. Sites for public housing had been chosen by the staff, the decisions based mainly on whether the land was vacant and land values low, without any negotiation with city leaders or neighborhood groups prior to public announcement. As Duncan Grant concludes, "THA's early years demonstrated its inability to accommodate opposing interests through private, covert negotiations, and thereby to maximize its chances for success in the public housing arena."[12]

When the federal urban renewal program was initiated in 1949, the Trenton Housing Authority was designated the city's Local Public Agency (LPA) for urban renewal. The first project, redevelopment of the Coalport Yards, was announced in 1952, with public support from the mayor and the city's daily newspapers. Relocation and clearance proceeded slowly, however, and demolition of the last buildings was not completed until six years later. During this period, THA experienced difficulties in its relations with Washington and with the city government. At one point, the housing authority found itself in violation of federal requirements regarding the number of professional planners on its staff. Progress on Coalport was also delayed while THA stumbled through negotiations with city agencies regarding complex technical problems relating to ownership and improvement of sewers, and other public facilities in the urban renewal area. Then, once the land was cleared, THA was unable to enlist enough private developers to complete renewal. In the summer of 1958, THA announced that 20 firms had shown a serious interest in Coalport. But this interest evaporated as commitments were sought. By 1961 only two commercial firms had signed contracts, and most of the land was still without prospective users.

Meanwhile, in 1955 THA had proposed a second renewal project for the Fitch Way area, which included about 100 acres near downtown Trenton. The

12. M. Duncan Grant, "Housing Authority Politics in Trenton and Newark," Senior Thesis, Princeton University, April 1972, p. 67. The analysis of the Trenton Housing Authority draws particularly on the perceptive discussion in Grant's research paper.

mayor, however, disagreed with the scope of the proposal, urging that it be expanded to encompass planning of the entire downtown area. The authority's commissioners found themselves divided on whether to broaden the project area, and activity on the project largely ceased for nearly a year. In 1957 the federal Urban Renewal Administration threatened to cut off all federal planning funds for the project if THA did not move forward. Early in 1958, the city government expressed its displeasure with the authority's inaction by taking the Fitch Way project away from THA, leaving the agency responsible only for Coalport. While unhappy with the action of the city commissioners,[13] THA staff also felt relieved. Already having difficulty carrying out Coalport, and lacking vigorous leadership and effective relationships with the city government, private developers, and the federal Urban Renewal Administration, THA officials were on balance glad to be free of the complex political and economic problems of the Fitch Way-downtown area.

City Hall found itself no better able to make progress with Fitch Way than THA, however. After a year the city commissioners returned the project to the authority, which proceeded to hold a blight hearing. But THA was soon torn by dissension within its ranks, as one member of the authority charged the agency with delay, waste of funds, and general incompetence. A group of local businessmen joined in the attack, urging that the city remove THA from all responsibility for urban renewal. The mayor agreed and the city fathers in 1960 ended the authority's role in the Fitch Way and future urban renewal activities. When THA was unable to produce firm contracts with developers for the use of land in the Coalport renewal area, that project also was taken from the agency in 1963. Thus, weak leadership cost THA whatever opportunity urban renewal provided for a role in shaping development in Trenton. Fourteen years after the bright beginnings of Title I, the authority was back at "square one"—limited to providing and maintaining public housing for the city.

### Building an Autonomous Base for Renewal in Newark

A striking contrast is provided by the Newark Housing Authority's renewal strategies and negotiations during the same period.[14] Like its Trenton counterpart, NHA was created in 1938 to construct and manage public housing projects. During the next decade it maintained close and effective relations with City Hall, and constructed seven projects without encountering any significant opposition. This relatively positive record—compared with the turbulent early years of THA—was somewhat marred by charges of political interference in site selection and awarding of contracts in 1948, and NHA's executive director resigned under fire.[15]

13. At the time both Trenton and Newark employed the commission form of government, with city commissioners exercising both legislative and executive authority.

14. The discussion of the Newark Housing Authority in this section draws primarily on Kaplan, *Urban Renewal Politics*. See also David Marshall, "Urban Renewal in Newark," Senior Thesis, Princeton University, April 1971: and James Schoessler, "Housing and Urban Renewal in Newark, New Jersey," Senior Thesis, Princeton University, April 1970.

15. The city commissioners' "close relationships" with the NHA apparently included an active role in deciding sites and all other NHA activities. The Essex County prosecutor had planned to bring charges of illegal interference before a grand jury, but suspended his investigation when NHA's executive director departed; see Kaplan, *Urban Renewal Politics*, pp. 39–40.

The new executive director, Louis Danzig, took over shortly before the passage of the Housing Act of 1949. When NHA was designated as Newark's renewal agency, Danzig and his staff moved quickly to meet what they perceived as the city's major redevelopment problem—the need for middle-income housing. Their early experience in attempting to fulfill this objective was much like that in Trenton. In 1952, having announced the agency's first project, to be located in Newark's North Ward, NHA encountered great difficulty in attracting developers. Active efforts to generate bids finally resulted in a contract in 1957, but the developer then withdrew. Not until 1958 was a firm agreement made with a developer for the site.

The difficulties encountered in this first project led the NHA staff to adopt a different strategy. Unlike the Trenton agency, which selected a massive 100-acre site and became enmeshed in complex political and economic debates on how to proceed, NHA decided to focus on parcels of 10 to 30 acres. NHA also altered its strategies to ensure that projects would in fact be built and that public criticism and debate would be muted. Rather than attempting, within NHA, to decide what specific types of projects—middle-income housing, luxury apartments, light industry, office complexes, etc.—should be located at each site and then seeking a developer, Danzig and his aides now defined their mission more broadly. NHA's goals would be to "tear down substandard housing" and attract capital for new construction, with the expectation that these efforts would serve as "significant steps to reverse Newark's decline." With these revised objectives, authority officials then began negotiations with private developers, and after "long months of pressure" were able to overcome Newark's negative image and persuade developers to undertake projects in the city.[16]

It is important to note that the characteristics of particular projects—housing, office buildings, etc.—were substantially shaped by the developers, within the broad guidelines of federal statutes. But the role of the local NHA staff was also crucial. In contrast with the Trenton authority, Danzig and his aides were able to use political skills to attract wary developers, build an alliance, and insulate that alliance from a range of diverse constituencies, thus permitting them to attract millions of dollars of investment into Newark. In the absence of these activities, the pattern of housing and commercial development would have been far different.[17] In shaping the renewal system, NHA's public entrepreneurs were motivated far less by a desire simply to "support" the private market than by a broader concern with Newark's future as a city—and by the lively and perhaps essential interest in enhancing their own power and reputation.

Once tentative agreement had been reached between these two central actors—NHA and a private developer—Danzig's staff negotiated with the

16. Ibid., pp. 26, 28.
17. From the vantage point of 1980, two students of Newark—no friends of NHA—underscore the beneficial impact of urban renewal on the city: "In the absence of the efforts that have gone into development the city would be far worse off than it is. The thousands of units of public housing, the improvement of transportation systems, and the economic growth that development has involved—not to mention the impact of physical construction on employment in the city—all these are and have been important to the city and kept bad from being the worst." Robert Curvin and Duane Lockard, "Newark: Another American Tragedy," typescript, 1980, p. 297.

Urban Renewal Administration and other federal funding sources. The regional URA office was under some pressure to support NHA proposals, since the New York and Philadelphia areas were strewn with vacant sites and incomplete renewal projects during the late 1950s and early 1960s. Even so, on some projects NHA spent several months working out detailed plans to meet the requirements of the private developer, URA, and other federal agencies.

At this stage, an agreed-upon project was taken to City Hall for ratification by the mayor and other officials. Local rejection at this time was "extremely unlikely," as Kaplan points out, since any effort to alter the project would "disrupt the balanced network of negotiations and probably stop the flow of capital into Newark."[18] Often the mayor was given the project plan shortly before a federal deadline for action, increasing the pressure for him to agree. The mayor also was permitted to announce the project, thus taking credit for the benefits expected to flow from the redevelopment activity. And by letting local political leaders get credit for its projects, NHA built support for its future efforts.

As a result of these complex, low-visibility operations, NHA was able to announce two or three new projects every year between 1957 and 1965. Underlying these results was a high level of planning and technical skill within the NHA staff, combined with considerable political sophistication. Equally important was the authority's deference to the basic imperative represented in the federal renewal laws: Urban renewal projects would have to meet the preferred goals of developers, and those goals generally involved central location, an attractive and relatively safe environment, and—crucial for most developers—the likelihood of making substantial profits. Consequently most of NHA's projects involved high-priced apartments or commercial and educational buildings in the downtown area.

The importance of political skill to NHA's activities can be seen most clearly in the way the authority staff dealt with constituencies other than those with which it was closely allied. One of the primary factors in determining whether an organization will be able to achieve its goals is its ability to restrict the intervention of other groups whose interests are affected by its actions. For NHA and other functional authorities, this task is made easier by narrow functional scope and often by access to external sources of funds. Nevertheless, as the Trenton Housing Authority experience shows, the urban renewal process offers considerable opportunities for outside intervention. NHA's staff devoted substantial amounts of energy to neutralizing potential sources of intervention. A large part of Harold Kaplan's book is devoted to describing these efforts, which included five major dimensions:

**Neutralizing the NHA commissioners.** Before 1948, NHA's commissioners frequently intervened both in project details and in the authority's general policies. During those years, executive directors at times "came to Board meetings without carefully prepared proposals, permitted aimless and chaotic debate among the commissioners, and often proved unable to answer questions" on NHA activities.[19] These conditions ended when Danzig took

18. Ibid., p. 30.
19. Ibid., p. 47.

over the authority, just when the agency prepared to expand into urban renewal. Danzig and his aides prepared the agenda, brought project proposals to the board after obtaining commitments from developers and federal agencies, and had a detailed knowledge of all issues that might be brought up at board meetings. Between 1948 and 1962, NHA's commissioners never modified a staff proposal, and its endorsements of the staff's recommendations were usually unanimous.

**Offering minor concessions to local political leaders.** Soon after he assumed the leadership of NHA, Danzig developed a working arrangement with Newark's elected officials. The city commissioners tacitly agreed not to interfere with general policies such as site selection and naming of redevelopers. In return, NHA's staff gave considerable weight to political sponsorship in making appointments to minor positions, as well as on matters having constituency impacts such as tenant selection and eviction. Many of these latter activities concerned NHA's public housing projects rather than urban renewal. Thus the authority was able to use its resources in one policy area to help maintain general control over another activity that NHA's staff regarded as more essential.[20]

**Denying the city planners a role.** Under state law, Newark's Central Planning Board (CPB) had important responsibilities in the field of urban renewal, since it was required to determine whether blight existed in a renewal site, and to certify that the redevelopment plan was consistent with the city's master plan.[21] Consequently, the city planners expected to be involved in the early stages of all NHA renewal planning. Danzig and his aides viewed the situation quite differently. Like Robert Moses and many other leaders of functional agencies, NHA's top staff viewed citywide planning as an infeasible, utopian ideal. Moreover, they recognized that to include the CPB as part of the main negotiating alliance would add both to the complexities of the process and to the range of interests that would have to be accommodated. Also, during this period the CPB lacked staff resources and thus could not be expected to add much to the renewal agency's analyses of complex economic or technical issues. Thus the NHA decided to confer with the planners only after a project had been formally announced, a position that was maintained despite occasional CPB grumbling.

**Winning the support of other city agencies.** As the Trenton Housing Authority learned to its dismay, renewal projects require support from local agencies involved in sewer relocation, street widening, and other public construction activities. NHA used the need for cooperation as an opportunity to

---

20. Compare the similar strategy of the Tennessee Valley Authority in electrical power generation and agricultural development; see Philip Selznick, *TVA and the Grass Roots* (Berkeley, Calif.: University of California Press, 1949), pp. 57 ff. For a discussion of comparable activities by the Port Authority, see Jameson W. Doig, *Metropolitan Transportation Politics and the New York Region* (New York: Columbia University Press, 1966), pp. 67 ff.

21. These powers were conferred on the Central Planning Board by the New Jersey Redevelopment Agencies Act of 1949, which empowered local agencies to take part in the federal renewal program.

strengthen its own position. NHA staff members pointed out to the Department of Public Works and other city agencies that they could expand their own activities if they participated in the growing, federally funded renewal program. The Board of Education was willing to cooperate in projects that included new schools, since part of the capital cost would be paid by the federal government. Such cooperative efforts between the NHA and local agencies made it more difficult for City Hall to control the NHA by direct manipulation of the one-third local share, or by encouraging dissension among the various city bureaucracies. Before the elected officials were brought into project planning, a complex net of mutual financial and psychological obligations had been woven by Danzig and his aides. And these other city agencies, having less concern than NHA with overall planning and development issues, left the formulation of particular projects in the hands of the executive director and his staff.

**Muting those to be displaced.** Many of NHA's projects required the demolition of residences and small business properties. Recognizing that the people who would be displaced formed an important potential source of opposition, the authority neutralized this threat in several ways. Most important was the strategy of silence—a lack of publicity about new projects until support had been obtained from the Urban Renewal Administration, developers, other city agencies that would be involved, and the elected officials. When a project was announced, NHA was required by the federal government to provide detailed information on relocation requirements, but this information—some of which suggested ways tenants could resist vacating renewal sites—was conveyed in only cursory fashion. Moreover, NHA kept in close contact with leaders of the black community, where most of the displacement occurred, and authority officials were able to convince them that on balance NHA efforts were helpful to their constituency. Vocal critics from the affected neighborhoods sometimes were given NHA jobs and other rewards. Because of these efforts, little effective opposition to authority projects developed during the first 15 years of renewal in Newark. Other constituencies, such as the downtown business community, also were attended to by NHA's politically sensitive leaders without hampering the basic structure of the authority-URA-developer alliance.

Thus its political skill enabled NHA to restrict the variety and intensity of constituency demands. While its counterpart in Trenton—with similar structural characteristics—succumbed to onslaughts from local interests in the early 1960s, the Newark agency kept these pressures at bay. Working in close alliance with private developers and federal funding agencies, NHA steadily expanded its renewal activities. By the end of 1966, the urban renewal alliance had produced 18 projects in Newark—either completed or in process—covering more than 2,400 acres. NHA's program ranked fifth in the country in terms of federal funding, and as the authority exclaimed in a brochure entitled *City Alive!*: "the strength and vision generated by this alliance of government and business have enabled Newark to undertake more urban renewal, on a per capita basis, than any other major city in the nation."[22]

22. Newark Housing Authority, *City Alive!* (Newark: 1966), p. 6.

## The Fragile Structure of Newark's Success

"In the world of urban renewal," Harold Kaplan commented when the Newark Housing Authority was riding high in the early 1960s, "project building seems to yield more project building. . . . After a certain point successful agencies can do nothing wrong. They are rarely involved in political skirmishes because they are rarely challenged."[23] In a few short years, however, the world of urban renewal in Newark collapsed. Constituencies that had been quiescent became active and influential. Ghetto blacks, whose previous role in renewal had been only an occasional irritant, became a major force. This challenge to NHA's policies—sparked by an ill-conceived proposal to use a huge tract of land in the ghetto for a state medical college, and dramatized by a devastating riot in 1967—fundamentally altered the politics of redevelopment in Newark. Faced with new and intense pressures, the alliance that had shaped urban renewal shivered and fell apart. Federal and state roles altered sharply; private developers faded in importance; Danzig, the skillful public entrepreneur who had molded and maintained the renewal alliance in Newark, departed. And the most "successful" urban renewal program in the New York region lost much of its capacity to make a significant impact on the pattern of development in Newark.[24]

Underlying these changes was increased dissatisfaction and political activism on the part of Newark's black residents. Rapid escalation of ghetto demands for more relevant programs and a meaningful role in the development process occurred in cities across the nation in the early 1960s. In Newark as elsewhere, blacks began to question programs that provided neither benefits nor a meaningful role for community and minority interests. By the mid-1960s, Newark's urban renewal had cleared nearly 6,000 dwelling units in neighborhoods selected by NHA for redevelopment. Yet 40,000 of the city's 136,000 housing units remained below national standards, giving Newark the highest proportion of substandard housing of any major city in the United States. From the perspective of NHA, "housing conditions in Newark [were] better than they have been in our time."[25] But for ghetto dwellers, housing conditions were "indescribably bad."[26] Moreover, urban renewal reduced the amount of housing available to poor families. A tight housing market, poverty, and racial discrimination compromised the ability of NHA to relocate the uprooted in the "decent, safe, and sanitary" dwellings called for in the Housing Act of 1949. As a result, large numbers of those displaced by redevelopment were resettled in slum housing, where they often paid higher rents and soon were uprooted again by the public bulldozer. To a state investigating

23. Kaplan, *Urban Renewal Politics*, p. 35.

24. The discussion below is based mainly on the following sources: M. Duncan Grant, "Housing Authority Politics in Trenton and Newark"; Robert Curvin, "Black Power and Bureaucratic Change," Graduate Seminar Paper, Princeton University, December 1971; David Marshall, "Urban Renewal in Newark"; New Jersey, Governor's Select Commission on Civil Disorder, *Report for Action* (Trenton: 1968); and Harris David and J. Michael Callan, "Newark's Public Housing Rent Strike," *Clearinghouse Review*, 7 (1974), p. 581.

25. Louis H. Danzig, executive director, Newark Housing Authority, quoted in New Jersey, Governor's Select Commission on Civil Disorder, *Report for Action* (Trenton: 1968), p. 55.

26. Committee of Concern, a black civic group, quoted in "Asks Study of Violence," *Newark News*, July 18, 1967.

commission reporting in 1968, it seemed "paradoxical that so many housing successes could be tallied on paper and on bank ledgers, with so little impact on those the programs were meant to serve."[27]

Significant black opposition to NHA first emerged about 1960, in connection with the authority's effort to renew the Clinton Hill area of the black Central Ward. The Clinton Hill Neighborhood Council fought to protect the interests of the area's black residents. Also during the early 1960s, the Congress of Racial Equality and the Students for a Democratic Society generated protests on housing and other problems, such as job discrimination and police brutality. But these early efforts were sporadic, and made little impact on NHA and its allies. Newark's urban renewal alliance continued its normal pattern of decisionmaking well into the decade, with no significant involvement by the city's growing and increasingly alienated black community.

### The Medical College

Business as usual for NHA and its allies led to a spirited effort to persuade the trustees of the New Jersey College of Medicine and Dentistry to locate the state medical school in Newark. From NHA's perspective, the prospect of attracting the $60 million educational facility was another potential milestone in the process of converting "badly used land to higher and better uses," another step in making Newark a "city alive."[28] Danzig, Mayor Hugh Addonizio, and other city officials met privately with the medical school's trustees, while the city's newspapers and downtown business leadership waged an intensive public campaign during 1966 to convince the college that central Newark was a better site than suburban Madison in Morris County, the location preferred by most of the school's officials.

Initially, NHA and the city government offered the medical school a 20-acre site in the Fairmount Urban Renewal Project. The trustees responded by praising Newark as a potential home for the medical school, but insisted that the college needed 150 acres, presumably much more land than could be made available in crowded central Newark. NHA and City Hall were dismayed, but not ready to quit despite the college officials' obvious desire for a suburban location. If the medical school had to have 150 acres, Newark would provide 185 acres in the black Central Ward. A city official later explained the strategy developed by Newark in the fall of 1966:

> We thought we would surprise them . . . and we drew a 185-acre area which we considered to be the worst slum area. It included Fairmount and surrounding areas, which was clearly in need of renewal, and we were going to proceed with the renewal in any case in that area. . . . We felt in the end they would come down to 20 or 30 acres in Fairmount, or in a battle we might have to give up some more acreage. We never felt they would ask for 185. We felt it was a ploy on their part.[29]

27. Governor's Select Commission on Civil Disorder, *Report for Action*, p. 55.
28. Newark Housing Authority, *City Alive!* p. 8.
29. M. Donald Malafronte, assistant to Mayor Hugh J. Addonizio, quoted in Governor's Select Commission on Civil Disorder, *Report for Action*, pp. 12–13.

Responding to Newark's bold offer, the medical school continued to demand 150 acres. The trustees then upped the ante by specifying that the college would come to Newark only if NHA and the city government were able within 10 weeks to "complete legal and financial assurances that will provide the college with a site of some 50 acres upon which it would begin initial construction by March 1, 1968 . . . [and] irrevocably commit approximately 100 additional acres for future college use to be promptly cleared and deeded to the college as the need for the land is determined . . . solely by the trustees."[30] To make things even more difficult for the city, the initial fifty acres was not to come from cleared land in the Fairmount urban renewal site. For city officials, the trustees' demand for uncleared land "was a slap in the face. . . . It was our opinion that they were attempting to get out of the situation. . . . What they wanted was across the street from cleared land. This to us was insanity and enraging because they knew this was not an urban renewal area. They knew that the urban renewal process is three years and perhaps five."[31]

Despite the dismay over the trustees' intransigent position, Newark's leaders were determined to secure the prize of the medical college. The medical school's offer was accepted in December, with the mayor expressing confidence that "we can meet all the provisions set by the trustees."[32] To ensure quick assembly of the initial 50-acre parcel, the city was prepared to use its power of condemnation, and NHA was ready to cut back other urban renewal projects to make funds available to underwrite land acquisition for the medical school. Trenton offered a helping hand, as the state legislature with the blessing of Governor Hughes authorized Newark to condemn land for the college, and to extend its debt limit by $15 million to provide the funds for the initial land acquisition. Support also came from NHA's allies in Washington. Officials at the Department of Housing and Urban Development (HUD) agreed to the methods employed by Newark in shortcutting the normal urban renewal procedures for the medical college. They also, in Mayor Addonizio's words, assured "us it will qualify as an urban renewal project."[33]

During the complicated bargaining that brought the medical college to Newark, none of the principals paid much attention to the views of the several thousand black families living in the 150-acre target area. For proponents of the project, replacement of a ramshackle black neighborhood by the medical school meant new vitality for Newark, $15 million in new jobs, and the elimination of a slum that was estimated to cost the city $380,000 more annually in public services than it generated in taxes. But from the perspective of the Central Ward's black dwellers, a medical school "in the heart of the ghetto," like Newark's "vast programs for urban renewal, highways, [and]

30. Statement of the Board of Trustees of the New Jersey College of Medicine and Dentistry, quoted in Malcolm M. Mamber, "Newark Is Given March 1 Deadline to Provide Medical Center Land," *Newark Sunday News*, December 11, 1966.

31. Malafronte, quoted in Governor's Select Commission on Civil Disorder, *Report for Action*, pp. 13–14.

32. Mayor Hugh J. Addonizio, quoted in Bob Shabazian, "City Pledges Land Med School Asked," *Newark News*, December 23, 1966.

33. Quoted in "Council Pledges Med School Funds," *Newark News*, December 27, 1966.

downtown development . . . seemed almost deliberately designed to squeeze out [the] rapidly growing Negro community that represents a majority of the population."[34]

In NHA's vast renewal projects of previous years, grass-roots protest had been haphazard and ineffective. But by 1967, the black population in Newark had grown to a majority, and the increasing political sophistication of black citizens and their organizations made it possible to develop sustained opposition to this latest renewal scheme. Resistance to the medical school plan mounted rapidly in the Central Ward during the spring of 1967. Residents of the target area enlisted the support of many black leaders in organizing the Committee Against Negro Removal, which argued that the medical college's benefits to the city "would be less than the misery it would cost."[35] Newark's antipoverty agency, the United Community Corporation, publicly opposed the project. Underlying black opposition to the medical college was a lack of communication between official Newark and the ghetto, development priorities that largely ignored the poor, and the pervasive fear of relocation. Commenting on the third factor, a state commission later emphasized:

> Many residents did not believe official reassurances on this subject. People hear that in the past families have been displaced by urban renewal and forced to live wherever they could, and they see few vacant apartments of decent quality in which they know they can afford to live. The statistics on the quality of vacancies support the view of the people in the area. . . . The Medical College case simply brought these fears to a head.[36]

The rising chorus of black protest made little impression on NHA and City Hall, which focused their energies on the difficult task of meeting the medical college's stipulations. Negotiations between HUD representatives and city officials led to a federal agreement to rush $15 million to Newark to aid the project. Mayor Addonizio and NHA then pressed for City Planning Board approval of the large area as blighted, and the board held blight hearings in May and June. Despite vociferous opposition from blacks at the hearings, NHA was ready to move forward rapidly with clearance.

But NHA's opponents did not fade away as they had in the past. Discontent over the medical college combined with another racial controversy—in school politics, where the appointment of a white official to a top Board of Education post drew vigorous black protests—to make black Newark a tinderbox. The spark was provided by a confrontation between blacks and the police, and a devastating six-day riot erupted in July 1967. When the smoke cleared from the Central Ward, 26 were dead and over $10 million in property had been destroyed. Black dissatisfaction with the medical school project in particular, and the city's renewal process in general, had been tragically underscored.[37] Business as usual was over for the Newark Housing Authority.

34. Tom Hayden, *Rebellion in Newark* (New York: Vintage, 1967), p. 6.
35. See Douglas Eldridge, "Displacees Fight Med School Site," *Newark News*, January 11, 1967.
36. Governor's Select Commission on Civil Disorders, *Report for Action*, pp. 61–62.
37. The riot and its causes are summarized in *Report for Action*, especially Chapter One. On the evaluation of protests against the medical school project, see Grant, pp. 126–131.

### The Collapse of the Urban Renewal Alliance

Of the Newark riot's many lessons, one of the clearest was the hostility of the city's black population to urban renewal and the kind of "successes" produced by NHA and its allies. With their opposition to the medical school and NHA's approach traumatically dramatized, black interests were able to enlist new allies in their opposition to the renewal alliance, and to exercise increasing influence within the city. The state government abandoned its passive role, and became an active participant in the effort to redesign the medical school project. Federal policy also changed, placing more emphasis on relocation needs and on community involvement in the renewal process. Within three years of the riot, the growing numbers of blacks and increased political sophistication resulted in the election of a black mayor in Newark. These and related changes eroded the independent power of the Newark Housing Authority, and thus destroyed the basis for the alliance which NHA had so skillfully constructed in the 1950s.

Traditionally, state officials in Trenton had deferred to the federal/local alliance in determining the direction of renewal programs, becoming active only to facilitate agreements already made by the alliance when legislation or other state concurrence was required. As noted above, this approach had been followed on the medical school, as Governor Hughes signed legislation in March permitting Newark to condemn, buy, and sell the land needed for the 150 acres demanded by the trustees. Two weeks after the riot, however, the state administration began to reverse its course. Hughes and his aides pressed the medical school to reduce the campus to 50 acres. They sought to convince the city to use the remaining land for low-income housing, child care, health centers, and other community projects. State officials also urged the city to ensure that representatives of the renewal area take part in planning for the projects. Little support for the state's proposal came from NHA and City Hall, which were fearful of losing the medical school, and of sharing their power over redevelopment decisions with the rebellious ghetto. Equally unresponsive was the medical college, whose president continued to insist that "we have a contract for 150 acres," and whose trustees responded to pressure by threatening to seek a site outside Newark in the suburbs.[38]

The resistance of NHA and elected Newark officials to the state initiatives ensured that state officials would become central participants in working out a compromise between the city, the medical school, and the host of local interests now seeking a piece of the action. At this juncture the state's efforts received a powerful assist from Washington, for HUD would not approve the use of urban renewal funds to clear the site in the face of strong community protests, and in the absence of an acceptable relocation plan. Responding to these pressures, the city and the medical school reduced the campus to 98.2 acres, and shifted the site slightly to reduce the number of families to be relocated.

These proposals, however, did not satisfy black demands on relocation and participation. At this point, Washington sided with the neighborhood forces. Early in 1968, HUD and the Department of Health, Education and Wel-

---

38. Dr. Robert A. Cadmus, quoted in Ladley K. Pierson, "Med School Debate Seen 'Historic,'" *Newark News*, March 3, 1968.

*The completed campus of the New Jersey College of Medicine and Dentistry. Even though the plans for the campus were scaled down after the Newark riot, a large amount of land still was cleared for the project, displacing low-income blacks from housing similar to that surrounding the campus.*    Credit: New Jersey Housing Finance Agency

fare—which provided much of the funding for construction of the medical college—indicated that the $43-million in urban renewal and medical facility grants would be approved only if there were agreement with the community on seven issues: (1) the amount of land to be used by the college; (2) community health services to be provided by the medical school; (3) relocation of residents from the campus site; (4) employment practices during construction of the school; (5) employment and training policies of the college; (6) future housing programs in Newark; and (7) community participation in the federal Model Cities program, which was just getting underway in Newark.

In the face of these federal, state, and community pressures, Newark officials and the medical college had no alternative but to compromise. The college agreed to limit its campus to 57.9 acres, and to provide a wide range of community and medical training services. City Hall and NHA agreed that neighborhood representatives would have a veto over development programs in the area surrounding the college, as well as a role in planning the construction of new housing in the city. In addition, the state promised to provide rent supplements where necessary for the 580 families on the site, each of whom was guaranteed relocation.[39]

NHA emerged from these negotiations a much weaker organization. In the future, it would have to share important powers with neighborhood interests, most of whom were hostile to the agency. Equally important, NHA could no longer count on the support of federal renewal officials. As we have seen, NHA's central role in urban renewal was closely linked to the financial support and program concurrence of the agency's federal allies. Before the riot, HUD had rushed to provide $15 million in support of the medical school project. Now, HUD was dealing directly with representatives of Newark's black and Puerto Rican communities, supporting their demands for improved relocation practices, and insisting that these groups be represented in NHA decision making. Moreover, as the complex negotiations over the medical college evolved after the riot, the role of state and community representatives became increasingly important, and NHA faded into a relatively minor role. The traditional pattern of NHA leadership was broken.

Not long after the medical school negotiations were completed, Louis Danzig resigned as NHA executive director. Danzig cited reasons of health, but he obviously was dissatisfied with the restricted role of his Authority in the medical college project and other programs in the post-riot era. In any event, the most important individual in making the renewal alliance work was gone. Moreover, his successor, promoted from within the agency, lacked the basic ability and political skills of a Louis Danzig.

At the same time that NHA was losing its control over the renewal process, the agency came under attack from the residents of its housing projects. NHA's tenants traditionally had been submissive, and had acquiesced in the authority's strategy of creating and controlling "tenant" groups. But the rising political consciousness of Newark's poor blacks and Hispanics, combined with their success in the medical school negotiations, led to increased militancy among residents of NHA's massive public housing projects. Independent tenants' associations were organized in 1968 and the following year a rent strike was initiated in protest against inadequate NHA facilities, repair programs, and safety measures. A second rent strike began in 1970 and continued for more than four years. The second strike had a particularly devastating effect on NHA's financial position, as several million dollars in rent payments were withheld from the agency during these years.

As the second rent strike began, NHA's ally in City Hall, Mayor Hugh Addonizio, was challenged at the polls by a black candidate, Kenneth A. Gibson, who was supported by a broad coalition of community and minority interests. One of Gibson's major campaign themes was to attack NHA's renewal policies and housing management programs. Gibson also endorsed the rent

39. The state also pledged that at least one-third of the journeymen and one-half of the apprentices employed in the construction of the college would be black or Puerto Rican. For the details of the final agreement, see Paul N. Ylvisaker, "What Are the Problems of Health Care Delivery in Newark?," in John Norman, ed., *Medicine in the Ghetto* (New York: Appleton-Century-Crofts, 1972), pp. 108–116.

strike. His election in June 1970 as Newark's first black mayor severed another tie that had supported NHA policies and independence. City Hall now joined the federal government, state officials, and community groups in insisting that NHA pursue different objectives and be more responsive to lower-income needs.

Another blow fell on NHA from the agency's one-time allies in HUD. Increasing concern on the part of federal officials about the administrative and financial capacity of the authority led to an investigation of NHA by HUD in early 1971. The resulting report criticized management inefficiency in the authority and urged that NHA be split into two separate agencies, one for public housing management and the other for urban renewal programs. The authority resisted dismemberment, and HUD retaliated by threatening to cut off all federal funds unless NHA complied.[40] This impasse gave Mayor Gibson an opportunity to act as mediator. He persuaded HUD to provide emergency funds to meet utility bills and other immediate costs, and to drop its demand for complete separation of housing and renewal functions. In return, NHA consented to accept a "consultant" designated by Gibson, providing the mayor a means to exercise considerable influence over the authority's decision making. Thus, power over NHA actions shifted toward the mayor's office, although conflict between Gibson and the city council prevented the mayor from exerting commanding influence over the authority.[41] Meanwhile, the rent strike continued until 1974, and NHA limped along, little more than a pale shadow of its former position as one of the nation's preeminent renewal authorities.

In the years since 1974, the mayor's office has used its appointing power, federal guidelines, and its negotiating skills to increase its control over NHA activities, turning the authority into an arm of City Hall's development efforts. Those efforts, which have included several housing, commercial and industrial projects, have had a modest impact on economic vitality and housing quality in Newark.[42] But the evidence bearing on the central theme of this discussion—the impact and strategies of a functionally autonomous development agency—ends with the NHA's collapse in the early 1970s.

### The NHA's Urban Renewal Program in Retrospect

At each point in the series of events that reduced NHA's capacity to influence development, one might ask, would the urban renewal alliance have survived had this or that factor not been present? For example, would Newark's development still be shaped by a vigorous, relatively independent renewal alliance if there had been no medical school project? Or if there had been no major riot in 1967? Perhaps, but in view of the broader demographic and political changes in Newark during the 1960s, the nature of that alliance

40. See U.S. Department of Housing and Urban Development, (Newark Area Office), "Comprehensive Consolidated Management Review Report of the Newark Housing Authority" (Newark: January 1971).

41. During 1971–1973, the city council turned down three of Gibson's five nominees to the NHA, and as Gibson's first term drew to a close at the end of 1973, only three of the six NHA commissioners were Gibson appointees.

42. See Newark Redevelopment and Housing Authority, *1977 Annual Report* (Newark: 1978) and Greater Newark Chamber of Commerce, *The Newark Experience, 1967–1977* (Newark: 1978).

probably would have been significantly changed, and the pace of renewal greatly slowed. Similar forces were at work elsewhere in the region's older cities, with similar overall impact on urban development, as illustrated in the discussion of New York City in the next section.

The rise and fall of the Newark Housing Authority underscores some general points that are important to an understanding of the variables that determine whether a governmental agency will be able to concentrate resources over time to influence urban development. NHA's experience emphasizes the crucial role an organization's leaders can play in determining the impact of constituency factors and the availability of funds. Robert Dahl's comments on urban renewal in New Haven apply to Newark as well. "Changes in the physical organization of the city," he notes, "entail changes in social, economic, and political organization." To develop a coalition that can continue to operate effectively amid such changes demands unusual leadership abilities. A strategic plan must be "discovered, formulated, presented, and constantly reinterpreted and reinforced." The skills required to identify the grounds on which coalitions can be formed, the "assiduous and unending dedication to the task of maintaining alliances over long periods, the unremitting search for measures that will unify rather than disrupt the alliance: these are the tasks and skills of politicians."[43] In Newark's successful urban renewal program, these political dimensions were located in the authority's headquarters rather than at City Hall. Because of these skills, the alliance grew and prospered, federal funds flowed in, and Newark like New Haven won a national reputation for urban renewal productivity.

As necessary as it is to construct a supporting coalition, the strategies used to neutralize potential opposition are equally crucial. The events recounted above illustrate the importance of these strategies. They also suggest the impact of constituency changes, which can generate serious resistance and undermine an apparently firm alliance. Opposition stemming from alterations in constituency factors may affect an agency or an alliance only in minor ways, or more centrally. An area of agency policy may be attacked, to be followed by remedial efforts that reaffirm or even strengthen the organization and its ability to achieve its goals. But other attacks from aroused constituencies can go to the "heartland" of an institution, fundamentally altering its direction and effectiveness, and perhaps impairing its ability to function at all. The Newark Housing Authority is a "heartland" case as far as its urban renewal program is concerned.

The NHA case in particular illustrates the potential importance of new constituencies that arise and become politically relevant to an agency. The ability of these groups to exert political influence may depend not only on increased numbers, wealth, and other "internal" resources, but also on *dramatic incidents*—or more precisely on a group's ability to link its concerns with such dramatic incidents which can generate support among other constituencies that are already influential in the policy arena. The leaders of successful functional agencies and alliances are often vulnerable to such strategies, being more likely than most political leaders to develop a "trained

43. Robert A. Dahl, *Who Governs? Democracy and Power in an American City* (New Haven, Conn.: Yale University Press, 1961), pp. 201–202.

incapacity" to perceive and respond to these new constituencies. Compared with leaders of less "successful" agencies and with elected officials, their ability to scan the political horizon for new threats and challenges becomes attenuated. They come to believe, with Kaplan, that "after a certain point successful agencies can do nothing wrong." This was the fatal weakness of Danzig and his allies in the late 1960s, just as it was a limitation of Robert Moses in his slum clearance activities in New York City a decade earlier, and of the leaders of the Port Authority in the early 1970s. Thus, we see that "some princes flourish one day and come to grief the next"; for such a leader, "having always prospered by proceeding one way, . . . cannot persuade himself to change."[44]

## Enlarging the Renewal Arena

Mobilization of new constituency interests also brought fundamental changes to urban renewal in New York City during the 1960s. New York's urban renewal program was initially directed by Robert Moses, who brought his distinctive entrepreneurial style to the city's Slum Clearance Committee. As indicated earlier, Moses undertook a vast renewal program, clearing hundreds of acres for the construction of luxury apartments and a variety of educational, cultural, and health facilities. Particularly devastating for the poor were the relocation practices of the Slum Clearance Committee. Responsibility for relocation was turned over to the private sponsor, along with title to the property to be redeveloped. In one project:

> 82 percent of the tenants received neither moving nor rehousing assistance or payments. Many residents had been handed eviction notices without court orders. Others were merely "relocated" to remaining buildings on the site (thus continuing the sponsor's income), although the buildings had no heat, hot water, or basic maintenance, and in spite of the fact that such rerenting was against City laws.[45]

Moses' relocation practices, along with urban redevelopment's conspicuous failure to improve housing conditions for the poor, produced increasingly vocal demands for fundamental changes in New York City's renewal program. Of the many battles fought in the city, perhaps the most significant was the prolonged struggle on Manhattan's West Side between representatives of the poor and New York's urban renewal alliance.[46] Conceived in the mid-1950s, urban renewal on the West Side was designed to restore a rapidly deteriorating neighborhood to its former role as a bastion of the upper middle class. The city's original plan for the West Side Urban Renewal Area called for 5,000

---

44. Niccolo Machiavelli, *The Prince*, translated by George Bull (Baltimore: Penguin, 1961), Chapter 25.

45. Jeanne R. Lowe, *Cities in a Race with Time* (New York: Random House, 1967), p. 83. Moses's urban renewal activities also are discussed in Robert A. Caro, *The Power Broker: Robert Moses and the Fall of New York* (New York: Knopf, 1974), pp. 703 ff.

46. For a detailed discussion of urban renewal on the West Side, and particularly the role of neighborhood groups, see J. Clarence Davies, *Neighborhood Groups and Urban Renewal* (New York: Columbia University Press, 1966), pp. 110 ff.

luxury apartments and 2,400 middle-income units. For the West Side's poor, urban renewal planners offered a pittance—only 400 of the 7,800 apartments would be low-income public housing. To clear land for the project, 6,000 families would have to be relocated. Most of these were Puerto Ricans and blacks, and many had previously been displaced by Moses's upper-income Manhattantown renewal project to the north, and his largely nonresidential Coliseum and Lincoln Center projects to the south.

Announcement of these plans provoked immediate neighborhood demands for more low- and middle-income housing. In response, urban renewal officials changed the housing mix from 5,000–2,400–400 to 3,600–3,600–600. Opponents rejected these modifications, which increased the low-income share by only 200 units, as inadequate in the light of the area's housing needs and the dislocations that urban renewal would cause. To press their case more effectively with the city, local resources were mobilized through the organization of the Strycker's Bay Neighborhood Council, a coalition of block associations, ethnic groupings, parent-teacher organizations, and political clubs. As Davies points out, the campaign was facilitated by the presence of middle-class residents, who supported a wide range of community organizations. Foremost among these were the liberal, issue-oriented, reform Democratic clubs that dominated political life on the West Side during the second decade after World War II. Most of the poor in the target area were Puerto Ricans, and their influence in negotiations with the city was enhanced by the assistance of representatives from the Commonwealth of Puerto Rico, whose officials commanded more attention at City Hall than did local Puerto Rican leaders. After three years of intensive political activity, the West Side coalition won substantial compromises from the city, with the final plan calling for 2,000 luxury apartments, 4,900 middle-income dwellings, and 2,500 units of public housing, a more than sixfold increase in the number of low-income homes over the city's original proposal.

Virtually every renewal project developed in the region's older cities in the 1960s reflected the increased political influence of the poor, and the greater willingness of renewal agencies to respond to minority and low-income city dwellers. Other grass-roots interests also were listened to, making urban renewal no more easy to undertake in working-class ethnic neighborhoods than in impoverished black or Hispanic communities. Greater involvement of the heterogeneous constituencies of the older cities has had a predictable impact on the ability of urban renewal agencies to concentrate resources on development goals, as Jeanne Lowe points out in an analysis of renewal in the 1960s:

> The more the city tried to please the people, the slower execution of the program became, and the more government subsidy was required. In fact, so much time was spent listening to the people and trying to make plans acceptable to diverse community and citywide groups that it was hard to advance projects. The city agency had to deal not only with the officially recognized local renewal councils; self-appointed spokesmen for various communities and independent citizens committees also would spring up in project areas. Often the latter developed plans which, they maintained, more truly represented what the community

desired, and the newspapers were quick to pick up the protests of any articulate critic.[47]

Moreover, citizen groups urged that housing programs be used to advance a great variety of social goals, including "balanced neighborhoods, community preservation, integration or deghettoization." As Lowe comments, few city officials or community advocates were willing to admit, however, that "these goals could not coexist within one project area, or perhaps were impossible to realize," given financial constraints and sharp divisions in priorities and attitudes within local communities.[48]

Many of these problems were illustrated by the efforts of the Lindsay administration to focus redevelopment resources in the poorest areas of New York City, and to involve residents of target areas in the planning and development of renewal projects. Awaiting John Lindsay when he took office in January 1966 was a $3.25 million planning commission study of housing and renewal which urged City Hall to concentrate its renewal activities where they were needed most, "in the Harlems and Bedford-Stuyvesants of the city."[49] Immediately after the report's release, HUD indicated that all future renewal projects in New York City would be evaluated in terms of the ghetto priorities established by the planning commission. Within six months, the Lindsay administration had moved to concentrate its urban renewal resources in Harlem, Central Brooklyn, and the South Bronx. One of the first neighborhoods chosen for renewal was Fulton Park in Bedford-Stuyvesant, a black community where 60 percent of the housing units were unsound. Another new target area was a section of Central Harlem with residential densities in excess of 150,000 people per square mile. The last of the three neighborhoods chosen was Bronxchester, a blighted industrial area lacking a single adequate home among more than 900 dwelling units.

Lindsay's renewal priorities were strongly endorsed in a 1966 report prepared for the mayor by Edward J. Logue, who had directed large redevelopment programs in New Haven and Boston, and who soon would become director of New York State's Urban Development Corporation. To bring renewal closer to the people, Logue urged the creation of area administrators to direct redevelopment within the target areas. Area administrators were named in 1967 as part of the reorganization of the city's housing agencies into the Housing and Development Administration. The new Housing and Development Administrator called "decentralization . . . essential to the effectiveness of urban renewal,"[50] while his deputy believed that the poor should control the redevelopment of their communities.[51]

Despite these changes and the commitment of top officials, renewal strategies focused on the needs of the poor proved extremely difficult to

47. Lowe, *Cities in a Race with Time*, pp. 104–105.
48. Ibid., p. 105.
49. New York City, City Planning Commission, Community Renewal Program, *New York City's Renewal Strategy/1965* (New York: 1965), p. 44.
50. Jason R. Nathan, quoted in Steven V. Roberts, "City to Decentralize the Administration of Urban Renewal," *New York Times*, January 16, 1967.
51. The official was Eugene S. Callender, who headed the New York Urban League before joining the Lindsay Administration; see Steven V. Roberts, "Top Role for Poor in Housing Urged," *New York Times*, December 17, 1967.

implement. A basic problem was the nature of urban renewal. The federal program, with its heavy dependence on the private developer, was not designed with the poor in mind, a reality that no amount of rhetoric by local or federal officials could alter. Without substantial public subsidies beyond those involved in the acquisition and improvement of land for redevelopment, the economics of urban renewal's public-private partnership were not easily met. Moreover, private developers were wary of investing in an urban renewal project that included substantial amounts of low-income housing. In the West Side renewal area, only 1,500 of the negotiated 2,500 low-income units were built, largely because developers persuaded city officials that too much public housing would jeopardize the market for the project's luxury and middle-income apartments.

Involving a wide range of interests in renewal—particularly in poorer areas where a variety of new groups and leaders jockeyed for influence— inevitably delayed the development and implementation of projects. Community participation is a confusing and time-consuming process. "A community always comes up with 60 different ideas," a New York official points out; "there is never any unanimity."[52] Complicating the process further was the emergence in the late 1960s of a group of community participants skilled in the politics of development, many of whom were employed in antipoverty, Model Cities, and other inner-city programs. To satisfy these varied constituencies, renewal agencies tended to propose more projects than they could handle, to promise more than they could deliver, and to find themselves enmeshed in ever more complex funding, policy making, and administrative arrangements. Perhaps a bit wistfully, New York's top housing and renewal official told a reporter in 1969 that there was no turning back the clock to the less complex and more productive arrangements of urban renewal's early years: "You can't do it any other way today. The old Moses approach of condemning 700,000 units of housing and expecting everybody to sit still— those glorious unsophisticated days are gone."[53]

## The Lesson of Urban Renewal

Urban renewal provided the region's older cities with a potential means of concentrating resources on development objectives. Federal renewal funds increased the resources available to the city for shaping the pattern of development. But the Housing Act of 1949 predicated renewal on the involvement of private developers, which meant that local renewal objectives had to be congruent with those of developers. Within this context, skillful leaders such as Danzig in Newark or Moses in New York could concentrate substantial resources on whatever objectives were shared by the renewal agency and developers. The result was a set of activities in some of the region's cities that indeed did shape development—by improving downtown areas, increasing

52. Eugene S. Callender, deputy administrator, Housing and Redevelopment Administration, quoted in Roberts, "Top Role for Poor in Housing Urged."

53. Jason R. Nathan, Housing and Development Administrator, quoted in David K. Shipler, "Urban Renewal Giving the Poor Opportunity to Increase Power," *New York Times*, November 9, 1969.

the supply of upper-income housing, and adding important cultural and educational facilities.

"Success" in these terms depended heavily on insulating the urban renewal process from the demands of diverse constituencies. Over time, the impact of renewal projects on city neighborhoods, along with broader demographic and political developments, eroded the protective wall that successful agencies had constructed. Responding to the same set of changes, federal officials revised the rules of urban renewal in ways that enhanced the role of neighborhood, minority, and lower-income interests. Urban renewal survived these changes, but in the process lost much of its particular capability to concentrate resources in the older cities. Instead renewal became another program in the older cities, beset with all the problems of other development activities. Renewal programs continued to achieve some successes, as land was cleared and new facilities such as the New Jersey College of Medicine and Dentistry constructed. The result was programs more responsive to the needs of the diverse constituencies of the older cities, and certainly programs less disruptive to the interests of the poor. At the same time, renewal agencies lost the capacity to concentrate resources possessed by NHA under Danzig or by Moses and his Slum Clearance Committee.

# 10

---

# Patterns of Government Action

---

Standing silent as two ghosts through most of this study, the twin towers of the World Trade Center now step forward. For in a curious but powerful way, sensed but not fully understood by the citizens of the region or by visitors, the Trade Center symbolizes the urban metropolis in its power, its energy, its complexity, and its waste. What Mont-Saint-Michel was to the eleventh century, a stupendous product of the combined energies of Church and State, a symbol of what was valued most highly in society, the Port Authority's two 110-story towers are to America in the late twentieth century.

Mont-Saint-Michel was erected on the coast of France, on a giant rock of granite from which, as Henry Adams reports, "the eye plunges down . . . to the wide sands or wider ocean, as the tides recede or advance, under an infinite sky, over a restless sea. . . . " Inside this Norman church, we find "Church and State, Soul and Body, God and Man are all one. . . . " Yet the structure is "ambitious, restless, striving for effect," and the "overmastering strength of the eleventh century is stamped on a great scale" in the spans, the transepts, and the triumphal columns.[1]

To anyone who has visited the Port Authority's massive towers, the resemblance of the two structures must already be apparent. Moreover, like the great church, the World Trade Center symbolizes the joining of major forces—now economic and political—to shape modern society and the modern metropolis. Thus the Center illustrates our view, elaborated throughout this volume, that government is not a passive or ineffectual institution, that Wood and Vernon and their colleagues erred in concluding that "public programs and public policies are of little consequence" in the urban region.[2]

The development of the World Trade Center also underscores the complexity of the economic and political forces that shape growth and change in the modern metropolis. In this case, the key elements were influential commercial interests, bureaucratic egotism, political rivalry, and substantive concerns with improving economic vitality and transportation, which combined to produce "the most important project for the economic future of the Port of New York launched for many a year."[3]

---

1. Henry Adams, *Mont-Saint-Michel and Chartres* (Boston: Houghton Mifflin, 1913), pp. 1, 7–8.

2. Robert C. Wood, with Vladimir V. Almendinger, *1400 Governments* (Cambridge, Mass.: Harvard University Press, 1961), p. 175.

3. "Downtown's Big Future," editorial, *New York Times*, January 27, 1960. As the project proceeded, it was given other characterizations and titles, some of them not so favorable: a "UN of

A crucial element in the creation of this new building project was the desire of David Rockefeller and other downtown Manhattan business leaders for such a complex—as a focal point of their effort to maintain lower Manhattan's position as the "dominant center of finance, world trade and shipping." After a preliminary study of lower Manhattan's future, Rockefeller and his colleagues urged in 1960 that a complex of buildings devoted to world trade be constructed on the East River south of the Brooklyn Bridge. The complex would include one structure fifty to seventy stories high, and several smaller buildings, with a total price tag of $250 million. The downtown business leaders urged that the Port Authority, with its large planning staff and interest in international commerce, make a more detailed study of the value and feasibility of the project.[4]

The Port Authority's response in this case was not simply to "ride with ... the main currents in the private sector."[5] Instead, the port agency saw the proposal as a well-timed, well-placed opportunity. First, the project would provide an opportunity for the authority to aid in the economic growth of the Port District, a goal clearly included in its statutory purposes.[6]

But the World Trade Center proposal had far more to commend it to the authority's staff than its economic development potential. Throughout the 1950s, the Port Authority had been continuously engaged in public debates and private negotiations regarding its proper role in mass transportation. As recounted in Chapter Seven, the authority had financed the MRTC study and had hoped that a transit district would be formed to remove the rail transit albatross from its own neck. When that strategy foundered, the agency agreed reluctantly in 1959 to take part in Governor Rockefeller's commuter-car program, and it had broken ranks with its fellow highway coalition member, the New Jersey Turnpike Authority, endorsing the view that excess Turnpike tolls should be devoted to mass transit. Meanwhile, most of the region's commuter railroads teetered on the edge of bankruptcy; the Port Authority was under renewed attack because of its alleged indifference to the transit problem and because of its efforts outlined in Chapter Four to locate a site for a fourth jetport; and the authority's ability to resist deep involvement in deficit rail operations was increasingly precarious as its reserves mounted—from $37 million in 1956 to $65 million in 1958 to $79 million in 1960.

For the authority, association with the World Trade Center project offered an opportunity to brighten an image tarnished by its jetport forays and

Trade," "Manhattan's Tower of Babel," and "the Colossus Nobody Seems to Love." These and other views of the center are summarized in Thomas Schiavoni, "The Port of New York Authority's World Trade Center," Senior Thesis, Princeton University, 1972, Chapter 1. The discussion in this section draws upon Schiavoni's perceptive analysis and on the documents he gathered in the course of his investigation.

4. See Downtown-Lower Manhattan Association, *World Trade Center* (New York, 1960), p. 3, and *Planning for Lower Manhattan: Third Report* (New York, 1969), pp. 6–7. The association included top officials of major banks, utilities, shipping companies, and other corporations between Canal Street and the lower tip of Manhattan.

5. Wood, *1400 Governments*, p. 174.

6. Preliminary assessments by the RPA and the *New York Times* concurred with the Rockefeller group's report that the project would have a favorable impact on the region. See for example Regional Plan Association, press release, April 12, 1961 and "Downtown's Big Future," editorial, *New York Times*, January 27, 1960.

its mass-transit aversion. Moreover, if the Port Authority's study showed the Center to be feasible as a project financed, built, and operated by the authority, a great part of its excess revenues would be committed for many years to come, thus reducing pressure to divert these funds to transit.

So in 1959–1960 the authority's officials readily agreed, in discussions with the Downtown-Lower Manhattan Association, that the bistate agency be named in the business group's report as the appropriate organization to carry out the detailed study. Once named, the authority shaped "the main currents in the private sector" to fit its organizational goals. By 1961, the original $250 million project covering 5 to 6 million square feet had been refashioned by the Port Authority into a $355 million complex extending to 11 million square feet. The authority also concluded that the World Trade Center's operation ought to be motivated "not by the development of maximum economic return, but by the improvement of the competitive position of the Port to assure its continued prosperity."[7] And significantly, the authority's study showed that in the long run the Center would be self-supporting, so the authority itself could be builder and entrepreneur of the colossal project.

Plans for the World Trade Center became enmeshed in 1961 with bistate negotiations for Port Authority purchase of the Hudson Tubes. As noted earlier, this problem in interstate rivalry was overcome by shifting the Center from the East Side to the West Side of Manhattan, and combining it with the rail project. Then the plans were delayed by lawsuits brought by some of the 325 merchants who were to be evicted from the site, and by other business interests. Meanwhile, the Port Authority's strategists began to explore the possibility of expanding the original plan. Could the businessmen's relatively modest scheme, centered on a fifty- to seventy-story building, be amplified to twice its dimension? Suppose the port agency could construct the tallest, the largest building in the world—this surely would be a testimony to its financial strength, its regional importance, its visible leadership. A monument equal to Robert Moses's Narrows Bridge, to Richard II's Mont-Saint-Michel, facing the same restless sea.

The authority's leaders recognized, however, that the Center could not be carried out on a really dramatic scale, and also be self-supporting, if its tenants were restricted to private and government activities engaged in international trade. What was needed was a major, guaranteed tenant, committed from the beginning to renting millions of square feet. Fortunately, David Rockefeller's brother Nelson was a strong supporter of the project, and in early January 1964 the governor announced that most New York State offices in New York City—including those in such areas as mental health and welfare, as well as international trade—would move to the World Trade Center, where they would occupy a major portion of one section of the complex.

Now the preferred plan could be unveiled. In late January 1964 the Port Authority announced that it would construct a "great new World Trade Center," featuring "twin towers of gleaming metal, soaring 110 stories," thus displacing the Empire State Building as the world's tallest building.[8] With

7. Port Authority, *A World Trade Center* (New York: 1961), p. 31.
8. The quotations are taken from Port Authority, *Annual Report 1963* (New York: 1964), p. 41. The Sears Tower in Chicago soon supplanted the World Trade Center as the world's tallest building.

each floor extending nearly an acre, the complex also formed the greatest aggregation of office space in the world, far exceeding the Pentagon, which was then the leader. And with an expected 50,000 people at work in the Center each day, with vast electrical needs to run its 230 passenger elevators, lights, and other operations, the World Trade Center was expected to be—and would turn out to be—a vast, complicated, energy-absorbing city within a city.[9]

Although attacked and sued by private real-estate interests when the real-estate market collapsed in the late 1960s, the Port Authority held firm to its Center's dimensions. As its costs mounted—increasing nearly $200 million to $525 million in 1965, and to $575 million in 1966—even the enthusiasm of the *New York Times* wavered. "No project has ever been more promising for New York," the *Times* exclaimed in 1964. By 1966, the *Times* wondered editorially whether the project was so costly that it would "divert the energies and the resources of the Port Authority" from important responsibilities in such areas as mass transit. A few months later, the *Times* found the authority scheme "enormously expensive and grandiose," and urged that the state reconsider plans to centralize its offices in the Trade Center; greater benefits to the city and state might be derived from decentralizing state offices to sites "in and around Harlem, Bedford-Stuyvesant or the South Bronx."[10] State Controller Arthur Levitt also questioned whether moving state offices into the Trade Center was preferable to keeping those offices where they were or moving some of them to Harlem.[11]

Still the Port Authority pressed ahead, for this was "one of the greatest of public service projects," whose creation, said the authority, was "motivated by the need to expand world trade on which the port's economic health depends,"[12] whose builders were motivated, as are men of wealth and influence in all ages, to create monuments to their own power and to their own particular gods. By 1980 the World Trade Center, at last nearly completed, had consumed over $1 billion and was now a vast, functioning complex. Into its rail-transit bowels are drawn men and women from throughout the region,

9. In reviewing a draft of this chapter, Port Authority staff members questioned whether the World Trade Center should be characterized as "wasteful" of energy. They noted correctly that the convenience of the Center to rail and bus transit is an "energy plus"—reducing transportation energy costs for workers and other users. On the other hand, the design of the Center includes a variety of energy-wasting features. The great height of the towers is one factor, since energy demands for elevators, pumps, and other mechanisms increase disproportionately with a structure's height. Other characteristics include sealed windows, air conditioning that cools multifloor sectors, and a lighting system that illuminates large areas even when only a few offices are in use. In these and other ways the World Trade Center is surely wasteful of energy resources. See Leonard I. Ruchelman, *The World Trade Center* (Syracuse, N.Y.: Syracuse University Press, 1977), Chapters 4–5, and Ruchelman, letter to the authors, April 9, 1980.

10. "The World Trade Center," editorial, *New York Times*, January 20, 1964; "Questions on the Trade Center," editorial, *New York Times*, December 24, 1966; "Reviewing the Trade Center," editorial, *New York Times*, April 12, 1967.

11. See Will Lissner, "Harlem Studied for State Office," *New York Times*, July 25, 1966; Thomas A. Johnson, "Harlem Presses State Office Plan," *New York Times*, August 18, 1966. While holding to its agreement to relocate many offices to the World Trade Center, the state also constructed a more modest office building in Harlem in the 1970s.

12. "They'll Raise Trade on Acres in the Sky," *Via Port of New York 16* (January 1964), p. 16. The periodical is published by the Port Authority.

*The World Trade Center towers loom over the Center's hotel, the abandoned West Side Highway, and new land created for the Battery Park City project.*    Credit: Port Authority of New York and New Jersey

who work in more than 1,000 firms and public agencies located in the Center's six buildings, as well as in hundreds of other downtown locations, symbolizing and helping to maintain the employment magnet of Manhattan.

The impact of the World Trade Center on the region's economy is, at this point, difficult to ascertain. The Center probably has helped, as the Regional Plan Association and the City Planning Commission thought it would, in generating economic growth in lower Manhattan.[13] Meanwhile, the role of the Port of New York in international trade has declined relative to other major ports, but the causes seem largely unrelated to the internal efficiency of Port Authority services. In fact, interviews with tenants at the World Trade Center indicate that in their view the complex has improved their communications efficiency, sales, and profits.[14] At the same time, the Trade Center has not been self-supporting; instead, it has generated millions of dollars in deficits during the past decade. And so we see a final parallel between the French abbey church and our World Trade Center. For those who lived in Norman France in the eleventh century, part of each year was spent in constructing Mont-Saint-Michel. In the twentieth century, the public's contribution to monuments is more indirect: each time this region's motorists are tolled to cross the Hudson, a small portion is husbanded to keep the Trade Center's lights burning, and the Port Authority's bonds solvent.

For our purposes, the World Trade Center is an instructive case. Here we have a government agency, the Port Authority, which demonstrates great skill in modifying and advancing a major project in order to meet the professional and personal goals of its own officials. The authority does far more than ratify and facilitate decisions made in the private marketplace; needs perceived in the private sector—for a trade center, for the revitalization of lower Manhattan—become a vehicle for the authority's own goals.[15]

Yet the impact of the massive project on the region's economic growth remains uncertain—particularly with regard to the avowed primary goal of improving the ability of the region to compete in international trade, thus

13. See Regional Plan Association, press release, March 30, 1967, and City Planning Commission, City of New York, *The World Trade Center: An Evaluation* (New York: March 1966), pp. 29 ff.

14. Major factors inhibiting foreign trade growth in the New York region include "shifts in the national economy which have seen other regions of the country prosper in contrast to our region's decline in the 1970s; changes in international trade patterns; relatively higher costs; and lapses in rail service quality in this region." Committee on the Future, Port Authority, *Regional Recovery: The Business of the Eighties* (New York: 1979), p. 31. Cf. Mitchell L. Moss, who emphasizes the development of the St. Lawrence Seaway and inland ports, and "discriminatory rates" set by the ICC, which favored southern ports, in addition to the factors noted above. See Moss, "The Urban Port," *Coastal Zone Management Journal*, 2 (1976), pp. 232 ff. On the views of Trade Center tenants, see for example Port Authority, *1974 Report* (New York: 1975), p. 14.

15. Our analysis of the World Trade Center case is erroneous, some of our Port Authority readers comment, in maintaining that authority activities were substantially shaped by "its desire to soak up excess reserve funds, by its need to relieve rapid transit pressure, and by its thirst for monumentality." The authority's concerns regarding rail transit and its excess reserves are discussed in Chapter Seven. As to the "thirst for monumentality," the comments in the text can be amplified, based on documents and interviews, as follows. It is true, as the text indicates, that the Center was viewed by its promoters, both within the Port Authority and without, as a project that might add economic strength to the port and the region. For Austin Tobin and some of his aides, however, a major attraction of the complex was indeed its monumental quality. Soon after the question of creating a World Trade Center was broached, Tobin embraced the enterprise with enthusiasm. While much staff effort was devoted to analyzing the efficiencies that might result if government agencies and private firms involved in international marketing were brought together on one site, the scope and height of the buildings also received great attention. Indeed, to some staff members it appeared that the primary goal was a large and striking edifice, with improvement of the New York region's trade position only a secondary consideration. As authority planners saw the possibility of exceeding the early seventy-story maximum height, the opportunity of overtopping the Empire State Building as the world's tallest building took hold and won out.

strengthening the region's economy. So perhaps the World Trade Center underscores the limitations on the ability of government units—and indeed of public and private organizations working together—to alter development trends, when major variables are external to the region. In addition, some critics have suggested, the project may illustrate the ability of some public agencies—with insulated funds and skillful leadership—to resist devoting their resources to programs that would truly help aid regional development, preferring to carry out less important projects that will benefit their own agencies and their leaders.[16]

## The Complex Role of Government

Do governmental organizations simply "ride with" actions taken in the marketplace, or—through their conflicting actions—"tend to cancel one another out," thus permitting the private sector to determine the direction and pace of urban development? Wood and Vernon have argued that public action is largely limited to these relatively ineffective roles. Our view, as suggested by the example of the World Trade Center, and demonstrated by our analysis of transportation and other development areas, is that the process is far more complex, the directions of influence far more diversified. The initial step in analyzing these patterns of influence involves three general points:

1. The activities of government, especially in a democratic political system, are closely linked to the predominant patterns of values and preferences held by the citizenry. Similarly, the patterns of marketplace actions by households and firms are significantly shaped by the preferences of society's members, acting as consumers. It is understandable, therefore—though not always to the liking of urban reformers—that the initiatives and responses of government and the marketplace activities of private units are often interrelated—and directed toward mutually reinforcing goals.

2. Even so, in some important policy areas and with regard to a number of crucial decisions, it is possible to determine whether particular clusters of government units, or private economic organizations (or religious or other kinds of organizations) have had—and are likely to have—a *crucial role* in initiating new patterns of urban development, or *moderate influence* (significantly altering activities initiated elsewhere, or deciding upon a specific course of action within a broader set of preferences), or only *minor influence* (for example, by simply ratifying actions essentially determined elsewhere).

3. In order to evaluate the influence of any public body (or of any other participant), the meaning of the elusive term "influence" must be clarified. As explained in some detail in Chapter One, the extent to which government actions are influential in shaping urban development can be measured by examining two variables: the *impact* of the actions on the distribution of jobs

16. As the *New York Times* expressed this critical view in 1967, the Port Authority's "gargantuan project" should be cut down to "realistic and efficient size," so that the authority's "management and money" could also be used to improve marine terminals and reduce traffic congestion in the region. Otherwise, a Trade Center would be only a monument "to the city's former glories as a port and to the Authority's audacious ability to get its own way." "Reviewing the Trade Center," editorial, *New York Times,* April 12, 1967.

and residences, and the degree to which specific government programs are decided *independent* of the demands and preferences of economic units or other groups. Fairly strong ratings on both dimensions would suggest that a government agency reaches a level of "moderate influence" or higher.

Exploring the forces that shape urban regions in terms of these dimensions raises some interesting difficulties in gathering and assessing the evidence. A public agency clearly is acting independently (vis-à-vis designated economic units) if its operative goals and those of the economic units are in conflict; our analysis of suburban zoning, in Chapter Three, illustrates this relationship. However, when the preferred outcomes of a public agency are much the same as those of major economic groups, different kinds of evidence must be sought in order to determine the degree of independence of the actions of a highway agency, city hall, or port authority. In such cases, as seen in the discussion of the highway alliance in Chapter Six, and in the World Trade Center vignette, we must search for motive and perception.

With regard to the impact of government action on urban development, we again find some cases that are fairly easy to evaluate, and others that are quite difficult. As described in Chapters Three and Six, the impact of suburban governments, through their land-use regulations, seems clear and extensive, as does the impact of the highway builders. The impact of government in other contexts is less direct but still clearly important. For example, suburban governing bodies were important participants in the grass-roots coalitions which halted the Port Authority's plan to build a fourth jetport, and which finally reined in the powerful highway agencies. In these cases, the suburbs exercised their influence primarily against regional government bodies, whose development plans were thereby modified or halted. These conflicts, outlined in Chapter Four, remind us also that "government" is not a monolith, taking unified action on development issues; instead, any large metropolitan area includes a wide range of government agencies whose development goals and strategies differ and often conflict.[17]

Like the suburban governing bodies, the impact of older-city mayors, councils, and line departments is relatively easy to evaluate. As we conclude in Chapter Eight, these government bodies have by and large been *unable* to concentrate resources on coherent development goals. Spreading their investments and their political energies widely, they seem to fit the model of an organization that usually must react to broader economic and social forces, with relatively little capacity to mold the shape of the urban region.

The field of mass transportation is, however, considerably more complex. Here, determining whether government has had significant influence or

17. These differences among government agencies are well understood by Wood and Vernon, who view such crosscutting effects as a major reason why government efforts are "of little consequence." Although less clearly described by those authors, similar conflicts occur in the private sector, so that the "private marketplace" does not always generate a clear set of demands—to which public agencies presumably could respond. For example, the Port Authority argued that its proposed fourth jetport was a necessary response to market demand, i.e., that because of an increasing number of air passengers, airport capacity must be expanded. But some of the major airlines disagreed with the authority's view; although not prominent in the public battle against the jetport, they believe—and argued behind the scenes—that the preferable strategy would be to remove small business aircraft and private planes from the three major airports, thus freeing more airspace and landing space for large carriers.

only a minor role in shaping development depends very largely on the *standards* applied. In our view, as set forth in Chapter Seven, government activities in the transit field have had a crucial impact on the distribution of jobs and residences in the New York region. Robert Wood and Raymond Vernon disagree, not because of factual differences or emphasis on different time periods, but because they apply a very exacting standard in determining when public action has a *significant* impact on development.

For Wood and Vernon, mass transportation is a particularly important domain, because government activities in that field—especially if joined with vigorous land-use controls—have the potential to modify substantially the direction and pace of metropolitan growth. The continual dispersal of jobs and residences might be checked, they argue, if there were a "great initiative" by government, involving "massive changes in passenger transport policy" and a regional public organization with the authority to make decisions about development throughout the New York area.[18] Such vigorous efforts meet their standards for influential government action; but all lesser efforts are viewed as only temporary palliatives. As we argue in Chapter Seven, such stringent criteria for evaluating influence may be appropriate for gods, but among men—at least in this region—they ensure that government will be judged as powerless.

The standards for influential government action outlined by Vernon and Wood, and the closely related hopes sometimes expressed by regional planners, raise further implications worth exploring briefly.[19] Imagine for a moment that sufficient political support existed to permit a "great initiative" by government, entailing the "massive changes" in policy suggested by Vernon and Wood. What actions would be taken, and with what results?

First, large amounts of public funds would be allocated to improve mass transit services, permitting faster and more frequent rail and bus services. But would such actions check the trend toward diffusion of residences and jobs, as Wood hoped?[20] Possibly, but it seems equally likely that commuters would not reduce travel time, so that faster transit services would permit them to search farther out for housing locations.[21]

Consequently, improved transit services alone might not check the tendency toward diffusion; instead, they might accelerate the trend. But perhaps this should not surprise us. The underlying dynamic—which Wood asks us to counter with government power if public action is to be considered "signifi-

18. Raymond Vernon, *Metropolis 1985* (Cambridge, Mass.: Harvard University Press, 1960), pp. 182–183; Robert C. Wood, *1400 Governments* (Cambridge, Mass.: Harvard University Press, 1961), pp. 170, 192–193.

19. For recent views of urban planners, see Lee K. Koppelman, "Land Use: Changing the Ground Rules," *New York Affairs* 5 (1978), pp. 66 ff.; and Boris Pushkarev, "Transportation: Crawling towards Consolidation," ibid., pp. 79 ff.

20. Wood, *1400 Governments*, p. 170.

21. See for example John W. Dyckman, "Transportation in Cities," in *Cities: A Scientific American Book* (New York: Knopf, 1966), p. 144; and Edgar M. Hoover and Raymond Vernon, *Anatomy of a Metropolis* (Cambridge, Mass.: Harvard University Press, 1959), pp. 210 ff. Improved public transport services would also make some suburban employment locations more accessible to older cities' residents via "reverse commuting." This improved access to these labor pools would increase the willingness of some employers to consider suburban rather than central-city locations. However, these transportation changes would probably have much less influence on job location than on housing location.

cant"—has been the evolving interaction between personal values and expanding individual wealth during the past 75 years and longer. Historically,
as Hoover and Vernon note in *Anatomy of a Metropolis*, a large portion of the
region's workforce labored long hours—roughly ten to twelve hours a day, six
days a week. This work pattern compelled them to seek living quarters, generally in densely developed apartments, very close to their places of employment. Moreover, the great majority lacked adequate income to permit them to
allocate a portion of their money for the luxury of daily commuting, or to bid
for the more spacious dwellings and land available outside the older cities. In
the past few decades the number of hours worked per day and the number of
days of work per week have declined, while real income has increased. Consequently, an increasing proportion of the region's residents—especially since
the late 1940s—have been able to allocate time and money in order to seek
greater space and privacy.[22]

Meanwhile, changes in factory technology and other forces, as noted in
Chapter Two, have permitted some plants and other employment centers to
move to the suburbs, both following the locational choices of many of their
employees and encouraging other workers to migrate with their families.
Unless there were a sharp and widespread drop in consumer preference for
space and privacy, a significant decline in real income for much of the
region's populace, or a continuing severe energy crisis, the pattern of behavior found in earlier decades seems very likely to continue. That is, any effort
within the region to improve the quality or to reduce the cost of individual
travel—whether by highway or rail—would lead individual residents to
respond in terms of *their own* preferences, not those of the Regional Plan
Association or the *New York Times*. On balance, such decisions would promote the dispersal of residences and probably employment locations in the
New York metropolis.[23]

By themselves even "massive funds" for transit therefore are not likely
to halt the trend toward dispersal of jobs and housing. As Wood suggests, we
might also need to create a regional agency that could overrule local land-use
policies and local controls.[24] As to job locations, the new agency would need
the power to nullify local zoning which attracts headquarters' offices, research
units, and factories unless it were "in accord with a general plan." Indeed, to
meet the Wood-Vernon test of significance, this authoritative general plan
would prevent suburban actions that might add to diffusion of industrial and
commercial development. As to residential growth patterns, this powerful
regional agency would have to ensure that farms and vacant land in outlying
areas were *not* converted to housing—since such conversions would add to
the tendency toward diffusion.

If such efforts by a regional agency were successful, they would surely
demonstrate that government can play a significant role in urban development. However, to define the concept so that only such actions qualify as

22. See Hoover and Vernon, *Anatomy of a Metropolis*, pp. 221–228.
23. In the short run, some households and businesses would opt for a return to central-city
locations, but these would probably comprise only a small minority, in view of the costs and other
problems associated with older-city housing, and considering the difficulties in attracting industries
to city sites. See our discussion in Chapters 8 and 9.
24. Wood, *1400 Governments*, pp. 170, 192.

influential would be to equate government influence with a single value-laden view of how public policy should help to shape regional development. And that, in effect, is what Robert Wood and Raymond Vernon do.

## Another View: Government Officials as All-Powerful

In contrast with the tendency of many observers to view government activities as having "little consequence" in shaping the pattern of growth, a few commentators have taken a quite different position. They argue that one public official or a few public agencies have had an overwhelming, dominating influence on the growth of the New York region. It should not be surprising that for this metropolis, and perhaps for any metropolitan region in the United States, the official most likely to be nominated for this role (and sometimes excoriated for his efforts) is Robert Moses, and the institution most likely to be honored or condemned in this context is the Port Authority of New York and New Jersey.

Perhaps the most extreme example of this view of government influence is that of Robert Caro, who in his Pulitzer Prize-winning volume explores the strategies used by Moses to gather unto himself the financial resources and government authority needed to construct a massive highway system, and the ways in which Moses used his vast intellectual and political energy to build that system. So it was, in Caro's interpretation, that Moses "flooded the city with cars," starved the rail lines of funds, and guaranteed that the "vast suburbs, rural and empty when he came to power, were filled on a sprawling, low-density development pattern relying primarily on roads instead of mass transportation. . . ."[25]

Caro's strong implication is that if Moses had decided upon a different program, oriented to mass transit, he could have shaped the pattern of jobs and residences across the region in a very different way. Rexford Guy Tugwell, onetime member of the New York City Planning Commission and a shrewd observer of American politics, takes a somewhat similar view. Reviewing Moses's efforts in building expressways, tunnels and bridges, parks, housing and a coliseum, Tugwell concludes that "most of them, or at least many of them, would not have come into existence if Moses had not created the circumstances for their beginning and maneuvered them into being."[26]

Theodore Kheel raises the Port Authority to an almost equal plane of influence. "Because of the Port Authority's failure to honor its vital mandate" to coordinate transportation in the region, Kheel argues, "we have inherited a chaotic system of transportation that is undermining the region's economy, polluting the air and driving out business and the middle class." Kheel asks us to imagine "what this region might have been like if the talent that produced the World Trade Center . . . " had been used instead "to

25. Robert A. Caro, *The Power Broker: Robert Moses and the Fall of New York* (New York: Knopf, 1974), p. 19.
26. Rexford Guy Tugwell, "The Moses Effect," in Edward C. Banfield, ed., *Urban Government* (New York: Free Press, 1961), p. 463.

produce a balanced system of horizontal transportation within the Port District."[27]

Our conclusions are quite different. Neither Moses nor the Port Authority nor any other public agency—nor a combination of banks and corporate leaders—is responsible for the automobile-dominated suburban sprawl of the nation's largest metropolis. Had their visions been quite different, neither Moses nor the Port Authority nor the Rockefeller brothers could have given us a sharply different pattern of urban development—even if they had labored in unison. The availability of the automobile, the desire of citizens for space and privacy, and the technical advantages of open space for new industrial plants were all beyond the control of any small group of actors. These factors both stimulated and were reinforced by government programs of home mortgage assistance, sewer connections, and road-building; and their interplay combined to shape suburban development in the New York metropolis, and to produce the very similar patterns of metropolitan growth across the nation.

We would not, of course, want to carry our disagreement with Caro and Kheel too far. While there are no all-powerful political leaders or government institutions in the region, both officials and agencies can shape the forces of urban change, and alter the rate and direction of development in quite significant ways. Tugwell captures some of these elements of influence in his perceptive essay on the potential impact of political leadership—which can break through islands of private power and bureaucratic lethargy, and channel funds as well as sustained and ruthless administrative energy toward identified goals—extending highways, rebuilding slums, or adding parks. Tugwell calls the successful concentration of such energy "the Moses effect":

> It involves ingenuity and aggressive pursuit of adopted objectives. . . . It is an increasing, a multiplying force; there is a gathering and discharge of energy which becomes a tide of change. . . . A Moses rides the tides when he can, deflects them where possible, and when necessary builds dams against them. But he is a restless force operating constantly to make out of what is happening what he wants to happen.[28]

## Sources of Influence

Like individuals, governments differ in size, shape, purpose, and influence. Wood and his colleagues divided all Gaul into two parts—local governments, and regional enterprises. We have chopped them up somewhat more finely, analyzing the influence of public agencies upon regional development in terms of several variables, summarized as areal scope, functional scope, and the ability to concentrate resources. As outlined in Chapter One, areal

27. Theodore W. Kheel, "The Port Authority's 'Failure,'" letter to the editor, *New York Times*, May 23, 1977. (Kheel, a labor negotiator and lawyer, signed his letter, "President, The Authority for Coordinating Transportation," which suggests that where power does not exist, titles may nourish hope.) For similar views of the Port Authority, see Edward T. Chase, "How to Rescue New York from Its Port Authority," *Harpers* (June, 1960) pp. 67–74; Chase's article is reprinted in Banfield, ed., *Urban Government*, under the title "The Trouble with the New York Port Authority," pp. 75–82.

28. Tugwell, "The Moses Effect," in Banfield, ed., *Urban Government*, pp. 466–467.

scope refers simply to the range or extent of the metropolitan area within which the agency operates, and functional scope to the number of program areas within which a government unit exercises its influence. The "ability to concentrate resources" refers to the factors that determine whether any given unit can focus political, administrative, and financial resources on identified goals over an extended period of time, and so accomplish those goals. As we have used the term, it refers to the interaction among seven important variables: extent of formal independence; variety and intensity of constituency demands; control over the use of land; financial resources; and three elements crucial to capacity for leadership—political skill, planning capabilities, and the extent of control over subordinate units. Unfortunately in terms of analytical clarity, but true to reality, these "concentration" variables are closely intertwined. Strength along one or two dimensions permits those so fortunate to gather increasing vigor across a wider front, while a growing weakness in one area makes the once-mighty vulnerable to decline or disaster.

In previous chapters we have analyzed the role of various government units in urban development with reference to these variables. For example, some suburban governments have made use of zoning powers and planning skills to shape decisively the pattern of development within their borders; because of its wide areal scope and sophisticated political leadership, Westchester's county government has been preeminent in the effective use of these resources.

Wide areal scope has also been an important factor in the Port Authority's ability to influence regional development. Its geographic range has meant that the authority's activities have helped to shape development quite directly in several of the region's largest cities—Newark, New York, Jersey City, and Elizabeth—and in the smaller towns near its major facilities. Moreover, wide areal scope has provided the bistate agency with some flexibility in deciding where to locate specific facilities. As a consequence, the authority has had significant leverage in negotiating with local and state governments and with private concerns as it has sought sites for truck terminals, marine terminals, and other facilities that modify further the shape of enterprise and job opportunities within the region.

Also crucially important to the Port Authority, and to other public authorities in the region, have been important elements providing insulation. These include control over revenues generated by their tolls and rents, and some ability to remain aloof from the wide-ranging constituencies that press demands on city hall and at state capitals, attempting to carry off bit-by-bit those resources that might have been husbanded and used on major development projects. An excellent illustration of the importance of insulation—and its interrelationship with the effective use of planning skills—is provided by the contrast between the Port Authority and the city governments in developing marine terminals.

## Contrasts in Influence: The Case of Marine Terminals

Historically, as emphasized in Chapter Two, the Port of New York— with its piers, docks, and related facilities for ocean-borne commerce—has been a central element in the settlement and economic development of the

New York region.[29] Despite the massive growth of economic activities that do not depend on ocean transport, the port has maintained an important role in the region's economy, with more than 170,000 of the region's jobs in 1978 directly involved in port-related activities.

Much of the port's 750 miles of waterfront is privately owned, but New York City, Newark, and other waterfront cities have long had city-owned port facilities, with ownership motivated both by hopes of generating income directly for the city, and by the perception that thriving city-sponsored port activities will encourage private industries that rely on ocean transport to locate and expand in their municipalities. Luther Gulick captured the significance of this latter potential in a 1947 essay, noting that a public agency "has the power to determine whether a community as a whole will expand as a raw material center or as a manufacturing center by the priority it gives to port facilities, loading and unloading equipment, wharfage rates, and rail and road connections."[30]

Alas, such hopes of city-government entrepreneurship are often disappointed. The city of Newark, for example, officially launched "Port Newark" in 1915 and began dredging its marshland to attract "great argosies of commerce . . . carrying the world's goods to Newark and Newark's wares to all points of the earth."[31] The marsh was partially dredged, some port facilities were begun, and a few industrial firms were attracted to the area. But because of the disruption of two wars—when the port area was in military hands—and the Great Depression, combined with a lack of adequate capital funds, Port Newark was only partly completed by 1946. Moreover, its buildings and piers needed rehabilitation and modernizing; and thirty years of effort, far from generating revenue for the city, had drained $10 million from city coffers.

The basic problem, as viewed by Newark city officials and business leaders, was the city's inability to allocate sufficient funds and managerial talent to develop the port area into a source of major economic benefit. "Forced to spread its limited resources on such projects as housing, schools and other civic improvements," Newark "could not spare capital funds to improve the waterfront. . . . "[32] By 1947 the city fathers had agreed to lease the seaport (and Newark airport as well) to the Port Authority, which would modernize and expand Port Newark. Using its growing bridge and tunnel revenues, the authority moved quickly—spending more than $3 million on rehabilitation and development in the first year, purchasing or leasing an additional 100 acres for expansion, and using its international promotion skills to bring added ocean freight traffic to the port.

By 1955 the Port Authority had invested more than $22 million in Port Newark, cargo handled at the port had expanded steadily, and the authority announced plans to create a new marine terminal adjacent to Port Newark, in

---

29. See Vernon, *Metropolis 1985*, Chapter 2, and Benjamin Chinitz, *Freight and the Metropolis* (Cambridge, Mass.: Harvard University Press, 1960), Chapter 1 and *passim*.

30. Luther Gulick, "Authorities and How to Use Them," *The Tax Review* (November 1947), p. 50. Gulick's essay refers primarily to the potential of port authorities, and in fact his article was drafted during the period in which the Port Authority was negotiating for control of New York's port facilities. The argument applies, of course, to any government agency with control over terminals and related port facilities.

31. A Newark newspaper article, circa October 1915, as quoted in Port Authority, "Port Newark," mimeographed, October 1965, pp. 2–3.

32. Ibid., p. 6.

Elizabeth. Then, working closely with private transport operators and using a highly skilled staff, the authority laid out plans, continued to modify them as dredging was carried out and as technology for marine terminals rapidly altered, and in 1962 opened the new facility, a prototype for container terminals worldwide.[33]

By 1965, the Port Authority's investment in Port Newark exceeded $86 million, and its deepwater berths had more than doubled compared with the old city-owned terminal. In 1947, its last year of city operation, Port Newark had handled only 450 vessels and 800,000 tons of cargo, with 1,500 workers. In 1965, 1,500 ships berthed at Newark, and four million tons were handled by 4,500 workers. Port Elizabeth, in the midst of a $150 million construction program, added another 2 million tons of cargo, and dramatic additional growth was expected at the adjoining terminals during the next decade. As to the impact of these developments on the region, it was estimated that each ship generated $100,000 in direct business for companies in marine and international trade, with additional benefits to banking, wholesaling, and insurance industries.[34]

Compared with the expansion and vitality of the Newark-area marine terminals, the evolution of port facilities owned by New York City during these first two postwar decades was negligible. In 1947 Mayor William O'Dwyer, with unseemly foresight, had perceived the difficulty that City Hall would face in attempting to rehabilitate its 130 piers and miles of other waterfront facilities. "The City is now faced with making capital improvements for hospitals, schools and its transit facilities, which will tax its present power to raise funds," O'Dwyer explained in a letter to the Port Authority in October 1947. Since other demands prevented scarce city funds from being used to meet port needs, the mayor asked the bistate agency to consider whether it might redevelop city-owned terminal areas.

The Port Authority responded quickly and enthusiastically, urging that New York City join with Newark to permit the development of the port's marine facilities "on a truly regional basis"—under Port Authority management. By February 1948 the Port Authority presented a detailed proposal, involving expenditure of $114 million of authority funds for new piers, rehabilitation of existing structures, and other improvements. In addition, the port agency would make payments of $5 to $6 million per year to New York City during a fifty-year lease period.[35]

33. On the development of Port Newark and Port Elizabeth by the Port Authority, see Port Authority, *Twenty-Sixth Annual Report: 1946* (New York: November 1, 1947), pp. 7–10; Port Authority, *Twenty-Eighth Annual Report: 1948* (New York: April 15, 1949), pp. 45–51; Port Authority, *1955 Annual Report* (New York: n.d., ca March 1956), pp. 7–11; Port Authority, *Annual Report: 1963* (New York: n.d., ca March 1964), pp. 8–13; John T. Cunningham, "Port Elizabeth: The Reshaping of Shipping," *New Jersey Business*, March 1970, pp. 31–35, 65.

34. See Port Authority, "Port Newark," October 1965, pp. 1, 7–10; Chinitz, *Freight and the Metropolis*, Chapter 3; "A Showcase for Integrated Transport," *Business Week*, November 27, 1971 (reprint, 3 pp.). By 1978, the Port Authority's New Jersey marine terminals, which include Hoboken as well as Newark and Elizabeth, handled 2,100 ships and 10 million long tons of cargo; the three terminals employed 6,300 persons.

35. The O'Dwyer-Port Authority exchange of letters and the authority's plan are included in Port Authority, *Twenty Seventh Annual Report: 1947* (New York: November 1, 1948), pp. 35–36; Port Authority, *Twenty Eighth Annual Report: 1948*, pp. 54–68.

Having just seen its two great airports slip from its grasp into the embracing arms of what some city leaders saw as the port octopus, New York's Board of Estimate was not eager to lose control of its piers and docks as well. And the politically influential labor unions controlling the docks urged that the offer be rejected. Moreover, the city's Department of Marine and Aviation, hoping for at least half a future, said it could do the job for half the cost. So the Board of Estimate turned a deaf ear to the pleas of the mayor and civic associations in the city, rejected the Authority plan, and urged its own agency to go forward with a $55 million program.[36]

Unfortunately, with two-thirds of the city's piers more than forty years old, and half in poor condition, $55 million was insufficient; and the Board of Estimate failed to provide the Department of Marine and Aviation even that modest amount.[37] So the piers rotted away and floated out to sea, along with the city's hopes for economic revitalization of its waterfront.

By the mid-1960s, city officials concluded that something had gone wrong. "The expansion of modern cargo-handling facilities in Port Newark and Port Elizabeth," the City Planning Commission asserted in 1964, "have made serious inroads into the economy of the New York City sectors of the Port." The commission urged the city to develop a more vigorous "port development policy" in order to "preserve its economic stability and job base." Pressed by short-run problems in schools, subways, and sanitation, City Hall responded in its usual fashion, and two years later the planners lamented: "Our side of the harbor has no counterpart to the new, modern facilities which are attracting containership operations to Port Elizabeth."[38]

Now the cause of the "obsolescence of our port facilities" was, in the Planning Commission's view, readily found; it lay in the Port Authority's failure to "balance" its terminal developments in New Jersey with an equal share in New York. The Planning Commission therefore urged the city to press ahead—although just how, was less clear. The commission warned that constitutional limitations and existing budgetary commitments "caution against" the city's assuming any major new capital programs. Yet, in considering whether the Port Authority should take on a major role, the commission argued that the mayor would have to weigh the "long-range gains to the City's prestige and economy" against the "surrender of City land and its earned revenues" to the bistate agency.[39]

36. The actions of the city are summarized in Port Authority, *Twenty Eighth Annual Report*, pp. 56–57. After the authority's proposal was rejected, Mayor O'Dwyer urged the authority to submit a second, more modest plan. Its 1949 proposal for $91 million in expenditures was also turned down by the Board of Estimate. See Port Authority, *Twenty Ninth Annual Report: 1949* (New York: July 15, 1950), pp. 70–71.

37. While the Port Authority plan had called for it to spend $114 million by 1960, and the city department had urged $55 million, the actual expenditures by the city as of 1960 were only $30 million. A student of the port's economy pointed out, however, that "current plans" called for additional expenditures of $200 million. Noting that these plans "must compete with other City needs" for limited funds, he concluded with admirable restraint: "One cannot readily assume that this program will be realized as rapidly as planned. . . . " Chinitz, *Freight and the Metropolis*, p. 82.

38. City Planning Commission, City of New York, "The World Trade Center: An Evaluation" (New York, March 1966), p. 48. The 1964 statement in the text is from the Commission's report, "The Port of New York" (September 1964), as quoted in ibid., p. 46.

39. Ibid., pp. 48–50, quoting in part from commission reports issued in 1964 and 1965. Despite the city's rejection of a major Port Authority program in the 1940s, by the mid-1960s the

*An important factor in maintaining the region's economic vitality has been the modern port facilities developed by the Port Authority in Elizabeth and Newark.*    Credit: Port Authority of New York and New Jersey

As part of the Lindsay administration's negotiations on construction of the World Trade Center, Deputy Mayor Robert Price picked up this broken lance in 1966, making a series of demands for immediate Port Authority commitments, totalling about $230 million, to improve city marine facilities.[40] Price also attacked plans for additional investment by the authority in New Jersey terminals as "another example of the Authority's discrimination against our side of the harbor," and complained that "meanwhile, the New York side continues to deteriorate, and to lose business, jobs and much-needed new construction."[41]

---

agency had three terminal projects on the New York side of the harbor, though none was on the scale of Port Newark-Port Elizabeth. The three were the Brooklyn-Port Authority Marine Terminal, Erie Basin-Port Authority Marine Terminal, and the Columbia Street Pier.

40. Once the World Trade Center had been approved by the two states, the authority needed permission from the city to close streets so that construction could proceed. Lindsay and his staff initially refused permission, and put forward a number of proposals for Port Authority assistance to the city. These are set forth in the letter from Robert Price to Austin Tobin, May 27, 1966 (17 p.). The marine projects included a new passenger ship terminal ($100 million), a containership terminal in Brooklyn ($80 million), additional development in South Brooklyn ($15 million), a new container-ship terminal, probably on Staten Island ($30 to $40 million), and removal of old Manhattan piers ($3 million).

41. Quoted in Edith Evans Asbury, "Port Agency Scored on Jersey Project," *New York Times*, July 17, 1966.

Not much came of this foray. One project already under negotiation, a $40 million passenger ship terminal, was built and years later, in 1974, a joint agreement provided for authority construction of a $33 million container terminal in Brooklyn. At the end of the 1970s the authority's facilities in New Jersey were handling 10 million long tons, seven times the cargo passing through its New York terminals. The city department, now renamed Ports and Terminals, still controlled large numbers of piers and other waterfront facilities. A few of these piers had been rehabilitated, and in the city's 1980 budget the department noted that it was "planning several major projects, including the development of marinas and floating restaurants."[42] But perhaps the time for major terminal construction projects had passed;[43] and in any event it seemed likely, given New York City's budgetary constraints, that the City would have great difficulty simply keeping its aging piers in good repair while putting a few restaurants out in the harbor, under the haughty gaze of the World Trade Center.

## Constituencies, Insulation, and Leadership

Limited constituencies and insulated financial resources were crucial to the Port Authority's ability to devise plans for Port Newark and Port Elizabeth, and to follow through promptly and effectively in executing those plans. In an important sense, however, those elements of insulation were only necessary preconditions; they gave opportunity and scope to the authority's leaders, who could then attract imaginative and skilled staff to develop major and innovative projects, and use immense organizational talent to implement these plans. A similar combination of political and technical skill characterized the Port Authority's tortuous negotiations leading to the construction of the World Trade Center, the activities of the Moses empire in developing parkways, bridges, parks and beaches, and the vigorous slum clearance efforts of the Newark Housing Authority under Louis Danzig.

These and other examples of government action in shaping urban development demonstrate the crucial role of leadership skills. Once top officials had a vision, or even a glimpse, of what might be done they had great resources which could attract men and women who were less interested in managing complex programs—hoping simply to keep the ship of state or city afloat—than in getting something done. Something concrete, measurable, perhaps visible and impressive. For such individuals, the Port Authority, the Newark Housing Authority, and similar enterprises could offer an assured flow of funds for planning, experimenting, building, and—equally important—constituencies that would applaud their efforts or remain silent. So insulation could be used by leaders to attract and retain staff members of initiative, energy, and great competence at the second, third, and fourth layers of the enterprise.

42. City of New York, *Executive Budget—Fiscal 1980* (April 26, 1979), p. 165.

43. In 1979, the Port Authority concluded that "the port's general cargo facilities are equal to or better than any in the world," and that facilities already in place or underway would meet the region's needs through 1990. Port Authority, *Regional Recovery*, p. 31.

If insulation of funding and constituencies was only one element in the capability of public agencies to shape the metropolis, it was a crucial element nonetheless. The importance of isolation is best understood when it is lost, when the intricate pattern of arrangements that seemed to make the agency invulnerable frays and falls apart. In the New York region the evolution of the Newark Housing Authority, outlined in the previous chapter, provides one of the clearest illustrations of this point. Led by an individual possessed of great political and administrative skills, encased in a network of agreements and habits of cooperation extending to Newark's city hall, private developers in the region, local business leaders, and Washington's financial angels, with a quiescent black community enduring "Negro removal" in the service of economic revitalization, and a somnolent state government, the NHA seemed nearly invulnerable. Yet while Newark's urban renewal program swept forward, the disruptions involved in slum clearance stimulated the silent constituency to organize, press its demands through demonstration and riot, and acquire allies in Trenton and Washington, where once they had had no friends. So the state awoke, federal officials stopped sending in money, "one of the most successful renewal programs in the country"[44] ground to a halt, and its powerful leader departed.

The final collapse of the Moses empire in the 1960s, and the fall of Austin Tobin and the Port Authority in the 1970s, find part of their explanation in a somewhat different line of analysis—the clash of strong egos, sometimes mixed with missionary zeal, that often characterizes men and women who command leadership positions both in the great authorities and at state and national capitals. A decade ago the press could focus upon and dramatize the battle of Tobin vs. Cahill, and the conflicts between Rockefeller-Ronan and Robert Moses. And indeed these contests were partly personal. But the *incentive* for Trenton and Albany to take on these powerful authorities and their leaders, when many other issues could have absorbed their time as they did their predecessors', lay again with constituency changes. So did the *capacity* of the governors to make sustained and successful forays against the King of the Narrows and the Hudson River Empire. In transportation, as we note in Chapters Four and Seven, the rise of the environmentalists and the new power of other antihighway forces meant that state leaders could act—indeed had to act—to undermine the influence of public-works alliances that earlier governors had helped to build and to insulate from direct public accountability.

Two other points should be made regarding the constituency problems facing insulated organizations. One concerns the role of the media. There is little doubt that a favorable press was and is of critical importance to these agencies. Stories that applauded the clearing of slums in Newark or New York, and that spoke rapturously of the George Washington Bridge, the Narrows span, and the World Trade Center kept the general public a friendly audience, and made it difficult for opponents—those removed forcibly from homes and small shops, those who saw environmental decay in the rush

44. This was the evaluation of the NHA's leading scholarly observer in the early 1960s; see Harold Kaplan, *Urban Renewal Politics: Slum Clearance in Newark* (New York: Columbia University Press, 1963), p. 3.

toward new roadways—to gain wider sympathy. The authorities' leaders recognized the crucial role of the media. The Port Authority's hundreds of press releases a year, and Robert Moses's news conferences, brochures, and regular column in *Newsday* (titled "On the Bridge") were motivated by more—and less—than a desire to keep the public fully informed. The battalions of press and information activities were carefully aimed at maintaining a favorable public image, devastating opponents, and ensuring that editorial writers and governors would proclaim without fear of public skepticism that these agencies, through their "great public works," have "set an example for the administration of public business on a sound and efficient basis."[45]

Unfortunately for those who prefer to control their own public image, the press is a complex beast, sometimes not controllable. At the top are men and women with strong attractions to the values of business: their newspapers and broadcast stations are businesses, and the "businesslike" stance of the public authority provides a certain affinity. Moreover, the owners of broadcast outlets and newspapers know that their own growth and profit margins are enhanced by a vigorous business community that can pour money into media advertising. So they and their editorial writers are eager to support the additional commercial growth, influx of shoppers, and image of downtown vitality that are signaled by a Lincoln Tunnel, a Coliseum, the revitalization plan of the Downtown-Lower Manhattan Association, or a Westway.

But down in the press room, out in the street, journalism attracts men and women—at least a small proportion of the working press—who like to dig behind press releases, who are skeptical of large bureaucracies and demonstrations of wealth and lordly power, who want to write about the Davids who might slay some Goliath. And since such tales sell newspapers and aid advertising rates, these scribes are sometimes permitted to pursue their inclinations. Moreover, these relationships are often symbiotic. As the anti-highway and pro-environmental movements have expanded during the past twenty years, the protestors have sought and encouraged a more critical brand of journalism; and the ranks of journalists—many themselves veterans of college protests against government programs, at home and abroad—who confront public agencies and "official explanations" with aggressive skepticism has grown.[46] Thus the anti-highway protestors found more sympathetic hearings among the local weeklies, the metropolitan press, and the local broadcasters; and so the media aided those who opposed large public projects, and once-quiet constituencies grew as their members could see, through the press, that their numbers were legion, and their objections, as certified by press coverage, were legitimate.

Finally, the battles of the 1960s and 1970s underscored the important connections between constituencies and expertise. Here we might note a similarity between the evolution of protest in the Stockholm region and the New

45. Governor Thomas E. Dewey of New York, quoted in Port Authority, *Thirty-Second Annual Report: 1952* (1953), frontispiece. Dewey's compliments were directed specifically to the work of the Port Authority.

46. Robert Caro is particularly effective in describing the work and frustrations of the investigative reporter confronting the secretive world of the public authority. See Caro, *The Power Broker*, Chapter 45 and *passim*. On relationships between the media and protest groups more generally, see Michael Lipsky, *Protest in City Politics* (Chicago: Rand McNally, 1970), Chapter 6.

York area. Writing of a rising dissident group in Stockholm, Thomas Anton comments:

> During the battle, plans and arguments put forward by various city "experts" were repeatedly shown to be inconsistent, misconceived, or inaccurate. Expertise thus became less compelling as support for a policy position, and experts themselves were shown to be not really different from other political figures with axes to grind.[47]

Thus efforts to defend the need for a new transport facility in terms of traditional standards of commuter-service needs were attacked by the protestors because "alternative conceptions of service and transportation needs" had not been considered. And when established political leaders spoke of need to accommodate "increased traffic caused by growth," the protestors challenged the desirability of growth. As Anton concludes, the traditional leaders "were using the language of economy and functionality, but the protestors had something different in mind—an 'Alternative City.' "[48]

What happened in Stockholm, what has happened in the New York region, is that the deference to expertise, as traditionally nurtured and used by public authorities and by other large bureaucracies, has been challenged and the power of expertise weakened. The opposition in both urban regions has been of two kinds. First, the experts have been questioned, and sometimes been found wanting, on their own terms. For example, the Port Authority, armed with sophisticated studies of traffic growth, argued that a fourth jetport was essential and, when that alternative was blocked, poured millions of dollars into enlarging Newark Airport. As the new buildings rose, however, air traffic fell, and with it the authority's reputation in traffic projection and revenue analysis. The continuing deficits of the partly empty World Trade Center also raised doubts, even among its supporters, in this core area of the authority's expertise. The financial difficulties of the World's Fair of 1964–65 had a similarly damaging impact on Moses's reputation.[49] And in other areas of central importance to all public authorities—financial integrity, and professional integrity in contracting—the Moses domain, the Port Authority, and the Newark Housing Authority all found their reputations damaged by charges and sometimes clear evidence of illegal use of funds, patronage, and other practices associated with urban political machines. Constituencies had been courted and skeptics held at bay by the widely accepted view that public authorities were run according to "sound business principles" and staffed by "the best available experts". By the early 1970s these were indeed tattered banners.

There has been a second challenge too, in New York as in Stockholm, based on differing views as to the range of values appropriate for judging public programs. Highway engineers in Westchester and Morristown, urban renewal experts in Newark and Brooklyn, air traffic planners at the Federal Aviation Agency and the Port Authority, were as comfortable as Anton's Stockholm leaders with the "language of economy and functionality." As long

47. Thomas Anton, *Governing Greater Stockholm: A Study of Policy Development and System Change* (Berkeley, Calif.: University of California Press, 1975), p. 206.

48. Ibid.

49. See Caro, *The Power Broker*, pp. 1102 ff.

as these experts spoke within the boundaries of their certain competence, and as long as these boundaries and criteria went unchallenged, the media and public could accept the inevitability that some people—poor, black, or simply "in the way"—would be hurt by the march of progress. Similarly, suburban planners could speak in sophisticated terms of the importance of tight building codes and detailed zoning controls in ensuring a balanced town treasury and avoiding the esthetic costs of high-density development. By the late 1960s, however, court suits, organized protests, and riots compelled the media and elected officials to acknowledge and weigh the costs of breaking up neighborhoods, of increasing pollution, of encouraging greater and greater amounts of vehicular traffic, of fencing out the less wealthy from the suburbs. Now the domains of the traditional professionals were breached, and the once-impotent constituencies could argue their views—against jetport, highway, and large medical school—on more equal terms.

In reviewing these interconnections of insulation and constituency, it is important to note the increasing role of "participation" as a separate value in itself in shaping inner-city and suburban demands, and in adding legitimacy to those demands. In the 1960s, the civil-rights movement and demands for "black power" emphasized that minorities, however poor, had a right to be heard and to help shape their own futures. In urban regions, this demand for a right to participate—in society, in government programs intended to "serve" them—was dramatized by the disruptions and riots in Los Angeles, Detroit, Brooklyn and Newark, and by sustained demands for community control of schools and other programs in inner-city neighborhoods—against the impersonal and often hostile bureaucracies of the educational establishment, police, and urban renewal authorities.

In the suburbs too, as noted in Chapter Four, there was increasing skepticism of the right of large institutions to cut highways through settled areas and to carve out airports in the hinterland, based on the agencies' "expert studies." Like their city counterparts, suburban residents demanded the right to be directly involved—the right to participate in decisions that would alter their own communities in major ways.

These demands for participation were rendered more legitimate and more salient to policymakers because—as noted above—they often were reported sympathetically and sometimes endorsed by the media. Television's on-the-spot coverage of disturbances and confrontations also dramatized demands to a broader public, often attracting new recruits to the cause. Among those attracted to local groups were individuals with public-relations and legal skills who then used demonstrations on the steps of city hall, television coverage, and public forums generally to force the resistant and sometimes somnolent bureaucracies to listen and respond.

As the right of local groups to be involved won a sympathetic hearing at the state capitals and particularly in Washington, changes in administrative procedures provided new levers and added legitimacy to those who demanded the right to participate. Thus Newark's protests led Trenton and HUD to establish revised guidelines permitting greater community involvement in renewal decisions. And the federal highway agency adopted new hearing rules which required that local communities be allowed to comment formally on the specific routes for new highways, thus providing a forum and an incentive for wider participation, and increased difficulty for the highway coalition in carrying out its preferred plans.

So it is crucial, if a government agency is to be able to concentrate resources in a sustained way on specific development projects, to limit the breadth of pressures on the agency by restricting the range of constituencies that can effectively demand a "piece of the action." The highway alliance, the urban renewal coalition, and many of the region's suburban zoning boards have demonstrated how this can be done, and with what impact on metropolitan development. However, in a complex society with a wide range of possible routes through which expertise can be challenged and participation encouraged, the necessary degree of insulation is, as we have seen, a highly fragile commodity.

## Broader Values and the Shackling of Government

When insulation does break down, the impact of the new constituencies on government action depends not only on the intensity of the new demands and on the number of citizens actively involved, but also on the particular values advanced by the newly admitted group. In the present era, the major additions to the social calculus are environmentalism with its cousin "neighborhood effects," and "social equity." These broader values are wide-ranging in their implications for government activities, particularly for public actions that shape regional development. Moreover, these particular value clusters are highly limiting for government action, particularly in a densely developed older area like the New York region.

Environmental concerns and "neighborhood effects" (also called externalities or third-party effects) have a rather straightforward constraining impact on government's ability to shape regional development. The underlying thesis, drawn from microeconomics, argues that the actions of any participant in the social system should take account of indirect as well as direct effects of the participant's activities. In the preceding chapters we have seen this concern particularly in the debates on highway expansion and the fourth jetport, and in the growing pressures beginning in the 1960s for public action to reduce air and water pollution.[50] The same perspective is directly relevant to understanding the special nature and evolution of limited-purpose public authorities. Initially, those peculiar institutions were so fashioned that they would be insulated from some of the broader impacts (the neighborhood effects) of their program activities; having a more focused lens, they could more easily take account of institutionally relevant factors and thus act rationally. So the Port Authority could dredge and fill parts of Newark Bay in order to create two massive marine terminals; whether the wildlife of the bay would be harmed was not a matter to be carefully weighed. Similarly, the Newark

50. In the public debates of the past 20 years the issues of air and water pollution have been especially prominent, but such concern for environmental protection is actually a subset of the broader argument that the actions of governmental institutions and private firms should take careful account of indirect effects of all kinds generated by their activities, especially when those effects are harmful to others. For a thoughtful discussion of these issues, see Charles L. Schultze, *The Public Use of Private Interest* (Washington, D.C.: Brookings Institution, 1977).

Housing Authority, in its most active period, could designate an area for renewal and then bulldoze, leaving the real costs of relocation to be borne largely by others, mainly the former residents. Moreover, while only the authorities were formally insulated from concern with such effects, other government officials—such as the state highway engineers—were able to use the shield of professionalism and prevailing political sentiment almost as effectively to shroud some burdens of their well-publicized activities in quiet darkness.

During the past two decades such comforts and protections were mostly stripped away: laws required, and vocal segments of the citizenry demanded, that the impact of any public project on air and water, on nearby residents, fauna, and flora all be weighed. Negative externalities can extend very widely, as the jetport opponents persuasively argued. The disruption of homes and communities near the site due to construction and increased traffic, the additional noise and fear of crashes, and the loss of marshland, with broader implications for the ecology of the eastern United States, all could be seen to flow from a jetport in Morris County.[51] Critics also pointed to the opportunity costs—the losses to society if public funds were absorbed by a jetport (or a freeway, or a gigantic building) rather than being employed to modernize a rail line, or improve the schools, or heal the sick.

In a careful calculation, indirect *benefits* as well as indirect costs of a proposed project would, of course, have to be assessed. Historically, agencies engaged in regional development programs made some effort to identify these blessings, such calculations being central to the arguments put forward by sophisticated planners in urging support for dramatic undertakings such as the George Washington Bridge, Mitchell-Lama housing projects, and the World Trade Center. But the new constellations of the 1960s and 1970s were far more sensitive to the *costs* of change—of a Westway, or a slum clearance project, or the completion of Route 287 in Bergen County—than to the benefits. In part this "negative" orientation which predominated among the newly organized groups illustrated a broader principle of community organizing: those whose lives are likely to be disrupted by new projects are concentrated in space and time, and so are more apt to be a fertile ground for organizing. In contrast, the beneficiaries of new highways and urban renewal projects are more dispersed.[52]

There were other reasons for the emphasis on costs more than benefits of new projects. By the late 1960s, those in the path of urban renewal and highway bulldozers, and broader segments of the public as well, had become skeptical of the unceasing demands for public support—and public funds—by federal, state, and authority officials whose turnpikes were still clogged with cars, whose cities were still decaying. And when state governors and city

51. See Chapter Four in this volume.

52. Of course some beneficiaries of development projects had long been well-organized through such groups as the American Trucking Association, real estate boards, and the construction unions. But in the past two decades the grass-roots opponents of development have only occasionally found counterparts in the form of community groups *favoring* slum clearance projects, new highways, and other major development projects. On motives for community organizing, cf. Robert A. Dahl, *Who Governs?* (New Haven: Yale University Press, 1961), p. 197 and *passim*, Douglas Yates, *The Ungovernable City* (Cambridge, Mass.: MIT Press, 1977), especially pp. 104–107.

planners sought in the 1970s to interweave road and rail bond issues, and to meet redevelopment and pollution goals as well as traffic needs through multipurpose projects such as Westway, wide segments of the public resisted. Opponents feared that official rhetoric favoring "balanced transportation" and environmentalism would mask a reality of community disruption, heavy taxes, and continued traffic congestion and urban deterioration. Finally, the critical cast of the newly emerging groups was due in part to their association with the broader movement to "curb growth, limit population and stop useless consumption. . . ."[53] The result, then, has been a range of new constituencies whose concern with environmental costs and other negative impacts of new development programs have tended to generate delay, higher costs, and often the abandonment of major public projects.

The heightened concern with enhancing "social equity" has had a less direct influence on the exercise of government power. By "social equity" we mean the extent to which individuals are equal in their opportunities and in their current situations, and (where inequalities exist) the extent to which such inequalities are "fair."[54] With regard to government's role in the distribution of jobs and residences, the concern with enhancing social equity is directed toward government actions that restrict the opportunities of some citizens more than others, or that might harm areas of the metropolitan region which already are relatively weak as measured by social and economic indicators.

For example, attacks on restrictive suburban zoning have been directed mainly toward the goal of increasing the opportunities for less-wealthy citizens to live in such middle-class or affluent suburbs as Madison or Greenwich if they wish to do so. It would hardly be accurate to say that there is widespread disapproval of these local zoning and other land-use regulations that screen out those of lower incomes and of darker hues. In suburban towns that maintain such practices, most of those who are already "zoned in" are not eager to lower the land-use barriers. Responding to concerns with equity and racial segregation, some judges—as described in Chapter Three—have declared some exclusionary zoning practices to be unconstitutional. The impact of the Mt. Laurel decision in New Jersey and similar court findings elsewhere, though much less revolutionary than their advocates had hoped, is to constrain the major lever through which suburban towns and county agencies shape development in the region.

Concern with social equity also motivates the Regional Plan Association and older-city officials as they criticize federal approval of multimillion-dollar highway interchanges, as well as other government actions that encourage businesses and middle-class residents to relocate from older cities into

53. The quotation is from an address by Robert Moses, who felt the new mood as target of its vengeful arrows. Moses also commented: "If you buck the environmental trend you will be shunned as a germ carrier. Your name will be mud. They tell me everyone in public life must be an environmentalist, ecologist and ekistician . . . the rage may not last, but join or be bludgeoned." Robert Moses, "Engineer and Environment," remarks to the Metropolitan Section of the American Society of Civil Engineers, February 18, 1970, p. 1.

54. For a perceptive recent exploration of this complex terrain, see J. Roland Pennock, *Democratic Political Theory* (Princeton, N.J.: Princeton University Press, 1979), especially pp. 35–37, 143–149, 191 ff.

suburban enclaves.[55] These criticisms, reinforced by heightened sensitivity to the energy and environmental costs of suburban dispersal, led the Carter administration to reconsider making federal grants for the kinds of projects that have encouraged the nation's "spread cities."[56]

The growing concern with social equity and neighborhood effects is a nationwide trend, affecting the role of government in all urban areas. The influence of these values in shaping government activities may be especially salient in the New York region and other older areas. In such regions, the density of existing development within and near the core is especially great, increasing the sensitivity of citizen groups, public officials, and the general public to environmental problems and other third-party effects of new highways and other kinds of development. Also, the differences in financial vigor and residential style between inner cities and suburbs are especially stark in most older regions, attracting more support for central-city mayors and citizens' groups who urge that government programs be strongly informed by social equity considerations.

Moreover, the New York region has a more fragmented structure of governmental responsibility and political leadership than any other urban region in the United States.[57] Fragmentation makes it difficult for major officials in the region to analyze trade-offs, for example between environmental costs and job-creation benefits, and when the cost-benefit ratio is favorable, to press ahead vigorously with needed projects. Consequently, as the number of active groups interested in an issue increases, fragmentation tends to aid those who counsel delay and inaction in the use of government power to advance development projects.

## The End of Growth and the Role of Government

At the same time that public officials must grapple with new values and constituencies, several other factors are making it more difficult for govern-

55. For example, in the summer of 1979 New Haven's mayor appealed to the White House to halt the issuance of a wetlands permit for a suburban shopping mall, which he alleged would attract shoppers from downtown stores. Reviewing a series of such criticisms, the *New York Times* commented: "Federal agencies have located interstate highway interchanges and off-ramps for the convenience of regional shopping centers. Water and sewer lines have been extended to such centers with Federal funds. In metropolitan areas with stable or declining populations, the resulting competition is costing cities sales, businesses, jobs and taxes." ("Restraining Suburban Sprawl," editorial, *New York Times*, September 10, 1979.) The RPA has argued that social equity, environmentalism and energy conservation require government policy changes to discourage highways and sewer systems that would facilitate suburban sprawl, and to encourage businesses to remain in or relocate into the region's downtown areas. (See Regional Plan Association, "Where Transit Works," *Regional Plan News*, No. 99, August, 1976 and Regional Plan Association, "New Jersey Cities, 1978," October 4, 1978, Chapter 12.)

56. In November 1979 the White House issued a new directive on "Community Conservation Guidance," which concluded that federal policies and grants should not "have unintended effects of eroding existing commercial centers." For a discussion of political conflict after publication of the directive, see Carter B. Horsley, "Suburban Malls and Urban Centers: Rivalry Intensifies," *New York Times*, June 15, 1980. This federal initiative seemed unlikely to be maintained by the Reagan administration, with its emphasis on a reduced federal role in the oversight of grants.

57. See Chapters One and Six in this volume. On the relative coherence of political leadership in other regions see, for example, Michael N. Danielson, Alan M. Hershey and John M. Bayne, *One Nation, So Many Governments* (Lexington, Mass.: Heath-Lexington, 1977), Chapter 4.

ments in the New York region to influence the shape of the future metropolis. One of these is the significant slowdown in the region's growth, in terms of population and jobs.[58] Since public agencies have more leverage in influencing new development—through land-use controls and highway construction, for example—than in shaping redevelopment of older urbanized areas, this slow-growth trend reduces the leverage of the region's governments. Moreover, a continuing economic slowdown in the New York area, extending into the 1980s and beyond, would make it more difficult for states, cities, and even public authorities to gather sufficient tax revenues and other monies to engage in significant redevelopment efforts, such as the creation of industrial parks, or major investments to reduce energy costs.[59]

It is possible, of course, that state officials and the federal government will respond to the weakening economic position of the New York region (and other older regions) with new infusions of funds and government power. As our earlier analysis of the highway and urban renewal programs amply demonstrated, national legislation and the federal treasury can be important sources of new money for cities and states, and of new programs that can dramatically reshape downtown areas and the suburban terrain. The states' role in mass transit and highways has also, as we have seen, been crucial for the region's transportation patterns and derivatively for its pattern of development.

New initiatives by federal and state agencies might, for example, focus on particular geographic sectors of the region, assisting in their rebuilding to make them attractive centers for new industry and residential development—as well as magnets to aid broader regional revitalization. But such initiatives raise difficult political questions: Will an attempt to concentrate resources on specific parts of a region be harmful to the economic and social vitality of other sectors of that region, or to other regions? And even if these issues of intra- and interregional equity can be answered to our intellectual satisfaction, will the reality of decentralized political power in the American system generate too many obstacles from congressmen, mayors, and other elected officials who will oppose a federal government initiative if it is not spread to include their own political turf?

Beyond these questions, which are always central to understanding the reality of federal and state programs (whatever the rhetoric of their officials), there are important economic complexities. As urban renewal planners discovered in the 1950s and 1960s, often to their dismay, great uncertainties attend any effort to use public powers to generate economic growth in older areas. Careful calculations are needed regarding subsidies and other incentives required to attract private firms to downtown Newark or inner Brooklyn. And fundamental analyses of labor-market characteristics, transportation

58. Regional employment fell by nearly 7 percent in the period 1969–1976; however, following a net increase in jobs in 1977 and 1978, officials predicted a modest upward trend during the next 10 years. See Port Authority of New York and New Jersey, *Regional Recovery*, pp. 5–13.

59. The declines in jobs and in population growth rate in the New York region during the past decade were partly linked to general U.S. trends, and a nationwide economic resurgence might be expected to generate upward trends in this metropolitan area. However, the downward economic and population trends of the New York region are caused in part by the loss of jobs and people to the "sunbelt" and other regions of the nation. Underlying these movements are long-term disadvantages of the New York region, such as higher labor expenses in manufacturing industries and higher transportation and energy costs.

costs, and other factors are essential for effective long-term stimulation of economic growth. Finally, the rise of environmental issues and a heightened concern with social equity further complicate political and economic analysis, and thus make more difficult the strategic use of government power to achieve chosen goals.

The well-publicized efforts in the South Bronx, triggered by President Jimmy Carter's dramatic announcement in 1977 that the revitalization of this area would be a central goal of his administration, illustrate some of these difficulties. Blessed with the President's support, high-level federal officials joined with state and local officials to devise both short- and long-range plans. The first major element of these plans to emerge—a housing project on the devastated street which the President had visited—provided a lightning rod for public officials and private interests to attack the Bronx effort, and to urge that the federal funds linked to this effort be allocated instead to help Brooklyn, or Staten Island, or other deserving and needy areas inside the New York region or elsewhere. The effort to reclaim the South Bronx continues, though at a greatly reduced funding level, and it can expect to face a continuing stream of attacks from those who say it is too little a plan, or too large, or is absorbing federal and state funds that should be spent elsewhere.[60] For the federal government, the advantages of wide areal scope and large financial resources are in this effort again offset, as they have been historically, by the existence of widespread and varied constituencies, each demanding a piece of the public pie, and most with ties on Capitol Hill and in the executive agencies which ensure that the pie will indeed be very finely divided.

In view of these constituency problems, which confront the national and state governments and most general-purpose governments in every region, there may of course be substantial advantages in looking elsewhere. If, because of limited resources, government's redevelopment efforts should be focused on discrete areas and projects, and if the economic complexities require a skilled and experienced staff, perhaps we need to create or find an engine of governmental power that can assemble the resources and overcome these difficulties, somewhat insulated from the buzzing confusion of constituent demands. Thus, it could be argued, we need to apply to current and future efforts the advantages which the Port Authority brought to the George Washington Bridge project in the 1920s, and to the marine terminals in the postwar era, and which the carefully crafted alliances of the NHA brought to Newark's redevelopment in the 1950s. Indeed, this is the perspective that underlies the Port Authority's current initiatives in the region.

In attempting to overcome widespread criticisms of its limited efforts in mass transit (described in Chapter Seven), the Port Authority created a staff

60. The ups and downs of the South Bronx rebuilders are summarized in Charles Kaiser, "$870 Million Revitalization Plan for South Bronx Unveiled by City," *New York Times*, December 21, 1977; Glenn Fowler, "$55.6 Million by Fall to Help South Bronx Is Pledged by U.S.," *New York Times*, April 13, 1978; Joseph P. Fried, "Is South Bronx Revival Plan Simply Folly?," *New York Times*, June 19, 1978; Steven R. Weisman, "City Hall Split; Gloves Are Off," *New York Times*, February 10, 1979; Paul Goldberger, "For Urban Planners, A Case Study in Frustration," *New York Times*, February 11, 1979; "South Bronx Debate: Dig It Now or Plan It Later," *New York Times*, February 25, 1979; "Badillo Deplores New Koch Plan on South Bronx," *New York Times*, August 15, 1979; Frank Lynn, "Kennedy, in South Bronx, Says Carter Broke Aid Vow," *New York Times*, March 23, 1980.

unit in the mid-1970s to explore possible new initiatives that might help revitalize the region's economy. The authority's staff soon saw opportunities for the region and for itself, and by 1975 a detailed analysis of "physical, economic and marketing steps required to stimulate economic development" in the region's cities was completed. The authority proposed to take the lead in assembling the land needed to create several new industrial parks in Jersey City, Newark and Brooklyn, in assuring "continuity of capital funding and management," and in developing new sources of fuel for these areas, thus generating more than 26,000 jobs. The Port Authority offered to devote $300 to $400 million of its own funds to this new enterprise.[61] Within a few weeks, both governors and regional leaders had applauded the agency for its efforts, both states had passed legislation to enable the authority to go forward with its plans, and the agency's image had once again brightened.

Meanwhile, the authority's staff was set to work on a wider range of issues relating to the region's future, and in the summer of 1979 it released a series of reports identifying a strategy for "regional recovery." The bistate agency proposed to expand its own role by including additional major responsibilities for waterfront development, energy diversification, regional marketing, and "transportation systems management." In undertaking these elements of a "new major economic development mission," the authority emphasized that it would need to work closely with the two states to form a "broad alliance for recovery among local leaders, state governments and business, labor and civic groups."[62] Executing the industrial-park plans—and finding ways to move ahead with broader regional strategies—will surely confront the Port Authority and the two states with great difficulties as issues of intraregional equity and environmentalism, among others, are raised. However, the authority's sophisticated approach and vigorous efforts again illustrate the advantages which wide areal scope, skilled staff leadership and planning skills, and partially insulated financial resources provide for the agency, and through it, potentially, for the New York region.

It should be noted that the Port Authority is not the only semiautonomous agency working to strengthen the region's economy. Following its financial collapse in 1975, the Urban Development Corporation has arisen phoenix-like to become the primary economic development agency for New York State—including a central role in the South Bronx program, in plans for a convention center in Manhattan, and in other major projects in the New York sector of the region. In New Jersey, the Economic Development Authority, criticized earlier for spreading its low-cost financing assistance thinly and for having little job-creating impact in older areas, has begun to target its activities in economically disadvantaged communities.[63] However, these and other economic-development agencies in the region inevitably risk neutralizing each other's efforts if

61. See Port Authority of New York and New Jersey, *Industrial Revitalization in the New York-New Jersey Region* (New York: May 1, 1978), pp. 3–5, and "Growth From Within," *Via Port of New York-New Jersey* (June/July 1978), pp. 2–4.

62. Committee on the Future, Port Authority of New York and New Jersey, *Regional Recovery: The Business of the Eighties* (New York: June 1979), p. 55.

63. See Carter B. Horsley, "New Directions for the U.D.C.," *New York Times*, February 25, 1979; Joseph P. Fried, "Goodbye, Slum Razing; Hello, Grand Hyatt," *New York Times*, July 15, 1979; New Jersey Economic Development Authority, "Targeting Authority Assistance" (Trenton: December 1978); and recent annual reports of the UDC and NJEDA.

they use tax incentives and other tactics to bid against one another for new manufacturing plants, retail stores, and other job-creating enterprises.

Certainly, it is conceivable that the widely felt concern regarding the region's economic decline will curtail such narrowly based competition for jobs and will reduce the other conflicts that have historically separated the New York area's myriad governments and interests, and that cooperative strategies among cities, suburbs, and authorities will then generate effective wide-ranging action that will ensure "regional recovery." This perspective underlies the Port Authority's plan, and it is a hope expressed fervently by the Regional Plan Association and the Tri-State Regional Planning Commission as they look forward to the 1980s.[64] Thus far, however, the evidence of increased willingness to cooperate is largely rhetoric. Conflict and competition among the region's governments continue to be the rule, as illustrated by the demise of the Metropolitan Regional Council in 1979, the partly successful efforts to dismantle Tri-State, the recurring attempts of other cities to lure the New York Stock Exchange out of Manhattan, and the responses of local officials to the South Bronx plan. Moreover, as long as local tax resources are important to the financial viability of cities and suburbs, substantial cooperation across the region is difficult to envision—particularly if that cooperation is asked to fly under the banner of the Regional Plan Association, which would revitalize the cities by discouraging industry from locating in suburban enclaves.

The dispute that arose in 1979 over the efforts of the Hackensack Meadowlands Development Commission to foster large-scale commercial and office development on a site in the heart of the New York region illustrates the conflicts inherent in the issue of economic revitalization. Created by New Jersey in 1969 to guide the comprehensive development of 31 square miles of marshland and garbage dumps adjacent to the Hackensack River in Hudson and Bergen counties, the state commission had substantial land-use controls and planning resources, and was empowered to allocate the tax benefits of new development among its 14 municipalities.[65] As the 1970s unfolded, the commission's wide-ranging development powers combined with the locational advantages of the Hackensack meadowlands to attract more than $1 billion in private and public investment. By 1979, over 100 office and warehouse buildings, more than 600 condominiums, and a 300-room hotel had been constructed under the commission's supervision, and numerous other projects, including three large shopping mall-office complexes, were being pressed forward by major corporations and developers. Among the public investments in the meadowlands, most striking were the facilities of the New Jersey Sports Authority—a race track, football stadium, and $55 million indoor arena completed in 1981.

From one perspective, the meadowlands boom was an important contri-

64. See, for example, Regional Plan Association, "New Jersey Cities, 1978," and Tri-State Regional Planning Commission, *Regional Development Guide, 1977–2000* (New York: March 1978).

65. The complex story of the creation of the Hackensack Meadowlands Development Commission, and the preparation of the master plan for the area, are outlined in Clifford A. Goldman, "The Hackensack Meadowlands: The Politics of Regional Planning and Development in the Metropolis," Doctoral Dissertation, Princeton University, 1975. Goldman was the commission's acting executive director during its early years.

bution to regional revitalization. New jobs were being created near the core of the region rather than along the sprawling suburban periphery, and thus were much more accessible to residents of Newark, Paterson, and Hudson County's older cities than jobs in suburbia's distant shopping malls and office parks. Moreover, development in the meadowlands was under the jurisdiction of a powerful public agency committed to an ambitious master plan that featured environmental protection, innovative transportation improvements, and the creation of public amenities. But to others, the meadowlands was just suburbia in a swamp, whose malls, offices, and apartments would drive one more nail in the coffin of northern New Jersey's older cities. For one elected official with a large urban constituency, "every cent those gigantic malls" in the meadowlands earn is going "to come out of either urban centers like Newark, Jersey City or Paterson, or from older suburban towns whose quality of life is equally threatened."[66] The 19-million square feet of new offices planned by the Meadowlands Commission was seen as undercutting office investment in the surrounding older cities. One of the loudest voices raised against the meadowlands agency was that of the Regional Plan Association, which urged that development along the Hackensack be restricted to warehouses and other projects that posed no threats to the older cities. Similar views were expressed in a staff study prepared by the Tri-State Regional Planning Commission.

Responding to these pressures, state officials in late 1979 prevailed upon the Meadowlands Commission to scale down its plans substantially. Office development was cut back two-thirds, future job creation halved to 70,000, and only one of the competing mall plans was approved. What none of those who sought so passionately to focus public efforts on the older cities could guarantee, of course, was whether the jobs kept out of the meadowlands would locate in the adjacent cities, or for that matter anywhere in the region. What could be guaranteed, however, was that consensus on economic development was unlikely in the highly competitive political economy of the New York region, even when a public agency has been given substantial ability to concentrate resources on a comprehensive set of development objectives as in the case of the Meadowlands Commission.

What then of the future? Even standing astride the World Trade Center which looms over the Hackensack meadows, we confess difficulty in seeing the future, particularly as measured by the level of economic vitality and the distribution of jobs and residences in the New York metropolis of 1990 and beyond. Fortunately, that kind of prediction is not the major concern of this volume. Instead, our interests have been primarily political. We have sought to demonstrate that the behavior of government officials, market forces, and the attitudes of the region's citizenry are closely intertwined, and that careful study of the patterns of areal and functional scope and of the variables that permit concentration of resources is crucial to an understanding of the ways government officials of cities and suburbs, state and federal agencies, and public authorities behave, and why they are effective (in quite varying degrees) in shaping an urban region. In exploring these general points, we have also attempted to provide some flesh for the bones—some richer detail on

66. Peter Shapiro, county executive, Essex County, quoted in Neal R. Peirce, "Malls Are Newest Threat to North Jersey's Old Cities," *Sunday Times Advertiser* (Trenton, N.J.), October 14, 1979.

how Westchester County, New York City, the Port Authority, Robert Moses, and other parts of the complex contraption called the political system of the New York region evolved and came to shape the spreading metropolis. If we are to make any prediction, then, we would expect the variables that underlie the past behavior of the region's public officials will also be central to understanding their activities, their failures, and their successes in the next several decades. And we expect that the same themes and patterns underlie the political economies of other metropolitan regions.

# Index